PRAISE FOR

KAITEN

"A powerful tale about how an intersection of youth, patriotism, and sacrifice ended in a fiery suicidal assault on an American warship. More than recounting a battle, this is a very human story that relives one of the most painful episodes of World War II."

—James P. Delgado, author of *Silent Killers: Submarines and Underwater Warfare* and *Khubilai Khan's Lost Fleet: In Search of a Legendary Armada*

"Mair and Waldron masterfully interweave World War II documents, interviews, and oral histories of two opposing nations in mortal conflict to create a rare and intimate view of the Pacific War that provokes the reader to rethink the boundaries of individual courage and national patriotism."

—Larry E. Murphy, Chief (Ret.), Submerged Resources Center, National Park Service

"A crisp, persuasive narrative about a little-known but startling World War II attack . . . Mair and Waldron portray the story from both perspectives, constantly building to a dramatic, fiery crescendo. Their profiles of American and Japanese sailors add poignancy to a compelling story of battle disaster, death, and survival."

—David Sears, author of *Pacific Air* and *At War with the Wind*

"This doomed mission almost became lost in history after the atomic explosions at Hiroshima and Nagasaki. But the authors of *Kaiten* have pulled together the story and populated it with flesh-and-blood warriors on both sides of the conflict . . . This book can take its place alongside *Shadow Divers* and *Unbroken* as a graphic, living story from the worst war the world has ever known."

—Richard McCord, journalist, editor, and publisher of the *Santa Fe Reporter*, and author of *The Chain Gang: One Newspaper versus the Gannett Empire*

"If you like reading history with the details to bring it back to life, you'll enjoy *Kaiten*."

—Ralph Wilbanks, underwater archaeologist and NUMA expedition leader

KAITEN

Japan's Secret Manned
Suicide Submarine and
the First American Ship
It Sank in WWII

MICHAEL MAIR and **JOY WALDRON**

BERKLEY CALIBER, NEW YORK

THE BERKLEY PUBLISHING GROUP
Published by the Penguin Group
Penguin Group (USA) LLC
375 Hudson Street, New York, New York 10014

USA • Canada • UK • Ireland • Australia • New Zealand • India • South Africa • China

penguin.com

A Penguin Random House Company

ISBN: 978-0-425-27270-1

The Library of Congress has catalogued the Berkley Caliber hardcover edition as follows:

Mair, Michael.
Kaiten : Japan's secret manned suicide submarine and the first American ship
it sank in WWII / by Michael Mair and Joy Waldron.
p.   cm.
ISBN 978-0-425-27269-5 (hardback)
1. Kaiten (Warship)   2. Mississinewa (Tanker)   3. World War, 1939–1945—Naval
operations—Submarine.   4. World War, 1939–1945—Naval operations, Japanese.
5. World War, 1939–1945—Naval operations, American.   6. World War, 1939–1945—
Campaigns—Pacific Ocean.   I. Waldron, Joy.   II. Title.
D783.7.M35 2014
940.54'5952—dc23
2013044199

PUBLISHING HISTORY
Berkley Caliber hardcover edition / May 2014
Berkley Caliber trade paperback edition / April 2015

PRINTED IN THE UNITED STATES OF AMERICA

10   9   8   7   6   5   4   3   2   1

Cover photo by Simon Harris.
Interior text design by Tiffany Estreicher.

For the American and Japanese soldiers and sailors
who were there and for those who loved them

Valor is a gift. Those having it never know for sure whether they have it till the test comes. And those having it in one test never know for sure if they will have it when the next test comes.

—NAPOLÉON BONAPARTE (1769–1821),
military and political leader of France

Heroic? I suppose it was temporary insanity. You don't wake up thinking "I'm going to be a hero today." You do your best because you don't want to lose any more lives. Your fellow soldiers were closer to you than your family.

—DANIEL INOUYE (1924–2012), late U.S. senator from Hawaii,
on the battle April 21, 1945, where he lost an arm but took out a machine
gunner's nest with a hand grenade; his military awards included the
Distinguished Service Cross, the Bronze Star, and two Purple Hearts

Bushidō . . . is the code of moral principles the samurai were required or instructed to observe . . . It is a code unuttered and unwritten . . . an organic growth of decades and centuries of military career.

—NITOBE INAZŌ, *BUSHIDŌ: THE SOUL OF JAPAN* (1899)

CONTENTS

PREFACE

Long after the USS *Mississinewa* exploded and sank in the western part of the Pacific in 1944—the home stretch of World War II—survivor John Mair was still filled with sadness and grief over the death of his shipmates and the suffering experienced by all who lived through that day. As much as he wanted to tell the story of the *"Miss,"* he felt the world also deserved to know about the strange and secret weapon Japan had created and used to sink his ship at Ulithi Atoll. Years later, in 2005, while John Mair lay dying, he made his son, Mike, promise that he would write the *Miss* story.

Mike, a businessman in the highly competitive field of audiovisual equipment and systems, took hundreds of hours from his busy life, which included a wife and children, to research the story of the *Miss* and the suicide submarine, called *kaiten*, that sank it. He read thousands of pages of books, articles and Navy action reports, consulted Japanese historians and former *kaiten* submariners, and interviewed dozens of surviving crewmembers of the oiler, and in some cases their sons, wives or other relatives. As he began to study the *kaiten* program and specifically the *Kikusui* Mission that went to Ulithi for the kill on November 20, 1944, he was struck by the realization that the men on both sides of the war held ideals and goals that were often the same, perhaps the greatest being the salvation of their own country and their own way of life. The means they chose to attain their goals were, perhaps, different, but their hopes for the future mirrored each other, at least on the level of the individual men who took up guns or dived deep in submarines. It is another matter why governments go to war.

As Mair began to piece together the massive amount of data he was gathering, he realized there was a big story to be told, bigger even than the tale of his father's ship, the story of how a country like Japan could instill in its men a belief that their suicide could be the turning point for an otherwise all-but-lost war, and how one man's choice to live out that destiny would take so many American lives with him.

When Joy Waldron joined Mair to coauthor the book in the making, she brought with her three decades of journalistic experience and a specialty in underwater archaeology that had resulted in a WWII book, *The USS* Arizona: *The Ship, the Men, the Pearl Harbor Attack, and the Symbol That Aroused America.* Her extensive experience as an investigative journalist and her interviewing skills merged with Mair's years of research. The two uncovered previously unpublished documents and interviewed people who in some cases had never before spoken of their wartime experiences. They ultimately located and interviewed the pharmacist's mate who, long ago, had made a very important discovery in the waters of Ulithi Lagoon, a discovery that is brought to light in this book and helps to resolve a long-unanswered question.

This is the story of how destiny brought all those lives together, a very human story set against the backdrop of the Pacific War.

TIMELINE

1941

December 7   Attack on Pearl Harbor; United States officially enters World War II

1942

June 4–6   Battle of Midway: victory for Allies, loss of four Japanese aircraft carriers

1943

March 3   Petition from submariner Hiroshi Kuroki to Admiral Isoroku Yamamoto to develop *kaiten* suicide submarines

April 19   Death of Yamamoto in Solomon Islands aerial ambush

1944

February 26   Project team set up at Kure Navy Yard for experimental development of *kaiten*

May 18   Commissioning of USS *Mississinewa* ("the *Miss*"), a fast-fleet oiler (AO-59)

June 6   D-Day Invasion of Normandy

June 19–20   Battle of the Philippine Sea, also called "the Great Marianas Turkey Shoot" that forces Japan to change strategy

July 25   Two *kaiten* prototypes are delivered to coinventors Kuroki and Nishina for sea trials

August 1	Japanese Navy orders one hundred *kaiten* for completion in thirty days
August 23	The *Miss* crosses the Equator en route to the Admiralty Islands
August 26	The *Miss* arrives in Manus Harbor, Admiralty Islands
August 31	Fueling the Fleet: *Mississinewa* earns its first Battle Star for support on the September 8 attacks of Bonin, Volcano and Yap islands
September 6	Death of *kaiten* coinventor Hiroshi Kuroki in training accident at Kure
September 6	Allied forces capture and occupy Southern Palau Islands, including Peleliu in October 14 invasion, for which the *Miss* earns its second Battle Star
September 9	Third Battle Star for the *Miss:* air assaults on the Philippine Islands
September 20	Capture of Ulithi (Caroline Islands) by American forces; established as forward base
October 10–11	The *Miss* earns a fourth Battle Star for support of the air attacks on Formosa and Okinawa
October 20	After overwhelming losses in Formosa, Japan's First Air Fleet forms the Special Attack Corps *kamikaze* (Divine Wind), a cadre of suicide aircraft pilots
October 21	USS *Mississinewa* enters Ulithi Lagoon for the first time
October 25	Battle of Leyte Gulf: first organized attacks by *kamikaze* planes
November 2	The *Miss* departs on its last sortie, a fueling at sea for the Luzon attack
November 9	Departure from Japan of *Kikusui* Mission; mother submarines *I-36*, *I-37* and *I-47* sail from Kure, each carrying four *kaiten*; *I-37* is bound for Palau on a diversionary mission; *I-36* and *I-47* head for Ulithi
November 15	The *Miss* returns to Ulithi for the last time
November 19	Sinking of Japanese submarine *I-37* by USS *Conklin*, with loss of all hands, at Kossol Passage, Palau

November 20   Attack and sinking of *Mississinewa* at Ulithi Harbor; sixty-three officers and crew lost; death of *kaiten* pilot Sekio Nishina

1945

January 23   *Kaiten* from *I-48* attack Ulithi; *kaiten* pilot Kentaro Yoshimoto dies

May 8   VE Day (Victory in Europe)—war in Europe declared over; war in Pacific continues

July 24   USS *Underhill* rams a *kaiten*, with disastrous consequences

August 6 and 9   United States drops bombs on Hiroshima and Nagasaki

August 14   VJ Day (Victory over Japan); Japan surrenders

August 15   The Imperial Japanese Navy, Sixth Fleet, orders all documents burned

September 2   Peace is signed on USS *Missouri* in Tokyo Harbor

2001

April 6   Discovery of *Mississinewa*'s resting place in Ulithi Lagoon, Federated States of Micronesia, by dive team headed by Chip Lambert

2013

July   Return to Ulithi for research dive on *Mississinewa*

PROLOGUE

Far out in the western Pacific Ocean, almost as far west as the Philippines, lay a string of tree-studded coral islands named the Carolines, newly won in September 1944, in the third year of the War in the Pacific, as a forward base for the United States Navy. Tiny islands connected by coral ringed an azure lagoon called Ulithi, one of the largest anchorages in the world. Gone were the outrigger canoes and small fishing boats from the lagoon, now filled with warships whose long guns and crow's nests seemed to scratch the sky.

Hours had passed since a Japanese commander of submarine *I-47* reached the open sea outside Ulithi with four smaller torpedo submarines attached to the mother submarine's deck. The four pilots of the waiting craft—known as *kaiten* or "heaven shaker"—left the interior of *I-47* and climbed into their torpedo subs in the predawn darkness.

Each man knew he was taking his last ride. The steel hull where he sat on a small canvas seat in the *kaiten*'s cramped cocoon would soon become his coffin.

In the southern curve of the lush tropical harbor, the USS *Mississinewa*, a Navy fast-fleet oiler, lay at anchor in the sparkling water. Hundreds of ships of the United States Third Fleet kept it company. Scattered across the deep-water reaches, American ships of war bristled with long guns, while supply ships threaded their way through the flock with fuel, food and mail. The early morning was calm, a respite from the carnage of the past few weeks in the Philippines.

As the fighting roared to a crescendo in late 1944, officers and crews of the U.S. fleet savored the recent victories at Leyte Gulf, Formosa and Okinawa, where Japanese airpower had been hit hard. Everyone felt that the tide had turned in favor of the Allies, and victory seemed attainable, despite the craziness of the most recent threat: *kamikaze* pilots. Even in the European Theater, the Nazi grip was starting to crack open. On this very day in late November, while heavy artillery pounded the German countryside, Adolf Hitler finally left Wolf's Lair, the headquarters he had occupied since the war's beginning; he was bound for Berlin, where he would meet his fate.

For a few days anchored in the quiet lagoon it might be easy for American sailors to forget war. On the tiny islands ringing the atoll, delicate plumeria petals shivered in the dawn's warm breath, while in the lagoon water lapped the lead-painted hulls, the shadows playing with camouflage designs that made the vessels harder to spot at sea. From deck to deck on board the ships, sailors on watch heard the wind rustling hundreds of palm trees on the fringe, a welcome change from the sounds of island bombardment. Hawksbill turtles plied the sands in search of dinner, and coconut crabs raced along the rock crevices. The unspoiled islands that made up the Carolines seemed a dreamlike respite to the deckhands far from home.

But the war still had its course to run. Every day carried intense preparations for the planned invasions yet to come. On this morning the enemy had come to Ulithi, and the limpid waters held an unimaginable terror.

Stealing into the harbor was one of five newly released *kaiten*, a tiny manned submersible carrying a torpedo just launched from its mother submarine. The Japanese suicide pilot fought to concentrate as his forty-eight-foot vessel rolled and pitched, reeling like a long cigar in the water. He felt his hands slippery on the wheel, but he moved forward through the silvery water, picking his course to navigate among a hundred enemy ships. The craft was difficult to maneuver in the tight reaches of the harbor, and the warrior's band around his brow was damp with sweat. On the launch from the parent submarine *I-47* he had been given a certain trajectory to follow, and he approached the immense field of warships to search for a target. Every moment was perilous. He risked detection by U.S. Navy forces all around.

He thought of his life and he thought of his death. He thought of the men who would follow after him, inspired by his success, and the family he had left behind in his island nation. Most of all he thought of the emperor and the sacred mission to save his country. All these fragmented images flashed through his mind in seconds, then he was consumed by the task of holding his craft on course. He popped the periscope tube above the water to sight a target ship.

At that moment the alert officer of the deck aboard the oiler *Cache* noticed a swirl in the water, four hundred yards away from his ship. He watched a trail of ragged foam, saw a periscope move through the waves and disappear. He reported it instantly.

At the same moment aboard the nearby *Lackawanna*, the bow lookout jumped when his eye caught the periscope's tiny wake as it deposited frothy bubbles on the surface. The time was just a hair after 0530.

"Periscope," shouted the seaman, lunging for the phone at his watch station to call his own officer of the deck on *Lackawanna*'s bridge. Everyone knew what that one word implied: An enemy submarine was lurking, maybe more than one. After reporting the threat to the captain, the OOD returned to the bridge. He spotted the periscope again and tracked the feathery wake as it moved slowly past the ship's bow and headed for the starboard side of the oiler *Mississinewa*, anchored eight hundred yards away.

As the *Cache*'s radio crackled with submarine alerts relayed from ship to ship, the officer could picture the U.S. destroyers outside the channel entrance; he knew they'd be circling in the water like crazed hornets looking for an invader to sting. He felt a deep sense of foreboding.

The ship in the periscope's crosshairs was a fleet oiler with an Indiana river's name—the *Mississinewa*. The oiler had just swung around on its anchor chain and now presented its starboard side to the oncoming trail of foam. Full of fuel for the next duty at sea, the ship held 404,000 gallons of hundred-octane aviation gasoline in its centerline tanks and 90,000 barrels of Navy special fuel oil in tanks aft of the bridge. It was a recipe for disaster, a fire waiting for a spark.

Underwater, the submarine pilot knew his time was almost over. The end of a capital ship would mean the end of his own life, given gladly for his country. All his existence had led to this point, this day, this mission. His tension ebbed as the rightness of his decision lulled him, held him in his last moments as the droning of ships' screws vibrated in his metal cocoon.

On the ships of the U.S. Third Fleet, officers and crew feared the intrusion of submarines, but the submarine nets over the channel entrances surely would keep them out. The Americans never could have imagined the top-secret suicide weapon unleashed in the harbor waters below them, a submarine small enough to penetrate the harbor through the side passages away from the main shipping channel. Nor could they have imagined that in a few weeks newspapers in New York, San Francisco and Boston would be shouting headlines about the cruel fate that befell them in this remote place called Ulithi.

The periscope disappeared, dropping even as the craft weaved through a school of striped orange fish and thrust forward at thirty-five miles an hour toward the massive hull. The drama unfolding underwater played out as the submariner raced to the finale. Rocketing forward in the turquoise water, the pilot hoped his deadly weapon would strike the starboard side of the oiler's hull.

Suddenly a quick series of deafening explosions from depth charges reverberated through his hull, rocking him, nearly taking the craft out of his hands. Clearly the enemy had discovered the presence of the Special Attack Force. *Kikusui*—the sacred suicide mission—was now. He steeled himself to face a noble death.

CHAPTER 1

Heaven Shaker

The fiercest serpent may be overcome by a swarm of ants.

—Admiral Isoroku Yamamoto,
commander in chief of the Imperial Japanese Navy (1940)

MARCH 5, 1943
Tokyo

The commander in chief of the Imperial Japanese Navy Combined Fleet opened a letter. Six sheets of paper spilled out, revealing 874 delicate characters written in a man's blood. The reader, Admiral Isoroku Yamamoto, hero of the brilliantly conceived and executed Pearl Harbor attack, found himself gritting his teeth as he read a most unusual petition.

The request was like nothing he'd seen in this war, not a request for supplies or fuel, no bureaucratic infighting, no resistance to battle tactics. Instead, it was an impassioned plea asking for the greatest risk of all and therefore was penned in blood to show the author's deepest sincerity. The writer begged for permission to develop a manned torpedo for suicide attacks against enemy ships.

The request came from Sublieutenant Hiroshi Kuroki, a brilliant young submariner and a rising star in the Imperial Navy. He acknowledged that his idea was radical but argued that it would mean the sacrifice of only one life to sink an enemy ship. Such a strategy could turn the tide of war: one hundred men, one hundred U.S. capital ships destroyed.

The wisdom of the centuries drove Kuroki, who believed that fervent devotion to duty and sacrifice invoking the ancient warrior code of *Bushidō*—valuing loyalty and obedience and honor above life—could defeat the overwhelming might of American forces. The idea of suicide as part of military duty had been embedded in Japanese culture for thousands of years. An honorable warrior's death, embodied in the chivalric code of *Bushidō*, was revered in Japan; its core tenets included honesty, loyalty, and honor unto death.

The admiral's thoughts turned back to the attack on Pearl Harbor in late 1941 and the five midget submarines deployed there to bombard the American ships. He had considered the mission to be suicidal, yet it had achieved some good, even though nine of the ten submariner pilots lost their lives. Just before the attack on Hawaii, a photograph had been taken of the ten pilots, two to a midget submarine, who would chance fate at Pearl Harbor. The submariners who perished received almost more adulation in Japan than the aircraft pilots who dropped bombs on the harbor. The death and subsequent deification of the Nine Hero Gods reinforced the idea of submarines as suicide weapons and inspired other young men to follow their example.

Suicide in the course of military duty was a highly honorable course, but by contrast, to fail on a mission was an unbearable disgrace. The tenth man from Pearl Harbor's original submariners evaded glory, as he washed up on the beach and was captured. Reviled as a traitor, his image was painted out of the original pre-attack photograph, leaving only the remaining Nine Hero Gods.

Admiral Yamamoto reread the petition. Here the concept of suicide submarines took on a new twist, as passionately argued by the author. Accepting death if it came was not the same thing as intentional suicide. Death in battle was always a noble end, but it was not always required. That distinction created an essential difference between the midget submarines and the *kaiten*, as the suicide submersibles would come to be called. The difference was the pilot's fate. Midget submarines were designed to release torpedoes, but it was certainly possible for a pilot to escape and still fulfill his mission; the destruction of his submarine was not automatic with an attack. A *kaiten* submarine, however, meant certain death for the pilot, who must aim his vehicle at an enemy target ship and ride it to its disastrous conclusion.

Whether Admiral Yamamoto would have supported Kuroki's fervent request was never recorded. Only a month later the esteemed leader was killed when U.S. pilots attacked his plane over the Solomon Islands.

And yet Kuroki soldiered on. Despite the crushing loss of Yamamoto and his hoped-for support, the submariner continued to urge other decision-makers in the Imperial Japanese Navy to develop the suicide submarine as an offensive weapon.

Another submariner, Ensign Sekio Nishina, joined him in the quest to produce a suicide torpedo craft. Their mutual passion arose in part from the Battle of Midway, when four Japanese aircraft carriers had been destroyed and the momentum of the War in the Pacific shifted to the Allies. The Midway engagement in June 1942 had been a humiliating defeat for Japanese air and naval forces, a dreadful lesson hinting that conventional tactics might not win the war. None took the lesson more seriously than Kuroki and Nishina.

The Imperial Japanese Navy had been appalled and shamed by the shocking losses to their fleet when in the space of a few short hours four carriers sank to the bottom of the sea. Admiral Yamamoto had monitored the battle from a remote location, submariners Kuroki and Nishina on tenders nearby. The two veteran submariners never overcame their shock, which turned to a growing realization that a different strategy was necessary if Japan was to win the war. Their chagrin motivated the search for a new weapon, one able to provide the necessary speed, range and explosive power to break the back of a battleship or aircraft carrier.

Both Kuroki and Nishina burned with a desire to turn the tide of the Pacific War and claim victory, or at least create a better position for negotiating peace. On December 28, 1943, the two traveled to Tokyo to propose the development of *kaiten* and its suicide tactics (*tokkō*) to the minister of the Navy and his staff. The poised, articulate and impassioned presentation by the pair was characteristic of the dedication of the two young officers who were utterly consumed by their mission.

Kuroki first pleaded the case to officials high up in the Imperial Japanese Navy.

> If left as stands, this country will surely perish. Some decisive means must be taken immediately, otherwise our regret will remain forever. Though we are mere combatants, we should devote ourselves to this task.... We have already made up our mind to sacrifice our lives but we want to use our lives in the most effective way. This weapon is the device to fulfill our purpose.[1]

The Japanese Navy planners all knew they were faced with increasing losses in the Pacific and agreed with the doomsday sentiments. But did it make sense to use such drastic measures at this point in the war? Of course, *kamikaze* airplane pilots had already been discussed, and a few of the air attacks on Allied ships may already have been deliberate suicide attempts. However, there was no organized strategy yet to ask young men to commit to die—and take the resources of the Imperial Navy with them. As the naval experts listened to the young officers, they nodded and agreed earnestly with the sentiments. Yet they hesitated to move forward, indicating they would hold the concept in the abstract, but not wanting to advocate such a drastic measure at this point in the war.

Even so, the secret weapon Kuroki and Nishina proposed fit logically into the spectrum of war resources. Weapons technology was evolving rapidly just before and during World War II, and many Allied and Axis countries fielded scientists to develop innovative and competitive designs.[2] There was good reason to think that special attack submarines might be critical to the war's outcome.

One weapon that had devastated America's battleships at Pearl Harbor was the long lance, a formidable torpedo fitted with wooden fins to allow the normally deep-submerging torpedoes to arm and run in shallow depths; it was probably the best torpedo in the world at the time, and certainly superior to those of the United States. Also used with great success in the sea battles around Guadalcanal in 1942, it slowly became obsolete as the tone of the war changed. By 1943 and early 1944 the usefulness of the long lance was all but over, as major naval battles were now fought by aircraft at ranges of two hundred miles or more, rendering the torpedo's short-range advantages quite useless against surface ships. The Pacific War had become an aerial battlefield where the best weapons against enemy fleets were carrier-based planes.

Other specialized submersibles had been developed for war. In World War I the Italian Navy had distinguished itself by daring raids made by small torpedo boats and other special attack craft. The concept of a manned torpedo led Italian engineers to develop a craft that would be ready by the early months of World War II. It was called the *Maiale,* meaning "pig boat," due to its unusual shape.

Working independently at first, co-inventors Engineer-Major Raffaele Rissetti and Surgeon-Lieutenant Raffaele Paolucci developed the *maiale* using a design based on a twenty-seven-foot-long German torpedo powered by compressed air that ran a single-shaft forty-horsepower motor. Two men would ride astride the weapon, totally submerged except for their heads that were just visible above the water. Two bow-mounted metal canisters, each containing 375 pounds of explosives, could be removed and fastened to the hull of an enemy ship by means of magnetic "limpet" mines. A time-fused detonation could occur up to five hours later. A trip underwater on a *maiale* was not intended to be a suicide mission. If the pilots eluded enemy detection, they returned to a safe haven.

The development of the *maiale* was pushed forward in 1935 at the urging of Italy's dictator Benito Mussolini. The original design was refined by Sublieutenants Teseo Tesei and Elios Toschi, who submitted plans for a manned torpedo that significantly improved the earlier model, most notably by augmenting its ability to travel submerged over short distances. In January 1936 the First Submarine Flotilla conducted secret trials of two prototypes, crewed by the inventors. The results were successful.

Early in 1940 three manned torpedoes were launched from the Italian submarine *Ametista* in the Gulf of Spezia, in a mock attack by night. One manned torpedo succeeded in penetrating the harbor and fixing a dummy charge on the hull of a target ship. A shortwave radio link was tested to guide the manned torpedoes back to the mother boat but in the end was not installed on the *maiale*, largely because torpedo operators felt that any provision for their return might affect the men's determination to succeed at all costs.

The pig boat operators sat astride their craft with their feet in metal stirrups. The officer-pilot forward was protected by a chest-high curved metal screen that mounted a luminous magnetic compass, depth gauge, spirit level and instruments to monitor the electric motor. He controlled the torpedo's rudders with an aircraft-style steering column. Trim levers allowed seawater into or out of the ballast tanks. The copilot sat behind the pilot with his back to a metal storage locker containing spare breathing gear and tools. A six-hour oxygen supply was provided for the two crew members and they wore protective rubber suits.

The *maiale* was 22 feet long, 1.8 feet in diameter and displaced 1.5 tons. An electric motor provided the power, giving it a maximum speed of 4.5 knots and a range of 17 miles. The "pig" could submerge to a safe depth of 100 feet and had a detachable bow warhead of 485 pounds. Eighty pig boats were developed between 1940 and 1943, but at the midway mark of late 1941 they had seen only limited success. Italy's collapse stalled further development of the weapon.

The British Royal Navy recovered Italian *maiale* pig boats in Spain, Gibraltar and Alexandria in late 1940 and 1941; the capture of intact weapons led the British to build a prototype copy named the chariot. The British chariot was similar to the Italian pig, measuring 25 feet long, 21 inches in diameter, and displacing 1.5 tons. The added length of three extra feet was due to a larger 700-pound warhead. The electric motor, superior to the Italian design, gave it a top speed of 4 knots and a range of 21 miles. The safe depth for submergence was only 35 feet, but pilots exceeded the recommended depth in training and operations on a regular basis. The rubberized suits worn by British charioteers were more durable but bulkier than the suits worn by the Italians, partly because the British expected to deploy their chariots in colder northern waters.

The first deployment of the new British weapon in late October 1942 ended when the two chariots, slung underneath the Resistance-owned Norwegian fishing boat *Arthur*, broke loose from their slings and sank in Trondheim Fjord, Norway, only nine miles from the German battleship *Tirpitz*. The *Arthur* was scuttled and charioteer A. B. Evans was captured and executed by a German firing squad to satisfy Hitler's notorious anticommando order of October 18, 1942.

A common theme ran through these weapons, a theme of daring and death, even suicide. Despite its limited success, the Italian *maiale* program held at its core the philosophy of a noble warrior seeking death, and Italian leaders believed the attitude of their pilots was every bit as important as the developing technology. "What really counts is that there are men ready to die," said Tesei of the Italian Royal Navy, "to inspire and fortify future generations."

Officers Kuroki and Nishina used this same argument—the willingness to die—two years later in Tokyo, before the Imperial Navy officers. The craft they envisioned, a tiny submersible carrying a powerful warhead, would be piloted by a well-trained warrior prepared to make the ultimate sacrifice in exchange for a capital ship. Reviewing the missions of the British charioteer and the Italian *maiale* manned torpedoes, the two submariners believed that the component of suicide would create the extra element to ensure the human-driven torpedo's success. Their torpedo would require suicide as intrinsic and essential to the mission, and to prove that point they resisted the insistence of Japanese naval staff to fit the craft with an escape hatch.

The submersible, launchable from a fleet submarine, would be called *kaiten*, whose Japanese characters literally meant "heaven shaker" or "world changer." To Kuroki and Nishina, *kaiten* meant a weapon that would change the course of the war and grant Japan dominance in the Pacific Basin. One Japanese life for one American warship seemed a worthy exchange in the quest for victory.

To the young men who would volunteer for the *kaiten* program, however, the mission came to be regarded as not only honorable but frightening. One such recruit, Yutaka Yokota, was utterly shocked by this modern revival of the ancient samurai code and the certain death the *kaiten* presaged. Speaking of the suicide craft, he called *Bushidō* "the search for a place to die."

CHAPTER 2

Rising Sun

And I believe that every one of you, my fellow countrymen, will not care for your life but gladly share in the honor to make of yourself His Majesty's humble shield . . . The rise or fall of our Empire and the prosperity or ruin of East Asia literally depend upon the outcome of this war. Truly it is time for the one hundred million of us Japanese to dedicate all we have and sacrifice everything for our country's cause.

—Prime Minister Tōjō Hideki, December 8, 1941,
radio address in Tokyo[1]

Under the midnight sky laced with stars, a Japanese strike force moved through the open sea. It was called *Kido Butai*, a deadly cluster of six aircraft carriers laden with planes well armed and pilots ready to attack. By the time the pearly dawn softened the waters of the Pacific Ocean, the strike force lay 230 miles north of Hawaii.

It was December 7, 1941, in Hawaii. In Tokyo, across the international date line, it was December 8. As per the prearranged signal, the Japanese were to "climb Mt. Niitaka," the signal to bomb Pearl Harbor.

Seaplane scouts flew reconnaissance at 0600. Swinging into the wind, the carriers *Akagi*, *Hiryu*, *Soryu*, *Kaga*, *Zuikaku* and *Shokaku* launched the first wave of 183 planes. By 0620 they had massed together in the sky, the blood-red symbol of the Rising Sun on their wings. The formation of dive bombers, Zero fighters and the Nakajima B5N2s called "Kates" headed south. Pearl Harbor was ninety minutes away.

Just then in Hawaii the destroyer USS *Ward* sighted a submarine within the defensive sea area outside Pearl Harbor. The ship fired a round through its conning tower and depth-charged the submarine as it sank. It was an omen of more danger to come, but the significance was not realized at that moment. A report of the sinking made its way slowly through bureaucratic channels and took more than an hour to reach Naval Command. By then time was running out and a random submarine didn't seem to matter.

When the clock read 0702, Army radar operators on Oahu's north shore noted a very large formation of planes on their radar screens. After rechecking the equipment, they radioed the Fort Shafter watch officer in Honolulu. The American carrier *Enterprise* was due to arrive that day with a contingent of planes. Believing the planes to be fliers from the *Enterprise*, or else a flock of B-17s due in from California, the watch relaxed.

To the north, where *Kido Butai* lay in elegant splendor on the high seas, a second wave of 170 Japanese planes rose off the aircraft carriers. More Nakajima Kates flew with Mitsubishi AGV12 Reissen Zero fighters and Aichi P3A1 Val dive-bombers. The first and second waves, totaling 353 planes, would terrify Battleship Row and Hickam Field.

Just before 0800 the skies darkened over Oahu. Planes crested the mountains in a steady stream, blocking out the sun and filling the sky with a dull rumble like thunder. Zenji Abe, a bomber pilot from the carrier *Akagi*, noted how peaceful Oahu appeared. As the first wave approached Pearl Harbor, he said, "a faint haze of kitchen smoke from houses preparing breakfast hung over the water."[2] The torpedo bombers split into two attacking groups and approached Battleship Row, launching their "fish" just before the battleships prepared for colors. Splashing into the water, the torpedoes found their mark: Five exploded into the *Oklahoma*, seven tore into the *West Virginia*; the *California* took two, and another two capsized the *Utah*. Other ships, including the cruisers *Raleigh* and *Helena* and the battleship *Nevada*, were hit.

Three minutes later ten groups of high-altitude Japanese bombers flew over Pearl Harbor in formation and began dropping their 1,760-pound bombs; within seconds the U.S. fleet was engulfed in fire and smoke. Suddenly a gigantic shock wave rattled aircraft overhead and reverberated throughout Oahu. A column of smoke and fire reached to the heavens, as pieces of debris and bodies rained down over Battleship Row and Ford Island. The USS *Arizona* had exploded.

Nearly five thousand miles away, in Clinton, Wisconsin, a radio announcer interrupted the Sunday afternoon broadcast of the Chicago Bears football game with a chilling message: "The Japanese have bombed Pearl Harbor in the territory of Hawaii!" The city rivalry between the Bears and the Chicago Cardinals halted while the announcer at Comiskey Park told all servicemen to report to their units.

The message echoed in the living room of the Mair family as high-schooler John leapt from his chair and bolted out the door, shouting to his mother, "I've got to tell my brothers!" An acre away, the older boys were toting rifles with frozen breath and scouring the woods for rabbits when they heard the seventeen-year-old yelling as he raced across the brittle, frosty cornfield. "The Japs are bombing Pearl Harbor in Hawaii," he gasped. In seconds they were on the run back to the house, where the whole world seemed to close in on the radio announcer's shaking voice.

The Mairs listened as more reports came in, both parents reeling from the news of the attack that certainly would catapult the United States into the war. Two of their four boys were old enough to fight, and the reality unnerved them. John, still in high school, might follow.

The day after the attack, John gathered with his fellow students in the assembly hall at Clinton High. A teacher had brought a radio so that faculty and students could listen to President Franklin D. Roosevelt address the nation. The President's voice resonated in majestic, somber tones. He sounded calm and reassuring, despite his controlled outrage, but the Wisconsin air was full of fear. Judging from the newspaper stories that day, the entire nation was gripped with disbelief and terror.

The destruction to the U.S. fleet at Pearl Harbor was almost unimaginable: battleships sunk, overturned, crippled; the *Arizona* a battered hulk in the mud, nearly thirteen hundred men entombed within its hull; the battleship *Oklahoma* rolled over like a metallic beached whale, its keel thrust up to the sky; the *Nevada* run aground in the channel. Only the aircraft carriers out at sea had escaped the devastation.

The threat to the United States now came on two fronts: the European Theater, where Hitler still stormed like a madman, and the Pacific Theater, where Japanese commanders slowly moved easterly, taking island chain after chain, dreams of a Hawaii conquest in their minds.[3]

In Wisconsin, as in Massachusetts, California and all over, recruiting stations began to see long lines of volunteers. The United States would never be the same. Young men rushed to sign up, inspired by the posters featuring the mangled, smoking wreckage of a battleship and the slogan "REMEMBER THE ARIZONA!"

John Mair had to wait for his parents' permission to enlist, but he knew he wanted to join the Navy. In 1941 he couldn't know that in three years he would be part of Pacific War history, when his ship would be lost to the first suicide attack by a Japanese submarine pilot.

Two days after the Pearl Harbor attack, the *Arizona* still burned in the harbor, its twisted superstructure horribly askew, a searing reminder to everyone on Oahu of the devastation that had befallen them. Dozens of ships needed repair; others were trashed in the harbor, some to be salvaged and refitted. Even before the smoke cleared, the Navy knew it faced a grave and immediate problem—rebuilding the Pacific Fleet.

The War in the Pacific would require the largest shipbuilding program the country had ever attempted. Repairing the damaged ships was a massive undertaking, compounded by a demand for new auxiliary ships to maintain the flow of supplies—in particular, gas and oil—needed to fuel ships and planes. Although battleships and aircraft carriers were the visible vessels of attack and defense, they were only as good as their fuel supply. The auxiliary ships that fueled them didn't attract media attention but were nonetheless critical to the success of any naval mission.

Keeping Navy vessels in the Pacific supplied with fuel was a significant challenge, seeing that the anchorage of the Pacific Fleet was Hawaii, twenty-four hundred miles away from the West Coast of the United States. The round trip to shuttle oil from California or the Northwest to Pearl Harbor by tanker took two weeks.

When boats traveled with the wind, fuel was no issue, but that all changed in the second half of the nineteenth century when ships switched from sail to steam, and fuel replaced the unpredictable wind. It was a good change—except that wind is freely available and fuel must be supplied.

Steam could be generated by burning something—wood, coal, oil—to kick up the heat in a ship's furnace. Wood fires, always dangerous and a frequent cause of tragic fires on board, progressed into the hotter and more efficient coal fires as Appalachian mines yielded their riches. In those days of coal power a warship's mobility depended on adequate supplies of coal, and a warship cruising at ten knots could easily consume three or four tons of coal in an hour. Since the sailing range of a warship was limited to the size of its coal bunkers, it became critical to secure coal at various ports.

However, the idea of fuel ships actually traveling with the fleet wasn't seriously considered until the Great White Fleet's round-the-world cruise ending in 1908; although the feat had proved to be an engineering triumph for the United States, the fourteen-month journey by sixteen coal-burning warships caused much embarrassment to the Navy when the colliers failed to keep the ships supplied. The inability of foreign colliers to provide fuel on a timely basis was perhaps the most important lesson learned from the cruise.

Even with timely deliveries, the transfer of coal was time-consuming and inefficient. Oil was an attractive alternative. When oil became the Navy's fuel of choice for the fleet in 1909, transfer problems were largely resolved by fueling hoses, whose efficiency was unquestionably superior to the cumbersome transfers of bulk coal.

The First World War further illustrated the need to refuel ships at sea. Mare Navy Yard in northern California laid down the keels of the first two U.S. Navy auxiliary vessels to carry oil. The two ships, *Maumee* and *Kanawha*, were originally classified as "fuel ships," but the name "oiler" soon supplanted the older term. In official Navy terminology, all oilers are auxiliary oilers or Combat Logistics ships, fitted to fuel U.S. warships at sea. By contrast, tankers are merchant ships manned by civilian crews; they are not equipped with at-sea fueling gear but instead carry bulk fuel from port to port. In World War II the tankers delivered bulk fuel to Pacific Fleet staging areas from ports on the West Coast; the oilers would periodically resupply from these staging areas and then refuel the warships at sea.

The first wartime fueling of U.S. ships at sea was accomplished in 1917; it took a remarkably short ten hours and thirty-five minutes. Six destroyers received twenty thousand gallons of fuel each at a rate of thirty-two thousand gallons per hour. The extraordinary feat was successful despite inexperienced crews and nasty sea conditions.

Fueling at sea was deemed increasingly important in the 1920s and '30s. The strategy for a theoretical naval war in the Pacific—ever a threat in the minds of most military men—called for the fleet to reach the western Pacific at the prevailing speed of ten knots in twenty days.

In April 1923 a Navy oiler, the USS *Cuyama*, successfully fueled eight destroyers in pairs while steaming at slow speed in calm waters. The oiler employed the riding-the-beam method, also referred to as the broadside method, with a destroyer on each side of the fueling ship.

But *Cuyama*'s skipper was concerned about damage that could result from broadside fueling of larger capital ships, especially in rough weather. Sailing so close alongside ships larger than destroyers was impractical in anything but calm seas, as swells of any magnitude could result in damage to the tanker hull and its rigging, and even loss of life.

Another oiler, the USS *Kanawha*, attempted over-the-stern fueling at sea using a stern-mounted towing tension engine, but the low delivery rate of sixteen thousand gallons of oil per hour was deemed unsatisfactory for fueling capital ships at sea. Over-the-stern fueling was canceled in 1931, and from that point on all Navy oilers under construction were equipped for broadside fueling.

A fuel-related question—and a serious concern for the Navy—was the short steaming range of the battleships *Nevada*, *Oklahoma*, *Arizona*, *Idaho*, *Mississippi* and *Pennsylvania*. Expanding their range was vital to naval victory in a Pacific war, so rapid fueling at sea was critical.

And fueling at sea was only as fast as the slowest ship: In order for oilers to keep pace with the ships they were fueling, they obviously had to be capable of sailing at the same speeds. The newer Navy oilers were designed to keep pace with the main battle fleet, but the slower merchant tankers that had been converted to naval auxiliaries were woefully inadequate. By the 1930s senior naval officers believed the Navy was ill-equipped to protect its interests in the Pacific, but the Hoover administration, struggling with the Depression, was in no mood to rebuild the fleet.

Franklin D. Roosevelt's inauguration as president in 1933 offered new hope to the U.S. fleet. FDR had served as an assistant secretary of the Navy during the First World War and enthusiastically supported the Navy. His New Deal advisors persuaded him that naval construction could act as a cure to economic crisis in the United States; thus, to stimulate jobs and money flow, FDR signed an executive order freeing 238 million dollars for new naval construction that would include thirty-two new warships.

The Navy's top war planners were troubled by the fleet's obsolescence.

So concerned were they about modernizing the Navy that an updated War Plan Orange placed a very high priority on building fast, modern auxiliary ships, including oilers. Senior admirals recommended that fast oilers be able to cruise at a speed of fifteen knots—a remarkable requirement, given that merchant tankers during this time were capable of only eleven knots; even the fastest tankers under design would make only thirteen knots. This momentous recommendation led to the building of twelve fast oilers of the new Cimarron class, named for the first national defense tanker completed, the impressive USS *Cimarron*. Launched on January 7, 1939, it was the first oiler to be delivered to the fleet since 1922. Measuring 553 feet long, with a beam of 75 feet, *Cimarron* was one of the largest fueling vessels in the world and the fastest ever built in the United States. Others of its kind were soon to follow.

Three years into the war, another fast-fleet oiler, *Mississinewa*, would come to life on a shipyard's ways. Young men like John Mair would join the ship's crew and sail in to the Pacific islands where the war was playing out. At the same time they would sail onto the pages of history.

CHAPTER 3

Midway

The defeated should not talk about the battle.

—Japanese proverb

The shipboard wireless crackled with static, but Admiral Yamamoto was standing by, reading in disbelief as the battle reports poured in. From far away to the west he spoke with his leaders directing the attack on Midway Island. It was June 4, 1942, and the battle in the middle of the Pacific Ocean was nothing short of a catastrophe. The success that had been achieved by the Japanese forces at Pearl Harbor was slipping away. The admiral was hearing news shocking and almost unbelievable.

The exuberance after the Pearl Harbor attack was gone. In chilling contrast to today's events, Pearl Harbor had opened the War in the Pacific with what appeared an almost insurmountable disaster for the United States and its allies. Now, six months later, the Battle of Midway put a whole new face on the war.

Yamamoto had envisioned the capture of Midway Island as the most effective way to distract and disable the U.S. Pacific Fleet and take it out of action long enough for Japan to fortify its defensive perimeter in the Pacific island chains. As he had done successfully at Hawaii, the admiral felt it necessary to make a decisive strike. He planned to draw the American carriers into a trap at Midway where the First Mobile Force would engage and destroy them. Afterward, his First Fleet—consisting of a light carrier, three cruisers, seven battleships and thirteen destroyers—would, in conjunction with the Second Fleet, mop up remaining American surface forces and complete the destruction of the U.S. Pacific Fleet.

Stationed in a remote location far from Midway, Yamamoto consulted frequently with the on-site commanders engaged in the battle. Among the many staff and military support surrounding him were two young submariners, Sublieutenant Hiroshi Kuroki and Ensign Sekio Nishina, both pilots of midget submarines called *Ko-hyoteki*. The veteran midget submariners, stationed aboard the converted seaplane tenders *Chiyoda* and *Nisshin*, were privy to the events unfolding. Their reactions to the defeat at Midway and their desire for Japan's ultimate victory factored importantly in decisions later made by the Japanese Imperial Navy and in the secret weapon the submariners devised.[1]

Pearl Harbor had been a very different story. At that moment of America's formal engagement in World War II, Japan's impressive armada was greatly superior to the inefficient and aging U.S. Pacific Fleet. On December 7, 1941, the Pearl Harbor attack caused massive destruction: Of the eight American battleships present that fateful weekend, five were sunk, and many other vessels and aircraft were destroyed or damaged. But World War II was a different war from the old conventional ship-of-the-line engagements. Now the battles were shifting to the open seas, and battleships were yielding to the strategic power of aircraft carriers, the new queens of the sea.

Both Pearl Harbor and Midway pivoted around the role of aircraft carriers. At Pearl Harbor, six Japanese carriers had launched a dense horde of attacking planes that severely damaged the fleet of aging battleships. Conspicuously absent from the harbor that day, the three American carriers were many miles distant at sea and thus were spared, a most fortuitous event in an otherwise dismal time. It proved to be a deadly omen for the Japanese, for at Midway six months later, it was American carriers that commanded the victory, sending four Japanese carriers to the bottom of the sea.

Pearl Harbor came back to haunt Yamamoto now. His failure to strike U.S. carriers on December 7 had the smack of fate to it.

Why had he not done so? On December 6, the day before the attack, Japanese senior officers had expressed conflicting opinions on the importance of the American carriers, and a heated debate erupted over what should be the focus of their surprise attack, given the disparate positions of the U.S. battleships and carriers. Up-to-date intelligence reported that the U.S. battleships were anchored in the harbor while the carriers were at sea. Captain Minoru Genda lobbied to attack the carriers; he hoped the three ships might possibly return to Pearl Harbor in time to be attacked on December 7. If that should happen, he said, "I don't care if all eight of the battleships are away."

Commander Tamotsu Oishi, his senior staff officer, acknowledged the importance of the carriers but concluded, "I think it would be better if we got all eight of the battleships."

And so the strike took place and indeed Oahu was devastated. The *Arizona* and *Oklahoma* were utterly destroyed by Nakajima Kates that pummeled all the battleships. The U.S. carriers remained at sea, their absence having proven critical to the Japanese plan of successfully striking Oahu with little air defense on the American side. But the trade-off was coming: American carriers would figure prominently in the crucial Battle of Midway.

For many weeks the twisted wreckage of the *Arizona* loomed over the harbor, reminding every officer and sailor of the nightmare that had hit them on that "Day of Infamy," as President Franklin Roosevelt called it. As the superstructure was cut away and the other ships repaired or removed, the sense of despair began to galvanize into firm resolve. American men went to war.

The initially demoralized U.S. Navy had changed in the six months after Pearl Harbor into an increasingly armed and aggressive foe, but the Japanese continued to believe their forces were superior, an attitude later called the "victory disease." A number of battles went in their favor: Wake Island surrendered to the Japanese, followed by the fall of the Philippines and the expansion to Guadalcanal, and by May 1942 the Japanese high command began to look toward the West Coast of the United States, whose long and thinly defended stretch of mainland would yield a strategic land base to control the Pacific and the Panama Canal. As part of the strategy to take the mainland, the next Japanese offensive was planned for Midway Island, the halfway point in the Pacific between the United States and Japan, northwest of Hawaii.[2] After two months of planning and maneuvers, Admiral Yamamoto felt they were ready to attack.

Then the worst fate befell Yamamoto, and it was something every military commander fears: The enemy learned of his plans. Shortly before the attack, U.S. intelligence experts broke the Japanese naval code and discovered where they intended to strike. Ground Zero was Midway. The U.S. Navy mounted its own force, centered around three aircraft carriers: USS *Enterprise*, which had been spared on December 7, and USS *Hornet* and *Yorktown*. As the rosy skies paled on the morning of June 4, 1942, the Japanese and American forces met in the battle that changed the course of the war.

The Americans possessed three advantages: superior intelligence, the longer reconnaissance range of their Midway-based aircraft, and the element of surprise.

The first American planes left Midway at 0400 on the search for the Japanese fleet; a half hour later, the carrier *Yorktown* launched ten American reconnaissance SBD planes. The first sighting of enemy aircraft occurred at 0520, followed ten minutes later by the sighting of a Japanese carrier. Events moved quickly. A VMSB-241 Marine bombing squadron took off from Midway, and by 0616 Japanese planes were attacking the island. The battle was joined.

At precisely 0755, the exact minute bombs had first fallen at Pearl

Harbor six months earlier, American planes were massing to place the Japanese aircraft carrier *Soryu* under attack. A minute later the carriers *Akagi* and *Hiryu* fell under fire.

For the next three hours American airmen hammered Japanese ships like ducks on a pond, as they sent wave after wave of torpedoes and dive-bombers to attack the battleships and carriers. When U.S. dive-bombers dropped their loads on the enemy carriers, the decks were crowded with refueling aircraft that popped like firecrackers on a string. Flames erupted hundreds of feet into the sky.

The two-hour slice of time on June 4, when three of the four Japanese carriers present were mortally wounded, constitutes one of the most intense military events in modern naval history, second only to the attack on Pearl Harbor. The carrier *Kaga* was dive-bombed and fires broke out. *Soryu* was hit twice; within thirty minutes the officers gave orders to abandon ship. The *Akagi* succumbed to torpedo and bomber attacks when its fighter planes caught fire.

As American planes zeroed in on the carriers, they dropped five-hundred-pound bombs that exploded on the decks and ignited refueling planes. The intense conflagration melted through the teak-and-metal flight decks, hitting munitions and igniting gas and oil stored below, causing enormous fireballs of black, oily smoke and shooting flames.

After the stunning hits from the U.S. dive-bombers, the *Akagi*, queen of the sea and heroine of the strike force of *Kido Butai*, didn't last long. Less than an hour after its planes were on fire, all surviving personnel had been ordered to abandon ship.

By late afternoon of June 4, the Japanese witnessed an unthinkable sight—three aircraft carriers, *Kaga, Soryu* and *Akagi,* were burning and crippled. The fourth, *Hiryu,* still in attack mode, was about to be hit with bombs from planes from the *Enterprise*; by 1705 the last Japanese aircraft carrier was on fire from several hits.

It had seemed that the stricken carrier *Soryu* might be saved. When its fire abated, Japanese firefighters prepared to go on board and reclaim the ship, but at seven in the evening a huge explosion sent a brilliant molten ball into the sky and the flattop sank below the waves. Ten minutes later a tremendous undersea explosion reverberated through the waters, rocking the ships on the surface.

The *Soryu* sank at 1915, the *Kaga* ten minutes after.

The order had been given to abandon the *Akagi*. Soon after *Soryu* went down, an emotional discussion was held between senior Japanese officers at the battle site and General Yamamoto, who was reached by radio on the battleship *Yamato* six hundred miles to the west. They debated the best disposition of the carrier. The question was whether to scuttle the ship, abandon it or rush in and take it under tow in hopes of a retreat across the ocean to a Japanese navy yard. One officer opposed to scuttling the *Akagi* argued impassionedly, "We cannot sink the Emperor's warships by the Emperor's own torpedoes!"

Yamamoto took the heavy mantle of humiliation on himself. He paused for what seemed like endless seconds to the listeners, then said, "I was once the captain of *Akagi*, and it is with heartfelt regret that I must now order that she be sunk. I will apologize to the Emperor for the sinking of *Akagi* by our own torpedoes."

At 0500 the following morning, June 5, his orders were carried out and the carrier was torpedoed and sunk. At 0900 that same morning the *Hiryu*, the fourth and last remaining Japanese aircraft carrier, slipped beneath the waves that filled the seas around Midway with blood and foam.

The United States sustained only one major loss in the battle, the aircraft carrier *Yorktown*. Under retaliatory strikes by the Japanese on June 6, the carrier took a torpedo hit shortly after noon and sank fifteen hours later.

Midway delivered a stunning defeat for the Japanese Navy. Perhaps as many as 98 percent of the aircraft carrier personnel who had bombed Pearl Harbor were wiped out. Admiral Yamamoto, esteemed commander of the Japanese forces who had opened the war so successfully on December 7, lost all four of his veteran carriers, and most of their planes and pilots—a devastating loss from the first victorious sortie six months earlier.

The irony of the role of the American aircraft carriers missing at Pearl Harbor was not lost on Yamamoto, for one of those very same carriers of the U.S. Pacific Fleet that so fortunately had been out to sea on December 7 came back to engage his own forces at Midway and utterly defeat them.

Chagrined by the appalling loss of four Imperial Japanese Navy fleet carriers, Kuroki and Nishina, the submariners of Yamamoto's fleet, began to imagine a new weapon that could change the war. Nishina envisioned a midget submersible that, unlike the Type A midget submarine, would be launchable from a submerged fleet submarine. They began working together some months later and from their fertile minds came the idea of the "heaven shaker," a weapon they believed could reverse the fortunes of war.

As 1943 passed into 1944 and strategic islands fell from Japanese hands, the attraction of secret weapons grew in the minds of military leaders. The sense of urgency began to change to desperation.

The range of suicide weapons included an aerial bomb transported by a balloon. In a little known campaign known as *Fu-Go*, Japan released about ninety-three hundred bomb-laden balloons that floated on air currents across the Pacific; they were intended to explode in the United States and cause forest fires, panic and death. The balloons were armed with a 15-kilogram antipersonnel bomb and four 4.5-kilogram incendiaries, as well as a flash bomb to destroy evidence of the devices. Only one fatal event is recorded. In May 1945 near Bly, Oregon, a minister's wife and five teenagers with her on a picnic spotted a balloon bomb and began playing with it. It exploded, killing them all. Although they are the only known casualties of the balloon bombs, many balloons—probably one thousand—reached U.S. soil, some as far inland as Minnesota.[3]

With the variety of suicide weapons discussed in 1942, it was clear that, for the Japanese military, Midway had become a turning point in attitude, a seesaw between hope and despair, a reawakening of *Bushidō*. In that climate, the search for "a place to die" became a priority for certain Japanese fighters, those who would volunteer as *kamikaze* pilots in the air and those who would seek salvation as *kaiten* pilots underwater.

CHAPTER 4

The Mighty *Miss*

War must be, while we defend our lives against a destroyer
who would devour all; but I do not love the bright sword for
its sharpness, nor the arrow for its swiftness, nor the warrior
for his glory. I love only that which they defend.

—J. R. R. TOLKIEN, *The Two Towers* [1]

March 28, 1944, was a bitterly cold day at Sparrows Point, Maryland, but a brand-new oiler was ready to slide down the ways for its official launch. At the long-awaited moment Margaret Pence, the ship's sponsor, looked up at the massive ship, "as big as a tall building," and struck the newly painted bow with a champagne bottle, christening the vessel after an Indiana river: Mississinewa. As with all commissioned ships of the U.S. Navy, the name was preceded by USS, meaning "United States Ship." The men simply called the tongue-twister the "*Mighty M*" or "*Mighty Miss.*"

Six weeks later, the ship was handed over to the commanding officer. The bo'sun's pipe pierced the knocks and clanging sounds of the bustling Bethlehem Steel shipyard at 1400 hours on May 18. Admiral Felix Gygax crisply saluted the officer of the deck as he reached the well deck of the Navy's newest oiler. A commissioning party led by Captain B. M. Ward followed the admiral as he walked amid the maze of pipes, catwalks, capstans, valves and rope coils that are the trademarks of an oiler. All took their places.

Despite the festivities, war was calling and every sailor knew it. The last officer to speak at the commissioning had closed with a stark phrase: "You boys are going to the South Pacific—and some of you aren't coming back. Good luck and God bless you all."[2] The commissioning pendant rose to the ship's masthead and fluttered in the breeze. A few of the young men wondered where it would be fluttering a month from now. Sailors turned to leave after the thirty-minute ceremony with those words echoing ominously in their ears. ". . . Some of you aren't coming back."

The men selected as *Mississinewa*'s first officers comprised a varied and talented group.[3] Commander Philip Beck, the ship's first captain—and its last—was respected as a confident, capable officer with an intimate knowledge of the sea. Beck, fifty years old, provided the *Miss* crew with solid experience from a vast seafaring background, though he was viewed with skepticism by a few sailors for his hard-drinking ways.

Born in New York in 1894, he enlisted in the Navy in 1911 as an apprentice seaman and went through stints in the Merchant Service as well. Rising through the ranks of the Merchant Service, from able seaman to boatswain to second mate, he spent 1918 to 1920 in the U.S. Army Transport Service as second officer, ferrying troops between Haiti, Puerto Rico and the Panama Canal Zone. Enrolling in the U.S. Naval Auxiliary Reserve as an ensign, he served aboard his first oiler, USS *Sara Thompson*, as part of the Atlantic Fleet.

A stint for the Pan American Petroleum & Transport Co. was his last private employment before he returned to active duty in the U.S. Navy in 1942. Ranked as first lieutenant of the USS *Kenmore*, he brought troops to Guadalcanal and was again promoted to commander, then reassigned to USS *Cossatot*. A year later he was assigned as commanding officer of the soon-to-be commissioned oiler *Mississinewa*. He would live to write the Action Report of the ship's demise, a mere six months after he took command.

Lieutenant Robert L. Rowe, 33, the navigator for *Mississinewa*, had been a seagoing Merchant Marine for years. He'd begun his naval career in 1933 as a reserve ensign and spent months in the South Pacific after the Pearl Harbor attack as his ship fueled the remnants of the devastated U.S. fleet. Known for a thick Boston accent and great sense of humor, Rowe made full lieutenant on January 1, 1944, and was reassigned to *Mississinewa* as the fleet oiler approached completion near Baltimore.

Chief medical officer Lieutenant John Bierley grew up in Bellevue, Kentucky, and graduated from the University of Cincinnati in 1933. First a Naval Reservist, he commenced active duty November 1943 as surgeon to the U.S. Naval Hospital in Puerto Rico, then was reassigned to the *Mississinewa* the following year. Not all ships had a trained doctor in the ship's company, and his surgical skills would be badly needed in the Pacific Theater.

Newly commissioned officers joined the fleet as "Ninety-Day Wonders," the Navy's term for the brand-new ensigns with a mere three months of midshipman training. One young ensign, Charles Scott, was destined for the *Miss*, but not before he got engaged. He penned a letter to his girlfriend with a marriage proposal, knowing he "didn't want to lose his girl to a shorebird." Her "yes!" came quickly, but the wedding would have to wait till his ship returned to the States. When it did, in early February 1944, Scott got orders to report to Newport Navy Base in Rhode Island to await construction of the *Mississinewa*, still on the ways at Bethlehem Steel's shipyard.

Officers came in with Merchant Marine experience as well as Navy training. It was all good for morale. The seasoned officers lent an air of stability that inspired confidence in the junior officers.

The *Mississinewa*'s crew complement was a mix: enlisted men who had signed up before the war began, those who signed up after Pearl Harbor and fresh arrivals recruited as the war dragged on. John Mair was one of the recent high school graduates who saw enlistment as a patriotic duty and a way to see a world more exciting than southern Wisconsin's flat farmlands. He remembered the day he was first inspired to fight—December 7. Three years later he graduated and waited for the call to arms. Six months after getting his diploma, he finally got an induction notice. Since marching knee-deep in mud with Army troops sounded dismal, he requested the Navy and was soon bound for Great Lakes Naval Training Center in Chicago. The center was a busy place in early 1944, as the Navy urgently needed crews for ships being built at a rapid rate in the nation's shipyards. Immunization shots, classroom lectures and close order drills filled the next seven weeks as the new sailors learned the basics of military life. Mair graduated as a fireman second class, destined for sea duty.

Sailor recruits soon learned that the Navy did things the Navy way. "Assign me to any ship but a tanker," fireman Mair proclaimed to anyone near enough to listen. The Navy assigned him to the new auxiliary oil tanker, the *Miss*, under construction. It *was* the Navy way!

Another fireman, Ohioan Bob Vulgamore, had studied chemistry in high school and worked in steel analysis at Wheeling Steel in Portsmouth, Ohio. Torn between patriotism and devotion to family, the thirty-three-year-old resolved to enlist if the draft board called him. One day the chief chemist in his lab came around to each chemist and analyst to hand out deferments. That didn't sit right with Vulgamore—he tore his deferment paper into little pieces and enlisted the next day in the Navy.

Selection of crew members was intentional at times, random at others. Fifty enlisted sailors arrived to board the *Miss* from Great Lakes Naval Training Center, all with last names starting with C or D, a clear sign that after a certain head count the C and D lines were summarily ordered to board the train for Newport. In fact, in late November 1944 when the *Mississinewa* reported its last full crew complement of 278 enlisted men, there were 44 with C last names and 45 with D. A man's destiny could depend on the most random and innocuous detail.

Many seamen on the deck force had never sailed on a Navy oiler, and the senior officers knew they had a formidable task ahead of them. Dozens of high school boys fresh out of training made up *Mississinewa*'s inexperienced deck force in the fueling divisions. It was clear that experienced men would be needed to turn *Mississinewa* into a capable fleet auxiliary oiler. Veteran sailors from the fleet and stateside posts were ordered to Newport in March 1944 to begin training the sailors to man the ship.

Several members of *Mississinewa*'s engineering division were seasoned regular Navy sailors who had enlisted prior to or just after the attack on Pearl Harbor. This core group of veterans in Engineering and Construction and Repair was critical in making sure that the ship put to sea as soon as possible after the June 1944 shakedown cruise on Chesapeake Bay.

Machinist's mate Gus Liveakos had joined the rest of Recruit Company 104 at Norfolk, Virginia, in August 1940. The son of a Greek restaurant owner from Greenville, Alabama, Liveakos graduated from high school two years late, after one school year was canceled during the Great Depression for lack of money for teachers' pay; another year was lost when his school closed down for a flu epidemic. He joined a cruiser as a seaman, where he made a great discovery—whereas unlucky deckhands slept in hammocks, the engineers slept in bunks! He decided a bunk would suit him "just fine," so the feisty Alabama man joined the so-called "snipes"—a term for anyone who worked below deck—as a fireman. In March he transferred to Baltimore to become a machinist on the *Miss*.

Florian "Bill" Brzykcy had worked for the Midwest Baking Co. in Burlington, Iowa, making syrup for cookie manufacturing. In 1941 at age seventeen he decided to join the Navy while watching a sternwheeler paddle lazily up the Mississippi River during a work break. Failing the

Navy's color blindness test the first time around, he got accepted months later when they dropped that drill. Before he knew it, he was off to boot camp at Great Lakes Naval Training Center in Illinois, where recruit training had been reduced to only four weeks by July 1942. Following a dizzying array of shots, Brzykcy learned to sleep in a hammock and carry out drills while taking classes for a variety of skills. The young Iowan tested well for mechanical ability and received his orders to report to USS *Weehawken* as a fireman second class, making him a member of the "black gang," so named because almost a hundred years earlier, when coal became the fuel for steam engines, the men who shoveled it into the furnaces got covered with coal dust.

Brzykcy was stationed in the fire room with old-type Scotch tube boilers that allowed the burner flames to surround the boiler tubes, a dangerous system similar to old steam locomotives. Explosions were common. The base of the boiler tubes developed a collection of hard water mineral deposits that veteran fire room sailors called "crown cheese." If the water disappeared from the base of the tubes, the crown cheese would glow red hot and a catastrophic explosion could follow. To prevent such an occurrence, the boiler tubes had to be immersed in water at all times, a dangerous job Brzykcy wanted no part of. He fantasized leaving *Weehawken*'s black gang and joining the "real" Navy.

Tragedy came all too close to the Brzykcy family. While serving aboard *Weehawken* the young man received a telegram advising him that his brother had been killed in a motorcycle accident. He got a nine-day leave, not realizing his ship would leave shortly for Casablanca. He arrived in California for the funeral just in time to learn even more devastating news: His father, a WWI veteran who had reenlisted in the Army, had been killed overseas three days after his brother died. Grief-stricken, Brzykcy overstayed his leave. He was picked up by the shore patrol as he returned later to his ship. A summary court-martial levied a $195 fine against him.

He rejoiced on being transferred to Brooklyn receiving barracks, a new building with clean heads and showers, even a stand with "geedunks," as the sailors called ice cream and other snack foods. Several sailors from other countries were quartered with the American sailors. Fistfights broke out almost daily, but Brzykcy managed to stay out of trouble. One night a drunken British sailor at a local bar toasted the Queen of England and insisted that Brits were better than Americans. When the braggart passed out, the Americans took him to a tattoo parlor where the Stars and Stripes were tattooed on his chest and underlined by "God Bless America."

Brzykcy's next stop was at Newport, where crews were training for the ammunition ship *Mount Hood* and the oiler *Mississinewa*. Now rated as a fireman first class, he reported to ammunition ship *Mount Hood* as part of the commissioning crew. When the shipbuilder fell behind schedule, some of the men originally assigned to the *Hood* were reassigned to *Mississinewa*, including Brzykcy.

Raymond Fulleman grew up in Bloomfield, New Jersey, where the main business was industrial manufacturing. Nineteen when the war started, the slender fellow had gotten a job as an apprentice steamfitter, seeking to join either the Navy or the Merchant Marine because he liked being on the water.

At that time, the regular Navy required six years, the Navy Reserves only two—officially. But unofficially, of course, everyone knew he would really be signing up for the duration of the war. Originally intending to enlist in the Navy for six years, Fulleman overheard the kid in front of him enthusiastically tell the old recruiter that he wanted to sign up for the full six years. "What the hell's the matter with you?" the recruiter yelled. "You don't know what you're doing. Take the two years."

When Fulleman's turn came, he wisely responded to the same question, "I'll take the Reserves." Basic training led to an assignment on the light cruiser USS *Mobile,* where he advanced to fireman first class and water tender third class. In April 1944 he got his next ship assignment: *Mississinewa.*

Machinist's mate third class Stanley Johnson grew up in Rhode Island. After Pearl Harbor he elected to perform war work at a local plant, then joined the Navy in November 1943. He finished boot camp, married his betrothed in February 1944 and received orders to report to USS *Mount Hood,* under construction in Norfolk, Virginia. When it became evident that the ship's construction was delayed, Johnson and others below the rank of chief received new orders—this time for the oiler *Mississinewa.* The switch would prove to be life changing. The fairly routine change of assignment sent some men to their deaths; for others it saved their lives. Both the *Hood* and the *Miss* would be sunk, ten days and 830 miles apart, in the tropical reaches of the South Pacific.

Black sailors served in ship wardrooms throughout the fleet, as black men were limited to just a few ratings during the war due to prejudice. The ship's officers required a skilled staff of black stewards and steward's mates to prepare and serve the officers' meals. Many black sailors with considerable experience held advanced ratings.

Steward third class Raleigh Peppers oversaw the officers' laundry and cold storage for the officers' wardroom. Like other black sailors, he experienced inequity in many places. On the parade field, blacks marched only with sticks while the white sailors shouldered rifles. Peppers described their bewilderment. "Hey, we enlisted to serve our country, too." On his first assignment to a transport ship that made regular runs to Puerto Rico for sugar, an experienced galley steward recognized that Peppers was a quick study and recommended the young man for promotion to steward third class. Reassigned to Newport Base for duty, Peppers then was deployed to the *Mississinewa,* where he served as the senior rated black sailor aboard. He supervised a team of cooks and stewards for the officers' cuisine.

Meals for the large crew of *Mississinewa* presented a monumental task every day, requiring much prior planning and efficient delivery. One of the oldest crew members aboard, chief commissary steward Frank

Lutz, led the challenge. The forty-nine-year-old was one of the most experienced sailors aboard *Mississinewa*, and the hearty meals testified to his skill and that of his young staff.

Fernando Cuevas, a skilled short-order cook, had come to the States from Puerto Rico in 1917 when his father immigrated to New York City to work for American Tobacco Company. By December 1941 Cuevas was employed as a hydraulic press operator. He'd been married for eight years and his wife was six months pregnant when he was drafted.

As the *Mississinewa* took on the officers and men who would take the ship to sea, one last group of sailors still awaited ship assignments. The enlisted men went into a room where the seating was divided: The chairs on one side were devoted to the new ammunition ship *Mount Hood* and the chairs on the other side to the soon-to-be commissioned *Mississinewa*. For no apparent reason, three sailors, Upchurch, McGarity and McLaughlin, moved to the seats marked *Mississinewa*. Given what happened to the *Hood* later that year, that choice saved their lives.

The troop train from Newport, Rhode Island, pulled up to the Baltimore dock and *Miss* sailors got the first look at their new home. The *Miss* was constructed as a twin-screw oil carrier with "three islands," meaning the deck held a raised poop deck, bridge and forecastle. Belowdecks, twin longitudinal bulkheads divided the main hold, and traverse bulkheads subdivided the ship's interior into twenty-four main cargo tanks.

Dressed in fresh camouflage paint, the brand-new fleet oiler dazzled even the seasoned veterans, but it was downright daunting to the young sailors, who had mostly seen only fishing vessels. Atlantic duty vessels were often painted blue, while ships destined for the Pacific were usually painted a deep slate referred to as "haze gray." When the ship's crew first saw the *Miss*, the oiler was painted in a completely different mix: the newest camouflage scheme, with jagged streaks of black, gray and white. Where, they wondered, was the ship going—the Arctic? Before boarding, the officers would learn they were bound for the Pacific, but the destination was kept secret from the crew.

On the day of the *Mighty Miss*'s launch in 1944, the War in the Pacific had already lasted two and a half years. The attack at Pearl Harbor had caused the sudden American pact with the Allies, but battles in the Coral Sea and the Solomons cost many an American life. The June 1942 Battle of Midway had been for the Allies a thrilling retaliation against the Japanese fleet. For the Japanese it was a renewed call for *Bushidō*. Both navies took inspiration from the events of Midway.

The war moved farther into the western Pacific, and island chains unknown to most Americans soon became daily headlines: the Marshall Islands, the Admiralties, the Marianas, the Carolines. The names rang with romance tinged with blood. A mere six months after its commissioning, the *Mississinewa* would carry its officers and crew to a rendezvous with fate, and Americans would read a name in the newspapers most had never heard of: Ulithi.

The men hoisted their seabags and headed up the gangplank. Sea trials were about to begin. War suddenly seemed closer than half a world away.

May 26. Norfolk, Virginia. Inspections and shakedown cruises filled the first week of the oiler's active life, and it was about to leave on another operational test. Before leaving the harbor, the *Mighty Miss* had to undergo the first of many degaussing operations to demagnetize the hull. Crews surrounded the hull with wires, and engineers then sent electrical currents through the wires, a process that altered the ship's magnetic field and offered at least temporary protection against the thousands of magnetic mines scattered by the Japanese around the Pacific islands. Magnetic mines had been a growing problem as the war progressed, and the Navy now required all ships to undergo frequent degaussing.

Watches could be inadvertently demagnetized during that process, so before the degaussing started on the *Miss*, a seaman collected watches, clocks and all other timepieces from everyone aboard, taking everything ashore for safekeeping until degaussing was finished.

Word passed among the crew that the ship was to depart on May 27 for more shakedown operations. Over the next five days, as the ship steamed on Chesapeake Bay, the crew tested machinery and conducted drills in firefighting, collision response, degaussing runs, general quarters (GQ), and cargo shifting for ballasting and gunnery. Firemen tested all the pumps, gauges, valves and the array of pipes and machinery that made up the pump room watch station.

The next day would hold a major gunnery drill. Pointers and trainers would man the large mounts, which required two to four loaders to transfer shells from ammunition hoists to the gun. A pointer aimed the gun while a trainer would crank a hand wheel that changed the barrel's elevation. A seven-man team was required for most large-caliber weapons aboard *Mississinewa*. Gunner's mates trained deckhands on each type of weapon in the ship's arsenal, and the sailors gained proficiency as a team.

June 4. The ship was finally deemed ready to go to sea, and the six shakedown advisors left *Mississinewa*. Captain Beck weighed anchor at 2111 and ordered the crew to GQ stations a minute later. John Mair raced to his duty station as trunnion operator on the starboard 20mm mount. The bridge rang up engineering and ordered eighteen knots speed. Gunnery crews commenced firing runs on a stationary target in the darkness. Number 5 mount, the stern 5-inch/38, and all four 3-inch/50 mounts had been test-fired in twenty-five minutes. Pain shot through Mair's left ear as the 5-inch mount unleashed nine rounds. The gun crew told him, belatedly, that he needed earplugs.

June 5. Late in the day word passed among the crew that the long-awaited invasion of Nazi-occupied Europe had begun, as the largest seaborne invasion force ever assembled attacked the beaches of Normandy on the coast of France. Due to superior forces backed up by mobile warships and air cover, the Allies prevailed and gained access to the coastal area. The *Miss* crew speculated whether they might be called to go to Europe and support the D-Day invasion. No such order came.

They turned to the training they needed to safely maintain an oiler. One of the most important operations was firefighting. Fires aboard a capital ship were extraordinarily dangerous, and an oiler carried its special cargo that made it extremely hazardous. For specialized training, on June 7 Captain Beck sent ten men to firefighting school in Brooklyn, followed two days later by another group of twenty. The training was not for the faint of heart: Instructors doused the interior of a metal building with 10 gallons of gasoline mixed with oil. Firemen, including Bill Brzykcy, suited up in asbestos garments with cuffs taped shut over asbestos gloves covering their hands. Wet rags covered their faces except for the eyes. As the building burned, the sailors headed into the blaze dragging a fire hose. The men struggled with the hose as the stream of water exerted tremendous pressure, making the hose jump like a crazed serpent. At the end of the drill, the trainees emerged from the building dripping with sweat, hoping they would never have to fight a fire at sea aboard *Mississinewa*.

The oiler remained docked after the second week of June, taking on stores and readying for sea. A few lucky sailors got liberty ashore.

Sailor Ray Fulleman sneaked off the ship for one last night of freedom. Like many men who had already seen combat, he believed he wouldn't make it through the war alive. With imminent death a possibility, Fulleman didn't mind stretching the strict Navy rules. Whenever he could, he visited local bars with his shipmates, trying to forget the hell that he'd have to return to all too soon somewhere on the front, be it the Atlantic or the Pacific.

A trick some sailors used to gain liberty from the ship involved a few props: a five-gallon bucket, some oily rags and a dress uniform. The sailor would put his dress uniform in the bucket, place sheets of paper over the uniform to keep it clean, and then throw some oily rags on top. He'd walk off the ship wearing dungarees, carrying the bucket as if to discard the rags, only to find a quiet spot on the wharf to change into his dress uniform and go ashore for a few hours. Fulleman used this gambit a few times, as did other crewmates.

One night Fulleman decided to stay out overnight. Off the ship he changed into his dress whites and left his dungaree uniform rolled up in the bucket. Bad luck. It rained that night, and the following morning when he peered in the bucket to retrieve his work clothes, he found it half full of water. He wrung out the soaked, oily clothing and slipped the dungarees on, but it didn't pass muster—the officer of the deck spied him coming, probably the wettest, most wrinkled sailor ever seen on dry land. An enormous grin crossed the OOD's face. But he turned his back on the gangplank and officially ignored the bedraggled sailor coming aboard.

Fulleman was lucky, but only for a few minutes. When he reported on board, it was June 15, and he was almost thirty-three hours overdue. At the captain's mast, Beck looked at the errant sailor with a sly smile and said, "Fulleman, you could have been back in time. It doesn't take that long to get to Norfolk from New Jersey."

Executive Officer Robert Lewis fumed, wanting to dismiss the errant sailor. "He wasn't in New Jersey, sir, he was in Norfolk getting drunk." The captain overruled him. "His records indicate he was in several battles with the cruiser *Mobile*. We really need water tenders—there's a big shortage of experienced tenders." The exec protested, but Beck ignored him and simply restricted Fulleman to the ship for ten liberties. The infraction also delayed for four months his promotion to water tender second class, a fact he regretted, as it meant a loss of $15 a month in pay. On the other hand, there was nowhere to spend it in the middle of the Pacific. Over the months on board, a dozen other *Mississinewa* sailors received disciplinary actions for their infractions. The Shore Patrol charged "Frenchy," the ship's talented baker, with failure to obey Shore Patrol orders. Even cooks broke the rules.

The new sailors discovered that duty on an oiler held unique challenges, and the duty was relentless. Hoses and cables, saddles and booms, aviation fuel and heavy oil—sailors learned a new lexicon as well as new trades. Dragging hoses, rigging booms, stoking the furnace—all the skills and hard work transformed the inexperienced young men into seasoned hands in a few short months.

June 19. *Mississinewa* lifted anchor at 1027 bound for the oil docks at Aruba, an island in the Netherlands West Indies close to the northeast coast of South America. The oiler cruised in the channel lined with buoy markers and steamed out of Hampton Roads at fifteen knots. At the general quarters klaxon call, gunnery crews manned the four gun turrets and fired rounds at a target sleeve towed by a Navy plane.

The destroyer USS *Straus* joined *Mississinewa* as escort. The two vessels began sailing a defensive zigzag pattern to avoid U-boats. Between watches the sailors took turns observing the destroyer thread the seas back and forth. They wondered if any submarines might be zigzagging a similar course, shadowing the cruisers like sharks in the dark waters below.

CHAPTER 5

Circle-Six Metal Fitting

If there are any among you who burn with a passion to die gloriously for the sake of their country, let them step forward.

—Instructor at Tsuchiura Naval Air Base
to potential *kaiten* recruits[1]

One afternoon in the late summer of 1944 a Japanese naval commander told two submariners of a new secret weapon that would save Japan: *maru roku kanamono*. It would be loaded onto fleet submarines, he said, to go to battle and turn the tide of victory.

"What are *maru roku kanamono*?" the two submariners asked, almost in unison. The words literally meant "circle-six metal fitting." The commander replied that it was the secret code name for a manned torpedo. Piloting such a craft would be a volunteer suicide mission, he said, and would result in the loss of the pilot in exchange for an enemy warship.

Such drastic measures seemed to be the last resort for the Empire of Japan. Short on fuel and other critical supplies, Japan was strangling in the grip of a vast military blockade. The lack of fuel to sail ships and war materiel had become critical, limiting training as well as military sorties and response to attacks. American carrier task forces had established air supremacy.

Submariner Hiroshi Kuroki's dramatic petition in blood to Admiral Yamamoto a year earlier had garnered little support among Navy staff, but as Japan's military losses in ships, aircraft and men mounted exponentially, Japanese strategists began to consider ever more desperate measures. An array of suicide weapons was considered, and the *kaiten* came under fresh scrutiny.

Debate about an undersea suicide weapon had escalated in January 1944 when four midget submariners from the Seventy-First Class of the Naval Academy debated the idea. From that time forward, interest in the manned torpedoes gained momentum. Some senior officers, including chief of staff to the commander of the submarine force, Kennosuke Torisu, thought the weapons would be most effective in high-seas attacks on American convoys, but his view was overruled in favor of using the new weapons to attack fleets at anchor—the "Pearl Harbor" model employed by the two-man midgets.

Prompted by the design theories of submariners Sekio Nishina and Hiroshi Kuroki, the Imperial Japanese Navy issued an order on February 26, 1944, for a Kure-based engineering team to develop an experimental manned torpedo. A construction program to produce *kaiten* was set up at Kure Navy Yard, and production was later extended to other bases at Yokosuka and Hikari.

The Kure team consisted of the chief designer, Captain Shimizu Watanabe, an authority on oxygen torpedoes; an assistant designer who was an engineer, Lieutenant Hiroshi Suzukawa; and a technical expert and veteran torpedo designer, Atsushi Kusunoki. Engineer Suzukawa took a leading part as the principal proponent of the *kaiten*'s development. The design team was instructed to produce three working prototypes for sea trials.

Then came the June 1944 "Great Marianas Turkey Shoot," as American military officers triumphantly called it. The two-day battle in the Marianas Islands devastated the Japanese Navy, when 476 planes and

445 pilots were lost. The dreadful loss of Japanese life and materiel seems to have convinced Japanese naval planners that suicide weapons such as *kaiten* were now critical to stopping the slide to disaster.

Kaiten development raced to the forefront of naval planning. However, in order to maximize its effectiveness, such a suicide weapon required secrecy, which meant the weapon must not physically appear to be a suicide craft, *even to military higher-ups*. To disguise its true mission, Nishina and Kuroki proposed adding an escape hatch below the pilot's seat so that it would appear that the pilot, after steering on a collision course with an enemy ship, could eject fifty to one hundred yards before the strike. Yet, in truth, the escape hatch was only a theoretical benefit, an add-on that gave the appearance of last-minute salvation but offered no such thing, for once the *kaiten* was on a collision course there was no escape, and no pilot could survive the detonation of the high-explosive warhead. That fact was officially ignored, and the escape hatch was planned into the design solely to allay the misgivings of military men who did not completely support the suicide approach.

As the *kaiten* began to be taken seriously, Kuroki and Nishina emerged from relative obscurity to become leading players of the program that hoped to produce Japan's most effective secret weapon of World War II. Both were enthusiastic Japanese Navy men, brilliant and driven. Both would lose their lives to the suicide weapon they designed.

Hiroshi Kuroki, the son of a physician, was born September 11, 1921, in Gifu Prefecture. As a teenager already in the Japanese Navy, he had sailed on the battleship *Yamashiro* before the war. Transferring to the submarine force, he became the first engineer to skipper a midget submarine. Confident and assertive, the young man had mastered the operation of the *Ko-Hyoteki* midget submarine and used his engineering talents to improve the craft, introducing a number of innovations, most important the diesel generator propulsion system that increased the submarine's cruising range. His design additions were superlative. In addition, he developed new craft. The sophisticated Type D midget submarine with a crew of five was almost exclusively his design. The

Imperial Navy quickly recognized its potential and ordered the construction of 550 craft for coastal defense.

A high-spirited young officer with a deep devotion to duty, Kuroki was smart, sincere and zealous, seeking excellence in everything he did. One influential mentor was Dr. Kiyoshi Hiraizumi, professor of Japanese history at Tokyo Imperial University, so perhaps it was not surprising that Kuroki focused on a long-term view of life nourished by centuries of art and culture, warfare and aggression, a ribbon of time leading into a future almost certainly as glorious for the empire as the victory-studded past.

Yet he worried about the war's direction. He looked beyond the present conflict and prayed for peace and serenity; he pictured a victorious Japan guided by the emperor as spiritual leader. The future of his holy country became his obsession. It was his deep sense of purpose that drove him to contemplate a weapon that would sacrifice the life of a person for a patriotic cause.

Kuroki never knew if his *kaiten* invention was successful in war, for he was fated to die two months before the first attack against U.S. ships.

The other *kaiten* coinventor, Sekio Nishina, was born to two schoolteachers on October 10, 1923, in Otsu City, Shiga Prefecture. He graduated from Osaka Tennoji Middle School near the head of his class; he had taken the naval exam in his fourth year of middle school and passed with the highest grade. On graduation he joined the Navy. It was 1939 and he was sixteen.

Getting accepted to the Navy was an unbelievable coup for the young man, given that the competition included the most outstanding students in the country. So difficult was the Japanese Naval Academy's entrance exam that only the most brilliant students had a chance, and the facts told the story: Ten percent of the academy students had placed at the top of their class at first-rate schools, 60 percent had made it into the top five in their class, and all others had ranked in the top twenty.

It was well known that only the most elite students were accepted to the Naval Academy.

The Academy had been founded in 1869, during the reign of the Emperor Meiji. Each class was designated by its entry year, numbered since the Academy's beginning. Thus Nishina's class, entering in 1939, was the Seventy-First Class.

Disciplined in mind and body, Nishina distinguished himself in school. After graduation he was stationed at Ourasaki Base, a *Kohyoteki* submarine base established in 1942 in Kurahashijima, not far from the large Kure Naval Base. It was there that he met Kuroki. The two discovered they shared a mutual philosophy and a passion for patriotism, and together they began in earnest to refine the concept of their suicide submarine called *kaiten*.

Nishina was promoted to sublieutenant in March 1944, when only twenty years old, and sent to the naval base at Ozushima. Trainees there found him an impressive leader. He was remembered vividly by a younger Naval Academy student, Toshiharu Konada of the Seventy-Second Class, who trained with Nishina for several months.

"He was honest, frank and positive," Konada said, "and he grasped the substantial point exactly: striving to reach the goal. Nishina was always at the forefront of research and training on behalf of fellow *kaiten* pilots and other personnel of the base." Nishina's creed was simple: "A commander takes the lead." Following that tradition, he would lead the first sortie of *kaiten* on the *Kikusui* Mission to Ulithi in November 1944.

The Naval General Staff insisted on conditions of strictest secrecy. The code name for the *kaiten* program—those innocuous words *maru roku kanamono*—was essential for security, and it was such a dull, bureaucratic-sounding label it was sure to disinterest spies and intelligence gatherers. The weapon was also referred to as the national salvation weapon (*kyukoku heiki*).

"Strangers will assume it is some kind of spare part or shipboard equipment," an officer explained to *kaiten* volunteer Yutaka Yokota. "They will have no idea what we are doing here, and our activities cannot leak out to the enemy."[2] Indeed, so effective was the security surrounding circle-six metal fitting that even years after the war's end many Japanese naval officers remained completely unaware of the suicide program's existence.

Now *kaiten* had a design, a code name and a strategy. It was time to begin construction.

Kuroki's and Nishina's concept of the *kaiten* was based on the Japanese Navy's interest in large-diameter torpedoes, which dated back to the period following the Russo-Japanese War in 1905. By the 1920s Japanese engineers, stimulated by intelligence reports of British experiments with hydrogen peroxide and oxygen systems, were experimenting with enriched-air propulsion torpedoes. In fact, the Royal Navy's effort ceased after 1928 because of the instability and high corrosion factor of the liquid oxygen used in the excessively bulky Mark VII torpedo. However, a team of Japanese designers at Kure, led by Vice-Admiral Toshihide Asaguma and Rear Admiral Kaneji Kishimoto, persevered in torpedo development.

By 1933 they reached the fleet testing stage of the *Shiki Sanso Gyorai*, called the Type 93 torpedo, or known in English as the Long Lance. It was a formidable weapon, outweighing and outranging the torpedoes of other major navies. Unlike compressed-air torpedoes, it left no telltale wake as it streaked toward its target. An aerial version of the Long Lance used compressed air rather than oxygen. Used to deadly effect at Pearl Harbor, nearly a year later in the fall of 1942, the Long Lance lived up to its reputation as a much-feared weapon when it was used with incredible success against Allied ships in the sea battles off Guadalcanal.

Stretching nearly thirty feet long, the Long Lance measured twenty-four inches in diameter with an eleven-hundred-pound high-explosive warhead. The torpedo had a range of 34,995 yards at a speed of forty knots and could actually reach nearly fifty knots. The torpedo weighed 6,107 pounds and contained a gasoline/oxygen propulsion system. Unlike other torpedoes, it was accurate and dependable; failures were rare.

In contrast, the primary torpedo used at the time by Allied forces in the Pacific, the Mark 15, was inferior. The Mark 15 torpedo was six feet shorter, with a smaller diameter, and carried a warhead far smaller—660 pounds. With a range of only 6,100 yards at forty-two knots and a maximum speed of forty-eight knots, the U.S. torpedo weighed 3,289 pounds and was a turbine design, leaving a visible wake in its path—a very serious drawback, as it was more easily detectable from the surface. Another problem with the Mark 15, the failure of the detonator, plagued U.S. destroyer skippers and submariners until the fuse mechanism problems were finally remedied in 1943. All in all, it couldn't hold a candle—or a fuse—to the Long Lance.

The Long Lance torpedo and its proven propulsion system became the basis for the new terror weapon of the seas that Hiroshi Kuroki so fiercely advocated. Little did he know he would become its first victim.

Based on that superior Type 93 Long Lance oxygen propulsion system, the Kure design team drafted a craft that enlarged the space for the warhead to include room for a pilot, and named it the Type I *kaiten*. All the major components of the original torpedo were retained, the only major new addition being the pilot's compartment between the massive warhead in the nose and the oxygen motor. In this space the craft was fitted with a periscope and a set of controls enabling a man to direct the torpedo run. By spring of 1944 the designers had completed their drawings. They calculated that the Type I manned torpedo, fitted with a 3,418-pound high-explosive warhead, would have a range of forty nautical miles. The Long Lance had proven at Pearl Harbor it could destroy a heavy cruiser—the Type I *kaiten*, with a warhead three times more powerful and a man directing it, could do the same to a battleship or an aircraft carrier.

Although other prototypes were envisioned and planned, the one-man *kaiten* Type I was the only model actually carried into action during the war. Three hundred and thirty Type I *kaiten* were built, each measuring forty-eight feet, four inches long and thirty-nine inches in diameter, displacing 8.3 tons and deploying a 3,418-pound warhead. Its range varied from forty-eight miles at twelve knots to fourteen miles at thirty knots. A *kaiten* traveling at top speed could cover seventy-five feet in one second.

Kure Navy Yard employed workers to produce the new killer weapon; two other sites were later brought on line, at Yokosuka and Hikari. By July 25 two *kaiten* prototypes had been fitted out and turned over to Kuroki and Nishina to commence sea trials at the Dainyu torpedo test site at Kure. The results were excellent. Enthusiasm was high as the exultant submariners reported their success.

The Department of the Navy officially adopted the *kaiten* as a weapon on August 1 and ordered the immediate manufacture of one hundred submersibles for completion by the end of the month. No longer would the airborne *kamikaze* be the only suicide weapon—the Special Attack Corps would employ a similar weapon at sea. The man who would oversee the Special Attack Forces utilizing *kaiten* would be Vice Admiral Shigeyoshi Miwa, who had taken over the command of the Japanese Sixth Fleet submarines a year earlier, in July 1943.

The *kaiten* were unstable and unwieldy craft not designed for long solo journeys, so larger craft were necessary to transport them to their place of deployment. To meet that need, Japanese naval engineers refitted large fleet submarines of the I-class to carry up to six *kaiten* manned torpedoes. During the mother sub's approach to the target, the *kaiten* pilots would climb into their *kaiten* torpedoes through the so-called escape hatch below the pilot's seat.

Along with mastering his craft, a pilot would have to master his own fear, including the fear of shame, for if he failed, he would be disgraced. And if his mission was successful and he hit his target, he would not return alive.

Although suicide was an honorable philosophy in Japanese culture, the reality was frightening to many men. The real meaning behind "circle-six metal fitting"—the horror of a death the moment of which was unknown—was terrifyingly different from a *kamikaze* pilot's choice to down a damaged plane and end in a fireball. Simply having the choice to live or to die made a *kamikaze* pilot much more likely to make that glorious decision in the heat of battle. But certain death in the black waves when darkness and noise surrounded you? The *kaiten* program had its marketing problems, and it was quickly obvious that recruiting pilots and keeping them healthy and motivated would require special incentives.

Of course, the legacy of Japanese military history was "death for country," and the call to honor was significant. In addition to the accolades for the warrior, a pilot's noble suicide in combat would provide benefits spiritual and tangible for his family. Upon his death, a *kaiten* pilot would receive an automatic two-step promotion and enshrinement at Yasukuni Shrine in Tokyo in recognition of his patriotic sacrifice.

Yasukuni War Shrine had been created in 1869 to honor the 7,751 men who died in the war that ended the Tokugawa Shogun's rule and brought the imperial family to power in the Meiji Restoration. *Yasukuni* means "to govern the state peacefully." Since then, all Japanese warriors who perished in war have been enshrined at Yasukuni, and the place has become the most important symbol of the official state religion, Shinto. The war dead are enshrined as *kami*, meaning gods or spirits. During World War II, enshrinement at Yasukuni, which gained the prayers of Emperor Hirohito the living god, was the highest honor given to a military man who fell in battle.

Other incentives were offered to attract and sustain recruits. Living conditions were very good at Ozushima at a time of general shortage in Japan. *Kaiten* trainees received ample food, cigarettes and sweetmeats. The buildings, though spartan and constructed of plain wooden siding, were much more comfortable than accommodations on ships. Instead of sleeping on straw mats on the decks of warships, pilots in training received wide, comfortable Western-style beds, and although Japan's food shortage was growing worse, bountiful meals were served to *kaiten* trainees. But the amenities did not still the frightful voice inside, and the stress of their coming fate took its toll—despite the excellent cuisine, some pilots lost their appetites.

The vast majority of the recruits were very young men, some of them still teenagers. Most were now far from home. As military men, they faced more than the risks of danger in battle—as pilots in the *kaiten* program they faced certain death. It was a harsh psychological burden.

One woman, who has since been revered as "the mother of *kaiten*," tried to make a difference in their lives. To mitigate their loneliness and their fears, she assumed a role as a surrogate mother to the young recruits and has lived on in history as someone who welcomed them and provided a small oasis of stability. Asako Kurashige, whose nickname "*Oshigesan*" meant she was an honorable and venerated person, maintained an inn, or *ryokan*, in the village of Tokuyama (Yamaguchi Prefecture), outside the base at Ozushima. She welcomed the *kaiten* trainees on their visits to the base and treated them as though they were her own sons; she met dozens of them over the months, and in effect, they came to look on her as the mother of the *kaiten* pilots. She knew far less about the purpose of the submarine program than the young recruits quickly came to learn; later, when she discovered the true nature of the *Kikusui* mission and what her beloved boys were sent to accomplish, she broke down and wept. Over the years her compassion and devotion to the young men have been immortalized in poetry and song.[3]

In many ways the *kaiten* submarine pilots were treated considerably better than *kamikaze* airplane pilots. Japanese volunteers for *kamikaze* operations received only the most rudimentary training, for the simple reason that they were sent out to die quickly, before their enthusiasm could wane; many of them, in fact, could not even land a plane. This strategy was especially true for the *kamikaze* aircraft pilots in the last months of the war, when planes, fuel, qualified instructors and time for student flight training were all in miserably short supply; in those last desperate weeks of 1944 and '45, one volunteered to fly, learned the basics and flew off into the sky never to return.

However, such a cynical approach was certainly not used for the *kaiten* pilots, who spent many weeks training on land before even entering a *kaiten* in the water. The Imperial Japanese Navy was patterned after the British Royal Navy, and many of the traditions and customs of Japanese naval officers and training had their roots in the Royal Navy. The large number of officers and Naval Academy graduates at Ozushima Base indicated that only the very best naval candidates led the *kaiten* effort, and their training was commensurate with their great intellectual talent. Unlike the seemingly more dispensible aircraft *kamikaze* pilots, *kaiten* pilots were regarded as a very valuable commodity, highly trained and specialized, a commodity not to be wasted.

The first recruits for the *kaiten* pilot corps were chosen from volunteers throughout the Navy, primarily from aviator trainees, because few flight instructors—and very few planes—existed by then in the Japanese forces. Three criteria were essential: physical strength to master the difficult craft, a powerful will and a lack of family encumbrances. The need for strength was obvious, given the extremely difficult controls in a *kaiten*. The requirement for a strong will was meant to determine if the volunteer had a fighting spirit and a great sense of national responsibility. The third criterion ensured that recruits had a minimum of family ties and responsibilities to pull on them emotionally—or none at all.[4] Married men were excluded, and very few elder or only sons were chosen. The prime candidate was a young, fit man who would have little reason to look back. The criteria were so rigorously applied that initially very few men were chosen.

Day-to-day training moved slowly. Each *kaiten* required seven technicians, and few technicians had yet been trained to prep the submarines. By the time each weapon had been checked, deployed and finally returned to the base with its oxygen tanks recharged for another session, four or five hours had elapsed. Even after the in-water training, the days were packed with related activity; after training with the *kaiten* afloat and on shore, students underwent rigorous physical training in sumo wrestling, judo, rugby, rowing and baseball.

From the pool of thousands of volunteers, only 1,375 young men were selected as *kaiten* pilots, and few of those ever entered a *kaiten*. Only 50 suicide craft were ever launched in combat.

Yet as blood filled the seas at Okinawa, the Marianas and the Carolines—islands whose names glimmered like pearls on the necklace of Japanese desire—the admirals of the Imperial Navy saw their advantage eroding catastrophically, and by the second half of 1944 they were desperate to turn the tide. They needed a dramatic weapon to turn the spirit of the Japanese military and inspire their men. And it was not only ships they wanted to bring down; their goal was to shock and dishearten the enemy with the unthinkable: intentional suicide. As *kamikaze* pilots would kill from the air, *Kikusui* pilots would kill from the sea.

Japan had begun the war with formidable aggressive attacks at Pearl Harbor. Midway had changed the trend of victory. Perhaps now they could recapture dominance of the Pacific with their selfless noble warriors.

SUMMER 1944
Ourasaki Submarine Training Base

Training was about to begin for *kaiten* pilots. The naval base for the secret program was secure: Only relevant military personnel were allowed to walk these top-secret grounds.

Yutaka Yokota was one of the hundred men selected from the

Tsuchiura Naval Air Station's class of two thousand men to train for the deadly mission. Yokota had entered Tsuchiura's cadet training school to become a carrier pilot, but he came to understand that there was a mysterious new weapon.

"Your motherland faces imminent peril," the Tsuchiura recruits were told. "Consider how much the motherland needs you. Now a weapon that will destroy the enemy has been born. If there are any among you who burn with a passion to die gloriously for the sake of their country, let them step forward." The assembled men were each handed a piece of paper. Those who truly wished to volunteer were to mark the paper with two circles, while those who were *"merely willing to do this duty"* would mark it with only one. The number of men accepted had to be restricted, since facilities adequate to train large numbers of *kaiten* pilots were still under construction. Volunteers from Tsuchiura, therefore, were carefully scrutinized in order to pare down the final count of men to a manageable one hundred.

While many thought the idea of self-guided suicide in a dark waterborne machine was crazy, it appealed to some hotbloods. Nineteen-year-old Yokota was inspired by a sense of extreme patriotism. Once admitted to the Navy, he had been indoctrinated every single day by leaders: "If the need for it comes, one should give his life for the Empire gladly."

However, the other side of the coin held a different face: One should not die in vain. *Kikusui* lives were valuable, as these men were highly intelligent, highly motivated, and unique in their unparalleled specialized training. Therefore the sacrifice must be carefully chosen. "Death must have a purpose," one instructor said. "Do not accept death unless by dying you can hurt the enemy severely."[5]

Another recruit in Yokota's training group, Naoji Kozu, a former Tokyo Imperial University student, had been drafted in early 1944. While in antisubmarine warfare school, Kozu volunteered for what he knew only was a dangerous job: being willing to board a "special weapon" that would reverse the tide of the war at once. He applied for it carelessly, he said many years later, adding, "I never imagined I'd be going to a place from which I'd have absolutely no chance to return alive."[6]

Another volunteer, petty officer Yoshiteru Kubo, remembered his sense of shock when he learned the true nature of the assignment.

"When the volunteers were invited to become *kaiten* pilots," he recalled, "I understood that a high risk was involved, which was inevitable with newly created weapons. But when I saw it in front of me, I realized it was much more than this—it was suicidal. There was no chance of survival. This certainly made me feel we had been gravely misled."

Even top-level brass had reservations. Commander Kennosuke Torisu, a staff member of the Imperial Japanese Navy, took a dim view of a suicide mission, saying, "I believe that a kind of weapon such as a *kaiten*, guided by a human being who faced certain death, should not be regarded as a weapon but an act of desperation."[7]

However, as Japan's losses mounted, the sense of desperation grew. The idea of suicide submarines became increasingly palatable as the War in the Pacific turned against the empire.

Moving from Ourasaki to Ozushima

Lieutenant Hiroshi Kuroki had been assigned to Base P at Ourasaki in December 1942; nine months later, in late 1943, Lieutenant Sekio Nishina had followed him there. Both submariners took part in training *Ko-hyoteki* midget submariners. But for reasons of practicality and secrecy, by summer 1944 it was determined that *kaiten* operations and training would be moved to a new base, Ozushima, near the Kure Naval Base.

In July 1944 tugboats from Ourasaki carried a group of *kaiten* pilots to Ozushima, a short distance along the coast. Since 1937 Ozushima had been functioning as a launch, repair and recovery service for the Long Lance torpedo, and it possessed the facilities, equipment and manpower to handle *kaiten*. Torpedo maintenance experts accompanied the pilots and three experimental Type I *kaiten*.

Lieutenant Commander Mitsuma Itakura was assigned as the base commander, Lieutenant Y. Hamaguchi as the chief of torpedo fitting. Kure provided a number of torpedo experts who remained at the new site when the early *kaiten* began to arrive for fitting out and prelaunch inspections. Escort boats also were assigned to the base, to be used as high-speed pursuit boats for training drills. Torpedo boats, motor launches and, later, *Shinyo* suicide boats would be used as recovery craft for *kaiten* training in the bay. Kure Naval Yard provided many of the boats and their personnel on a temporary basis; later the boats and crews were permanently assigned to Ozushima.

Pilots and other personnel from various sources arrived at Ozushima: torpedo fitters, caterers, seaplane maintenance crews, boat crews, ever increasing as the number of *kaiten* pilots grew. As the new arrivals flowed onto the base, housing and working space became cramped on the small, narrow island. In a short time it became difficult to accommodate the numbers of military men.

As the *kaiten* craft and technicians were moving over to Ozushima Base, so was the training of the naval recruits. The *kaiten* teams quietly moved to the new location on September 1, where the corps could train under strictest secrecy.

In that first week of September Ozushima possessed only six *kaiten*, limiting the training to 32 officer pilots out of the 200 volunteers present. The remaining 168 would-be pilots had to wait for new construction to catch up.

The top-secret nature of the *kaiten* was supported in every possible way. One of the most significant efforts to conceal its presence from Allied reconnaissance planes was a hidden railroad constructed at Ozushima Base to bring the *kaiten* down from the mountaintop where they were assembled to the water below for "wet" training. Tunneling through the mountain, the railroad was underground for almost its entire length, away from the eyes of intelligence gatherers. At the maintenance yard up in the hills, the *kaiten* were loaded aboard a carrier, simply a type of cradle or dolly with railroad wheels and axles to roll on the track, and transported through the tunnel system. The carriers exited the tunnel at the pier in Tokuyama Bay.[8]

The shortage of *kaiten* was not the only difficulty. Also hampering training efforts was the critical shortage of skilled technicians to maintain and service the manned torpedoes at the training bases. The situation improved later that year, and by November a second training center, at Hikari, located on the coast just south of Tokuyama, stocked more than seventy *kaiten*.

The Ozushima site made a depressing first impression, according to recruit Yutaka Yokota. "Two large black buildings that resembled airplane hangars" and a barracks made up the facility, he said. Kure Navy Yard built the *kaiten* parts, but they were assembled and maintained at Ozushima, hence the construction buildings.

After receiving an official welcome from the base commanding officer, Lieutenant Commander Itakura, the volunteers were allowed to inspect a *kaiten*. After having seen the weapon in which they would attack the enemy and die, they were given a final chance to withdraw. Any man who wished to return to conventional pilot training could do so, with no questions asked and no imputation of dishonor. However, the code of *Bushidō* was strong, and perceived disgrace hung heavy in the air. Very few took advantage of this offer.

The ancient code of the samurai overrode all other constraints, including reason and the urge for survival. "Honor unto death"—the most sacred and central tenet of *Bushidō*—took precedence over fear and its companion, shame, and pushed the young military men to make the ultimate sacrifice for their country.

CHAPTER 6

Neptune's Ancient Order of the Deep

Americans love to fight. All real Americans love the sting of battle.

—General George S. Patton

Sailing south toward the Panama Canal, *Mississinewa* sailors fell into the rhythm of shipboard routine, mastering the hoses, the pumps, the engines of a working oiler.

The young ones learned naval etiquette. It was de rigueur to salute an officer the first time he was met each day, and not again after the first encounter. But all sailors had to salute Captain Beck every time he was met on deck during routine duties, regardless of the number of times a sailor saw him.

They wore the sailor's work uniform: light blue chambray shirt, bell-bottom blue jeans, regulation socks and shoes and the round white sailor's hat mandatory at all times. The shirts, long-sleeved to protect against flash burns, were typically rolled above the elbow in hot Pacific weather. Deckhands were required to carry a sheath knife on their belt in case a line or rigging became fouled and needed a quick cut; boatswain's mates strictly enforced the knife requirement.

The shape of the sailors' days was governed by their rank and their skills, and whether they were on watch, at general quarters or off duty, but the hours were always full. There was little time to watch the flying fish that sailed past the bow or the dolphins that occasionally followed in their wake.

Deckhands were split into two divisions, those that worked from bridge to bow and the others who worked from bridge to stern. Division One sailors were responsible for the fueling equipment and ship maintenance forward of the bridge, to the fo'c'sle, including the aviation gasoline tanks containing hundred-octane aviation fuel, commonly referred to as AV gas. The AV gas was carried in centerline tanks forward of the bridge. Wing tanks at port and starboard carried naval special fuel oil (NSFO) and flanked the centerline numbers 1, 2, 3 and 4 tanks. In the event of a torpedo attack, it was hoped that the wing tanks would serve as a buffer for the more volatile aviation gas in the centerline tanks.

Division Two sailors were responsible for fueling stations and ship maintenance from bridge to stern. Operating the four fueling stations aft of the bridge required several deckhands when fueling was done at sea.

Rated sailors, who possessed a special skill or training, wore a patch sewn on their left sleeve denoting their particular skill. Rated deckhands included boatswain's mates, coxswains, gunner's mates and fire control men, and they were assigned to Division One or Division Two. Division Three's rated sailors included quartermasters, radiomen, signalmen and radar specialists, all assigned to bridge duty; a special group called Construction and Repair (the C&R gang) was made up of ship fitters, electrician's mates, metalsmiths and carpenter's mates. Division Four held both rated and nonrated men; the nonrated engineering sailors being firemen, and the "rates" being water tenders and machinist's mates. Division Five included the yeomen, cooks, storekeepers and pharmacist's mates.

A typical watch lasted four hours and then the sailor got eight hours off. Engineers, like most sailors, performed other work duties when not on watch. Twelve-hour days were common, and fueling at sea would stretch the workday even longer. Sleep became a luxury.

Whenever the klaxon warned of enemy attack, crew members raced to their assigned general quarters stations. An engineering sailor's GQ station was usually in the same place as his regular assigned watch, but many sailors had GQ assignments elsewhere from their regular duty: Water tender Ray Fulleman switched at GQ to monitor the check valves in the fire room, while John Mair left off mess cooking to become a fireman and serve as trunnion operator on a 20mm mount.

The sailors in the black gang readied the ship for full steam to obtain the maximum flank speed, as ordered by the bridge. Orders from the conn for sudden speed changes or rudder control directions could spell the difference between life and death when avoiding the enemy.

Deckhands manned *Mississinewa*'s guns during general quarters. Deckhands stood a normal gun watch unless GQ sounded, in which case they would scramble for a different assigned mount.

After four days at sea the lush, sultry coast of South America came into view on June 23, the shores dense with coconut palms and the sky filled with seabirds. A few men got liberty and hit "the beach," meaning they sought out the watering holes for rum and beer or visited the shops for souvenirs. The next morning *Mississinewa* sailors, a few suffering from hangovers, awoke to find the ship showing only five feet of freeboard after loading fuel all night at the utilities dock. Laden with thousands of pounds of fuel and riding low in the water, the oiler was now called a "fat lady."

Captain Beck set the sea detail, and the ship moved away from the utilities dock at afternoon's end, using the cover of darkness to minimize detection by U-boats. *Straus* took up station as the pair left the safety of San Nicholas Bay at a speed of seventeen knots. The two ships were bound for the Ditch, the name coined by veteran sailors for the Panama Canal.

That night was peaceful, until a voice from *Straus*'s radar shack tore through the darkness and caused the destroyer escort's bridge personnel to spring to life. "Sub contact, Captain," called the radar man.

"Signal *Mississinewa*. Sound general quarters," the captain said. *Straus*'s crew sprang to their battle stations. Sailors readied the hedgehogs, the antisubmarine weapons that could be thrown ahead of the ship. Developed by the Royal Navy, the hedgehog fired a number of small spigot mortar bombs from spiked fittings. The bombs exploded on contact, rather than using a time or depth fuse as depth charges did; they also achieved a higher sinking rate against submarines. Nonetheless, they were supplemented on the *Straus* and other destroyers by depth charges, and on this day men on the fantail prepared to roll those "ashcans" off the stern.

On the *Miss*, the radar operator had also picked up the sub blip on the screen. He sent a message to the bridge. Beck barked out, "General quarters, flank speed, all ahead full. Commence zigzag pattern." *Clang, clang, clang!* The general quarters klaxon horn echoed throughout *Mississinewa* as the order came through the PA system. "All hands, man your battle stations."

Seamen raced for their battle stations and took up firing positions on the guns. One man on the bridge gun suddenly felt a hand grip his shoulder, squeezing his shoulder blade. It was Captain Beck. "Are you scared?" asked the captain. When the sailor nodded yes, Beck said, "We're all scared. It'll all be over in a bit."[1]

The escort's captain ordered the hedgehogs fired from the bow as the *Straus* separated from the *Miss*. The hedgehogs fired; the ship circled back to the point of original contact, and ashcans rolled off the fantail. From the depths they exploded in a spray of seawater, and the crew noted oil residue on the surface where the sub had dived. The results were inconclusive. The sub may have gotten away. Captain Beck knew enemy subs traveled in wolf packs. He kept extra men on watch until they were far away.

Mississinewa and *Straus* continued steaming to the Canal Zone all the next day, entering the Gatun Locks on the Atlantic side at noon on June 26.

John Mair watched in fascination from the deck, noting the 85-foot difference in water level from the lower Atlantic side to the Pacific side. The Panama Canal was 110 feet wide, allowing a mere 17 feet of clearance on each side of the ship. The loaded oiler was slowly pulled through the chambers by lines tied to electric "donkeys," sometimes called "mules." The tropical forest was so close Mair reached out and picked a leaf off a tree. He wondered if an aircraft carrier or battleship could squeeze through the Ditch. After going through the lower, middle and upper chambers of the locks, the *Miss* emerged an hour and twenty minutes later.

Arriving at Balboa Island off California, sailors were granted liberty, a gesture welcomed by the younger sailors who had stayed aboard in Aruba. Deckhands filed down the gangplank to see what Balboa had to offer. The shore patrol monitored the entrances to bars that were frequented by the locals, with sailors being told the establishments were strictly off-limits. The officers had to bear the brunt of corralling wayward young sailors. Drunk sailors came back from liberty, some staggering on their own, some escorted by the shore patrol. The crew all knew they were en route to a war zone and that this liberty was their last hurrah. Captain Beck and Executive Officer Lewis were very forgiving on this occasion, knowing it was the last relaxed liberty for some time to come.

The anchor rose the next day and the oiler headed north, hugging the coast of California then turning west for Pearl Harbor. Shipboard routine took over as the ship crossed the ocean headed for the Hawaiian Islands, where black lava reached its fingers into the sea on the Big Island and Waikiki welcomed visitors with bone-white beaches and hula dancers.

The *Miss* now sailed alone and unescorted, as the *Straus* had left for an unknown destination. Captain Beck ordered the speed increased on the twin screws to 90 rpm; the oiler sliced through the Pacific swells at a speed of eighteen knots. Japanese submarines were known to operate off California's coast, but at that speed, Beck knew they could never catch him.

Monday, July 10, Hawaii. John Mair, Bill Brzykcy and the crew lined the rails as Diamond Head came into view on the starboard side. All sailors not on watch were ordered topside, and Captain Beck called for dress whites for entering Pearl Harbor; the dress uniform was a sign of respect for the ships and officers of the naval anchorage.

One seaman, Joe Contendo, looked down at his dress whites and blanched on seeing a large grease line staining his trousers from one side to the other, the mark of the steel cable he had grabbed as the tugs escorted the ship into Pearl Harbor. No time to change, so he watched the deep blue of the Pacific Ocean as it turned to beautiful swirling colors of green, aqua and blue when they entered the channel to Pearl. The *Miss* steamed at seven knots, hardly more than a soft slide through the harbor waters. Yard tugs guided the *Mississinewa* to the southern end of Battleship Row, a few hundred yards north of the sunken battleship *Arizona*. For young *Mississinewa* sailors the battleship's sunken hulk was a sobering reminder of the stakes of war.

Captain Beck rotated the crew through watches so his sailors could hit "the Beach" after the long voyage. It was nearly a month since they'd left Hampton Roads; since then they'd touched down in Aruba and sailed across the Pacific. They began to feel like part of the Pacific Fleet, surrounded by battleships, carriers and destroyers. Even the younger men now felt they belonged to the ship that was their floating home.

A twenty-five-year-old New Yorker, seaman Joe DeSantis was determined to give the ship a mascot and one day came in from Honolulu after liberty carrying a special friend onto *Mississinewa*. No sooner had he toted his canvas bag aboard than out popped a small terrier barking and yipping and ready to go to sea. "I'm gonna' name him Salvo,"

DeSantis said to appreciative crew members. The little dog slurped beer from a saucer and barked for more.

"The dog is a typical Navy dog already," one man wrote to his wife about Salvo.[2] "He's careful about what he eats and can consume more cake and root beer than three sailors. Everybody plays with him and feeds him. He's just getting big enough now to go all over the ship. There are still hatch coamings he can't get over but he barks like anything until someone lifts him over." Salvo enjoyed a pampered life at sea and was everybody's friend, but DeSantis made it clear to everyone that Salvo was his dog.

Soon after arrival in Pearl, Captain Beck ordered the crew to assemble on deck in dress white uniforms for a photo. Sixteen officers took the chairs in the first row. Directly behind them stood six chief petty officers, clothed in their dark dress uniforms that contrasted sharply with the ocean of white surrounding them. On the right-hand side next to the officers stood the seven black mess stewards. At the back, ten rows of *Mississinewa* sailors filled out the photo, many of them boys still in their teens. They grinned for the camera wielded by a Navy photographer.

Five months later that picture would be the only consolation for some military families, a proof of their sons' passing from civilian to military life, of spending their days on a ship in the Pacific, whereabouts sometimes known, sometimes not, but always a place far from home. For the ones who never came back, it was the last official photo to mark their presence.

On July 15 duty called and it was time to go to sea. Leaving Pearl Harbor, the *Miss* was escorted down the channel by a tug, with Captain Beck taking over the conn from the harbor pilot when the open sea beckoned. As usual, Beck sounded general quarters at sunset, and the convoy began zigzagging to avoid Japanese submarines. When darkness fell, the escorts moved in close to the oilers.

The *Miss* was a "fat lady" again, filled with millions of gallons of NSFO, diesel, and aviation gasoline in massive tanks from stem to stern. The ship bristled with armament, ready to defend itself against any threat. The oiler carried fuel, provisions and cargo to thousands of sailors who would soon line the decks of warships anticipating the fueling convoy of auxiliary oilers. The *Miss* was a lady with a mission, her job to fuel the Pacific Fleet and satisfy the thirsty ships of the line who roamed the far reaches of the Pacific.

The ship sailed with Convoy PD-21-T as it navigated westerly. Memories of the last liberty at Pearl Harbor faded fast. Steaming southwest for ever-longer days as they headed for the equator, the convoy's next destination was Eniwetok, a small atoll in the Marshall Islands that served as a staging area for fleet operations.

Mississinewa ran in a darkened condition at night. Black canvas covered the hatches to the berthing quarters, and all lights were extinguished except for red lights that illuminated compartments belowdecks. At night those red lights allowed sailors going topside to see in the dark immediately, as their eyes adjusted quickly to the inky blackness.

Japanese subs usually attacked at sunrise and dusk, which mandated that every U.S. Navy ship enforce general quarters at those times, so shipboard routine began with a call to general quarters just before 0530 sunrise, and the day ended with a call to GQ as sunset neared at 1830. The *Miss* steamed at an average speed of fourteen knots, fast enough to make it difficult for Japanese submarines to keep pace with the convoy ships or maneuver into attack position. The benefit of fast-fleet oilers was demonstrable, as they were able to keep up with the warships and sail away from attackers.

As the ship prepared to enter the war zone, Captain Beck stepped up the drills: man overboard, gunnery practice, fire and rescue, and abandon ship.

Each sailor's routine during watch varied according to a man's rank and the duty. Water tender Ray Fulleman stood his watch on the cat-walk near the fire room boilers, regulating the flow of water by monitoring a vertical glass tube marked with levels. Among hundreds of chores, the fire gang was required to wipe down the floor plates and boiler surfaces with diesel oil to keep them clean.

John Mair got the duty of engine room phone communications and was taken under the wing of machinist's mate Alexander Day, a regular Navy man and an old salt. School was in session for Mair whenever Day clamped the Bakelite sound-powered headphones over the young man's head and ears, crushing his round white sailor's cap.

Mair's job as bridge phone man was to relay instructions from the conn as to the number of revolutions needed on the port and starboard shafts of the ship; he stood between two machinist's mates manning the port and starboard throttles. Each throttle man gripped a large steam wheel in front of him, one for each shaft, while watching the steam pressure gauges on the throttle board. Mair repeated instructions phoned from the bridge—"up one rpm, down one"—while *Mississinewa* steamed ahead. Hard turns necessitated moving the twenty-five-foot rudder toward the desired new direction while increasing rpms on the screw on the opposite side, so a hard turn to port would require a helmsman to move the rudder to port while revolutions were increased on the starboard screw and decreased on the port screw.

Belowdecks, away from the wind, temperatures could quickly become uncomfortably hot in the engine, fire and pump rooms; black gang sailors sometimes endured heat over a hundred degrees. Men standing watch would stay under blowers that circulated air from topside to below, but relief was marginal.

One afternoon machinist's mate Fred Schaufus, alone at his GQ station in the aft pump room, dozed off in the oppressive heat. An officer came down the ladder with his .45 colt sidearm strapped to his belt. Schaufus felt pressure against his chest from the .45 barrel and the twenty-seven-year-old sailor woke to find the man snarling in his face,

"You know I could shoot you." Schaufus, annoyed, called his bluff. "Go ahead and shoot." The officer stomped away.[3]

Officers often conflicted with the enlisted men and were taunted in less-than-subtle ways. Ensign Brown, a Ninety-Day Wonder whose name lent itself to mischief, had gotten used to ribbing and jeers from the old salts. "What color is shit?" someone might yell when the ensign's shoes appeared at the top engine compartment ladder.[4] "Brown" came the reply from an accomplice, as Brown hopped down the last rungs of the ladder to the deck. One time someone hurled a wrench that narrowly missed the ensign; a handwritten attached note said, "Next time the wrench may not miss you." Unable to isolate the offender, Brown retreated from the engine room.

Fireman Bill Brzykcy stood his watch in the aft pump room, watching pumps and pressure gauges and making sure the large bearings in the shaft alleys were well oiled to keep them cool. The shaft bearings used a lot of oil when the *Miss* ran at flank speed, so vigilance by the pump room watch was paramount. The noise in the pump room was deafening at flank speed, and sailors were forced to cup their hands around their mouths to shout in the ear of the next man in order to communicate.

One quiet day at sea when Brzykcy was down in the engine room alone, his gaze landed on the edge of a bilge plate. For some reason he decided to unbolt the plate and saw glass gleaming in the light. Down on his knees, he peered into the depths and saw row after row of gallon-size glass jugs lining the bilge, thirty or so in all, apparently filled with fruit juice. He knew in an instant he'd stumbled across someone's stash of homemade booze, and he quickly replaced the plate and tightened the bolts. He didn't mention his find to anyone, and he never learned whose booty it was.

Sailors' attempts to concoct homemade booze didn't always go undiscovered. On this southerly cruise two engineering sailors filled Coca-Cola kegs with a blend of fruit juice, raisins and other delectable fruit that would ferment in the hot fire room. The kegs were hoisted by ropes to the top of the boiler stacks in an effort to conceal the home-made still and allow the heat to ferment the brew. The plan was foiled one night when the ropes came undone, sending the kegs crashing into the pipes, valves and gauges below. The cascading liquid covered the once-spotless boilers with a thick coat of purple goo. Chief Water Tender Smith, furious at the sight of the boilers turned purple, rousted the entire fire gang out of their bunks in the middle of the night, and they spent the next several hours cleaning up the mess as officers looked on. No one ever took responsibility for the still, but the pungent aroma of fermented raisins and plums lasted for a few days.

Captain Beck often negotiated for commodities—one of them alcohol—from aircraft carriers that came alongside for fueling. Ice cream was a rare treat, as *Mississinewa* had no means to make the cold confection. Beck bargained with various ships for other treats, as well. Alcohol was forbidden aboard U.S. Navy ships, although small bottles of whiskey were stocked in sick bay for medicinal purposes. On occasion Beck traded merchant tankers freshwater in return for a case of liquor, but long periods at sea required a bit more ingenuity. To the crew's surprise early in the cruise, Beck traded freshwater from *Mississinewa* distillation units for cases of Aqua Velva aftershave lotion brought by a civilian merchant tanker. Soon afterward the captain requested the steward bring a fresh loaf of bread to the bridge. After that it became well known that the captain strained Aqua Velva through the bread to isolate the alcohol. After the first Aqua Velva event, the crew always knew when a booze transaction had been made with a merchant tanker: whenever saltwater showers replaced freshwater ones.

Mississinewa crossed the international date line on Wednesday, July 19, and suddenly the day was Thursday. The new time zone, officially called Time Zone Minus 11.5 (meaning the number of hours off Greenwich Time), required setting the ship's clocks back thirty minutes, so the clock-changer made his rounds above and below deck to adjust the nearly two dozen clocks on board. Later in the day the crew sighted one of the easternmost islands in the Marshalls. Their next port, Eniwetok, lay just a few miles to the west.

The radar crew aboard *Mississinewa*, who worked under the critical eye of the navigator, were striking for the rating of radar operator. Their duty station, the radar shack, was a small room on the bridge navigation deck where two men constantly manned the radar for surface searches. When both air and surface searches were conducted at the same time, four sailors crowded the tiny room.

Peanut butter on toast and hot coffee from the signal room supplied the only relief during the long and boring radar watches. Lieutenant Rowe frequented the radar shack and befriended the young strikers. He harassed the enlisted boys incessantly with such lines as "You'll be in the Navy fifty years and you'll never know what I know."[5] All six radar operators liked him and made every effort to perform their duties efficiently. He took the young men under his wing and cared about them, and they responded with intense loyalty.

Captain Beck also visited the radar shack often, but he intimidated some of the boys stationed on the bridge. The radar crew noticed a degree of tension between fifty-year-old Beck and the younger officers, too, including Executive Officer Robert Lewis, who often seemed to disagree with Beck over one matter or another, but such tensions were not uncommon on the floating cities where hundreds of men shared the space and their daily lives.

The radio shack copied Morse code messages twenty-four hours a day and relayed encoded communications to the coding room for Lieutenant Wilson and Scott to decode. While both communications officers operated the electric cypher machine (ECM) to decode messages, Wilson did so more often because Scott spent six hours out of every twenty-four on the bridge serving as officer of the deck.[6] The ongoing task of censoring mail home fell largely on the communications officers. Wilson and Scott corralled available officers to help with censorship duties, and the wardroom table was often littered with scraps cut out with scissors, and heavy dark marker lines would crisscross many of the letters home; gone were any mention of military maneuvers or places that might tip off the enemy if intercepted. The envelopes were imprinted with a rubber stamp and initialed by the censoring officer.

The communications specialists—radarmen, radiomen, signalmen and yeomen—created, interpreted or relayed the messages addressed to *Mississinewa* or the Fueling Task Group. The radiomen were not above a little horseplay. Bob Brautigam found a way to enter Captain Beck's cabin after the skipper left the bridge and play a prank. Beck liked sweets and often asked the steward's mates to bake pies and deliver the warm treats directly to his cabin. The smell of fresh pie would waft through the bridge area and tease the nostrils of the radiomen. Brautigam hatched a plan. The radiomen turned to thievery, routinely stealing Beck's tasty dessert, swiftly downing the pie and tossing the pie plate overboard. The pie crimes continued until Brautigam overheard a steward's mate complain to Beck that they were running out of pie plates. The crime spree was over.

Chief commissary steward Frank Lutz, a forty-nine-year-old Navy veteran, was admired by his galley crew, and his cooking buoyed ship's morale. Sailors marveled at the plentiful and tasty meals he put out three times a day; many of them had suffered through the Great Depression with little to eat, and they were enormously grateful for such steady fare. Many *Miss* sailors held closely guarded memories of soup kitchens and hungry nights.

A messenger from the bridge awakened the cooks each morning at 0300 to begin preparing breakfast. Three cooks were always on duty fixing food for each meal. Four other cooks acted as servers at large steam tables on the serving line. Eight enlisted sailors on mess duty cleaned the tables, helped serve the food, performed scullery duty, peeled potatoes and disposed of garbage.

Fresh eggs cooked to order were sometimes available in port. At sea, powdered eggs, powdered milk, bacon, toast and pancakes were the standard breakfast fare, served with strong coffee. Navy coffee mugs of thick white porcelain without handles offered a good hand warmer when the weather was cold and seas were rough. Navy beans as breakfast fare were palatable with enough ketchup.

Australian beef, gray and shoe-leather tough, was served often for lunch. Marbled with gristle and fat, the Aussie beef was not popular with the crew. Same with the tropical butter, which appeared to be normal table butter in color and consistency, but sailors said not even a blowtorch could melt the waxy substance. The ship's supply never seemed to dwindle.

"Horsecock and Joe" described bologna sandwiches and hot coffee. Frozen in long sausage shapes, the horsecock was cut in thick slices; the coffee was served so hot that sailors would wrap the frozen sausage around their coffee mugs to thaw the meat. Chief Lutz's special horseradish mustard added a spicy kick to the meal. Whenever the crew awoke to find cooks preparing hundreds of horsecock sandwiches, they knew the ship was headed for bad weather.

The Italian sailors from the Bronx and Queens boroughs of New York City enjoyed spaghetti and meat sauce prepared in the galley. After a long day of fueling other ships, Captain Beck, defying Navy regulations, often allowed them a can or two of beer with a spaghetti meal as a reward for a job well done. Canned vegetables, mashed potatoes and an endless supply of bread and coffee rounded out the crew's regular diet.

Fernando "Cookie" Cuevas and John D'Anna enjoyed cooking for the crew and had earned their ratings as strikers. Thirty-three-year-old Cuevas had worked briefly as a short-order cook in New York and was glad to use his culinary experience to avoid deckhand duties. D'Anna, an eighteen-year-old from Detroit, found it hard to get up in the middle of the night to cook. Captain Beck discovered one day on visiting the galley that the young man had slept through a GQ alarm without waking. "John, if we ever get hit, you're going to die," the skipper said to tease him. D'Anna replied easily, "Don't worry, sir, I'll be the first over the side."

The ship's baker, Marcel "Frenchy" Lamock, a French citizen who had volunteered to fight with U.S. forces, was the most popular sailor aboard. When asked why he had joined the U.S. Navy, Lamock replied, "The *Boches* [the Nazis] have invaded and occupied my country and I want to fight back." The talented baker delighted the crew with delicious pies baked with canned pears and peaches. Waking up to fresh cinnamon rolls for breakfast was a pleasant surprise on the mornings deckhands rigged for fueling. The smell of Frenchy's bread rising in galley ovens wafted through the aft crew's quarters every morning; he never failed to have fresh bread available.

One job of the *Mississinewa* steward's mates was to prepare and serve officers their meals in the wardroom. James Reeder was wardroom cook, and he took the lead in preparing the officers' meals. Reeder's chili, a family recipe featuring vanilla extract and a generous dose of chile peppers, was popular with Captain Beck, so it appeared often on the wardroom menu.

When Reeder wasn't cooking, he and his crewmates frequently took part in the mess hall casino gambling. The game of choice was craps. Fellow steward Raleigh Peppers often came to watch. One time Nathaniel Warren begged for a $25 loan from Peppers, who complied reluctantly, as he sent most of his $16 pay home to his family every month. Warren's mounting losses made Peppers anxious. A few weeks later Warren was transferred to another ship by high line; as he dangled between the two ships, Peppers waved good-bye, and realized too late that he'd never gotten his $25 back.

Eniwetok's sister island, Kwajalein Atoll, appeared out of the mist early on the morning of July 23. Eniwetok lay farther to the northwest, 326 miles away, a full day's cruise. Eniwetok's capture five months earlier had given control of the Marshalls to the United States, and the atoll was developed principally as a Navy and Marine air base and fleet anchorage.

Eniwetok Atoll, containing thirty small islands of sand and coral, measures sixty-four miles around, with an elevation of fifteen feet. Three entrances to the lagoon permit access to an island also named Eniwetok, a tiny outpost two miles long and a quarter mile wide. The day after passing Kwajalein, *Mississinewa* sailors lined the ship's rails as they entered Eniwetok's harbor, already crowded with ships from the Fifth Fleet. The island appeared to be covered with hundreds of telephone poles. As the *Miss* came closer, the crew saw why: Hundreds of palm trees had had their tops shot off from shellfire, and the protruding, naked stumps poked skyward, leafless and unadorned.

The *Miss* stayed anchored for several days, and the sailors didn't expect the ship to move within the harbor anytime soon. Seamen Eugene Cooley and Joe Contendo decided to play volleyball over the forward AV gas tanks with a couple of off-watch sailors. Deckhands didn't realize the anchor had already been hoisted for getting under way, and they started a spirited volleyball match. Leaping into the air near the port rail to snare a wild volleyball serve from Contendo, Cooley's outstretched hand tipped the high-flying ball, but not before he ran out of deck and tumbled overboard. The hull was gliding past Cooley when someone yelled, "Man overboard." Captain Beck ordered the launch to retrieve him and summoned the water-soaked deckhand to the bridge. Beck chewed him out, saying, "I won't stop this ship to pick you up if you pull a foolhardy stunt like that again."

Two weeks at anchor had passed. One morning *Mississinewa* received a visual message from the signalmen, universally known as "skivvy wavers," since the white flags they waved often looked like underwear from a distance. The message, relayed from Commander Service Squadron Ten, was to deliver aviation gasoline for the planes, so the oiler deckhands performed fueling in port for those warships.

Toward the end of August Admiral William "Bull" Halsey ordered *Mississinewa* to leave Eniwetok and head for the Admiralty Islands with the task force. The ship's degaussing system was energized to avoid triggering enemy mines near Eniwetok's entrance while the ship steamed at ten knots out of the channel and headed for open sea. As planned, a Navy plane towing a target sleeve appeared, and Captain Beck ordered all starboard guns to open fire on the target. The gun crews expended more than thirteen hundred rounds of ammunition.

Mississinewa took up the lead ship position as guide for the convoy, and the ships sailed in a standard zigzag pattern. Each day continued with GQ sounding before sunrise and again at sunset. Daytime temperature increased as the oiler steamed southwest for Seeadler Harbor in the Admiralties. Before the ship would reach Seeadler, it would cross the equator, an event of momentous import in the nautical world. The shipboard "ceremony" would give the men a respite from thoughts of war, when the seasoned sailors, called Shellbacks, would initiate the Pollywogs, as green sailors were called.

The crossing of the equator ceremony is a centuries-old naval tradition that sailors continued even during wartime. In the ancient ritual, King Neptune and his Royal Court allowed uninitiated sailors the privilege of joining the Ancient Order of the Deep. Once a Pollywog sailor completed his initiation, he became a Shellback. The initiation— part fun, part mock torture, part humiliation—was a memorable experience for all sailors who endured the ceremony.

Mississinewa Pollywogs had become somewhat anxious as the dog days of August grew hotter and the ship neared the equator. The Shellbacks ribbed the Pollywogs for days with comments like "You sure have nice hair, but don't get used to it." Adding to the tension, Shellbacks cut up old pieces of fire hose that they soaked for days in salt water, then dried in the hot sun till they formed hard paddles, called shillelaghs, to be used for disciplining the Pollywogs.

On the morning of August 23 King Neptune, played by chief commissary steward Frank Lutz, ordered his assistant, Davy Jones, to report to the bridge and present Captain Beck with the Royal Court Summons to be read over the ship's loudspeakers.

From: His Royal Highness, King Neptunus Rex,
Ruler of the Raging Main
To: The Commanding Officer, USS Mississinewa

At about 1200 today, August 23, 1944, your vessel will be visited by my
Royal Scribe, Davy Jones, and his party. You are directed to muster at
quarters all of the slimy, landlubberish Pollywogs in your crew by 1300.
At this time, all your lowly Pollywogs will be served with your summons
to appear before my Royal Court. Failure to comply will invoke my
Royal displeasure and bring disaster to your Pollywog cargo-hauling
slop barge.

Signed:

King Neptunus Rex
His Royal Highness
Ruler of the Raging Main

At noon the festivities began. Davy Jones, the Royal Scribe, and
his party of Shellbacks reported to the bridge to converse with Cap-
tain Beck over the ship's loudspeakers. A figure representing Davy
Jones asked: "Are you the commanding officer of this scurvy-looking
Pollywog-packing sand scow?" and the ship's captain meekly answered,
"I am, sir."

The rites began. Sailor after sailor suffered the Shellbacks' antics,
while Bill Janas and Bill Brzykcy decided to bypass King Neptune's
Court and hide in the spud locker above the mess hall. An hour later a
Shellback opened the spud locker and spotted the pair of Pollywogs
under the pile of heaving potatoes; several sailors dragged the unfortunate pair to the well deck.

Ray Fulleman, wielding a fire hose, stood at the top of the ladder
leading down to the cargo deck while King Neptune's Court watched
from a wooden platform. Fulleman, already a Shellback from crossing

the equator, directed a stream of water at men scaling the ladder and soaked the Pollywogs. He heard Captain Beck's voice behind him, "Blast them off the ladder." Beck seized the hose and doused the Pollywogs with an even stronger stream of salt water.

King Neptune bellowed at Janas and Brzykcy, the recalcitrant spud sailors. "Kneel before the court. What are these Pollywogs charged with?" The Royal attorney replied, "Hiding in the spud locker without the spuds' permission, Your Majesty."[7]

King Neptune glared in royal disgust at the kneeling pair of firemen. "How do you plead, Pollywogs?" The pair knew only one answer was acceptable: "Guilty, Your Majesty." A royal deputy stepped up to the men, dipped a paintbrush in a bucket of black oil and swabbed their heads with the slimy ooze. Led to a barber's chair, Brzykcy got a haircut with tin snips from the royal barber. Then the royal doctor stepped up to the chair and ordered him to open his mouth. "This will cure what ails you," he laughed, squirting hot pepper sauce into Brzykcy's mouth; the Iowa fireman had a red mark down the left side of his chin for two days from the fiery mixture. A Shellback hit the lower lever of the barber chair, and Brzykcy catapulted backward into a canvas chute that dumped him into a pool of foul-smelling water laced with three-day-old garbage. Shellbacks dunked the Pollywogs repeatedly in the putrid filth.

The half-drowned Pollywogs were forced to crawl through piles of foul-smelling garbage until they exited the opposite end to terminate the ordeal. *Whack! Whack!* They crawled on their hands and knees through the canvas tube encouraged by painful swats on their backsides by Shellbacks swinging the dreaded shillelagh. Two sailors suffered scalp lacerations as Shellbacks inadvertently knocked their heads into nearby pipes; the pair received their Shellback certificates in sick bay. Other Pollywogs fought their way through a powerful stream of salt water to reach the end. Gus Liveakos, machinist's mate, played the part of the Royal Devil, dressed in a union suit dyed red with food coloring and a devil's skullcap with two horns. He rigged a 360-volt battery and attached the device to his royal pitchfork. Every Pollywog kneeling before King Neptune took a jolt for providing an answer, correct or not, to the Royal Court.

Ensign Brown had the ultimate humiliation. He knelt before King Neptune and was ordered to kiss the protruding belly of the Royal Baby, who was actually a steward's mate clad only in a diaper and boxing gloves. Brown adamantly refused. Liveakos gigged Brown with the 360-volt pitchfork, but the ensign refused again and again to perform the kissing ritual. As the Royal Devil poked him with the pitchfork one last time, Brown screeched and relented, kissing the Royal Baby's hideous belly. Afterward Liveakos joked that Brown was "just about ready to kiss anything" after the pitchfork jolts.

Captain Beck stood in the dunk tank in shorts and a T-shirt, dunking Pollywogs one by one as they came down the chute from the cargo deck. Executive Officer Lewis was dunked repeatedly in the putrid water. Several Shellbacks and Pollywogs thought Beck was drunk; at any rate, at some point during the ceremony, he gave away his uniform insignia. By the time he left the dunk tank he was stark naked, his clothes having disappeared during the Pollywog ordeal.

When the rites were finished, the cold, wet and oily ex-Pollywogs lined up on the cargo deck to receive their Shellback certificate, a handsome paper graced with an artful tableau portraying King Neptune and several shapely topless mermaids with long blond hair. The ancient ceremony had been again made fresh. By 1800 hours on August 23, 1944, *Mississinewa* had crossed the equator and steamed into Time Zone Minus 10, headed for the Admiralty Islands near Papua New Guinea. Every man aboard was now a Shellback and a member of King Neptune's Ancient Order of the Deep.

It was the last merriment before the war began in earnest for the men of the *Miss*. Within weeks they would see carnage and death, *kamikazes* and fire. War loomed ever closer.

CHAPTER 7

Suicide Submarines

This brave man, so filled with love for his country that he finds it difficult to die, is calling out to his friends and about to die.

—Hiroshi Kuroki, as he waited to die in a *kaiten* accident[1]

On September 1, 1944, the first group of *kaiten* pilots had made the switch from Ourasaki Base to begin training in their suicide craft at the top-secret Ozushima Base. It was the first official day of their special attack force known as *kaiten*.

Sekio Nishina and Hiroshi Kuroki were assigned as chief instructors to the incoming pilot trainees. At the time they were the only veteran midget submariners to train *kaiten* pilots; not until March would another midget sub trainer finally arrive, months after the two coinventors were gone.

The first class numbered thirty trainees, who were tasked with instructing new recruits while completing their own training. The number of pilots grew, and by September 8 thirty-two officer pilots were in training. Thirteen of those officers had graduated from the Naval Academy, fourteen were reserve officers and ex–torpedo boat students; five came from the Naval Engineering School. All had volunteered, of course, for the dangerous assignment.

Petty officers who were torpedo men assisted this early group of *kaiten* pilots. After several weeks ten of them volunteered to join the ranks of the pilots. As additional support, nine non-rated sailors experienced in torpedo fitting joined the first group of sixty personnel. Operations were set to begin at Ozushima.

The *kaiten* had been assembled up in the hills overlooking the water at Ozushima. The underground rail system now began to bring the craft down to Tokuyama Bay.

Mastering a *kaiten* required as much skill as piloting a fighter aircraft, but other reasons influenced the length of the training period. The highly specialized piece of technology was not only difficult to operate, it was acutely uncomfortable to operate, and even to enter. It measured only a meter in diameter, so even a small man was cramped. Unfortunately, due to a critical shortage of fuel, men sometimes trained two at a time to maximize the training time. It meant sharing the space barely big enough for one. Every day pilots were reminded that fuel was "as precious as a drop of blood."[2]

The need for rapid proficiency meant that training runs in Tokuyama Bay were vitally important. In addition to daytime in-the-water training, pilots spent their nights studying, reviewing manuals and onboard training reports.

The *kaiten* controls were simple, but considerable skill was needed to operate the craft efficiently. Directly in front of the pilot's face was the viewing glass of a short periscope that could be raised or lowered by a simple hand crank on the pilot's left. Above the pilot's head was a valve (*chout-su*) regulating oxygen flow to the motor immediately behind him.

Buoyancy was a challenge. Overhead on the pilot's left was a lever connected with the *kaiten*'s diving planes, which controlled the rate of descent or climb underwater. But controlling depth was very tricky and the craft often unexpectedly broached the surface, an event that would place a pilot at great risk of detection. Thus training emphasized buoyancy control.

Below the depth-control lever was a valve for letting in seawater for ballast to replace the oxygen fuel as it was used up, a critical component for maintaining stability. The last control touched by the pilot when he set his final course for an enemy ship was the rudder-control lever, which steered the weapon right or left.

Kaiten pilots felt they needed six hands and the same number of eyes for watching the control panel. There was no instrument panel, only a gyrocompass, a clock, and depth and fuel gauges. The space was so tight that any sudden change in the controls or contact with an underwater obstacle always caused the pilot to bang his head on the instruments, so bandaged heads were a frequent sight on Ozushima Base.

Keeping a target in sight was one of the greatest challenges to a successful suicide mission. Isolating a target was one thing; keeping it in your sights was infinitely harder. Initially the pilot of the mother submarine would give the *kaiten* pilot the coordinates of the intended target, which was prepared to launch and go forward in the recommended direction. At the optimum moment the *kaitens'* engines were started, and they were released at five-second intervals from the mother submarine.

Once in motion, the pilot could observe the target through his own hand-cranked periscope and make corrections to his course. As the submarine closed on its target, a telephone link between the submarine's conning tower and the *kaiten* enabled the captain to keep the pilots informed on the relative positions of their targets. At about five hundred yards from his target, the pilot would take a final bearing and begin a high-speed attack, remaining submerged at fifteen feet below the surface.

On an operational mission, the captain of the mother submarine aligned his ship with the target and each *kaiten* pilot checked his own compass bearing. The navigator of the mother submarine was responsible for plotting the attack course of each individual *kaiten* to arrive within range of the target. Relayed by telephone, a typical order might be "Go right thirty degrees on leaving. Speed twenty-five knots for twelve minutes and thirty seconds." The pilot was expected to raise his periscope and set the controls for his final approach, a high-speed run at thirty knots to hit the enemy ship.

The task was difficult. The "cruel weapon" tested the pilots in every way, pitting their mental and emotional resources against the knowledge of certain death if they succeeded, shame and disgrace if they did not. Even in training it caused great embarrassment if a pilot failed to control his craft and arrive at the intended destination, so every in-water session was highly stressful.

The pilots trained doggedly, determined to succeed. Every day was a new ordeal, every night an exhausted slumber too short to refresh their tired bodies. They pushed themselves hard, drilling in mock attacks in the bay, deploying and returning, finding a target, losing it, finding it again.

Fifteen *kaiten* pilots were killed in accidents during training between September 1944 and August 1945.

The first two casualties died on September 6. They perished together in the same *kaiten*, and one victim was none other than Hiroshi Kuroki, a guiding light of the "heaven shaker." Kuroki and trainee Lieutenant Takashi Higuchi had set out riding tandem in one of the three prototype *kaiten*, when their craft suddenly dived and hit the bottom of Tokuyama Bay. Unable to free the craft and return to the surface, they sat for hours in a dark and increasingly hot and airless crypt, hoping their absence would be noticed in time.

Word of the missing men spread quickly through Ozushima Base. An emergency call from Base Commander Itakura required all pilots to man available boats and launches. The *kaiten*'s location was unknown, so Itakura ordered the seabed of Tokuyama Bay to be swept with a long wire rope secured between two boats. The news of the lost craft reached

Ensign Toshiharu Konada, a volunteer selected from the Naval Submarine School who had been on-site only a few hours. Konada joined in the search for the two pilots, but at first he didn't realize the significance, for few of the new recruits knew the names of the missing men.

The search continued all night. Rescuers hoped the pilots' air supply could hold out until they were found.

At dawn a search boat noticed air bubbles rising from a spot on the sea bottom. A diver discovered Kuroki's *kaiten* stuck in the muck deep in the bay, where the escort boat had last sighted it. After becoming stuck in the seabed, Kuroki had wisely stopped the engine and released its compressed air, in hopes that the air bubbles would alert rescuers. The clever move was to no avail; the bubbles had risen unseen until it was too late. Kuroki and Higuchi had slowly suffocated from lack of oxygen. The sunken torpedo sub was raised to the surface by a boat fitted with a crane.

At dockside Ensign Konada stood by with other long-faced watchers as Kuroki's body was removed from the *kaiten*, then wrapped in a white blanket and laid on the floating pier. While more and more pilots learned of the shocking death of the *kaiten* coinventor, the body was placed on a stretcher and carried to the headquarters office up the steep stone steps leading from the waterfront. Older than most of the trainees, Kuroki was still a young man; in five more days he would have turned twenty-three.

Kuroki's companion, Lieutenant Higuchi, was wrapped and also carried to the office. Young recruits and senior officers alike tried to control their sense of shock and loss. In particular, Kuroki's death greatly touched Lieutenant Yoshinori Kamibeppu and Sublieutenant Nishina; the three had been classmates at the Naval Academy, and all three had piloted midget submarines.

The searchers discovered that in the last hours of his life Kuroki had written a report of the sinking, even as he awaited death in the confines of the *kaiten*. In two thousand graceful characters he wrote of his hopes for the success of the training program.[3] The posthumous battle cry inspired the newly arrived trainees, and Ensign Konada, like the others, vowed that he would honor Kuroki's sacrifice by making the most of this new weapon.

In the saddest of testimonies, Kuroki wrote a short poem. He had hours to contemplate his chance of rescue, ever less likely as the time slipped by. As the air grew foul and it became harder to breathe, he was forced to confront the growing certainty of his death. In graceful calligraphy he wrote his own epitaph:

「国を思ひ死ぬに死なれぬ益良雄が
友々よびつ死してゆくらん」

This brave man, so filled with love for his country that he finds
it difficult to die, is calling out to his friends and about to die.

After the tragedy, both *kaiten* pilots were cremated. Sekio Nishina took Kuroki's ashes and placed them in a small white box. He vowed to carry the remains of his friend on the very first *kaiten* sortie to Ulithi, so the pair could still attack the Americans "together," ensuring they would be enshrined as gods at Yasukuni Shrine. Nishina kept his vow when the heaven shaker was unleashed at Ulithi two months later.

Lessons were learned from the accident. After Kuroki's death, the *kaiten* was altered to include a vitally important valve. If a pilot's weapon dived too deep and became stuck in the depths of Tokuyama Bay, he could free the *kaiten* by using a blow valve that forced compressed air from the steering apparatus into the water-filled practice warhead. The resulting buoyancy would raise the *kaiten*. However, the blow valve was positioned next to the fuel valve, creating a potential hazard, as it would be easy to open the wrong valve; too much fuel would force the *kaiten* deeper into the mud.

The design team carefully analyzed Kuroki's last report, and the changes he recommended from his tomb were incorporated into future *kaiten* designs. One important consideration was recovery time, the interval or window of opportunity to locate and raise a *kaiten*. Recovery of the craft required sending a diver down to attach lines, but that often occurred too late to save the pilot. After much experimentation, engineers devised an air purifier that could enable an undamaged *kaiten* to remain submerged for up to twenty hours with breathable air.

Other changes were instigated. The tops of the training *kaiten* were painted white to allow for better detection in case of accident; the white top also had the benefit of allowing training boats to better track the craft in training maneuvers. Because collisions with underwater objects were a major cause of *kaiten* loss and malfunction, the training boats would now throw signaling charges into the water to alert a submerged *kaiten* pilot that his craft was approaching a dangerous object.[4]

Immediately after Kuroki's death, Nishina took over the project's leadership. A week after the tragedy the team of trainers headed by Nishina held an important briefing for the incoming pilots in training. First the instructors discussed the dire outlook of the fighting in the most recent Pacific battles. Nishina would make the closing remarks.

Unlike the upbeat messages of all-but-certain victory given to the public, the briefing revealed an unusually stark analysis: Japan was losing the war. The pessimistic message hit one recruit especially hard. Pilot-in-training Yutaka Yokota, who had arrived on the base just days after Kuroki's death, recalled the message conveyed that day. "Again and again, they told us, the enemy has been able to range forces of ships and planes against us in overpowering strength. His ships can open fire at greater distances and much earlier than ours, because of his superior radar. He sights our ships and planes before they spot him. Confidence was draining from us."

Still, hope for victory continued, and the *kaiten* program was a morale booster to a discouraged military force. Instructors pumped up the recruits.

"When the American fleet moves closer to Japan, we will attack it with 'seeing' torpedoes," the trainers said. "You and men like you will be the eyes of the greatest sea weapon ever devised. If each one of you scores a hit, what do you think the result will be? Even America, for all her industry and riches, cannot afford the loss of a hundred warships."[5]

The bravado inspired Yokota and his shipmates. Then Nishina, the last officer to address the group, stood up. It was the first time Yokota had seen him, and he didn't yet know his name. He wondered who the man was, so coarse was his appearance. It seemed strange for him to be here in this place with distinguished Navy officers.

"I gasped at the sight of him," he said. "He had extremely long hair, an oil-stained messy uniform, and a dirty face that looked drawn and tired. Surely he could not be a naval officer. He looked like a vulgar person, with no standards of dress or cleanliness."

And yet Yokota found something compelling in the man with the fierce bright eyes. "As he looked upon us, I told myself that whoever this man was, he would throw himself, body and soul, into whatever he undertook."

Then he spoke. "I am Sekio Nishina," he said in a gentle voice. The room was hushed. Yokota could hardly reconcile the man with the growing legend. Nishina's nondescript appearance contrasted sharply with his engineering prowess and intellectual brilliance. "He hesitated before going on," Yokota said, hardly able to believe this was one of the *kaiten* creators. "He looked more like a dreamy poet than anything else."

Nishina's words touched and inspired all who listened. "I am happy to meet you," he said, "and hope all of you will have as great a spirit as my dear, intimate friend Hiroshi Kuroki. Although I may not be with you long because I hope for the honor of going on the *kaiten*'s first mission, I will do my best to teach you everything I can in the time remaining to me."

Training at Ozushima resumed and intensified after Kuroki's death. Now looking primarily to Nishina as the leader, the recruits knew they had a lot to learn and a short time to do so. They practiced every day for long hours, starting at the launching site.

A trainee entered his *kaiten* as it lay on a launching trolley on the dockside, secured the entrance hatch, and checked his instruments and controls. A crane lifted the *kaiten* into the water, where it was lashed to a launch for transport to the training area. Specialized working boats were ordered for *kaiten* training, but few were built; instead, old torpedo boats and other light escort boats were pressed into service. These training craft consumed more fuel, and each trainee was constantly reminded of the fuel shortage, the consequence of which was to make training in the bay a stressful experience. The seawater quickly rusted the hulls of the *kaiten* craft except for the brass fittings, and the mix gave the craft a splotchy brown appearance. (The "unusual rusty brown color" of the *kaiten* was noted in the Action Report of USS *Case* following the attack at Ulithi.)

A simple code of knocks on the *kaiten* hull allowed instructors to check if the pilot trainee was ready for launch. Reaching up and back, the pilot pulled the starting lever and moved away from the training launch. The pilot would next test the diving controls, sometimes descending as deep as seventy-five feet. Navigation tools were very limited, a pilot having only a stopwatch, a gyrocompass and a short, hand-cranked periscope to guide him.

Students spent many hours mastering the skills to hold the unwieldy craft steady at fifteen feet below the surface, the optimal depth to attack an enemy ship. Breaking the surface meant failing the test; even so, it was a familiar sight to see a *kaiten* broaching the surface of Tokuyama Bay. Such an event was extremely shameful for a pilot.

In the weeks that followed Kuroki's accident, the trainees examined the torpedo and learned how it was built and maintained. They trained in mock-ups of *kaiten* cockpits to familiarize themselves with the instruments and controls. The new recruits also worked every afternoon, sometimes as crew and assistants aboard the torpedo boats that towed the *kaiten* into the bay, sometimes as targets for the first class recruits to "strike." Yokota called it hard work, but said they enjoyed it, "for we were learning much about the *kaiten* while waiting for one of our own."[6]

Even as the craft were still under construction, recruits practiced being sealed inside the *kaiten*. As more *kaiten* were finished, more men were able to get their own craft. Naoji Kozu remembered his first view of his own *kaiten* as overwhelming—and frightening.

"At last we saw the weapon we would ourselves board," he wrote. "I sensed something larger than the power of a human being glowering down at me. I lost my reason and emotions. I was dumbfounded. I felt that I had myself turned into something no longer human."[7] Once inside and moving through the water, he compared the experience to "being put inside an oil drum and spun around and around until you were dizzy—and then ordered to go on a run!"

Mastering a *kaiten* during an attack would be a very difficult task. While training in a bay with calm seas was relatively easy, conditions on the ocean changed the equation; it was an entirely different matter to peer through a periscope on the open sea, where waves could obscure the view, and the undersea currents could so greatly affect buoyancy.

The pilot had three criteria to consider for a successful attack: the enemy's course, speed, and bow angle from the *kaiten*. Even a slight miscalculation in judgment could force the pilot to use his periscope and thus expose his position to the enemy.

The question of positioning was first addressed by an operator on the mother submarine, who could telephone the enemy's course, speed and angle to the *kaiten* pilot before his launch from the submerged mother sub. The pilot would be given a specific course and time to follow after leaving the cradle on the deck. At the end of his timed run, the pilot would raise his periscope to take a final bearing on the target, then submerge to fifteen feet and run full speed at the target. In training, seven seconds was the maximum time a pilot was allowed to make a final bearing "fix" with his periscope—even just a few seconds longer might allow the enemy to see the periscope wake.

———

The initial launch was a critical element of success. Weather permitting, the ideal position for the mother submarine was a depth of fifty-five feet below the surface; the *kaiten*, strapped to the submarine's deck, would thus be situated at a depth of thirty-five feet. The immediate challenge for the *kaiten* pilot at the moment of launch was to maintain the same depth after the release from the mother sub. To do so, he had to create a slight downward angle on the diving planes, allowing the *kaiten* to dip a little after leaving the deck and compensate for any push toward the surface. It was nonetheless risky, as too much downward thrust would propel the *kaiten* toward the ocean floor. Getting stuck in the mud would be disastrous in an enemy anchorage.

Maintaining the correct buoyancy after launch and during target-seeking was also hazardous, as the system of ballast replacement—seawater for lost fuel—was a major concern. Any miscalculation of the correct amounts needed could very quickly change the buoyancy and shoot the *kaiten* to the surface, where it would be spotted by the enemy.

Knowing they might miss an enemy target on their first try, pilots in training practiced making a second run on a target. Observed by the instructors, their tactics were studied and critiqued. Had their tactics worked? Or did the enemy detect them? If they had revealed too much wake or evidence of the periscope, they would have met with surface guns or depth charges. In short, they would be dead, mission unfulfilled.

Running out of fuel at sea was a possibility, a hazard that must be confronted. A long pursuit by an enemy destroyer could throw a *kaiten* off course and cause it to go dry on fuel. What then? The trainees discussed what they would do in such a case. Yutaka Yokota had a plan that was a different twist on the suicide mission.

"If I ever ran out of fuel, I would come to the surface and lie there," he said. "We knew the Americans were great souvenir hunters. It seemed very likely that they would try and recover my *kaiten* so their ordnance experts could look it over. If they tried, I planned to remain perfectly still. I would let them hoist me out of the water. Then as soon as I felt my weapon touch the deck, I would throw a special switch each *kaiten* had in case the nose detonator did not work—and [I would] take everyone on the American ship to eternity with me."

The pressure grew intense, and the pilots in training grappled with fear and exhaustion.

"We trained desperately," Yokota said. "You couldn't complain of pain or anything. You had to push on: If I don't hit the target, if I have to self-detonate, I'll die without doing what I must. It was agony for everybody."

Once you became a member of an attack force, he explained, it became deathly serious. After all the training and resources that had gone to train a pilot capable of the task, the idea of losing that valuable commodity was horrendous.

"If you had two lives, it wouldn't have mattered," he said, "but you were giving up your only life. Life is so precious. Your life was dedicated to self-sacrifice, committed to smashing into the enemy. That is why we trained like that. We practiced that hard, because we valued our lives so highly."[8]

Naoji Kozu also felt that the training was agonizing, particularly because of the weapon's major difference from other suicide craft. In a *kaiten* the moment of death was unknown. With other suicide weapons—like the *kamikaze* planes—young men charged into the enemy and died, but they had their eyes open and they chose the time of their death. A suicide attack by a *kamikaze* plane, an *Ohka* (cherry blossom) flying bomb or a *Shinyo* suicide boat allowed the operator to decide the moment of impact and death. Not the *kaiten*.

Kozu talked about the very worst stress, which he said was the uncertainty as the pilot sought the target but didn't know exactly when and where he might hit it. At the same time his body was fighting with the very difficult controls, his mind was tortured by not knowing when the impact would come.

"You're underwater," he said, "and you can't look out. You've determined your course, peering through the periscope. The enemy position in one minute and thirty seconds will be this; I set my angle of attack at this. You submerge. You run full speed at the estimated enemy attack position. From the moment you commence your attack you see nothing. You have a stopwatch. You know how much of the one minute and thirty seconds has elapsed. But you may have made an error in measurement. You keep thinking. *Now! Now! Now!* But you never know when that moment will come. *Time's elapsed*, you realize. *I missed the target.* You come to the surface. You search again for the enemy. You realize you passed astern. Once more you set your course. But again, you don't know the moment of your death. You may die ahead of schedule. You don't even know that. I can't imagine a crueler weapon."[9]

He wondered, in the months to follow, how others felt at the moment of the attack. Did they suffer the same misgivings, the same fright, the same terrors? "I can't ask anyone how they felt at that moment," he said, "because no one who experienced it came back alive."

CHAPTER 8

Battle Stars

Sure, we want to go home. We want this war over with. The quickest way to get it over with is to go get the bastards who started it. The quicker they are whipped, the quicker we can go home. The shortest way home is through Berlin and Tokyo.

—General George S. Patton Jr., addressing his troops before
Operation Overlord, June 5, 1944

Two days after the *Miss* crossed the equator, it arrived close to Papua New Guinea, where the tropical forests and mountains of the Admiralty Islands came into view. Manus Island in the Admiralties was now designated a forward staging base for the Third Fleet. Its large harbor, Seeadler, named by Germans for the plentiful sea eagles that nested among the rocky outcroppings there, would be the fleet's new anchorage. Twenty miles across and protected by a horseshoe-shaped natural breakwater, the harbor was comparatively easy to defend. To the northwest lay the Philippines.

Shortly after the 0800 crew muster on August 26 the *Mississinewa* steamed into the harbor. A harbor pilot guided the ship to berth 374, where the *Miss* dropped anchor in twenty fathoms. Beck ordered the port and starboard number 1 tanks to shift NSFO to the ship's bunkers. Sailors went about their routines that week, and deckhands prepared for their first combat operation with the Third Fleet.

One day soon after arrival, Captain Beck's drinking habits, ever a cause for speculation, were called into question again. After spending several hours ashore, he came aboard in a most unusual way: via a cargo net that was hoisted from the captain's gig. A commotion ensued as sailors witnessed the hoist moving the net with Beck in it, elbows and legs gangling like a bug's. They assumed their captain had been drinking, as he often did, and was too drunk to navigate the starboard side ladder. Minutes later he awkwardly crawled out of the net and stepped onto the cargo deck. Scuttlebutt flew. The story was told and retold in the next few minutes, each time more dramatic than the last. Scuttlebutt always flies fast and furious aboard Navy ships. The word comes from the days of old wooden sailing ships when every sailor feared fire, so a spot to smoke was designated and cigarette butts were safely scuttled in a sand barrel. Naturally the sailors talked as they smoked, and rumors, hearsay and speculation came to be called scuttlebutt.

Today the rumors flew thick and fast. Boatswain's mate Junior Haskins knew for a fact the stories of the captain's drinking weren't exaggerated, for several times he'd personally brought Beck aboard cross-eyed and inebriated. Beck often had business ashore or on other vessels when the *Miss* was in port, and plenty of sailors had seen him return "three sheets to the wind," in Navy parlance. Haskins and the crew figured that alcohol was simply one of the perks for officers in the U.S. Navy.

This time it was different. Dr. John Bierley knew exactly why the captain had boarded in this manner—it had been Bierley's own suggestion.[1] Beck was bringing the ship's payroll with him in a very heavy metal box and was worried about the valuable payroll dropping into the sea if he climbed up the ladder. It had been known to happen. The solution was to bring Beck and the payroll box safely aboard in the cargo net. This time onshore hadn't been a pleasure trip.

In any case, deckhands certainly had fewer pleasures than officers. Pretty much the only breaks from the endless drills were gambling aboard ship and the occasional liberty "on the beach," and on the beach at Manus was not going to be hotels and dance halls, only very modest shops. And sometimes the sailors had a bigger complaint than just boredom: their ship assignment. Although tankers were generally considered good duty, a few sailors were unhappy. One boilermaker wanted to transfer off the *Mississinewa*. One afternoon he created a game-changer to get off the ship. As sailors were bringing stores aboard, he spotted a crate full of fruit juice destined for the officers' wardroom. In full view of Captain Beck and other officers, the rogue boilermaker opened the crate, pulled out his knife, punched a hole in the top of a can and slurped the contents, juice spilling down his beard. He was speedily transferred off the ship, leaving the other boilermaker jealous and angry.

Boredom could make sailors careless. One evening Ray Fulleman was tired as he passed his watch in the fire room. While the crew assembled on the deck for the night's movie, Fulleman got careless as he changed boilers and opened a burner that wasn't hooked up. Oil squirted across the fire room under two hundred pounds of pressure. He secured the oil leak and started another boiler, but he opened it too quickly and the pressure was low. Thick black smoke billowed out of the main stack, enveloping the cargo deck occupied by dozens of moviegoers. The movie screen was completely blacked out and the air stank. The crew was hopping mad, and angry voices yelled at Fulleman through the fire room hatch, "What the hell is going on down there?"

Movies weren't the only entertainment on Manus, and occasionally big-name performers visited the troops: comedians Bob Hope and Jerry Colonna and beautiful Hollywood actress Frances Langford performed at Seeadler Harbor with a USO tour right after the *Mississinewa* arrived. The men in uniform eagerly anticipated the USO shows with gorgeous young starlets, the first women they'd seen in months. The songs and dances and slapstick theater brought a little bit of comfort to the fighting men in the middle of the Pacific War, and if a tropical rain fell during a performance, it never dampened the spirits of the cheering servicemen.

By August's end the fight for control of the western Pacific was ratcheting up. No more movies, no more USO tours. Formosa was calling. Yap and Volcano were calling.

The *Mississinewa*'s crew, still untested under fire, was about to earn its first battle star fueling ships for the attacks on the islands of Bonin, Volcano and Yap. On Friday, September 1, Captain Beck read his orders to fuel Task Unit 30.8.1 and assumed command with the *Miss* as lead oiler. With dozens of other ships, they cleared the harbor and headed for the open sea.

Deckhands watched the Admiralty Islands fall away from sight and disappear in the blue haze of the Pacific. The ship steamed northeasterly at fourteen knots, zigzagging in the number 6 plan that called for all oilers to travel in circular formation. To further protect them from submarine or air attack, they were escorted by a jeep carrier and destroyers.

The task unit arrived at a spot three hundred nautical miles northeast of Manus. It was time for the young deckhands aboard *Mississinewa* to put their training to use: For the first time, they would be fueling U.S. Navy ships not in port but on the open sea.

The first ship to fuel from the *Miss* would be the aircraft carrier *Hornet*, flagship of Vice Admiral John McCain. As commander of Task Group One, McCain was part of four fast-carrier groups to conduct Operation Stalemate II maneuvers. His ship and its destroyer escorts would fuel on September 2 prior to launching air strikes four days later on Palau.

Fueling a ship at sea was a major challenge but a necessary part of winning the Pacific War, as it allowed the fleet to remain for long periods at sea thousands of miles from the West Coast, even from Hawaii. High-speed fueling increased the danger of accident, but the advantage was obvious: The fast pace meant less time and therefore less exposure to enemy submarine attack.

The dynamics of maneuvering a thirty-thousand-ton aircraft carrier and a twenty-four-thousand-ton oiler safely alongside each other—a mere fifty feet apart and steaming ahead at ten knots—are frightening.[2] Oil surges out from the oiler to the carrier through rubber hoses suspended from saddles rigged to booms hanging off the oiler's sides, while seawater cascades down between the two ships in white-water rapids. Heavy seas could cause the bows of both ships to pitch up and down, and millions of gallons of salt water would rush across the oiler's well deck, sweeping aside everything in its path.

September 2 was a typical fueling day during this intense period. The morning started with Captain Beck ordering deckhands to their fueling-at-sea stations at 0512. The sun rose at 0556, and the bridge phone talker relayed orders to the engine room to reduce the shaft speed on both screws to 50 rpms. Speed dropped to ten knots as deckhands waited for the first ship to come alongside for fuel. A heaving line sailed through the morning air at 0710 and landed on the deck of destroyer USS *Bell* on the starboard beam; three minutes later, fuel was flowing through the four-inch hose. The *Bell* was fueled in less than an hour, just in time for *Mississinewa*'s crew to muster on stations at 0800.

During the same time but on the port side of the *Miss*, the carrier *Hornet* approached and received the first line at 0733, as the *Miss* crew winched six-inch hoses suspended from saddles over to the carrier. It took *Hornet*'s crew only thirty minutes to connect all hoses to fuel manifolds, and fuel started flowing shortly after morning muster.

At the same time as the *Hornet* drew its oil and gasoline, other ships took fuel on the starboard side, each one averaging thirty to forty minutes. All in all, it took less than three hours for *Mississinewa* to fuel the carrier while at the same time it topped off three destroyers with fuel and filled the bunkers of two others. The fueling detail finished at 1345. Booms, hoses and lines were stored for tomorrow, another fueling day.

Congress's money had been well spent on fast-fleet oilers. Beginning on September 2, with the Palau operation, and until the end of phase one of the Philippine operation on January 26, 1945, fleet oilers delivered an unprecedented amount of fuel to Third Fleet carrier forces—8.25 million barrels of fuel oil and 14.5 million gallons of aviation gasoline—more than half of that dispensed before the end of October.

When fueling was finished that day, the *Miss* resumed a zigzag plan for the night. Fueling at sea began anew the next day, Sunday, for two more ships. When finished, the sailors on *Mississinewa* had completely fueled Task Force 38 vessels at sea, a job they had trained for since May.

All over the western Pacific, contact with the enemy was escalating, and random encounters with enemy planes and submarines were commonplace. On September 4 an unidentified plane approached the *Miss*, causing the ship to change course abruptly with an emergency turn. There was no radio contact. The plane few off, and the oiler resumed its position in a circular formation with the other oilers and escorts on a zigzag course. No harm was done.

The ships continued to zigzag in three columns to avoid submarine attacks in the early morning hours of September 5. They sighted the Admiralties by the coconut palms ruffling in the wind. As they approached Seeadler Harbor, Captain Beck ordered degaussing coils energized as a submarine preventive measure.

Needing to replenish its own fuel supply, the *Mississinewa* maneuvered alongside civilian merchant tanker SS *Ball's Bluff* and connected the first line at 0909. Two minutes later a jarring blow shook both ships as the upper port side of *Mississinewa's* bridge collided with the forecastle of the tanker. Metal screeched as the two ships scraped past each other in berth 379. Both angry captains demanded to know the reasons the accident had happened, and three *Mississinewa* officers met with SS *Ball's Bluff* officers to determine the damage. Dented and bent stanchions, pipes and deck frames were the only fallout from the minor collision.

After refueling from the merchant ship, *Mississinewa* moved back to its mooring, fully loaded and ready for further assignment. Big military operations were gearing up.

The Admiralties, where they were now anchored, had been secured in August, but a much larger anchorage called Ulithi lay to the north, in the string of atolls called the Western Carolines. Invading and controlling that immense lagoon now became the focus of the Pacific Fleet. The Carolines would be essential to Operation Stalemate—the invasion of Palau—that was ordered by Admiral Chester Nimitz, the fleet's commander in chief.

D-Day was set for September 15, 1944, when General Douglas MacArthur's Southwest Pacific Forces would advance across western New Guinea to invade Morotai Island close to the Philippines, and Nimitz would secure the Western Carolines.

Palau had become the most important second line of defense for the Japanese. Unless the American Navy could secure the island cluster, the Japanese could challenge the pending invasion of the Philippines. And by taking Palau, American forces would gain their own advantage: an established airfield, a bomber base and a large anchorage for supply and cargo vessels.

Back at Seeadler Harbor, even as the *Miss* sailors prepared for an extended sortie at sea, they had a day off. On September 6 most of the off-duty *Miss* sailors boarded launches and whaleboats for what would become a hell-raising beach party.

Pharmacist's mate John Bayak toted a seabag ashore containing baseball bats, gloves and balls.[3] Younger sailors started a ball game while veteran old salts headed for the beer tent, which was full of sailors from several ships. Men from ships of the line, the combat vessels, were limited to two beers each, but teetotaling sailors were allowed to sell their allotment to others. After months aboard ship, thirsty sailors would do just about anything to seek out more than the allotted two beers per man.

The weather was hot and the day turned sour, especially as the beer consumption went up. Sailors from the carrier *Princeton* taunted the

Miss boys: "Hey, you tanker guys, why don't you get into the shooting war?" Insults flew back and forth and someone threw a punch.

All hell broke loose as blows flew between the crews, and in the confusion much of the *Mississinewa* beer stash was liberated by *Princeton*'s enlisted men, but *Miss* sailors retrieved it and got the last word. A few *Mississinewa* sailors had pinched a lot of beer, their rain ponchos covering the cache as they brought it back to the ship. Back on the *Miss*, the bruised and battered oiler sailors lined up on the cargo deck for muster while Captain Beck walked down the ranks inspecting his crew. "I've got sailors lined up at sick bay . . . Couldn't you guys come out of this in better shape? Next time why don't you uphold the name of this ship? Dismissed," he barked.

He headed for the bridge. *Mississinewa* was slated to go back to sea and service the fleet again. No more beach parties were allowed. For the next few days many sailors sported black eyes and cut lips.

A last Mass was held on September 10, three days before sailing on the fueling mission. The aircraft carrier *Wasp* was the venue. The Mass was, for the Catholics at least, a welcome enhancement to the nondenominational services conducted every Sunday by Dr. Bierley.

"Attention all hands." The ship's PA system blatted to life early that Sunday morning, as recalled by a number of *Miss* sailors years later. "Catholics who would like to attend Mass, fall in on the quarterdeck in thirty minutes to catch the whaleboat." The majority of the crew was Catholic, and the men were enthusiastic, having waited a long time for the privilege.

This September day Bill Brzykcy ran forward to find his friend Buddy Akermann in the crew's quarters under the bridge; he urged him to run for the whaleboat. Brzykcy's mother's advice as he left home was simple: "Go to Mass every Sunday and God will look after you." He hoped so.

He'd met Akermann's mother and remembered his promise to look after her boy. Akermann had taken Brzykcy to his home in Scranton several times to sample his mother's home cooking. On their last visit, as the young sailors said good-bye, Mrs. Akermann had unexpectedly clung to her son, begging him not to leave. Buddy reassured her he'd be back "next weekend," but the *Mississinewa* had pulled out for the Pacific before the two sailors could get another weekend pass. Akermann would never come back.

Brzykcy and Akermann climbed aboard. The whaleboat, loaded with penitent sailors, approached the *Wasp*; the boys from the oiler climbed onto the carrier's immense flight deck and looked around in awe. Many had never been aboard a carrier.

After Mass, *Wasp* sailors offered a tour of the carrier for *Miss* sailors, and the group accepted, eager to see a carrier up close. Fireman John Mair looked in disbelief at dozens of Japanese flags painted on the side of the carrier's island and hailed a *Wasp* deckhand: "Did you guys really shoot down all those Jap planes?" He got a huge grin back.[4]

War still seemed far away to the men of the *Mississinewa*, but the serious faces of their officers told them it was coming close. On September 12, sailors noted that the commander of Destroyer Squadron Fifty-One had come aboard to meet with *Mississinewa* officers in the wardroom, and it was soon known around ship that they were planning to place a protective screen of destroyers around the vulnerable oilers during fueling operations. Speculation abounded, but one thing was clear: *Mississinewa* was soon going back to sea.

As part of the battle for Palau and the Philippines, the *Mighty Miss* would be fueling the fleet for the upcoming raids on Formosa in September–October 1944 operations, a major support effort that would earn two more battle stars:

Second Battle Star: September 6–October 14, 1944
    Capture and Occupation of Southern Palau Islands
    September 12, 1944, D-Day minus three (Peleliu Invasion)

Third Battle Star: September 9–September 24, 1944
Air Assaults on the Philippine Islands

September 13. Fire room sailors lit boilers number 2, 3 and 4 at 0406 that Wednesday morning. It was farewell to Seeadler Harbor. The ship weighed anchor at 0646.

Captain Beck stood at the conn on the ship's bridge, accompanied by Exec Lewis and Navigator Rowe. The degaussing system was energized as the oiler navigated the channel to reach open sea. *Mississinewa* led the two columns of oilers out of Seeadler; at a speed of fifteen knots the vessels took a zigzag course to avoid enemy submarines.

The Sea Logistic Services Group to which the *Miss* belonged was part of the Third Fleet, but it was almost a fleet itself, with thirty-four oilers, eleven escort carriers, nineteen destroyers, twenty-six destroyer escorts, ten seagoing tugs and twelve ammunition ships. The profile was high. In fact, so high that Bull Halsey, the feisty admiral in charge of the task force, had remarked, "We've been extremely lucky; our oiler groups for Stalemate were pure submarine bait."[5]

Their luck would run out in a few short weeks.

Mississinewa steamed northwest from Manus on September 14. Operation Stalemate, the invasion of Peleliu, was to proceed as scheduled on September 15. The already long year of 1944 roared onward.

The Japanese fully expected a Philippines invasion. Imperial Japanese Headquarters had correctly estimated that by March 1944 the American's two-pronged advance—the Southwest Forces and the Central Forces—would converge on the Philippines and push north via the Ryukyu Islands. The Japanese planned to conserve their air and naval forces until the actual invasion, then unleash their strength on the Americans in an all-out attack.

As the *Miss* steamed toward Palau in convoy on September 13, Rear Admiral Jesse Oldendorf stood on the bridge of the battleship USS *Pennsylvania*, 7,500 yards west of Peleliu's shoreline. "Commence firing!" The order came precisely at 0530, and Peleliu's beaches and highlands took a furious bombardment from the battleship's long-range guns for the next thirty minutes. The arcs of the shells were clearly visible, landing with a large orange flash as tons of earth and debris cascaded skyward, falling into huge craters. Twenty-four Navy Hellcat fighters and thirty-two Dauntless dive-bombers appeared to strafe and bomb.

During the two-day preinvasion bombardment of Peleliu, Admiral Bull Halsey's Third Fleet Task Force 38 flew more than 2,400 sorties, destroying 250 Japanese planes, wiping out ground installations and sinking a dozen cargo ships and a tanker. Task Force 38 lost eight planes and five pilots.

On September 16, the day after the initial assault on Peleliu, *Mississinewa* and the oiler group met the ships from Task Force 38 returning from the invasion beachhead. The destroyer USS *Marshall* came along the *Miss*'s starboard side to pick up 48 bags of mail; the destroyer *Gatling* followed to take an additional 106 bags. *Mississinewa* received a signal ordering it to the beachhead, where the USS *Franklin* and its destroyers needed the fueling task unit to arrive the next day.

In order to ensure that fueling stations would be manned by first light, Captain Beck ordered the deckhands to sound reveille at 0430 on September 17. Winch operators unsaddled booms in the predawn darkness, and sailors bolted together long sections of hoses. The sun cracked the horizon and fueling operations commenced.

Seamen took positions on the starboard side of the bow, preparing to rig a towline to the first destroyer to come alongside. The deckhands sent a small line over to the receiving ship by tossing a monkey fist at the end of a length of heaving line. Rougher seas or greater distances required a line gun to provide an explosive charge and propel the line over to the waiting destroyer. Today the seas held true.

A towline allowed the two vessels to maintain a precise distance of forty to seventy-five feet from each other while maintaining the recommended speed of ten knots. One vessel did not actually tow the other, the procedure simply helped maintain the distance between ships. Towline procedures were a dangerous task in heavy seas, darkness or during attack. Machinery could malfunction, hoses could separate. Winch heads and hawsers could crush fingers and bones in an instant.

One sailor arrived topside from belowdecks and saw a destroyer sailor sunbathing on top of a gun turret. At that moment the fueling operation from the *Miss* to the destroyer was almost done, when a hose separated from a manifold aboard the destroyer. The hose whipped around uncontrollably, spewing NSFO fuel under high pressure. In seconds a thick spray of black ooze covered the sunbather and everything around him. Destroyer deckhands tried in vain to dodge the black oil that quickly covered their deck and hull. Once the valves were secured by *Mississinewa* deckhands it took a minute or more for the pressure to ease. Oil-soaked destroyer sailors shook their fists in rage at the *Miss* deck crew.

The next day, September 18, *Mississinewa* began fueling the cruiser USS *Indianapolis* with 5,903 barrels of NSFO to use for the ship's power and 1,500 gallons of aviation gasoline for its OS2U Kingfisher scout planes. To replenish its own cargo, *Mississinewa* pulled alongside the USS *Tomahawk*, which emptied its partial tanks into the oiler. The *Miss* resumed course 190 degrees true at a speed of ten knots.

SEPTEMBER 20
Far from Land in the Western Pacific

The USS *Pennsylvania* pulled along the port side of the *Miss* at 0740 in the morning after spending the previous days bombarding the landing beaches of Palau. The towline was secured in four minutes, as the tanker deckhands had become skilled at sending lines over to vessels alongside. Six hours later, the battleship cleared *Mississinewa*'s port side, fully loaded and ready for battle.

That day American forces invaded Ulithi Atoll, a cluster of islands forming part of the Western Caroline Islands. They encountered no opposition and ceased firing after a few unanswered strafing runs. Ulithi would become a forward base, and its anchorage for a time would be the largest in the world. To protect the island from air attacks, the Army set up a searchlight, a radar station and an antiaircraft battery.

The day after Ulithi fell to American hands, the *Miss* was still out at sea, where the two task groups joined up to consolidate cargos. The seas were calm and the day seemed uneventful, as the oiler maneuvered alongside the tanker *Kennebago* and began to take on fuel cargo.

Suddenly, in response to an underwater sound contact, the captain of USS *Nehenta Bay* ordered Emergency Turn Six in hopes of averting a possible enemy submarine. Deckhands aboard the *Miss* scrambled to disconnect hoses, some having to be cut with a fire ax while the GQ klaxon rang insistently. Sailors aboard the *Kennebago*, connected to the *Miss* by a hose to their manifold, neglected to signal the *Miss* deckhands to cut the hose's pressure. As they disconnected it, oil spurted out under one hundred pounds of pressure and sprayed the chief petty officer's quarters on *Kennebago*'s port side with thick black oil. The *Mississinewa* sailors on deck watched helplessly.

Kennebago and *Mississinewa* began to turn away from each other in five-degree steps. A jarring collision sent seamen sprawling to the deck as the starboard quarter of the *Miss* collided with the port quarter of *Kennebago*. Metal ground on metal, but the ships were clear of each other three minutes later.

For the third time in three months a Hull Board was formed to investigate the damage. A trio of *Mississinewa* officers found one plate on the starboard side, at frame 62.5, dented, but all the adjacent hull welds remained watertight. One wooden fender had been crushed and lost over the side.

Mississinewa, sailing in a convoy of two columns surrounded by a destroyer screen, took the lead in the right-hand column. The escort carrier USS *Sargent Bay* followed, while the oilers USS *Marias* and *Manatee* steamed parallel to their sister ship in the left-hand column.

On the morning of September 24 *Mississinewa* and the other oilers formed a fueling line to fuel their escorts before the trip back to Manus. Captain Beck reduced speed to the usual working pace of ten knots. USS *Kadashan Bay* approached the port side of *Mississinewa* at 0704 and received a towline; naval special fuel oil began to flow to the carrier while the destroyer USS *McCord* took a towline on the starboard side and also accepted NSFO.

Camera at the ready, a U.S. Navy photographer stood on the hangar deck of the baby flattop USS *Sargent Bay* to capture the fueling on film. The ships glided through the calm seas with no visible wake. The photographer noted streaks of rust on *Mississinewa*'s steel flanks where salt water and air had bitten into the camouflage paint scheme. He saw clearly the silhouette of the aft port-side K-guns, with depth charges on the oiler's stern.

Click. The camera shutter snapped just moments before the towline was secured at 1405. The photos of the *Miss* steaming along would be the last in memory; the next ones would show the ship in its death throes.

The threat of Japanese submarines was ever present. To confound enemy subs suspected of shadowing the fueling task group, *Mississinewa* executed more than thirty course changes, including three emergency turns in the daylight hours of September 27. The next day the fueling group encountered heavy rain that limited visibility for the lookouts, so numerous course changes were initiated again as a precaution. *Mississinewa* headed for Seeadler Harbor on September 30 and refueled from the civilian tanker USS *Beacham*.

The target date to invade the Philippines was set for October 20, when Admiral Halsey's Third Fleet carriers planned to unleash massive air strikes against Formosa, Okinawa and Northern Luzon. General MacArthur had gathered troops from all over the western Pacific and clustered them at Manus to prepare for the invasion. The Seventh Fleet, known as MacArthur's Navy, had seven hundred ships in the area between New Guinea and Manus; the Third Fleet under Halsey comprised eighteen fleet carriers, six battleships, seventeen cruisers and sixty-four destroyers. It was the most powerful naval force ever assembled, surpassing even the Normandy invasion.

Japanese naval forces marshaled all their resources to defend the islands, although they had been forced by fuel shortages to stay based in the home islands, ready to sail at the first sign of a major American offensive. With their forces greatly weakened, they believed now that all-out defense of the inner empire was their only hope.

Halsey upset their plan when Third Fleet operations started in early October. Halsey intended to launch the powerful carrier air forces against Okinawa on October 10, followed by a strike on Luzon in the Philippines. Right after that he would hit Formosa, a Japanese staging area for reinforcements only two hundred miles north of the Philippines.

USS *Mississinewa* hoisted anchor on October 2, bound for fueling the fleet before the air strikes planned for Okinawa. Accompanied by sister ships *Marias* and *Manatee*, the *Miss* and its defensive convoy zigzagged northwest at fifteen knots. The Pacific Fleet encountered terrible typhoons, one striking Ulithi the day after the ships departed. Tremendous swells and high winds swept across the Pacific, and weather steadily worsened as the convoy headed northwest to reach the warships of Task Force 38. Many *Mississinewa* sailors never before seasick hung over the rail in misery. The tanker, fully loaded, plowed through mountainous waves, dropping violently into the troughs.

Deckhands were knocked around and bruised as footing became treacherous. Swells crashed over the well deck and cascaded off the port and starboard sides. John Mair, climbing topside in the storm, held on to the hatch and watched the well deck disappear under tons of seawater and emerge seconds later as the ship pitched and heaved. "There's more Pacific Ocean going over the well deck than there is under the keel," he said to himself.

Most of the crew succumbed to seasickness. One seaman who fared better than the others stood outside the mess hall as the ship plunged into another swell. A wobbly sailor approached, his face white as a sheet, saying, "What's for chow?"

"Fried pork chops, dripping with lots of grease."

"You son of a bitch." The other man gagged and leaned over the rail.

Despite the nasty weather, the *Miss* met up with Task Force 38 at the appointed latitude and longitude on an otherwise trackless ocean, where nine oilers began fueling in heavy seas. On the morning of October 8 the destroyer USS *Miller* was the first vessel to fuel from the *Miss*, starting at 0642. At 0702 another towline shot over to the fleet carrier USS *Hancock*. Engineering sailors on the port capstan struggled to keep the towline in place as *Mississinewa's* bow pitched and rolled in heavy seas. Deckhands slipped and fell repeatedly as seawater washed over the deck.

The work continued all day in bad weather. Captain Beck summed it up in his October 8 War Diary, noting that the seas were very rough and fueling exercises difficult.

> This was the crew's first heavy weather fueling at sea and everyone behaved splendidly . . . On the well decks, the men were handling gear in seas that buried them and it was with great satisfaction that I saw them hang on like old timers!

That night the waves were violent, but there was one more ship to fuel: Admiral Halsey's Third Fleet flagship *New Jersey*. Beck darkened the ship at sunset. Halsey's battleship came along the starboard side soon afterward to take a towline and start fueling. The seas were running rough and cascading over the well deck. *Mississinewa* sailors had yet to fuel a ship after sundown and never in heavy seas. At that moment the light carrier *Cabot* was still fueling on the port side, creating the threat of trapping the *Mississinewa* between the carrier and Halsey's huge *Iowa*-class battleship. Fueling was dangerous in the best of seas but nearly suicidal with capital ships flanking the oiler in foul weather and in full darkness. The fueling of the *New Jersey* began, but the towline parted several times as the ships thrashed and pulled against each other.

Captain Beck was unnerved at the nearness of the carrier, as the two ships lurched and tossed in the water, perilously close to each other. At one enormous rogue wave he yelled, his face nearly purple with rage, casting choice words at Halsey for endangering the oiler. "Tell that son of a bitch to get away . . . he's getting my ship all wet." Beck fumed to the ensign at his elbow on the bridge.[6]

Every time the *New Jersey* came down, water splashed over the young men who stood at the winch head at the bow, where the towline was rigged to the carrier. Lieutenant Rowe, ever worried about the young sailors, saw the danger and was concerned that someone would lose a hand or an arm, so he went out in the pouring rain to keep an eye on the deckhands. The other officers were shocked to see him leave the bridge and join the sailors in peril. Just then *New Jersey*'s bow came crashing down hard again in the heavy seas, drenching the men and sending a torrent of water over the well deck. Beck, enraged, ordered the fueling halted. By radio, Admiral Halsey agreed to stop. Even an admiral had to yield to weather conditions.

For the *Miss* sailors, it was a baptism in seawater, a precursor to the baptism in oil and fire that awaited them a month down the line.

CHAPTER 9

Kamikaze War

*You don't know the moment of your death . . . I can't imagine
a crueler weapon.*

—Naoji Kozu, *kaiten* pilot[1]

Shigeyoshi Miwa, commander of Sixth Fleet submarines, called a high-level meeting of officers at the end of July. With aircraft and pilots, carriers and other war materiel at a critically low level, the Japanese commanders were pressed to assess their strategy. Miwa, newly appointed as vice admiral, intended to evaluate the Sixth Fleet submarine actions of the last twelve weeks, when the Naval General Staff had begun to activate Operation Sho-go.

The submarine captains of the IJN fleet attended the meeting, grateful that they had survived the most recent battles and could appear at all. They had been savagely battered by American antisubmarine forces and considered themselves lucky to return alive to offer their reports.

Lieutenant Hisashi Watanabe, captain of submarine *RO-115*, criticized the submarine school, saying they were not offering any innovative weapons or tactics. He was opposed by Rear Admiral Keizo Yoshimura, chief of staff of Admiral Ozawa, who made a caustic reply to the criticism. "In the Marianas battle, the American submarines performed brilliantly. But where were Japan's submarines?" he asked tauntingly. "What were they doing to help us?"

Watanabe was furious. He and his comrades had fought bravely. He stood his ground with his superior officer, saying, "You know very well, Admiral, that Admiral Toyoda ordered us [submariners] to stay out of waters . . . expected to be the battlefield. Therefore you must know very well why we could not meet and strike the enemy."[2]

Watanabe's anger grew. His next comments to the admiral stunned everyone in the room. "Before criticizing us submariners for supposedly having failed you," he said, "you must first reflect on the defeat of your own air and surface forces, and on how well American submarines were able to perform against you. If our submarines are to enjoy any degree of success in the future, you will have to stop underestimating the ability of men the enemy sends against our submarines. It is excellent! You think of nothing but the clash between two great surface fleets. You completely ignored us and the men who fought against us."

The room full of officers, normally silent and respectful, erupted in chaos. Watanabe, angry, bitter, frustrated, had made his point.

Elsewhere that week, other submariners were getting grim reports from their superiors. Northeast of Tokyo, at Tsuchiura Naval Training Base, Captain Kenjiro Watanabe, the base commander, stood before his assembled cadets on August 25 to discuss the deteriorating conditions of the war. He reported that Sixth Fleet submarines were increasingly disadvantaged in fighting the enemy.

"It grieves me very much to tell you this," he told his men, "but the news from our Navy comrades on the front lines is not good. The difference between our power and the enemy's grows ever greater. In spite of the gallant fight our countrymen make, Saipan is in enemy hands and we are having great trouble supplying our forces."

Watanabe dropped a bombshell. Japanese technicians had developed a weapon of overwhelming strength, he said, and there was now a call for volunteers to man it. He warned the student pilots beforehand that it was a no-return weapon, and at his words a gasp went up from the ranks. It was the first time the secret suicide weapon was more or less publicly mentioned, and it was the first acknowledgment of a special attack (*tokkō*) weapon that had actually been designed for suicide.

Watanabe gave his listeners no details on the secret weapon, but they grasped the implication. It was clear that Japan's fight for survival was becoming increasingly hopeless. Any chance of victory would require ever greater sacrifice from its fighting men.

It was true that victory was slipping. Japan's 1942 "victory disease" had been forcibly replaced with feelings of doom and desperation, as by late summer of 1944 the momentum of the war was turning harshly against the Axis forces. In Europe the Allies had fought their way through France and were slowly approaching Luxembourg and the German border, as Germans were methodically purged from northern France. In mid-August the invasion of southern France had been successful, and the Mediterranean Sea was slowly yielding to Allied control; the British Fleet and three squadrons of American PT boats increasingly disrupted the German and Italian supply convoys. In rapid succession German radio stopped broadcasting in Paris and the Vichy government fled to Germany.

In the Pacific War, the picture for the Axis was even grimmer. Japanese-held islands had begun to fall rapidly. Guam was now occupied by Allied forces after being pounded by American planes and warships for a month and finally invaded on July 21, the same day the French First Army surrounded Toulon, France. The Marianas had been taken by the Allies. The Japanese Tojo-led government in Tokyo fell, and the old prime minister was replaced with a hard-line nationalist backed by the Imperial Army.

Commander Kenjiro Watanabe inspired a number of young recruits from Tsuchiura to join the ranks of *kaiten* pilots. For the time being they would join the first group already under way in training at Ozushima.

At Ozushima the training was intense for the *kaiten* pilots, but it was equally serious business among the fleet submariners, those who operated the mother subs that would carry the *kaiten* to their launch sites. Their role was essential to the success of the *kaiten*, and the risks were high.

One submariner who would play a key role in the planned *kaiten* attacks was Captain Zenji Orita, the man who skippered a Sixth Fleet mother submarine, the *I-47*. As planning moved forward, Orita learned he would be carrying four *kaiten* to an as-yet-unannounced destination, and one of his *kaiten* pilots would be Sekio Nishina. Orita had graduated in the Fifty-Ninth Class at Etajima, the Naval Academy. When Nishina met him at Kure, he had already built a reputation as a seasoned veteran in the Pacific and a man with impressive foresight: When the Philippines fighting had started up two years earlier, Orita was already training his crew in the Inland Sea.

As a distinguished submariner, Orita was in good company—one of his classmates was Lieutenant Commander Mochitsura Hashimoto, who would become famous in 1945 as the submarine commander who sank the cruiser USS *Indianapolis*. Both Orita and Hashimoto commanded 2,500-ton I-class fleet submarines belonging to the Fifteenth Unit.

Orita had first taken command of the fleet submarine *I-177* on August 30, 1943; at that time he was tasked with transporting soldiers and supplies to forward areas in the southern Pacific, where the fighting was then concentrated. Considered very aggressive even among the forceful Sixth Fleet submarine skippers, his intense attitude bothered many young officers. Some avoided him, a few sought to censure him, while others praised his skill and dedication. None were indifferent to the man.

A rigorous trainer, he drilled his men to perfection. Often when his sailors were standing watch on the bridge, he ordered a crash dive, which meant they must evacuate the bridge and enter the submarine in the shortest possible time. Precious seconds could mean the difference between life and death if an I-class boat was caught on the surface by a patrolling American plane. *I-47* watch sailors drilled incessantly, until they had reduced the time to a mere seven seconds from the order "Crash dive!" to the closing of the hatch—a record in the IJN submarine service.

Other crews competing for the record were very good, very capable, but they fell behind Orita's record. Minoru Yamada, the navigator of *I-53*, admitted that Orita's record beat his own crew by a full second; he admitted his team had never cleared the bridge for a dive faster than eight seconds, even with constant drills. The crew aboard *I-53* learned about the seven-second record set by *I-47* and trained until they finally reached that mark. No other submarine crew of the Sixth Fleet ever attained this feat.[3]

One September day Orita, who now captained fleet submarine *I-47*, received a message while he was performing checks on his sub at Yokosuka Naval Yard. He was summoned to Kure Naval Base and ordered to attend a conference on board the merchant cargo ship *Tsukushi Maru*. There he was joined by Captain Kiyotake Ageta, who commanded the Fifteenth Submarine Division. Also present were Orita's counterparts, the commanders of submarines *I-36* and *I-37*, Iwao Teramoto and Nobuo Kamimoto.

Two members of Admiral Miwa's staff, Commander Shojiro Iura and Lieutenant Commander Kennosuke Torisu, a key naval strategist, joined the officers. Iura began with a full briefing on the fighting in the Philippines going on at that time. The news was bad. All three submarine captains readily agreed. The outlook for a change in fortune was not promising.

It was then Iura made a dramatic announcement. "In order to turn the tide of war in our favor, the Combined Fleet and the Sixth Fleet have decided to load special weapons, called *maru roku kanamono*, on board large-size submarines and attack advance enemy anchorages with them." He watched the faces of the submarine captains. They looked puzzled.

"The plan is already under way," he continued, "and the first attack will be made about the middle of November, using *I-36*, *I-37* and *I-47*. Without waiting for formal orders you are to go ahead and make preparations."

Maru roku kanamono. The words meant simply "circle-six metal fitting." But what could that really mean? When Kamimoto and Orita asked for an explanation, they were told by Torisu, the other staff officer, that it was simply a cover name devised for secrecy. It really stood for a manned torpedo. The Model 93 Long Lance had been converted for steerage by a man, Torisu explained.

"The pilot will be the torpedo's eyes and steer it directly into a target," he said, noting the chagrin of the submarine pilots. "Once it is released from a submarine, there is no way to recover it, or its pilot. It is a *tokkō* [special attack] weapon designed especially for water use."

Kamimoto asked if pilots existed to man the weapons. He was told they were already in training at Ozushima on Tokuyama Bay. "Experimental attacks have been made," Torisu said, "using *I-36*. Results have been very favorable so far."

Orita wanted to know if the weapons were ready.

"Kure Naval Arsenal is producing them right now," Torisu said. Within the hour Orita was shown the Type I *kaiten*; he learned the rudiments of its structure and capability, and the role Nishina and Kuroki had played in its development.

Shortly afterward Orita walked alone with Kamimoto. He seemed stunned, Kamimoto said later. "Things must be really bad if we have to resort to this," Orita said to his colleague in a soft voice.

Kamimoto agreed, adding, "The pilots will certainly have to have the *tokkō* spirit. But so will we submarine crewmen, if we're going to help them do their jobs." Kamimoto, sympathetic to the *kaiten* pilots he would carry, could not know that he himself would not return from the first mission.

For Orita and Kamimoto on that solemn day of bizarre news, there was nothing to do but move forward. Circle-six metal fitting was the talk among submariners at the training bases, but nowhere else was it mentioned, except in private conversations among a very tiny group of high commanders. It could not be discussed even with the families of the young trainees when they went home on leave. No one could know of the heaven shaker, if it was really going to "turn the world" and save Japan.

The few high-level officers who even knew of the top-secret *tokkō* weapon had misgivings. Despite his brave words to Orita and Kamimoto, Commander Torisu had to stifle his own feelings about the desperate measures his navy was now setting in motion.

The number of parent submarines designed to carry *kaiten* increased as 1944 roared on. Despite the losses in Japanese materiel in other aspects of the war, resources were thrown into creating suicide weapons and the naval craft to transport and support them.

Between autumn 1944 and late spring 1945, fifteen fleet submarines and eight transport submarines were refitted to carry *kaiten* torpedo subs. The parent craft were stripped of their main gun armament and sometimes their aircraft hangars and catapults; chocks were built onto the decks to carry two to six *kaiten*. Among the fleet submarines so designed were *I-36, I-37* and *I-47* that would take part in the *Kikusui* Mission in November. Transport submarines that were equipped to handle *kaiten* included *I-361, I-363, I-366, I-367, I-368 and I-370*.

Surface ships were also refitted to carry and launch the suicide torpedoes, among them two *Minekaze*-class destroyers, *Namikaze* and *Shiokaze*; five *Matsu*-class destroyers and the light cruiser *Kitakami*. During the same time, twenty-one Type I fast-transport/landing ships were completed with stern ramps and launch rails for *kaiten*. In addition, engineers proposed several types of steel-hulled and wooden-hulled light escorts for construction in 1945, but only two had been completed by war's end.

Typical of the effort to reconfigure ships in support of the *kaiten* effort, *Kitakami* commenced repairs and modifications on August 14, 1944, at Sasebo; the end result would be a cruiser with the capacity to carry eight *kaiten*.[4] A twenty-ton crane, formerly from the seaplane carrier *Chitose*, was fitted to raise and lower the *kaiten* into the water. The stern was remodeled into an overhanging ramp configuration. The aft turbines were removed to make space for spare parts and tools, although the turbine removal reduced *Kitakami*'s top speed from thirty-six to twenty-three knots. All armaments were removed and replaced by antiaircraft guns and radars. The deck was refitted to contain two depth-charge launching rails at the stern; two depth-charge throwers were also installed. The refit would take five months to complete, so it was not until January 1945 that *Kitakami* was assigned to the Combined Fleet. The ship saw no battle duty; it was scrapped after the war. As with many of the new weapons and changing tactics and strategies, Japan's efforts to "shake the heavens" came very late in the war.

Although captains and crew members on board Japanese I-class submarines hoped to survive the battles, they shared many of the same dangers as the *kaiten* pilots. In order to deploy the *kaiten*, the mother submarines needed to maneuver close to anchorages and risk detection by U.S. forces. Danger could be even worse in the open sea, as the *kaiten* had to be launched close enough to American ships to allow the pilot to close the range to his target. If the large fleet submarines were spotted by planes or by a ship's watch, they would be pursued mercilessly with depth charges.

The enormous responsibility of transporting men to a death mission weighed heavily on the captains and crews of the mother subs; many of them reported heartbreaking scenes as they bid farewell to the *kaiten* pilots. The demeanor of the pilots and especially their last moments before launch left a lasting impression on Japanese submariners who manned the fleet boats. Years later their memories still haunted them.

Submariner Minoru Yamada vividly recalled the attitude of the pilots and how it affected him.

"We [the mother sub crews] were the same soldiers," he said, "but their attitude—spending days calmly until their *kaiten* were launched—made me feel strongly that their state of mind was nothing but those of persons of religion who had already risen above matters of life and death." He mentioned one man in particular, but added, "the same was true of the other *kaiten* pilots."[5]

The Empire of Japan was in peril. As air and sea losses mounted, top commanders believed the dismal situation called for extraordinary measures—perhaps with the blessing of divine forces. Suicide had become a modern weapon of war. It was showing many faces, and one of them was suicide from the air.

The spirits or gods of the wind had saved Japan many centuries ago by the almost miraculous appearance of typhoons. The country had been weakened by years of dissension and internal war, and in its weakened state was highly vulnerable to a takeover by hostile forces. When the great Mongol emperor Kublai Khan tried to invade Japan in 1274 and again in 1281, massive Pacific typhoons blew over the seas and devastated the Mongol fleet. Japan had been spared from invasion. The storms were hailed as an intervention by Ise, the wind god, and the sudden deflection of enemy forces led the Japanese to believe they were divinely protected, shielded by what they called "the Divine Wind." The Japanese word was *kamikaze*.[6]

Almost seven hundred years later, in 1944, Air Fleet commanders considered suicide from the air a modern way to repel the enemy—a new "Divine Wind." On October 19 Vice Admiral Takijiro Onishi was named commander of the First Air Fleet, effectively giving him leadership over all naval air forces in the Philippines. He gathered his senior officers that day to propose a radical solution to the plight of the Japanese forces facing a superior enemy. As in the days of the Mongol invasion, he told them, it would be called *kamikaze*.

"We must organize suicide attack units composed of Zero fighters armed with bombs," he said. "Each plane [will] crash-dive into an enemy carrier."

It was not the first time aviation suicide had been considered. Pilots on both sides had sometimes crashed their planes into enemy ships when damage to their plane or grievous injuries made it clear that they would not survive a mission. Japanese flyers had, in moments of patriotic emotion, willingly sacrificed their lives to harm the enemy. But Onishi's suggestion was the first time a commander openly advocated suicide tactics as a weapon against the enemy.

As the special attack force was becoming a reality for the Air Fleet, their counterparts in the Navy, the Japanese submariners, applauded the *kaiten* as a potential heaven shaker, an underwater echo of the *kamikaze* air attacks to come.

CHAPTER 10

Killer Steam, Killer Planes

Heroism is latent in every human soul. However humble or unknown, they [the veterans] have renounced what are accounted pleasures and cheerfully undertaken all the self-denials—privations, toils, dangers, sufferings, sicknesses, mutilations, life-long hurts and losses, death itself—for some great good, dimly seen but dearly held.

—Joshua Chamberlain (1828–1914),
Civil War hero, awarded the Medal of Honor
for bravery at Gettysburg[1]

As young men of the Imperial Japanese Navy sought to throw deadly weapons at their enemy, those American men in their sights were fighting their way across the vast expanse of the Pacific Ocean, taking island after island, in an increasingly lopsided series of battles that favored the Allies, bolstered as they were by the industrial might of the United States.

On a day that marked tremendous victories for Allied forces in the Pacific, a horrible shipboard tragedy ended with an American sailor buried at sea. The calendar said October 10. As Formosa and Okinawa were under Allied air attack, hundreds of miles to the east *Mississinewa* sailors witnessed their saddest day yet.

Agonizing screams pierced the air that morning right after reveille, screams that burst out from the chain locker of the *Mighty Miss*. Seamen Patrick Curran and Herb Daitch rushed to the compartment and saw a shocking sight. Ed Darcy, a fellow seaman, lay slumped on the deck, scalded, the skin peeling from his body. Daitch grabbed Darcy by the arm but let go when scalded flesh sloughed off in his hands.[2]

On a working oiler, danger could come from the most unexpected quarters, and every sailor knew it. In this case the culprit was super-heated steam, packing four hundred pounds of pressure in temperatures over seven hundred degrees Fahrenheit. It could be a killer, and on this day it was. Superheated steam was invisible to the naked eye, but a small leak could cause serious injury. A pinhole leak rarely offered a sound—not even a hiss—to warn a potential victim. It was all too evident that superheated steam had escaped from the steam line and literally cooked Darcy. He hadn't seen the ghostly wisps of death, never knew the danger until it was way too late.

The elbow joint in the steam line that scorched Darcy had burned Herb Daitch a few weeks before from a miniscule leak. Daitch had reported the minor injury to an officer. Evidently this morning the superheated steam hit the water condensate in the line with thousands of pounds of force and blew out the faulty elbow.

Darcy had entered the chain locker, his general quarters station, and dogged down the hatch behind him, a procedure he'd repeated every morning for five months. Then the line blew. From the myriad cuts and bruises covering his body, it appeared the stricken sailor had fallen to the deck, desperately trying to open the dogged hatch, but his burned hands were unable to grip or twist the hatch wheel. In moments the killer steam cooked him alive.

Panicked sailors summoned a stretcher, and Darcy was rushed to sick bay, where Dr. Bierley administered morphine and placed an oxygen mask over his face. The doctor inserted an intravenous needle to pump fluids into the terribly burned man and sprayed him with burn ointment. As pharmacist's mate John Bayak wrapped him in sterile gauze, he noted burns over Darcy's entire body except for a tiny patch on his abdomen that had been protected by his belt buckle.

Delirious with pain, Darcy said over and over, "Look what they've done to me." Bierley placed a stethoscope on his chest and listened to the breath gurgling in his lungs; he glanced at Bayak and shook his head, making no comment. The burns were fatal. Darcy wouldn't live long.

Though the smell of charred flesh sickened the pharmacist's mate, Bayak made Darcy as comfortable as possible. Late in the morning Bierley, on death watch, phoned the galley requesting a bite to eat. Cook John D'Anna, shocked to hear about the tragedy, recalled how he'd served Darcy at breakfast and exchanged friendly banter only a few hours earlier as he heaped eggs on the deckhand's plate. It was unimaginable that the young man lay dying.

As the morning wore on, life seeped out of Darcy's scalded body. At the dying man's request, Bierley summoned an ensign to sick bay to baptize him; Darcy clutched a rosary in his bandaged hands during the religious rite. He drew his last breath at 1110, five hours after the accident. Bierley called the bridge and notified Captain Beck, who signaled the commander of Task Unit 30.8 for permission to bury Darcy at sea. Permission was granted.

All hands not on watch were ordered to witness the burial. Bierley ordered a canvas bag stitched for the rite; in order to make certain the bag sank, the gunnery department delivered two 5-inch/38 shells to sick bay, where the heavy brass casings were stitched into the bottom of the bag. As all hands assembled on deck, *Mississinewa* ceased zigzagging with the rest of the task unit ships and sailed free on the tossing seas.

Darcy's body lay on a board, the end with his feet resting on the starboard rail, the other end supported by a sailor. Two others held the corner of an American flag draped over the body. Herb Daitch, one of the honor guard, touched his shipmate's body in a final farewell.

Captain Beck conducted the burial as prescribed by Navy regulations, first reciting prayers. After the ten-minute ceremony ended, he nodded to the honor guard. The board was slowly lifted, and Darcy was committed to the sea, his body sliding out from underneath the American flag. The sound of taps drifted mournfully across the deck. It was the worst day so far for *Mississinewa* sailors, who watched grim-faced as the bag containing Darcy's remains slipped beneath the waves.

Later that afternoon *Mississinewa* sailed north for a rendezvous with Admiral Gerald Bogan's task group, whose aircraft carriers had launched 1,396 sorties that day against the Ryukyu Islands, including Okinawa. The Ryukyus hosted formidable Japanese bases with hundreds of land-based aircraft and harbors glutted with ships, a target-rich environment for U.S. Navy carrier pilots. In the attack, the Japanese lost 12 torpedo boats, a submarine tender, 2 midget submarines, 4 cargo ships, several auxiliary sampans and 111 enemy planes. Task Force 38 lost 21 aircraft, 5 pilots and 4 enlisted aircrew. For the first time since the 1942 Doolittle raid the U.S. naval forces had come close to the Japanese homeland.

That morning Admiral Toyoda, the commander in charge of Japan's Combined Fleet, received news of the Okinawa strikes at his Formosa headquarters. The air bases had been alerted to make defense plans. Formosa, now supported with 230 operational fighter planes, was ready to defend itself against the American aviators.

The following day the American oilers, including the *Miss*, rendezvoused with Bogan's task group, and nine thirsty ships formed a fueling line: USS *Iowa, Intrepid, Independence, Miami, San Diego, Halsey Powell, Colahan, Stockham* and *Twining*. When the job was finally finished, Task Force 38, newly fueled and reinforced with planes, pilots and crewmen, steamed northwest at twenty-four knots. Admirals Halsey and Mitscher wanted to deliver a knockout blow to Formosa the next morning. *Mississinewa* left the area to rendezvous at another location with five other oilers.

By providing fuel for the attacking warships, the *Miss* had further distinguished herself and earned the fourth Battle Star:

October 10, 1944 (Third Fleet Supporting Operations, Okinawa Air
   Attacks)

October 11, 1944–October 14, 1944 (Northern Luzon/Formosa Air
   Attacks)

Early on October 12 Task Force 38 arrived at the designated spot for launching planes fifty miles off Formosa. The first strike began a three-day effort to pulverize the remaining Japanese air strength on Formosa and prevent the enemy from launching attacks during the upcoming American landing at Leyte planned for October 20. American pilots flew 1,378 sorties from the four task group carriers.

The Japanese Sixth Base Air Force covered Southern Kyushu, the Ryukyus and Formosa. As of October 10, the base commanded by Vice Admiral Fukudome held 737 planes, among them 223 fighter aircraft. In response to the American threat, nearly 700 more planes were flown to Formosa in the next four days, including 172 from Imperial Japanese Navy carriers. Captain Shuzo Kuno commanded the T Attack Force, the "T" meaning typhoon. Although the group was considered elite, half were army pilots with only two to four months of training; even so, they still managed to inflict damage on the Americans.

From his Formosa command post, Admiral Fukudome watched as the aerial battle developed over his head. Planes began to drop from the sky. Assuming the casualties were American, Fukudome clapped his hands and shouted, "Well done. Tremendous success."

But a second look revealed the falling planes were Japanese defenders. Fukudome stopped clapping. In the end, American planes leveled his headquarters and inflicted tremendous damage on Japanese ground installations. When the final tally was counted, Fukudome said bitterly, "Our fighters were nothing but so many eggs thrown at the stone wall of the indomitable enemy."

On the first day of fighting Japan lost a third of its air strength, including many veteran flight leaders. Against the second wave of attacks, only sixty fighter planes were left to defend. No planes at all rose to challenge the third wave. Fukudome lost another forty-two planes from his elite typhoon force of experienced pilots.

American losses were also heavy, and forty-eight planes failed to return, but no American carriers were damaged.

The air attacks by the Third Fleet on Formosa had piled yet more destruction on the already-dwindling Japanese forces, and the losses were nothing short of catastrophic. In the heaviest attacks, on October 10, 12 and 14, the Empire of Japan lost at least five hundred planes; some historians put it closer to six hundred.

Japanese air forces were now beyond recovery. They could no longer mount a serious challenge to American aviators, who were even now receiving fresh replacement pilots with more than three hundred hours of training time.

And yet, after the air attacks, Formosa Radio Tokyo announced a bold victory, citing an official Imperial Japanese Navy report issued on October 16 that indicated devastating U.S. Navy losses. The report claimed Japanese forces had destroyed eleven enemy carriers, two battleships, three cruisers and one destroyer or light cruiser, and it claimed other casualties—namely, damage to eight carriers, two battleships, four cruisers, one destroyer, and thirteen unidentified ships, and a dozen ships burned. Japan, believing a few exuberant pilots, was swept by a sudden wave of exhilaration and celebrated victory.

The Imperial Japanese Navy had taken their pilots' reports of sinking U.S. Third Fleet ships at face value. The pilots were gravely mistaken. When Admiral Halsey heard of the Radio Tokyo broadcast, he responded by sending a witty message to Admiral Nimitz in Hawaii:

All Third Fleet ships recently reported sunk by Radio Tokyo have been salvaged and are retiring at high speed toward the Japanese Fleet.

The message, released to the American press, further enhanced Bull Halsey's fighting image. The Allies were tasting victory, and they relished the fight.

Mississinewa reached latitude 18° 00' N and latitude 129° 00' E on October 18, and Beck got word that his task group was to fuel the ships of Admiral Sherman's fast carrier task group. The Philippines invasion, beginning with beach landings on Leyte, was two days away. Twelve oilers formed a line and the waiting ships approached. The fueling exercises began at 0711; the *Miss* would be filling the *Lexington*, the *Dortch* and the *Bronson*.

With a wary eye, fireman Bill Brzykcy watched the enormous *Essex*-class carrier *Lexington* approach *Mississinewa*'s port side for fueling. Carriers coming in so tight always made him nervous. This one's flight deck hovered over the oiler so close the Iowa fireman thought he could reach out and touch the carrier's gun tubs. Despite the carrier's enormous size and close proximity, all went well; the *Lex* took on 5,735 barrels of NSFO along with 14,000 gallons of AV gas and moved away.

Next the cruiser *Santa Fe* pulled along the *Miss*'s port side and began the difficult task of transferring survivors it was carrying from the crippled ship *Houston* that had been torpedoed at Formosa. In all, *Mississinewa* took on 196 survivors. The oiler suddenly was crowded, with 450 men now sharing meals, deck space and latrines aboard a 553-foot ship meant to accommodate only 275 men under the best of wartime situations. *Houston* sailors were everywhere on deck and waiting for meals, but *Mississinewa* sailors had to be served first so as not to compromise watches and shipboard routine.

Pharmacist's mates Kelly McCracken and Art Young sat in sick bay at the bedside of injured *Houston* sailor Robert Ulbrich, who had taken a turn for the worse. He begged McCracken not to leave him, and the vigil continued through the night. It ended when Ulbrich died at 0530 in the morning.[3] Dr. Bierley notified Captain Beck and medical staff prepared the body for burial at sea. Permission was granted.

Once again the crew of *Mississinewa* gathered on the cargo deck for a burial at sea, the second they had witnessed in nine days. Beck conducted the now-familiar Navy regulation burial, and radioman Robert Ulbrich was committed to the deep.

The Japanese government had not yet activated the special attack force known as the *kamikaze*, but as the magnitude of Japanese losses at Formosa and the Philippines became known, they would launch a wave of suicide pilots of both planes and submarines. Allied forces would soon experience the terrifying effects of this new threat.

October 20 was D-Day for the Philippine invasion. Leyte Gulf was the site of one of the world's biggest battles, and the skies were about to break out in terror. The initial landing was easier than most other amphibious operations up to this point in the Pacific: perfect weather, no surf, no mines and little Japanese response, but the full-scale Battle of Leyte Gulf that followed on October 23–25 was bloody.

While Leyte was being played out, the *Mississinewa* arrived at the new forward base: Ulithi Atoll. Located in the Western Caroline Islands, the massive lagoon was the perfect staging area from which to attack Japan and end the war, as U.S. naval commanders were hoping to strike a conclusive blow.

Ideally located, Ulithi was 360 miles from Peleliu to the southwest and an equal distance from Guam to the northwest. The distance to Manus in the Admiralty Islands was 830 miles, and Leyte was 900 miles away. A 1,200-mile radius from Ulithi cuts through Okinawa and Lingayen Gulf, and passes close to Formosa. Pearl Harbor lay 3,660 miles to the northeast. Situated in such an advantageous location, Ulithi was to become the largest port in the world, holding up to seven hundred ships. The lagoon is currently the fourth largest in the world, measuring almost twenty miles long by ten miles wide.

Miss sailors had greatly anticipated their arrival at Ulithi on October 21, as they would be getting mail and a break from the ship. Nothing prepared them for the atoll's beauty. Created by an ancient volcano that had sunk into the sea, the edging coral reef was all that was visible of the volcano, and it ringed the lagoon like a necklace of pearls, each one an island of coral and palm trees. Only four were normally inhabited, but the Navy had relocated the islanders to a slightly more distant location during the war.

The newly built recreation area on one of the small islands, Mog Mog, would allow the ships' crews to play baseball and football and walk the beaches when they weren't on duty.[4] But the respite was brief and the anxiety never went away these days. The men learned the recent news of Leyte, and it created new fears. They heard that the Allies had dealt unimaginable blows to the already-dwindling Japanese aircraft and pilots, knocking out hundreds of planes, but the three-day battle brought a new horror: the attacks on American ships by *kamikaze* planes.

On October 25, aboard the USS *Santee*, a CVE or "baby flattop," gunner's mate John Mitchell, a gun captain aboard the *Santee*, heard an officer shouting a warning just as a Japanese plane dived ferociously down toward his ship. Mitchell directed the pointer to bring the 40mm gun to bear on the attacker. The pilot kept flying toward them. All hands stared at the oncoming plane in disbelief—for some reason the plane wasn't pulling out of its dive. There was no good reason: The pilot couldn't be dead or wounded, because no antiaircraft guns had yet fired.

Sensing disaster, Mitchell screamed, "Pull out, you bastard, pull out!" but the plane flew straight into the flight deck. Debris blasted upward as it penetrated the hangar deck, causing bombs to explode and spraying shrapnel everywhere.[5] *Santee* had just experienced the first planned *kamikaze* attack of the war.

The Way of the Warrior—*Bushidō*—had created a wave of young recruits willing and eager to pilot the planes and fly into their own deaths. Dozens of suicidal crashes happened at Leyte as planes hurtled from the skies to explode on the decks of U.S. warships.

Across the Pacific, U.S. naval commanders took notice, concerned about the deadly turn the war was taking with the killer pilots attacking from the skies. They had no way of knowing that the same suicide mentality would come to them by sea.

CHAPTER 11

Blossoms on the Water

He wondered what the man's name was and where he came from; and if he was really evil at heart, or what lies or threats had led him on the long march from his home; and if he would not really rather have stayed there in peace.

—J.R.R. Tolkien, *The Two Towers*

The news of Ulithi Atoll's fall to the Allies in September was the trigger for a suicide submarine attack that came to be called the *Kikusui* Mission. The loss of Ulithi, such a large and critical anchorage in the Western Caroline Islands, prompted Japanese naval commanders to launch a strike against the target-rich enemy fleet that now anchored in the lagoon preparing for final invasion against the Philippines and the Japanese homeland.

It would be the first *kaiten* attack. Strategy and planning for the *Kikusui* Mission intensified through October, as Allied forces pummeled Japan's air and sea forces. As the casualties grew with every battle lost, so did the Japanese sense of urgency. Air attacks on Formosa and Okinawa had cost them hundreds of aircraft. In late October the struggle for Leyte Gulf in the Philippines took out more than forty warships; when that fight ended and the waters of Leyte Gulf calmed, the Imperial Japanese Navy had ceased to be a fighting force. From then on, hopes were pinned on *tokkō*—suicide weapons and tactics.

Twelve *kaiten* pilots were selected for the Ulithi strike. Eleven were new trainees who had drilled for more than two months on the suicide craft; the twelfth was Sekio Nishina, now holding the rank of sublieutenant at the age of twenty-one, who had already been a dedicated Navy man for five years. As one of the two creators of the suicide torpedo and the program's leader, he was an inspiration to the other *kaiten* pilots, most of them even younger than he was.

The target for the first *kaiten* mission was Ulithi Atoll, which had just become the major advance anchorage of Admiral Halsey's U.S. Third Fleet. Japanese prewar strategic predictions were being borne out, but not along the lines Japan's planners had hoped. The Americans were pressing westward from island to island, bypassing Japanese strongholds such as Rabaul and Truk, leaving those heavily fortified islands to wither on the vine from lack of supplies.

At the conflicts at Midway, the Solomons, the Marianas and Leyte, the Japanese had failed to win the one great decisive battle needed to stop the Americans. But now with the suicide submarines, the war might go differently. Just as Kuroki and Nishina had proposed in their original presentation of the *kaiten* scheme, Japan's Sixth Fleet might be able to successfully attack the U.S. Third Fleet in the anchorage. The first mission to Ulithi would be a decisive move on the part of Japanese submariners.

The element of surprise was essential.

The mission was given the name *Kikusui*[1], literally meaning "chrysanthemums floating on water." The name honored an ancient feudal lord named Kusunoki Masashige, who centuries earlier had withstood an onslaught of thirty-five thousand warriors for seven hours with only seven hundred men. Mortally wounded, Kusunoki is believed to have committed suicide, and reportedly his last words were "I wish I could be reborn seven times to fight the enemies of my Emperor." Those words have lived on as a patriotic declaration often used by Japanese military men.

The Kusunoki family crest, dating from 1331, contained symbols of floating chrysanthemums,[2] thus the aster-like pungent flower came to symbolize bravery in the face of tremendous odds. In 1944 in preparation for the *Kikusui* Mission to Ulithi and Palau, the Kanji ideographs for *kiku* chrysanthemums and *sui* water were painted on the conning towers of the three fleet submarines setting sail: *I-47, I-36* and the ill-fated *I-37.* Some of the *kaiten* torpedo submarines also bore the crest as a talisman.

Captain Zenji Orita was the overall commander of the *Kikusui* Mission. The lead mission pilot was Sekio Nishina. He was intensely focused on the task at hand, having faith in the weapon he and his now-dead partner Kuroki had devised. Nishina often told his men that no warship in the world could outrun the *kaiten* with its thirty-knot speed, and he sought to exhort them to brave deeds.

"We will lay the ground for Japan's further prosperity," he said, confident the mission would create a turning point. "We will not die for nothing."

Three more *kaiten* pilots joined Nishina as his counterparts in *I-47*: Sublieutenant Hitoshi Fukuda, a Fifty-Third Class Naval Engineering School graduate; Ensign Akira Sato, a law student at Kyushu University; and Ensign Shozo Watanabe, an economics student at Keio University. All would perish at Ulithi.

Mother submarine *I-36*, headed for Ulithi along with Captain Orita's *I-47*, also carried four *kaiten*; their pilots were Sublieutenant Kentaro Yoshimoto; Ensign Taichi Imanishi, formerly an economics student at Keio University; Sublieutenant Kazuhisa Toyozumi; and Ensign Yoshihiko Kondo. Three would return, but Imanishi would die inside the lagoon.

The *Kikusui* Mission was two-pronged: The main target was the ships in Ulithi Lagoon, but a diversionary tactic at Palau would be staged in hopes of distracting the enemy and obscuring the true mission. Fleet submarine *I-37*, commanded by Captain Nobuo Kamimoto, would split off from the other two fleet subs north of the Carolines and proceed on its own to Kossol Passage in the Palau Islands. The distance from Palau to Ulithi was 390 miles.

The four *kaiten* pilots selected for *I-37* and the Palau strike were all distinguished Navy men. Yoshinori Kamibeppu, a lieutenant and Seventieth Class Naval Academy graduate, was a close friend of Shunichi Shigemoto, chief navigator of the Ulithi-bound *I-47*. Kamibeppu's three colleagues were Katsutomo Murakami, a graduate of the Fifty-Third Class of the Naval Engineering School; Ensign Hideichi Utsunomiya, who left off his law studies at the University of Tokyo to join the Imperial Navy; and Ensign Kazuhiko Kondo.

Kaiten trainers had made recommendations for pilot selection for the *Kikusui* Mission, but it was the base's top officer, Lieutenant Commander Mitsuma Itakura, who had the last word. "Ultimately, I made the final decision who was to be sent and who was not,"[3] he said, no doubt as a statement of ultimate responsibility. "The final decision was made by me." Itakura made it known that, in the *samurai* tradition, he fervently desired to lead his men on the first mission, but Naval General Staff overruled his wish and did not permit him to join the pilots. He felt overwhelming humiliation at not being allowed to join his brave junior officers in the attack. His wife later recalled his devastation, saying, "When the first pilots went on the mission, he rolled on the floor crying."

Sublieutenant Katsutomo Murakami, an *I-37 kaiten* pilot, was described by friends as a strong-willed man and unquestionably honest, who showed great kindness and concern for others. On completing his *kaiten* training, Murakami visited a close friend, fellow *kaiten* submariner Mikio Samaru. When Samaru asked Murakami about his thoughts of the mission and impending death, he was silent; the *kaiten* was such a closely guarded secret that even submariners were discouraged from talking about it with their fellow officers. As they talked, the tension, unspoken, was palpable in the room. Murakami shuffled a deck of cards, then clenched the cards, creasing two of them; Samaru felt he understood.

The same evening Murakami presented his friend with a large black trunk. "This trunk was bought by my father and I have used it regularly," he said. "I think you are the only man that truly knows what is in my heart. I want you to accept this trunk. If you have the opportunity to make a sortie, I ask that you give the trunk to another man who understands our hearts and will follow us."

Murakami bid Samaru farewell. They both knew his place aboard *I-37* for the *Kikusui* Mission had been decided.

The departure of the *Kikusui* pilots was honored in a series of ceremonies that set a pattern for the rites of passage for later *kaiten* missions. On the afternoon of November 7, two days before their planned departure, the men chosen for the *Kikusui* mission paraded in new uniforms embellished on their left sleeves with the green chrysanthemum badge of the Special Attack Forces. They listened to an address given by Vice Admiral Shigeyoshi Miwa, who commanded the Sixth Fleet submarines. Members of the audience recalled that during his farewell address to the pilots, Miwa pointed often toward the submarines in plain view nearby, the *kaiten* strapped to cradles on their decks. The air was filled with words of bravado; the hearts of men held a mixture of emotions too complicated to untangle.

Admiral Miwa concluded his speech by presenting each of the *kaiten* pilots with a *wakizashi*, the short sword traditionally carried by a samurai warrior, and a *hachimaki*, the strip of cloth that a samurai warrior wrapped around his forehead to keep the long hair out of his eyes; the bandanna had come to stand for relentless determination. The *hachimaki* worn by the *Kikusui* pilots bore Japanese patriotic slogans.

It was understood the *kaiten* pilots were not coming back from *Kikusui*. Indeed, for the sake of personal honor and for the salvation of Japan, it was desirable that they *not* come back. Knowing their destiny, Nishina and the other pilots spent a few hours packing up their personal belongings for shipment to their next of kin; the parcels included their wills for disposition of property and last wishes, as well as personal letters to those they loved. Some letters contained more than one message, perhaps one written in conventionally patriotic terms and one more personal, genuinely thoughtful and moving. They even sent locks of hair and fingernail clippings to be placed by their families as an offering at the family Shinto altar.[4]

A farewell party for the officers and crews of the three *Kikusui* submarines and their *kaiten* was held that evening, when the officers of Ozushima wished to encourage the departing heroes with a brave send-off. Admiral Miwa gave another speech meant to instill courage. It was followed by comments in response from Lieutenant Yoshinori Kamibeppu, a *Kikusui* man bound for Palau on *I-37*, who spoke on behalf of his fellow *kaiten* pilots.

"We are determined to destroy the largest enemy ships we can find," he said. "On the eve of our departure, we are grateful to you for all that you have done for us. We wish all of you the best of health, and the best of good fortune."

Miwa lifted his glass and toasted the mission's success. They drank from special bottles of sake, sent as a gift from the emperor himself. It was a solemn moment. The banquet that followed included scarce luxuries, an extra acknowledgment that Japan was sending her distinguished sons to their deaths. Their last formal meal honored their sacrifice with such rarities at that moment in the war as fish, rice, canned fruit and dried seaweed. They finished with *kachi kuri*, the victory chestnuts traditionally served to express wishes for success.

At the height of the celebration Sekio Nishina slipped away from the toasts and bold speeches to say farewell to the new trainees just arrived from Tsuchiura Base. He wished them luck in their continued training and shook each man's hand.

The next day, November 8, was the last full day on Japanese soil before the men would depart on their mission. A ceremony was held at the Shinto shrine at Ozushima, the last home of Nishina and the other *kaiten* pilots accompanying him to Ulithi. The inspiring words of the Japanese national anthem, "*Kimigayo*," rang through the air: "May thy reign last one thousand, eight thousand generations." Each *kaiten* pilot of the *Kikusui* group bowed before the shrine, Nishina carrying the box of Kuroki's ashes.

The next morning they left for the journey of two thousand miles to keep their appointment with destiny. The skies were clear; the signs were auspicious if one could believe the waves, lapping peacefully at the docks of the Navy base. The cherry blossoms had fallen many weeks ago, but chrysanthemums still bloomed in the gardens at harborside.

The three mother submarines formed impressive silhouettes as they waited their turn to get under way, their monoliths a tribute to the best submarine technology perhaps in the world. Submarine *I-36* got under way by 0900 and slowly left the harbor, cruising along the surface. The *kaiten* pilots sat astride their weapons lashed to the decks, waving their swords and shouting farewell to the onlookers on shore.[5] *I-37* followed in similar fashion, the men waving to the crowds, and Orita came last in *I-47*, the vessel carrying Nishina. Small boats followed the three submarines out of the harbor, many of their decks crowded with other *kaiten* trainees, who waved their caps in a traditional farewell salute. Some of those left behind may have felt relief not to be part of the deadly mission, but others who recorded their thoughts later expressed sorrow at not making the first cut.

The three fleet submarines and their suicide cargo faced 2,000 miles of open sea before they would reach their separate destinations to the south, 390 miles apart from each other. The journey would take more than a week.

Soon after their departure from Japan, well before November 15, they parted company. The men of *I-37* said good-bye to their compatriots on *I-47* and *I-36*, as Captain Kamimoto was bound for Kossol Passage in the Palau Island group, to attack shipping there. Captain Orita sped toward Ulithi at a speed of twenty knots until he came within range of American patrol planes; like all the fleet submariners, he ran submerged during the daylight hours and surfaced only at night to charge batteries. Each night he received radio information in short transmissions from Kure headquarters, and when he surfaced he posted six lookouts on the bridge of the conning tower and ran the newly installed surface radar. Reconnaissance planes, flying from the Japanese stronghold at Truk Island, would reconnoiter the lagoon at Ulithi prior to the *kaiten* attack from *I-47* and *I-36*.

The *kaiten* pilots passed the time with the officers of *I-47* playing chess, cards, and the game *Go*. Hitoshi Fukuda was squirming uncomfortably after a day at sea aboard *I-47*. He had not used the complicated toilet with its maze of valves since leaving port, and he was too embarrassed to ask how it worked. His timidity led to a lot of teasing by *I-47* crewmen.

The voice of a trained singer enriched the passing hours. Chief Petty Officer Yukio Oka, the son of a Tokyo fish market vendor, was assistant diving officer aboard *I-47* but also an accomplished singer. He entertained the crew and pilots, and they admired his talent.[6] A few weeks earlier he'd almost been lost when his lifeline parted as he was inspecting *kaiten* on the mother sub's deck. When he was washed overboard, his fellow pilots took immediate action and rescued him from the water.

The men had ten days to prepare for their final mission. In the previous months they had written in their diaries "This is my last birthday," or "This is the last time I will see my brother." Now they wrote "This is my last Tuesday" and "This is my last voyage." Their doubts and fears were largely unexpressed, as it was not manly to cry, nor was it acceptable to diminish the courage of other pilots. Just before leaving Ozushima they had been briefed on the "incredible victories" by the *kamikaze* force that had launched its first attack at Leyte on October 25. Speaking for many of them, Yutaka Yokota said, "What they could do, the *kaiten* could do."[7]

They held that thought in their hearts through the dark passage to Ulithi.

CHAPTER 12

The Last Sortie

I learned that courage was not the absence of fear, but the triumph over it. The brave man is not he who does not feel afraid, but he who conquers that fear.

—Nelson Mandela, after prison release

Captain Beck wrote in his war diary on October 27 that the Commander Service Squadron (ComServRon) Ten led by Commodore Worrall R. Carter had worked well together in every way since *Mississinewa* first entered Ulithi on October 21. Beck noted that mail service had been very good, and Commodore Carter had freely given supplies, repairs, replacements and advice. Beck also praised the high morale aboard ship.

The crippled cruisers *Houston* and *Canberra*, both stricken by torpedoes in the Battle of Formosa, arrived under tow at Ulithi October 27. As they crept in, all vessels in the harbor blew their whistles for one minute as a salute to the gallant seamen who had escorted *Canberra* and *Houston* to safety. That day the weather took a turn for the worse, and strong winds were expected. Captain Beck ordered the port anchor let go, aiding the starboard anchor in keeping the *Miss* in its designated berth. All boilers were brought on line and small boats taken on board and secured in their davits. All loose gear was secured.

The storm blew in on October 28, bringing huge whitecaps to the normally peaceful waters of the atoll. Heavy rains battered the islands and pummeled the anchored ships all day long. By sunset the storm had dissipated and the seas calmed. Signalman Larry Glaser and his skivvy wavers had been serving as the visual signal relay ship, passing on messages from the *Mississinewa* to the other oilers nearby. The rear admiral in charge of communications issued a "Well Done" commendation to Glaser and the *Mississinewa* for prowess in signal communication.[1]

Navigator Rowe took a bearing on the ship's position in berth 32 on the morning of October 30 as he had done each morning for the past several days. The one-hundred-foot beacon tower on Mangejang Island and the forty-foot tower on Mas Island provided the bearings to fix the oiler's position inside the lagoon. Boiler number 3 was the only unit on line, creating auxiliary power. The *Miss* had received 326,211 gallons of hundred-octane aviation gasoline from the station tanker USS *Giraffe* on October 23 and was fully loaded for deployment to sea. Captain Beck awaited his sailing orders.

After reveille one morning soon after, *Mississinewa* buzzed with scuttlebutt. It seemed seaman Ed Coria was to appear at a disciplinary hearing—the dreaded Captain's Mast—at 1000 for a summary court-martial.[2] The charges were serious: abandoning a gun station while on watch. Coria had left his post for, of all things, permission from the boatswain's mate to take a shower! The officer of the deck had noticed the sailor's absence from the guns, and soon afterward the sailor was facing Captain Beck. Coria was sent to the brig, where he would remain until his trial.

Savoring its victory at Leyte Gulf, the Third Fleet retired to Ulithi with great fanfare, arriving on October 30. Warships circled the anchorage amid cheering sailors and the sounds of ships blowing their whistles in salute.

Within days of the victory at Leyte, the tactical situation there was already turning bad for the Allies; since the fierce battle the week before, Japanese forces had begun to recover some air control over the region. Halsey proposed to Admiral Nimitz that a series of air strikes by Task Force 38 be taken on Luzon; Nimitz gave permission to begin air strikes by November 5. Halsey then ordered three fast carrier groups to be fueled at sea by November 3, so the *Mississinewa* sailed from Ulithi in early November as one of the tankers of a fuel task unit. *Mississinewa* would soon fuel Admiral McCain's task group, whose mission was to attack Northern Luzon. Admiral Bogan's group struck Southern Luzon, the Mindoro airfields and the shipping lanes in the North Sibuyan Sea, while Admiral Sherman's task force concentrated on the shipping in Manila Bay.

McCain's force crept to within eighty miles of Luzon; his air groups claimed 439 enemy planes, destroyed both on the ground and in the air on November 5 and 6. His pilots also sank the Japanese heavy cruiser *Nachi*, once the flagship for Vice Admiral Shima in the Battle of Surigao Strait. The Americans lost only twenty-five planes and eighteen pilots in Northern Luzon, a victory of numbers as well as momentum, but they suffered a grievous loss when a *kamikaze* successfully targeted Admiral McCain's flagship, the fleet carrier USS *Lexington*.[3] Four *kamikazes* flew in like crazed hornets to attack the *Lady Lex*. Three were shot down by antiaircraft fire, but the fourth crashed into the starboard side of the carrier's island superstructure, causing terrible damage. Fifty men were killed and 132 injured.

On November 2 *Mississinewa* steamed out of Ulithi Lagoon on what would be her last sortie, although the oiler would return for a final rest in the lagoon. The date of the last departure is not proven, because no ship's logs exist after the oiler's sinking, but the logical date to meet her commitments at sea would place it as November 2. Accompanied by five other fleet oilers, including *Marias*, the *Miss* sailed to rendezvous with Fuel Task Group 38.1.

A seemingly minor event turned into a trick of fate. After most of the warships had been fueled at sea, the *Miss* was preparing to return to Ulithi. The last task before leaving was to top off the three oilers that would remain on station, the standard practice for fueling task units. But a winch broke on the oiler *Marias* that could not be repaired at sea, creating a wrinkle in the logistics. Captain Beck volunteered the *Miss* to accept cargo consolidation (the fuel in *Marias*'s tanks) and remain at sea for the next cycle of fueling the task force, another two weeks. Only after that would the oiler return to Ulithi Harbor, making the entry to the anchorage on November 15. The change of plan doomed the *Mississinewa*, for instead of being out to sea on November 20, she would be anchored in berth 131 on an intercept path with an underwater killer.

While the *Miss* still steamed on the open ocean, taking the place of *Marias* in fueling the ships, the calendar turned to November 10 and an extraordinary event occurred in the Admiralty Islands—the demise of the light cruiser *Mount Hood*. Earlier that year when getting ship assignments, a dozen *Mississinewa* sailors had passed up the chance to join the crew of the *Hood* and chosen the *Miss* instead. On November 10 it seemed Lady Luck was on their side, for in Seeadler Harbor on Manus Island—a location *Miss* sailors knew well, having anchored there the previous month—*Mount Hood* blew up, suddenly, inexplicably. All 295 men on board disappeared along with the ship; a dozen nearby ships were damaged and more than 300 men wounded. To some *Miss* sailors it seemed that fate had dealt them a lucky hand, and they thought for sure they'd cheated death.

Japan fought to regain control over the Philippines, and the Allies strategized to stop them. It was coming clear that if Task Force 38 was to have any hope of striking Japan's home islands by the year's end, Admiral Halsey would have to break off supporting the Leyte operation and deploy forces elsewhere. American military strategists agreed that the Japanese would fiercely defend Leyte despite the crushing losses of the recent naval battles and massive destruction of aircraft.

On November 11, Halsey conveyed to Admiral Nimitz that he wanted the planned strikes against Japan indefinitely postponed and the fast carrier forces to concentrate on the continued support of the Philippine campaign. Nimitz agreed, replying that Third Fleet fast carrier groups would be essential to support the Leyte operations until the Army Air Force could build airfields and amass enough strength to defend them.

The fast carrier units of Task Force 38 fueled from the oilers the morning of November 12. The watches on board the carriers saw Japanese planes circling in the skies on reconnaissance over their heads, but no air attack came.

On the *Miss*, the danger that day came from the Navy's own ships and the vicissitudes of the sea. The oiler had just finished fueling the heavy cruiser USS *Boston* when Bill Brzykcy climbed up the engine room ladder for a breath of fresh air; he saw the last of the fueling hoses hauled in from *Boston*. General quarters sounded on *Boston*, and the cruiser immediately went to flank speed, as it had to do on a general quarters call, but the result was a turn that cut right across *Mississinewa*'s bow.[4]

"Full astern," yelled the officer of the deck on the bridge. It was almost too late. Frightened deckhands, recoiling at the sight of *Boston* so close, grabbed for anything to hang on to in case the ships collided. Machinist's mate Jim Lewis could have reached over and shaken hands with *Boston* sailors. The two ships narrowly missed each other. The danger receded. Later that afternoon Brzykcy asked the officer of the deck how close they'd actually come to colliding. The OOD spread his hands about eighteen inches apart and said, "That far."

Mississinewa returned to Ulithi on November 15 and tied up to a merchant tanker in berth 131. It was the end of the oiler's last cruise. At anchor at the south end of the channel, the *Miss* rocked gently as ebb tide swung the ship 360 degrees around. A merchant tanker pumped 404,000 gallons of hundred-octane aviation gasoline into *Miss*'s number 2 and number 3 centerline tanks; 9,000 barrels of diesel oil were also delivered and 90,000 barrels of NSFO transferred into *Miss* tanks aft of the bridge. Fully loaded, the oiler was again ready to fuel Third Fleet ships whenever the call came. It didn't come in time.

A few days after the arrival in Ulithi, Ray Fulleman greeted a few merchant tanker sailors who worked the fire room on their civilian vessel. Fulleman was standing auxiliary watch while hoses pumped cargo over from the merchant tanker, and the talk among the sailors ran to pay—how much they got on different ships for the same work. Of course, the big difference was that sailors on the merchant ships were civilians, not the same as U.S. Navy. One civilian sailor, a third class engineer, did the same work as Fulleman.

"I get paid forty-five dollars a month," Fulleman said with pride. He heard a laugh. "I get paid five times that and a bonus for being out here," came the reply from one man, "and *no one* shoots at me."[5]

It gave Fulleman something to think about that day. Submarines stalked the fleet at sea, and enemy aircraft often surprised them with rogue attacks. One of these days, he thought, it might be his luck that a suicide pilot dived on the *Miss*.

The sailors aboard *Mississinewa* waited for sunset as the calendar inched its way to the end of a lazy Sunday, November 19. Thousands of U.S. Navy sailors went about their duties aboard the seemingly endless number of gray warships swinging at anchor inside Ulithi Lagoon late in the day on November 19, 1944. Small craft like shuttle bugs busied themselves going from ship to shore and back again.

On the *Miss*, a work party under the direction of cargo officer Lieutenant James Fuller shifted fuel oil and aviation gasoline cargo forward of the bridge. The tanker swung at anchor on placid waves. Hardly a ripple stirred on the water, and the bow watch sailor had no cause for alarm. *Mississinewa* rode at an even keel, thanks to the careful shifting of the liquid cargo to aid in ballasting. The day's work was almost complete.

At 1800 hours Captain Beck hailed his cargo officer from the bridge. "Lieutenant Fuller, secure the work detail and get the men below for a shower so they don't miss the movie." Fuller protested, saying the centerline tank number 3 and bow wing tanks 1 and 2 hadn't been purged.[6]

"It's eighteen hundred hours now, Fuller, and the movie is at nineteen hundred. Secure the detail," Beck ordered. Fuller could only say, "Yes, sir," but an uneasy feeling gripped his stomach. He knew that vapors built up if the tanks weren't purged; they were supposed to be filled with seawater to flush them out. He appreciated the captain's concern for the men's recreation, but all the same, he wondered what in the world Beck was thinking to ignore the standard procedure. He went to bed feeling upset.

The last night on board *Mississinewa* was tranquil. "No watch tonight for me on the ole *Miss*," Bill Brzykcy said to his buddy Bill Janas as they slung their hammocks beneath the aft cargo deck. "I have scullery duty at 0600, and that's a piece of cake." He'd never make that duty, for destiny was preparing a tiny submersible for the death blow of the fleet tanker.

Just before midnight, eighteen-year-old electrician's mate Joe Morris rewound the movie *The Black Parachute* on the ship's movie projector. The B-grade spy thriller focused on hero Larry Parks's method of entry behind enemy lines in German-occupied Europe. The drama included a night-time parachute drop, which was mandated by the need for a wartime mission to dispatch an evil Nazi general played by actor John Carradine. Liberating an occupied nation while simultaneously sweeping resistance fighter Jeanne Bates off her feet, the plot ended with the last reel Morris placed on the projector. Morris would only have an hour's sleep before his watch began. Exhausted, he fell asleep on the aft well deck surrounded by several engineering division sailors.

At the same time, Rocky DeMarco was gathering his winnings in the mess hall casino, his streak of bad luck at gambling over. DeMarco's buddies, considerably poorer, decided to quit the game. They started forward to bed down under the bow 3-inch/50 gun tub that offered shelter from frequent rain showers. They invited Rocky to join them on the bow.

"No, you guys go ahead and I'll be up there in a bit. I've got a winning streak going here," he said.[7] A few minutes later he quit the poker game, buoyed by the wad of cash in his dungarees. A warm rain shower greeted him by the time he had trekked halfway across the cargo deck. He turned back the way he had come. The rain shower stopped briefly. He decided to stay on the cargo deck and sleep there instead of risking getting wet again making his way to the bow. It was a lucky decision for DeMarco. Not so lucky for his friends on the bow.

Ed Mitchell, an electrician's mate, planned to sleep on deck, on top of the aviation gasoline tanks on the bow. He asked his friend Joe Morris to join him, saying, "Where you gonna sleep tonight, kid? Come up forward, it's cooler in the breeze."[8] Morris declined, and the fateful decision saved his life. Mitchell would die the next morning when the gas tanks exploded on the bow.

Even as they all went to sleep, two submarines were hovering outside the lagoon, far enough away that no sailor on watch spotted them as they surfaced under the tropical stars.

CHAPTER 13

The *Kikusui* Mission

Over a hundred ships at anchor in Ulithi. There are but two submarines and eight human torpedoes—a regrettable matter.

—Sublieutenant Sekio Nishina, diary entry, November 19, 1944

On November 17, while running submerged, Zenji Orita's alert sonar operators on *I-47* picked up the noise of a propeller screw. Distance and direction of underwater disturbances are hard to calculate: Sounds appear closer than they really are, but their direction is difficult to determine. When the noise faded away, Orita gave the order to raise the sub cautiously to periscope depth. He peered through the lens and saw an American destroyer heading away from him, angling to the northwest. He continued to his destination point outside Ulithi Lagoon.

Palau, Yap and Ulithi dot the Pacific in a slanting line from west to east, forming the backbone of the Caroline Islands. Each one is a cluster of islands made of coral that together form a larger chain of the Carolines, stretching across four hundred miles of ocean. The submarines of the *Kikusui* group, each carrying four *kaiten*, would pass the cluster of islands that formed Palau and then another cluster of Japanese-held Yap Islands on the way to Ulithi Lagoon.

The diversion planned near Palau for *I-37* would happen in two stages. The captain, Kamimoto, would first launch his four *kaiten* to strike and destroy four U.S. ships, then follow that attack with conventional torpedoes. His counterparts, Lieutenant Commander Zenji Orita's submarine *I-47* and Lieutenant Commander Iwao Teramoto's *I-36*, would proceed straight to Ulithi for their *kaiten* launches. By November 17, both elements of the *Kikusui* group had reached their assigned target areas at Palau and Ulithi.

The Palau Island group is ringed with a large barrier reef. On the north end, a large natural harbor contains two openings, named the Kossol Passage. That passage was where *I-37* arrived with its four *kaiten*. Here *I-37*'s part in the mission that had departed Japan ten days earlier came to a premature end.

It was morning in full sun. Captain Kamimoto wanted to reconnoiter, but daylight made a dangerous time for a submarine to leave the deep ocean and go to the surface, where an enemy destroyer or airplane might notice a silvery glint. He decided to chance it anyway, perhaps judging that he was far enough away from the inner harbor that he would go undetected. He decided to surface for a quick look to assess his location and direction. The decision was fatal.

At the western entrance of Kossol Passage, the net-layer USS *Winterberry* was on alert. Just before 0900 on November 19, a man on watch had noticed something breaking the water's surface for a few moments.[1] His commanding officer sent an urgent message to the port commander and also to the watch near the harbor's west entrance. *Winterberry* was ordered to investigate the contact. The submarine disappeared but surfaced again twenty seconds later, this time at a very steep angle, the bow nearly vertical and rising out of the water.

The commander of the task group ordered destroyer escorts USS *Conklin* and *McCoy Reynolds* under way at 0915 to form a hunter-killer group to destroy the enemy craft. Navy planes were dispatched from Peleliu to assist in the hunt. *Conklin* and *McCoy Reynolds* paired for a box search. To cover the selected box area, the two ships sailed parallel to each other three thousand yards apart, constantly pinging a 180-degree sonar arc from beam to beam. If the submarine came within range of the sonar, it would read out as a large object on the sonar screen aboard the ships. On the *Conklin*, the sonar technician searched the readouts for clues; the helmsman, Howard Higgins, strained to concentrate as the captain paced the bridge and ordered frequent course changes. "The captain was on my ass every minute," Higgins said. "Go this way, go that way."[2]

Hours went by with no sonar hits. The crews of both destroyer escorts had been at general quarters for six hours when the sonar operators aboard both *McCoy Reynolds* and *Conklin* sang out at 1504. "Sound contact, range 1,600 yards, course 130 degrees true."

The *Conklin*'s skipper ordered a course change to 130 degrees and ten knots, and then stood by while the *McCoy Reynolds* initiated a hedgehog attack. *McCoy Reynolds* fired the first hedgehogs at 1539 and a second attack shortly after, both unsuccessful. *Conklin*'s captain ordered rapid course changes to retain sonar contact with the target, making the helmsman grip the wheel and turn quickly in response to his commands. The hedgehogs seemed to have missed, and indeed *I-37* had dived to a depth of 350 feet. *McCoy Reynolds* pressed the attack with thirteen more depth charges but lost contact with the submarine as underwater explosions completely obliterated any sonar echoes.

The crew of the *Conklin* would be next to attack the submarine. They didn't have to wait long for their prey. At 1603 the sonar operator relocated the vessel within range, and the captain, Lieutenant Commander Edmund McGibbon, swiftly ordered a hedgehog attack. Less than a minute after the hedgehogs went barreling over the side, *Conklin*'s sonar man reported an explosion deep below. The crew knew a hedgehog wouldn't explode unless it made contact with a submarine's hull. *Conklin* had found the mark.

The exact fate of the submarine wasn't known, but the hit had clearly been mortal. It was confirmed nearly an hour later, at 1700, when the sailors aboard both destroyers felt the decks rock with a massive underwater explosion, almost eight hours since the initial sighting of the submarine. Minutes later a huge air bubble rose to the surface of the ocean. The *kaiten* were known to carry large oxygen tanks for submergence and steering; perhaps these tanks contributed to the massive air bubble. Topside sailors aboard *Conklin* spotted fuel oil, cork, decking, pieces of finished wood and bits of human flesh in the middle of the expanding oil slick.

The Action Report from *McCoy Reynolds* detailed the unusually large air bubble that surfaced from the grave of *I-37.*

> The bubble, about 25 feet in diameter, rose about 5 feet above the surface, darker in color than the surrounding sea and appeared to remain in a mushroomed elevated position for several seconds. Nothing more conclusively indicated a tremendous underwater explosion than was ever observed in this command in over 20 years of frequently dropping depth charges.

Captain McGibbon had no way of knowing that *Conklin* had very likely touched off the explosive power of the combined warheads of four Japanese *kaiten*—a total of 13,672 pounds of high explosives. In fact, the U.S. Navy was simply reporting the sighting as a submarine contact.

Pleased with reports of their success, Admiral Halsey sent a congratulatory message to the successful hunter-killer ships: "Well done on your job of recruiting for the Association of Nip Ancestors."

The demise of *I-37* would not become known to the other two submarine captains of the *Kikusui* Mission for several weeks. They continued on their own part of the mission to reach Ulithi, hopeful that their counterpart had staged his diversion successfully at Palau.

Lieutenant Shunichi Shigemoto, the chief navigator of *I-47,* learned two weeks later when he returned from the *Kikusui* Mission that all hands on *I-37* had been lost, including his friend Yoshinori Kamibeppu, one of the four *kaiten* pilots on board. The two men had been good friends, having been close since their days at the Imperial Japanese Naval Academy. A frank, honest and hot-blooded man, Kamibeppu radiated a passion for life. Shigemoto would miss him. At the moment of that sad discovery, he faced the sky in the direction of Palau and lamented the loss of his friend. "Kamibeppu, have a peaceful sleep," he prayed.

As Kamibeppu and his comrades sank to the ocean floor, Zenji Orita on *I-47* guided *I-36* onward, and the two submarines reached their launching area off Ulithi without incident. As mission commander, Orita made the tactical decisions for the attack.

They knew the pickings were good, with many targets waiting. On November 16 a Japanese high-altitude reconnaissance plane from Truk had reported that Ulithi Lagoon was crammed with U.S. Navy ships, including aircraft carriers and battleships.[3] The warships were located in the north central part of the lagoon, while the transports, oilers and other auxiliary vessels occupied the south central part of the anchorage. The intelligence relayed to the submarines from Japan was very detailed.

In fact, the American targets were far too numerous for the small number of Japanese submarines to destroy. Present at the time of the attack were four fleet carriers, three battleships, the cruisers and destroyers of Rear Admiral Frederick Sherman's Task Group 38.3, the heavy cruisers and destroyers of Task Group 57.9, a number of major and minor units under repair and the many fleet auxiliaries of Commodore Carter's Service Squadron Ten. About two hundred ships in all had taken anchorage in the pristine lagoon.

En route to Ulithi, the *kaiten* pilots practiced manning their weapons. The *kaiten*'s token escape hatch, insisted on by the high command, was put to practical use. By rigging a tube twenty-four inches in diameter between the submarine's casing and the escape hatch on the underside of the *kaiten*, the pilot was able to enter his weapon while the submarine lay submerged; it was a previously unforeseen but practical solution to escape detection. A mother sub crewman followed the pilot through the access tube to secure the escape hatch after he had entered the torpedo. Once the mother submarine's hatch was secured, the access tube flooded. A telephone cable running through the tube allowed voice contact between the pilot and the submarine's skipper up to the moment of launching. At launch, both cable and tube tore free from the *kaiten*. Only two of the four *kaiten* on the mother submarines of the *Kikusui* Mission had been fitted with the access tube, but on later missions all *kaiten* were so equipped.

At sunset on November 18 Orita surfaced *I-47* fifty miles west of Ulithi to check the condition of the *kaiten*, which were fastened to the deck using clamp rings and blocks of wood. Maintenance men loosened the first and fourth hold-down bands on each forty-eight-foot manned torpedo, leaving only the two center bands for faster release from inside the submarine at launch time. All *kaiten* were considered in good shape for the attack on Ulithi.

On the morning of November 19, an hour before sunrise, Orita prepared to approach the lagoon. He submerged *I-47* and stabilized the craft at 180 feet below the surface to avoid U.S. patrol planes. Creeping along the western side of Ulithi, the mother submarine arrived at a point within four miles west of Eau and Ealil islands. At 0930 Orita came close to the surface and raised his periscope. He made a quick sweeping look of the harbor and called out the bearings of three cruisers inside Ulithi to the navigator, Lieutenant Shigemoto. He dived and stayed at depth for two hours, then returned to periscope level again just before noon. He saw only open ocean; there were no close patrol boats. Orita raised his periscope four feet above the water to get a good look at Ulithi. The nearest cruiser was only three miles away.

He saw several cruisers beyond the nearest U.S. Navy ship, as he scanned for the very desirable battleships. Aircraft carriers—the most valuable targets of all—were located beyond that; he noted the patrol circling above the ships but could not see the ships themselves. All the clearly visible ships were located toward the south and southwest area of Ulithi. The central part of the harbor held ships moored in rows. To the north and east, rising columns of smoke marked the presence of other U.S. ships, but their configurations were unknown; Orita's vessel lay too far to the west of Ulithi to get a view. But what he saw was inspiring, and he called Nishina to the periscope to take a look.

Nishina peered into the periscope for two or three minutes, straining to see as much as possible. He drew in his breath slowly, gratified at the number of ships, then abruptly relinquished the periscope to Sublieutenant Fukuda. Ensigns Sato and Watanabe next took their turns at *I-47*'s periscope. Seeing the plentiful targets rich in armaments and aircraft lined up on the decks, the pilots were elated. Nishina commented in his diary for the day on the "golden opportunity to use *kaiten*."

I-47 submerged again while the sun was still well above the horizon. In the deep, the submarine moved slowly through the dark waters outside the lagoon, unseen by patrolling aircraft that occasionally swept the area. Captain Orita summoned his department heads and the four *kaiten* pilots to the officers' wardroom.

"We will launch *kaiten* in the morning," Orita said. "I intend to have *I-47* within four miles east of the westernmost channels of Ulithi. You will enter Zau Channel and attack large-sized carriers and battleships in the anchorage. In order to avoid having two *kaiten* attack the same target and so we [would be making] simultaneous attacks, Nishina will be launched at 4:00 A.M. He will penetrate the anchorage and go straight ahead as far as he can. Ensign Sato will leave four minutes later and move to the right after entering. Watanabe will depart five minutes after Sato and go left. Fukuda, launched five minutes after Sato, will seek as large a target as possible near the entrance."[4]

If the pilots implemented Captain Orita's attack plan successfully, all four *kaiten* released from *I-47* would run northwest and enter Zau Channel that funneled directly into the deep anchorage.

After writing the last words each wanted to leave behind, the four *kaiten* pilots accepted a gift from Chief Oka, *I-47*'s assistant diving officer. Oka produced a sketch he had drawn, a delicate, beautifully executed piece done with soft lead pencil in varying shades, depicting an American aircraft carrier breaking in two as a *kaiten* struck it. All four pilots autographed it; under his signature Nishina added the characters for *gochin*, meaning "sunk instantly." It was how he wanted to be remembered, dying honorably in an attack, as he had promised he would do for his country.

That evening at dinner on board the submarine, young submariners served the *kaiten* pilots a special gift from the emperor of fine *sake* in lacquer-ware cups. After their last meal, the *kaiten* pilots purified themselves with springwater, then shaved and trimmed their hair. Only Nishina did not shave or cut his long hair, saying, "I will not shave or cut my hair until I have obtained my hit against a U.S. ship." Of course, it would then be too late.

The pilots retired to their cabins to rest. In the darkness Orita brought his submarine to the surface and approached Ulithi at a moderate speed of twelve knots. The dark protected them from the ships at a distance, although the stars twinkled brightly over the coral lagoon of Ulithi that night.

Before going to sleep Nishina wrote a final entry in his diary. He was filled with exuberance after seeing the myriad enemy ships in Ulithi's vast harbor:

> Daylight observation disclosed over a hundred ships at anchor in Ulithi. Though this provides a golden opportunity for the use of our human torpedoes, there are but two submarines and eight human torpedoes—a regrettable matter.

He wrote more, words that seemed to express a need to bolster himself for the ordeal to come. His last words would be passed on to people who cared for him, and they would be recorded for posterity at Yasukuni Shrine:

On November 20, 1944, I shall dress in a six-inch loincloth and pilot suit with a Japanese sword. I will wear a white *"hachimaki"* headband cloth with the word *"Shichisho-Hokoku"* ("Serve the nation during seven existences") imprinted on it. A photo of my friend Kuroki will be in my left hand and the explosive handle of the *kaiten* in my right. I will have my canvas cushion that was sewn and presented to me by a sweet Japanese girl. I shall draw my sword, my hair standing heaven-ward, keeping the sunrise of [our] godly country in my heart, saying "May the Emperor reign for 10 thousand years." Run at a maximum speed of 30 knots, hitting a large aircraft carrier![5]

The submarine surfaced shortly after midnight, and ensigns Akira Sato and Shozo Watanabe emerged on the bridge. White *hachimaki* adorned the young pilots' heads. The pair entered the open hatches of *kaiten* numbers 3 and 4 secured on deck, while officers of I-47 scanned the sea and sky, worried about detection on the surface from U.S. Navy antisubmarine patrols. There were no access tubes from I-47's main deck leading to Sato and Watanabe's craft; their entry had to be done while the mother submarine was on the surface, a critical point that meant it would have to happen hours before their actual launch, well away from possible detection. It also meant the pilots would be forced to remain for hours squeezed into their narrow, dark quarters.

On the deck, technicians helped both pilots enter their craft. Under the star-filled sky with the sounds of waves slapping the submarine, the pilots bid farewell, climbed inside, and the hatches were pulled and bolted shut. No exit was possible now from the *kaiten*, whether the mission was successful or not. The assistants, nearly overcome with distress at the pilots' impending doom, finished their task of tightening the bolts of the hatches to prevent leaks, then collapsed with grief, sob-bing bitterly underneath the two *kaiten* that held the pilots.

Sometime before 0200, when the blackness of night still covered the ocean with a vast blanket, Nishina walked across the submarine deck to take a last look at the world he would be leaving. Starlight glinted off the metal of the sub's armaments, dulled as it was by rust and algae from thousands of hours spent underwater. He went back inside the submarine.

Field glasses in hand, Orita could see the sparks of welding torches inside Ulithi as the U.S. Navy repaired battle-damaged ships. The time was 0100 on November 20 and *I-47* lay five miles from the intended launch point. *I-47* slipped beneath the surface of the ocean as Orita submerged with Sato and Watanabe sealed inside their *kaiten*. The crew of *I-47* grew ever more somber as they thought of the brave young men who now waited in their *kaiten* for their deaths.

Next to board his killer weapon was Fukuda. He saluted the officers and men of *I-47*, face flushed, shoulders back. "I am much obliged to you. I shall go," Fukuda announced in a spirited voice, his trademark demeanor. He entered through the special tube and took a seat on his canvas cushion to wait for launch.

Next Nishina slowly saluted Orita and the men of *I-47*; he held in his left hand the box containing Kuroki's ashes. He spoke softly, as he usually did. "I am much obliged to you. Thank you very much" were his gentle words. Nishina praised the crew of *I-47* and Captain Orita for getting so close to the enemy without detection. "Please do not endanger your ship in observing our results, sir," he said. "*Kaiten* operations should always remain a mystery to the enemy, if possible." Nishina said he hoped *I-47* would leave the area quickly so that the Americans couldn't pinpoint the source of the attack. When he was finished saying good-bye at 0300, he entered his weapon, crawling through the access tube to *kaiten* number 1. He was the last man in, but he would be the first to launch.

All four *kaiten* pilots were now waiting for launch in the tight confines of their craft, still sitting on the deck, anticipating final directions from the *I-47* navigator, Shigemoto. He was connected by telephone to each pilot.

"Are you lonesome up there?" he asked Sato first, then Watanabe. "You've been waiting a long time." Both men had been confined for two hours, legs bent under them, their bodies nearly immobile in the cramped torpedoes.

"Not I," said Sato. "I've been singing."

Watanabe replied with similar composure. "That ice cream you served us at dinner was very good. Thank you very much for your thoughtfulness." He sounded calm and unruffled.

The navigator was impressed by their stoicism, and reported the conversations to Orita, who was so moved that he was able to recall the exact words years later. "They're acting as if everything is routine, yet death is only minutes away," Orita thought. Deeply troubled as he had been by the recent tactical changes proposed by the Japanese Sixth Fleet command, he was particularly chagrined by Admiral Miwa's decision to use suicide weapons. As captain of the submarine that housed the *kaiten* and contained other officers and crew not necessarily destined for death, Orita faced a great dilemma: how to offer the young lives the opportunity to make their great sacrifice while preserving the lives of his own crew. The risk to *I-47* was readily apparent to Orita, as his submarine crew would have to maneuver close to the enemy to deliver *kaiten*. "I will be taking to sea men who were determined to die and I have always felt it my duty, up until now, to not let one man under my command die if I can do anything to prevent it."

He had to provide *kaiten* pilots the means for death in order to save his country and give others a chance for life. He had come to a torturous solution. "My duty is clear!" he said to himself, as he recounted his top priority: "I have to get *kaiten* men to their launch points, disregarding the safety of *I-47* crew members. After *kaiten* are launched, I can resume responsibility for my crew and make our escape."

It was an agonizing question of life and death, or life *versus* death. The *kaiten* pilots were dying so that the Empire of Japan and the "sweet Japanese girls" yet in their adolescence could live. Ever since he first learned of the suicide torpedoes, Orita had struggled with the tragic philosophy; years later he said those thoughts never left him.

———————

Inside their human torpedoes, the pilots checked their instruments. When navigator Shigemoto sent them updated information by telephone about the sub's location and the ocean currents, they plotted their attack courses. At 0400 Orita surfaced *I-47* for a final periscope view to allow Shigemoto to determine the correct course and bearing to place the *kaiten* pilots near the entrance to Zau Channel. Orita reported in his Sixth Fleet Action Report that *I-47* was 13.8 nautical miles south of Ulithi; Zau Channel was on a bearing of 154 degrees to the northwest. The equilateral current ran east to west at a speed of 0.9 knots.

It is not known if navigator Shigemoto compensated for the estimated three miles *I-47* drifted in that east-west current during the window of launch. Given the analysis of other submariners years later, it is possible, even likely, that he did not.[6] *I-47*'s drift to the west, unrecognized by the navigator, may have compromised the mission, as one and possibly two *kaiten* pilots would soon lose their lives at a location far away from their intended attack point.

Shigemoto gave the final ranges and bearings to the four pilots anxiously waiting for launch. He asked the pilots to confirm their readiness, and they did so. The submarine held steady at thirty-five feet below the surface. From within the submarine, technicians moved to each *kaiten* in turn, releasing the bands that secured them to their cradles. As each *kaiten* was released, the pilot started his engine and adjusted his diving planes to hold a steady depth.

Nishina left first in *kaiten* number 1.[7] Orita tried to follow him through the periscope, but the line of white bubbles obscured his view. Sato and Watanabe left five and ten minutes later. Last to depart was Fukuda; a moment before his craft broke free from the cradle and parted from *I-47* for the last time, his final words came clearly over the telephone: *"Tenno heika banzai."* ("May the emperor reign for ten thousand years.")

Each pilot was to pursue a different attacking course after penetrating Zau Channel, a strategy that placed them in the lagoon just after daybreak on courses to strike targets in widely separated locations.[8] Based on their estimated launch times, Nishina's release would place him at the channel entrance twenty-three minutes before sunrise. Sato would arrive eighteen minutes before sunrise, Watanabe thirteen minutes before and Fukuda eight minutes before.

Sato was to move to the east after entering Zau Channel. Watanabe was to enter and go west to make his attack. Arriving last at the channel entrance, when presumably the other three pilots would be already inside the lagoon, Fukuda was to create a diversion, seeking as large a target as possible near the anchorage entrance. Nishina, the most skilled and experienced pilot on the team, was to penetrate north, deep inside the lagoon, in the vicinity of Mugai Channel, and search for a battleship or aircraft carrier.

Lightened by the release of the killer subs, a change of more than seventy-five tons no longer weighing down the mother submarine, Orita's craft bobbed briefly to the surface. He went to depth and headed immediately out to sea, intending to surface at a safe distance and watch for explosions through his binoculars.

Just after midnight on November 20, submarine *I-36* was waiting at a spot about eleven nautical miles southeast of Mas Island, which was on a bearing of 105 degrees northwest. Commander Iwao Teramoto's plans to release all four *I-36 kaiten* did not go smoothly. When *I-36* surfaced at 0030, Ensigns Imanishi and Kudo boarded their *kaiten*. Sublieutenants Kentaro Yoshimoto and Kazuhisa Toyozumi crawled into the others at 0300 via the access tubes.

Lieutenant Takashi Ozawa, navigator of *I-36*, indicated in his report to Sixth Fleet that at 0400 Teramoto had positioned *I-36* more than nine miles from Mas Island, which marked the right-hand side of Mugai Channel. The night had grown cloudy, making astronomical observation more difficult but not impossible. Although Ozawa had less complete data in determining the exact position of *I-36*, it appears he did a better job on calculating the current than *I-47*'s navigator[9] and was able to compensate, at least partly, on the rapid westerly current drift. The position had the submarine on a bearing 105 degrees southeast of Mas Island, taking into account the equilateral current that had washed Teramoto's submarine four nautical miles west during the four hours since the last position point fix.

The antisubmarine net stretched over the Mugai Channel, the main shipping entrance, for four and a half miles, reaching a point nearly two miles northeast of Mas Island. The one successfully launched pilot from *I-36*, Imanishi, cruised underwater to a point about fifteen hundred yards from Mas Island, where he encountered an antisubmarine net. In order to enter the lagoon, he was forced to slide over the net, and in so doing he exposed himself to detection. It was a necessary decision to cross the net, but it would prove fatal.

At about 0400 Teramoto discovered that *kaitens* 1, 2 and 4 had jammed in their racks and were not fireable. The engines of the first two *kaiten* had been started, but the weapons were stuck fast in their chocks. A third *kaiten* had leaked seawater into its propulsion mechanism and failed to start.

The *I-36* man responsible for launching the *kaiten* was Yoshihisa Arizuka, the chief engineer.[10] Devastated by the failure to launch, he explained the events.

"At launching, a handle in the submarine was turned to release the belts that held the *kaiten* to the deck of the mother sub. With turning the handle, I confirmed the belts were off, but I heard that the *kaiten* had not left the submarine. After a while, one of their screw sounds was heard to leave." He summed up, "It was an accident with the launching pad of *kaiten*."

The screw sounds he heard came from the one *kaiten* that successfully launched, piloted by Ensign Taichi Imanishi, who broke away from *I-36* at 0454. Imanishi was released and instructed to attack in the area of known occupation by aircraft carriers and battleships south of Mog Mog Island. His attack instructions, as reported in the Sixth Fleet After Action Report, ordered him to proceed and penetrate the lagoon fifteen hundred meters southwest of Mas Island to reach his assigned target area.

Failing to launch from *I-36* and immensely distressed at their misfortune, Lieutenants Yoshimoto and Toyozumi reentered *I-36* through their access tubes after the tubes had been blown free of flooding. Ensign Kudo was retrieved later when the submarine surfaced briefly that morning; it could have been discovered and attacked by a USMC Corsair aircraft still near the original launch area, but Teramoto dived and escaped. Only one *kaiten* pilot had launched on his mission.

Orita's *I-47* submarine and released *kaiten* had better luck.

In darkness the *kaiten* pilots approached the channel destinations, hoping to find the openings at first light. Their courses had initially been plotted according to directions provided by Orita, who had viewed the target area at a distance through the fleet sub's own periscope, factors that made the calculations a bit of a long shot. It was assumed that the directions would enable the *kaiten* pilots to accurately steer to a predetermined target without visual reference. Orita admitted later in his Sixth Fleet report that the bright navigation beacon on Mangejang Island had impressed him and was used for the final bearing for the *kaiten* launch from *I-47*. Because of the predawn darkness, there was little else for Orita to reference in offering a course for the *kaiten* pilots. The lack of other landmarks was a serious handicap, and without a doubt affected the mission. At Ulithi, the *kaiten* pilots' opportunities for finding targets diminished; at least two of the four *I-47* pilots seemed to have become disoriented.[11] They were forced to search for unfamiliar channels in darkness, a most difficult task.

The mood was apprehensive aboard the Japanese I-class submarines, as crews hoped for success for the *kaiten* pilots and also for their own survival. Moments ticked by, each one feeling like hours, as the tension mounted for the men of *I-47* and *I-36*. Mission commander Orita had come to some kind of peace with his difficult decision to launch young men to their deaths, but he wanted to know their fate, and he had yet to safely return his men to the homeland.

CHAPTER 14

Death at Ulithi

They fought together as brothers in arms; they died together and now they sleep side by side . . . To them, we have a solemn obligation.

—Admiral Chester Nimitz, U.S. Navy,
of those who died in the war in the Pacific

On November 20, 1944, at 0418 an explosion erupted with a soaring flash of light on a reef a half mile south of Pugelug Island at the southern end of Ulithi Atoll. Before sailing, the survey ship USS *Sumner* was waiting for the first rays of light on November 20, when the blast suddenly blinded the lookouts who had been straining to pierce the inky black of the equatorial night for signs of the enemy. Lieutenant Commander Irving Johnson, *Sumner*'s captain, was jolted as shock waves violently shook his ship. He immediately reported the event to Commodore Carter aboard the flagship USS *Prairie*.[1]

Explosions were commonplace, so neither the Atoll Command nor Commodore Carter seemed overly concerned. It appears they initially surmised that the current had carried an undiscovered Japanese mine onto the reef and the wave action had detonated it. Eventually it would be discovered that a *kaiten* had exploded on the reef, either a tragic accident for the pilot or a deliberate detonation he decided to implement when his mission looked hopeless.

Slowly the dark receded, and the sun creased the horizon at dawn and began to glint off the waves. The temperature soared to eighty-four degrees. Soft tropical breezes floated across the deck of the *Mississinewa* swinging at anchor directly in the center of Mugai Channel, the broad entrance of Ulithi Lagoon. Just before dawn came the usual sound of the master at arms beating the stanchion rail with a pipe, rudely awakening the sailors precisely at 0530.

"Reveille. Reveille. Hit the deck." Sailors jumped out of their hammocks, but a couple, Bill Brzykcy and Bill Janas, fell back asleep on their makeshift bunks. A very few minutes later they would be shaken awake and dumped on the deck by a death blow to the ship.

Sekio Nishina, cocooned in his *kaiten* and moving through Zau Channel, had entered Ulithi Lagoon under cover of darkness, through a place that had no submarine nets for protection. He moved through the water going about twelve knots per hour, a steady pace, assuming he found his reference points easily. Sighting a cluster of ships before him, he headed for the tall masts and conning towers, expecting a warship to be his prize. He was on a collision course with the *Mississinewa*.

Now the man who had designed the very death weapon that would kill him had come face-to-face with his destiny. Sekio Nishina was twenty-one years old, and he was ready to sacrifice himself so that others might live. Exhilaration and fear churned his stomach and made his heart pound. Yet the intense hours of his training in Yokuyama Bay took over. Like the samurai warriors before him, he would die by the code of *Bushidō*. His worst fear was not dying—it was dying without accomplishing his mission. All his training and experience was of great value in the currency of war, and it was measured against the value of an enemy capital warship.

"I must not fail," he must have thought, and surely he repeated his wish: "The Emperor will reign ten thousand years." He reached to his upper left to adjust the pitch of his diving planes. Slowly, edging dangerously close to the surface, he cranked the stubby periscope above the water, praying he would see a target.

Targets proved to be plentiful. The calm waters inside Ulithi Atoll, revealing its holdings in the brightening daylight, sheltered the largest naval fleet the world had ever seen. The deep-water anchorage of the lagoon circled by thirty small islands held hundreds of ships, gathered for the final drive against Japan's home islands.

Nishina couldn't know it, but many ships had left earlier that morning as he was speeding toward the lagoon. In the early morning darkness at 0448, Task Group 57.9 had gotten under way for a sortie to Saipan. The three cruisers *Chester*, *Pensacola* and *Salt Lake City*, escorted by destroyers *Dunlap*, *Fanning*, *Cummings* and *Case*, made up the task group. They sailed past the Mugai Channel entrance buoy just before sunrise, and the destroyers fanned out to create an antisubmarine screen for the cruisers.[2]

Outside the lagoon, at 0523 the minesweeper USS *Vigilance* steamed past the net buoys that marked Mugai Channel. The ship was thirteen hundred yards south of the entrance when a lookout spotted a periscope wake seven hundred yards off the ship's starboard quarter. The wake was fifteen yards long with a prominent bulge on the forward end; its trajectory indicated the submerged object was moving at a speed of seven to ten knots toward the buoys at the channel entrance. The wake appeared for five seconds, disappeared, and then reappeared for another three seconds.

Vigilance immediately notified *Cummings* by flashing signal lamp of the submarine's position, turned to starboard and increased its speed, while the crew rushed to battle stations and set depth charges for a shallow attack. By the time *Vigilance* reversed course, the wake had disappeared. Sound gear failed to pick up a clear echo because of the noise generated by patrolling destroyers.

Vigilance flashed a signal to *Cummings* warning of the submarine's suspected position. Moments later, as *Cummings*'s TBS radio signaled a possible intruder, lookouts on *Chester* spotted the periscope wake at 0532.

Nine minutes had passed since *Vigilance* first sighted the water disturbance. *Case* reported the target as a submarine of the midget type, and warned the task group commander by TBS radio that the submarine was close to *Chester*'s starboard beam. The sub periscope swung toward *Case* and made a turn inside the destroyer's own turning circle before it passed along the ship's starboard side at an estimated speed of fifteen to twenty knots. The attacker made several more radical turns to port at high speed, as if it were lining up for a shot at *Chester*. *Case* continued to turn with the submerged vessel, still believing it to be a midget submarine. It was actually one of *I-47*'s four *kaiten*, piloted probably by Fukuda, who had been assigned to create a diversion at the entrance to the channel.

The Japanese pilot kept his periscope trained on *Chester*. *Case* grabbed the opportunity and rammed the submersible, hitting it on the port side just abaft the small conning tower, at a speed of more than fifteen knots. The craft broke apart cleanly, the two halves drifting down the port and starboard sides of the destroyer. The destroyer's crew reported oil, smoky vapor and loose debris, along with a large amount of escaping air and finally a deep rumbling sound as the *kaiten* sank.

The sinking of the *kaiten* at 0538 barely two miles south of the Mugai Channel entrance sounded the alarm. TBS radios aboard the American vessels anchored throughout the harbor spread the word of Japanese midget submarines possibly attempting to penetrate the lagoon. Indeed, the safety of the lagoon had already been breached.

———————

A drama starring a different *kaiten* was about to play itself out within the coral atoll. The *kaiten* that had penetrated to the central part of the inner harbor near Mangejang Island was piloted by Sekio Nishina, who had successfully found his way in darkness to the Zau Channel, which was his entry into the lagoon. Even now he coursed through the gentle waves toward the vast cluster of ships.

On one of the harbor ships, the oiler *Cache*, the officer of the deck reported a swirl in the water. The disturbance occurred between *Cache* and a floating beacon on Roriparakku Shoal, with a bearing approximately 310 degrees true at a distance of four hundred yards. Lieutenant Commander Coleman Cosgrove watched the tiny maelstrom. He saw a periscope rise and sink three times, each time visible for a scant three seconds.

At the same time aboard *Lackawanna*, a tiny wake feathering the water startled the bow watch lookout, Jimmie King. Glancing at his watch, he saw it was just after 0530. "A periscope," he screamed, lunging for the phone near his watch station to call the officer of the deck, Lieutenant Milford Romanoff. He reported "something in the water off the port quarter, could be a periscope or it could be a stick floating." Romanoff notified the captain.

"Keep an eye on it," Captain Homan growled, annoyed that the twenty-three-year-old officer had disturbed his sleep.[3] Returning to the bridge, Romanoff spotted the periscope and tracked the tiny wake as the feather moved slowly across the ship's bow, heading for the starboard side of the oiler *Mississinewa*, anchored eight hundred yards away. Romanoff shivered.

Linus Hawkins, a bridge lookout on *Lackawanna*, watched two ships exit Mugai Channel at high speed, the cruiser *Chester* and the destroyer *Case*. After hearing the bow lookout's frantic call, he studied the waves to see if he could spot the periscope's wake. Minutes later, the destroyer *Case* alerted the command center that it had rammed an enemy submarine just outside Mugai Channel. All ships were instantly alerted that enemy intruders were trying to penetrate the lagoon.

Romanoff reported the second periscope sighting to the captain and returned to the bridge, scanning for the periscope track with his binoculars, sighting it for a third and fourth time. The TBS radio crackled with destroyers reporting their frenzied searches outside the channel entrance. He sensed something big was about to happen. He drew in his breath and felt a chill, despite the mild tropical breeze.

Sekio Nishina peered into the eyepiece as his periscope broke the surface of the water. It was time to make the decision that would end his life. More depth charge explosions boomed in the water, shaking the hull. He had only a few seconds to select his target. A mammoth oiler loomed ahead, so large it filled Nishina's periscope glass.

His last view was the numeral 59 painted on the starboard bow as he took his final bearing on the tanker's midships superstructure. *Mississinewa*, laden with 404,000 gallons of aviation gasoline and a full load of bunker fuel oil for the fleet, rode low in the water, a "fat lady" now. The oiler was a floating bomb. He quickly cranked down his periscope, retracting the eyepiece inside the cramped torpedo.

Nishina reached for the handle above his head to increase speed, and the *kaiten* surged forward at a depth of fifteen feet below the water's surface. The oxygen flow to the oxygen/kerosene motors increased, propelling the underwater missile ever faster toward its victim. Death was certain now. Nishina would honor his emperor.

"Torpedo wake," a sailor yelled aboard the nearby oiler *Nantahala*. The chief in the bridge decoding room heard him and ran out just in time to spot the submarine's wake passing astern.

Nishina's killer weapon worked as he had planned.[4] The cache of 3,418 pounds of explosives detonated as his vessel slammed into the starboard side of *Mississinewa*'s hull and ignited the number 3 starboard wing tank. The resulting fireball shot skyward, engulfing the forward half of the oiler in a swirling kaleidoscope of red, orange and yellow tongues of flame. Ships' logs around the harbor mostly agreed on the time, recorded as 0545. Seconds after the *kaiten* struck the hull and started the first fire, the flames encountered the volatile gasoline fumes of hundred-octane aviation fuel stored in the number 3 centerline tank and blew up with a tumultuous roar.

The *Mighty Miss* erupted in a fireball of molten metal and burning oil, a spectacle of horror witnessed for miles.

Death claimed sailors who had little choice for escape except leaping into water sheathed in flaming oil. Men wearing life jackets succumbed to the advancing wall of flame. Swimmers could not outrace the burning oil spreading in flashpoints from the ruptured hull. Men swimming in the water without life jackets ducked under the oily flames, reappearing repeatedly, surfacing for air. Many miraculously escaped through the burning oil, many did not. At the same time the aftermath of the fire was unfolding on the *Miss*, destroyers and destroyer escorts circled within the anchorage on the hunt for more submarines. They dropped hundreds of depth charges, further endangering survivors in the water.

Everywhere in the harbor, officers and men on board ships were stunned by the catastrophe. In the weeks to follow, they remembered the first moments after the blast, where they were and what they saw, in official action reports and in their private diaries. Their recollections haunted them.

At the moment the *Mississinewa* blew up, *Lackawanna*'s cook Ulus Keeling was dumping the morning's garbage off the stern. He saw the oiler's deck heel over to port as the blast rocked the ship, and within seconds a red fireball engulfed the *Mississinewa* from the bow to the bridge amidships, throwing debris hundreds of feet into the air.[5] Keeling dropped the garbage can and raced for his 20mm gun battle station. General quarters began sounding on ships throughout the harbor, and the lagoon was filled with frenzied activity on board every vessel.

Keeling reached his 20mm mount in time to see his own ship's launch already under way and heading toward the stricken oiler; the launch had already gotten halfway toward the burning oil spreading out from *Mississinewa*'s port side. Black smoke billowed in large rolls thousands of feet into the sky, blotting out the morning sun. The oiler was already listing to port. Without hesitation, small boats from nearby oilers headed toward the fire scene to begin rescue. Keeler sent up a silent prayer as he watched *Mississinewa* sailors abandon the burning ship: "Save these men, Lord."

Lackawanna's quartermaster Stanley Grimes, posted on the early morning watch, had listened to the ship's radio as *Case* reported chasing a midget submarine outside Mugai Channel. Dismissing the report, Grimes encouraged signalman Chris Wettingheller to send a Morse code blinker message to *Kankakee* to arrange a beer party on Mog Mog Island later in the day. Grimes was peeriing through the scope, his attention focused on the *Kankakee*'s bridge, when his eyeglass went black. It was a skyful of black cloud from an undetermined ship.

Thinking Wettingheller had played a joke on him, he growled, "You son of a bitch!" but a few seconds later he was jolted by the explosion and realized it was smoke from the oiler. He trained his glass on the mushrooming fireball and saw a sight he'd never forget: *Mississinewa*'s bow watch sailor was catapulted seventy-five feet in the air, rifle still slung over his shoulder.

Also on board *Lackawanna*, water tender Joe Fello had been midway through his 0400–0800 fire room watch when *Mississinewa* was hit. At the alarm sounding, he lit off the second boiler to raise steam in case the ship needed to get under way. "What's going on?" Fello asked in the now-crowded room, but no one answered him. He asked the engineering officer what was happening topside to cause such alarm.

"What in the hell is wrong with you?" the officer angrily replied. "Go topside and see for yourself." Fello dashed out and saw the largest fire he had ever seen, tongues of flame and munitions popping like firecrackers on the spot where *Mississinewa* was anchored. The massive ship was shrouded in smoke that completely obscured the superstructure.

Navigator Lew Davies had felt the concussion as the *Miss* exploded. He raced to the bridge to take his next watch as officer of the deck, only to find Captain Homan screaming at the outgoing OOD, Lieutenant Romanoff, "Why didn't someone tell me? My God, why didn't someone tell me?" Homan yelled. No one answered. The question seemed ludicrous.

Looking in the direction of the burning tanker, Davies saw men abandoning ship over the stern. The TBS radio was nearly jammed with rapid-fire traffic now, most of the language in plain talk rather than code. A radioman with a Southern accent was excitedly describing midget subs that he said had invaded the harbor by hiding under the keel of U.S. ships.

Lackawanna was a blur of activity. Romanoff ordered, "Away all boats." Captain Homan, pacing the bridge, exploded in anger. "You gave an order to launch boats? You're going to send our men in there?" Homan waved his arms at the flaming *Mississinewa*. "I'll court-martial you, Romanoff," the captain snarled.

Romanoff, "scared silly," as he later admitted, turned away and watched survivors jump into Ulithi lagoon to escape the inferno. He left the bridge and headed for the fantail, where the launch and whaleboats prepared to leave for a rescue run. Although shaken by Homan's threats, he concentrated on getting the four *Lackawanna* boats under way to the scene of the fire a thousand yards away.

Fifty-nine oil-soaked survivors would owe their lives to Romanoff's brave decision to disobey his captain. By 0555 all four of *Lackawanna*'s boats had cleared the boat booms and been dispatched to the disaster scene to pick up survivors. Romanoff's men had responded quickly and courageously to the cry of "Away all boats!"

"We need a bow hook man!" someone yelled in the direction of shipfitter Jim Anson. He had reached his damage control station at *Lackawanna*'s bow CO_2 tanks when the voice grabbed his attention. Anson saw men jumping off the stricken *Mississinewa* into oil and flames. "Go ahead, Anson," someone said. "You've been a bow hook before. Get aft." Anson sprinted, and ran into fireman Jim Factor, who was racing through the rain of hot oil after being jolted awake on the fantail. Both sailors leapt into the small captain's gig and sped off toward *Mississinewa*.

Boatswain's mate Willie Potter had started making his rounds inside *Lackawanna*'s crew quarters just after 0530 reveille to awaken the crew. The sailor who slept right below him was always reluctant to get out of the sack, so Potter had dumped him on the deck; the pair might have squared off over the rude wakeup call, but the explosion abruptly changed their world. Both raced for their GQ stations. Potter arrived at his assigned 3-inch/50 stern mount only to hear Romanoff's order, "Away all boats," so he ran for *Lackawanna*'s forty-foot motor launch tied to the port side boom. Motor machinist's mate Earl Ertel was cleaning the bilge in the *Lackawanna* motor launch at that same moment. They scrambled down the boarding ladder and raced at flank speed through the water toward *Mississinewa*.

Bill Depoy recalled the sickening sight of orange flames rising from *Mississinewa*. Heading for his GQ station as a loader on the port side bow mount, he got there just as the public address system squawked, "Away all boats." That command triggered his next assignment: bow hook for the motor launch. Running to the stern, he found the engineer and coxswain already taking duty. As they approached the burning oiler, the three men peered beneath the smoke and saw heads bobbing in the oily water. Their challenge now was rescuing those struggling survivors.

Cory Jaramillo, a *Lackawanna* yeoman, saw the fire and worried about his close friend Art Jaramillo, who had transferred to *Mississinewa* a few months earlier. The two men were unrelated, but both had grown up in New Mexico, twenty miles apart. Shipmates had often teased Cory about favoring his "brother" with snacks from the galley. Now Cory ran to the fantail, arriving in time to jump aboard Willie Potter's launch. As Potter steered, Cory scanned the water for any sign of his friend.

Approaching the fire scene, rescuers watched as some fortunate *Mississinewa* sailors escaped the flames and explosions while entering the water. The boat crews picked up several oil-blackened and burned survivors. Cory was relieved to see Art Jaramillo in the water and

USS *Mississinewa* (*AO-59*) at anchor in Hampton Roads, Virginia, on May 25, 1944. The ship's total service life would be a short six months and two days from the date of commissioning until its demise at the hands of Japan's new secret weapon *kaiten* at the U.S. Navy Third Fleet anchorage, Ulithi Atoll, Western Caroline Islands.

National Archives

USS *Cimarron* (*AO-22*) fueling an unidentified U.S. Navy warship using the "broadside" fueling method. The *Cimarron* was the first of the new T3 fast oilers capable of keeping up with the fleet in the Pacific. Note the "white water" between oiler and warship, as both vessels fuel at a speed of ten knots to avoid attack by enemy submarines.

National Archives

Lt. Commander Philip G. Beck poses with *Mississinewa* officers and enlisted sailors in dress uniform for a formal photograph at Pearl Harbor in July 1944.

Photo courtesy of Philip G. Beck and Steve Panoff

Lt. Commander Philip G. Beck, captain of USS *Mississinewa* (*AO-59*).

Courtesy of Philip G. Beck and Steven Panoff

Simon "Sid" Harris, Storekeeper Second Class, USS *Munsee* (*ATF-107*). Harris took thirty-seven dramatic photos of USS *Mississinewa* (*AO-59*) in its death throes. Sid's photos were carefully studied by the *Mississinewa* discovery team led by Chip Lambert, providing the vital link to the past that allowed the dive team to locate the wreck of the long-lost *Miss* on April 6, 2001.

Photo courtesy of Sid Harris

Florian "Bill" Brzykcy, Fireman Second Class. *Courtesy of Florian "Bill" Brzykcy*

John A. Mair Jr., Fireman Second Class. *Courtesy of John Mair Jr.*

Raymond G. Fulleman, Water Tender Second Class. *Courtesy of Raymond Fulleman*

Robert Vulgamore, Fireman First Class. *Courtesy of Robert Vulgamore*

Aboard the *Miss*, King Neptune (Frank Lutz, CCS) and his Royal Court deviously planned the initiation of the unfortunate Pollywogs, allowing them to become respected Shellbacks joining the Ancient Order of the Deep. The *Miss* crossed the equator on August 23, 1944, celebrating a centuries-old naval tradition that continued even in wartime. The initiation—part fun, part humiliation—certainly became a memorable experience for all sailors who endured the ceremony to become Shellbacks.

Courtesy of Margaret Pence Howell

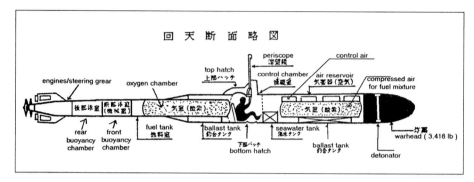

回 天 断 面 略 図

periscope 潜望鏡

top hatch 上部ハッチ

control chamber 後部室

control air

air reservoir 気蓄器（空気）

compressed air for fuel mixture

engines/steering grear

oxygen chamber

気室（酸素）

rear buoyancy chamber

front buoyancy chamber

fuel tank 燃料室

ballast tank 釣合タンク

seawater tank 海水タンク

気室（酸素）

warhead (3.418 lb)

bottom hatch 下部ハッチ

ballast tank 釣合タンク

detonator

Kaiten Type I drawing by U.S. Naval Technical Mission to Japan, April 1946, showing the major components of the manned torpedo by intelligence analysts.

*National Archives 000245 US Naval Technical Mission to Japan-
April 1946-U.S. Navy World War II Technical Intelligence-O-01-1 2 3-Japanese T~1*

Two Type I *kaiten* are cradled in V-shaped blocks forward of the bridge of an IJN I-Class fleet submarine. The bands securing the manned torpedoes to the deck were released from inside the hull. Two *kaiten* were secured in the same manner aft of the bridge.

Courtesy of Kaiten Memorial Museum, Japan

Oily black smoke billows skyward as fleet tug USS *Munsee* (*ATF-107*) steams southwest at flank speed to reach the stricken *Mississinewa*. *Courtesy of Sid Harris*

AP wire service photograph by Joe Rosenthal shows USS *Mississinewa* ablaze November 20, 1944. Rosenthal later took the famous photo of U.S. Marines raising the flag on Mt. Suribachi during the battle of Iwo Jima. *National Archives*

Tons of water from USS *Munsee (ATF-107)* fire hoses douses the 55-gallon lube oil drums on *Mississinewa's* cargo deck amidship as Harris takes this photo from high on his tug's bridge. USS *Mississinewa* booms are barely visible through the dense black smoke that envelops the sinking oiler. Lube oil drums caught fire and careened off the cargo deck like Roman candles. Survivors in the water feared for their lives as lube oil drums splashed among them, killing Chief Water Tender James "Smitty" Smith.
Courtesy of Sid Harris

Mississinewa rolls to port at 0825, slipping from sight. Sid Harris was loading film in his 35mm camera as the *Mississinewa* began the final roll to port, then capsized. Harris spun around and clicked the shutter without looking through the viewfinder—that photograph would prove to be the most dramatic image of the day's events.
Courtesy of Sid Harris

Ceremony for a sortie: Ensign Mizui receives a short sword prior to his mission with *kaiten* group "Tamon" on July 18, 1945.

Courtesy of Kaiten Memorial Museum, Japan

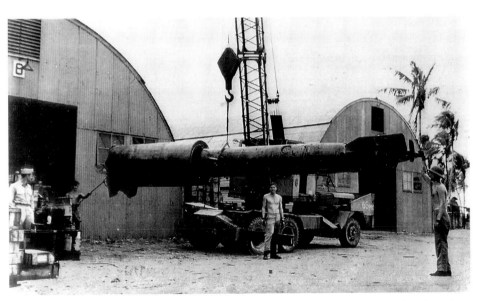

The Type I *kaiten* recovered from the reef south of Pugelug Island is shown dangling from a crane at Ulithi. The 3,418-pound warhead and pilot's cabin amidships are missing. *Kaiten* co-inventor Sub. Lt. Sekio Nishina had hoped Japan's new secret weapon would never be revealed to U.S. forces. The decimated weapon's remains discovered after the November 20, 1944, sinking of the *Mississinewa* revealed Japan's "Heaven Shaker" for the first time. Only after the occupation of Japan did the U.S. Navy discover the true nature of the *kaiten*'s destructive force.

National Archives

Chip Lambert with wife, Pam, and Pat Scannon after first dive to the *Mississinewa* on April 6, 2001.

Courtesy of Chip Lambert

Oil tank baffles from No. 3 starboard wing tank litter the sandy bottom of Ulithi lagoon on *Mississinewa*'s starboard side where Nishina's *kaiten* struck the oiler. The explosive force of the 3,418-pound warhead, combined with the explosion in No. 3 centerline AV gas tank full of 100-octane fumes, broke the ship from the well deck to the keel. The debris in the center of the photo was not from *Mississinewa*, according to Chip Lambert; the round shape of the metal housing and what appears to be a screw cage guard indicates the debris is a remnant of the kaiten stern drive propulsion unit. During the 2013 dive, no evidence of debris was found on the starboard side of the bow where the *kaiten* struck, probably due to the shifting sand on the sea floor of Ulithi lagoon.

Courtesy of Chip Lambert

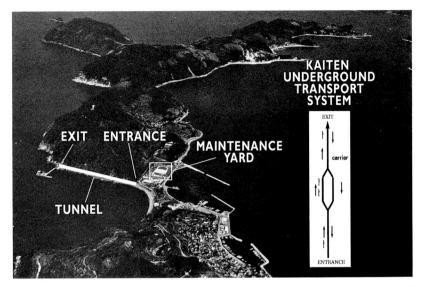

KAITEN
UNDERGROUND
TRANSPORT
SYSTEM

EXIT   ENTRANCE   MAINTENANCE
YARD

TUNNEL

Kaiten were loaded aboard a carrier in the maintenance yard and transported by rail through a tunnel system exiting at the pier for "wet" training. The tunnel concealed the rail system from U.S. reconnaissance aircraft.

Photo of rail system courtesy of Masami Ono

A Type I *kaiten* is lowered into Tokuyama Bay for "wet" training.

Courtesy of Kaiten Memorial Museum, Japan

Kaiten co-inventor Sub. Lt. Sekio Nishina (left) and Lt. Yoshinori Kamibeppu.

Courtesy of Kaiten Memorial Museum, Japan

Chief Oka, *I-47*, presented this sketch in soft pencil to the *kaiten* pilots depicting a U.S. carrier broken in two after being struck by a kaiten. The four *kaiten* pilots signed the sketch aboard *I-47* the night before the Kikusui attack on Ulithi Atoll; Nishina wrote "*Gochin*," meaning "sunk instantly."

Courtesy of Kaiten Memorial Museum, Japan

(Left to right) *Kaiten* pilots Ensign Akira Sato, Sub. Lt. Sekio Nishina, Sub. Lt. Hitoshi Fukuda, and Ens. Kozo Watanabe were carried to their Ulithi launch point by *I-47*.

Courtesy of Kaiten Memorial Museum, Japan

(Left to right) *Kaiten* pilots Ens. Taichi Imanishi, Sub. Lt. Kazuhisa Toyozumi, Sub. Lt. Kentaro Yoshimoto, and Ens. Yoshihiko Kudo were carried to their Ulithi launch point by *I-36*.   *Courtesy of Kaiten Memorial Museum, Japan*

I-47 kaiten pilots and crew waved their caps in a traditional farewell gesture on November 9, 1944, as the submarine departed Kure with four *kaiten* strapped to the deck. Note the Kiku-sui crest painted on the bridge of *I-47*.   *Courtesy of Kaiten Memorial Museum, Japan*

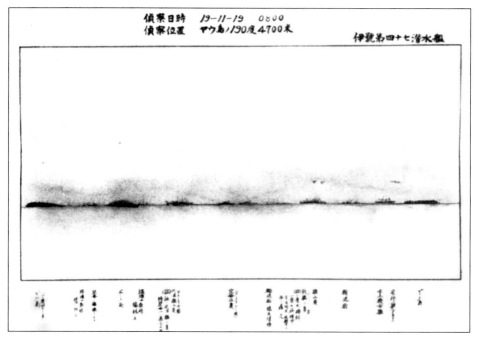

偵察日時 19-11-19 0800
偵察位置 ヤウ島ノ190度4700米

伊號第四十七潜水艦

Japanese fleet submarines were not equipped with periscope cameras, thus this historic *I-47* reconnaissance sketch of Ulithi Atoll on November 19, 1944, is extremely rare.

Courtesy of Kaiten Memorial Museum, Japan

Lt. Toshiharu Konada (1945). Toshiharu Konada was the founder of kaiten-kai in 1962. Konada formed the group as a "self-help" group for *kaiten* pilots, who were committing suicide at an alarming rate after being trained for a one-way "death mission." Kaiten-kai evolved into a memorial and reunion association over the years.

Courtesy of Kaiten Memorial Museum and Toshiharu Konada

Ensign Taichi Imanishi had been an economics student at Keio University before entering the Navy. The Japanese characters were drawn in his own handwriting. Imanishi was the only *kaiten* pilot to successfully launch from *I-36*. Imanishi touched off an intensive anti-submarine hunt within the atoll by U.S. forces after he penetrated the eastern anti-submarine net west of Mas Islet. His body was recovered on November 23, a few days after the attack, in the area where Third Fleet carriers, battleships and cruisers anchored.

Courtesy of Kaiten Memorial Museum, Japan

Author Mike Mair made six scuba dives on the wreck of the USS *Mississinewa* (AO-59) at Ulithi Atoll in July 2013. Mair poses with the starboard 3-inch 50-deck gun that is encrusted with hard coral, showing only the barrel of the weapon. Note the circular gun tub. The depth is approximately 125 feet. *Courtesy of Mark Hanna*

USS *Mississinewa* (*AO-59*) Reunion, Corpus Christi, Texas—1999 (seated, left to right), John Bayak, Ed Kinsler, Larry Glaser, Fred Schaufus, Andrew Johnson, Winston Whitten, Harold Ritchie, Bill Gimmeson, Al Bell, John Mair, John D'Anna, Fernando Cuevas, James Lewis. (back row, left to right) Robert Jones, Earl Givens, Ray Fulleman, Earl Van Orden, Jim Cunningham, Gus Liveakos, James "J. P." Hammond, Fred Caplinger.   *Photo courtesy of Mike Mair*

Marshall Doak, CPhM, USS *Arapaho* (*ATF-68*). Mr. Doak, Chief Pharmacists Mate aboard the fleet tug *Arapaho* was assigned the task of sinking flotsam within Mugai Channel that could pose a hazard to navigation. *Arapaho* placed a small boat in the water, and sailors proceeded to sink floating debris with rifle fire. One object bobbed in the water within 100 yards of where the *Mississinewa* had sunk. CPhM Doak pulled the badly disfigured body of *kaiten* co-inventor Sub. Lt. Sekio Nishina from the oily waters of Ulithi lagoon.

Courtesy of Marshall Doak

hoisted him into the launch. A wall of flame enveloped other men attempting to swim away from the danger, but their life jackets slowed them down. The onrushing flames engulfed them. The image haunted their would-be rescuers.

———

All around *Mississinewa*, the fleet was now at general quarters, with every man at his battle station. Explosions of U.S. Navy depth charges banged through the hull, sounding like thunderclaps to the crew. *Tallulah* had a boiler shut down for repair, but even so the skipper ordered a change of berths in order to distance the ship from the flaming tanker. The engine room relayed the message to the fire room, where water tenders sweated and swore at the uncooperative boiler.

Oil from the sky peppered seamen on deck as they scanned the skies. Scuttlebutt was rampant and all about doom. Even though the official word from the bridge said that all hands aboard *Mississinewa* had survived, not a man watching the blazing ship could believe that.

———

On USS *Sepulga*, sailor Bernard Beavin watched flames scampering up and licking the *Mississinewa*'s masthead. It was the precursor to the next eruption of aviation gas. He sensed a Japanese attack. The loudspeaker announced "Whaleboat away," and within moments a small craft cut a wake through the calm waters, headed at flank speed for the furiously burning oiler off the starboard side. He watched with a feeling of admiration at the bravery of the boat crews that steered directly into the flames as they sought survivors.

Twenty-one-year-old Ensign George Stefanco (Stevens) stood on *Sepulga*'s deck and felt a rush of air against his backside. He turned around in time to hear an earsplitting blast and see a billowing redorange fireball engulfing *Mississinewa*. Deck plates shuddered under his feet from frequent depth charge explosions. A destroyer escort sent 40mm shells over *Sepulga*'s stern that barely cleared the tanker's stack.

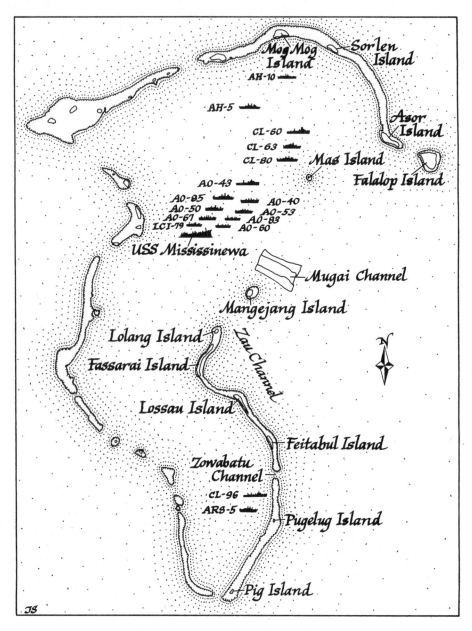

Location of Key U.S. Navy Ships, Ulithi Atoll, November, 20, 1944

The islands of Ulithi Atoll with the berthing location of key U.S. Navy ships anchored in Ulithi lagoon on November 20, 1944.

MAP BY JACK SCOTT.

Although the escort was responding to the possible sub sighting, the overanxious gun crews were unable to depress their weapons enough to reach the suspected target. The destroyer escort dropped several depth charges over the stern close to *Sepulga*, blowing one hundred rivets out of the old tanker's hull.

Two dozen sailors bobbing in oil-covered water struggled to swim away from the oiler's starboard side, but the burning oil patch moved faster than they could. In seconds the flame engulfed the swimmers. When it was gone, not one reappeared at the water's surface.

That morning seaman John Sidebottom on the USS *Enoree* had been sleeping in his hammock under a 5-inch/38 mount. The explosion woke him and five other sailors sleeping nearby. Once on deck the group scanned the sky for enemy planes and raced for their battle stations. Sidebottom arrived at his battle station on the bow 3-inch/50 mount in time to see Eugene Cooley dive overboard from *Mississinewa*'s bow. Sidebottom learned later that he had witnessed the escape of the only sailor forward of *Mississinewa*'s bridge who survived.

Across the lagoon, on Falalop Island, several miles to the northeast, a mailman's mate jumped out from the mail tent as he heard a loud explosion. The time was 0545. He saw a bright flash in the center of Mugai Channel, and it was instantly followed by a pillar of dense black smoke rising hundreds of feet into the air.[6] The mushrooming cloud billowed up from Mugai Channel, and he would learn later it was the oiler *Mississinewa*. Navy F6F Hellcat fighters and Marine F4U Corsairs parked on the crushed coral runway on Falalop began to warm up with a throaty roar as pilots rushed to get into the air and find the Japanese attackers.

Officers on the *Cache* reported at 0547 a violent underwater explosion forward of the midship house on the *Mississinewa* and saw the ship burst into flames. It was the approximate time the *kaiten* had slammed into the oiler's hull. The *Cache* immediately called away fire and rescue party and all boats; it also sounded general quarters and all stations manned and ready. The intensity and rapid spread of the flames made a fire-and-rescue party impracticable, so all boats were instead dispatched to assist in picking up survivors of the *Mississinewa*.

———————

Aboard the fleet tug *Munsee* riding at anchor two miles northeast of *Mississinewa*, Simon "Sid" Harris woke up to the blast. Immediately the gangway watchman raced through the crew's quarters yelling, "All hands up!" The twenty-year-old rolled his sleeves down for protection against flash burns and headed on the double for his battle station on the bridge, where he operated the communications and relayed commands from Captain Pingley. The tug roared at flank speed toward the column of black smoke, while the crew readied the fire pumps, salvage pumps and firefighting gear.

Harris, the tug's recreation director, had acquired a camera months before for the crew's use. As the *Munsee* went to general quarters and raced off to fight *Mississinewa*'s fires, he had just come off his watch. Standing on the bridge, he asked the commanding officer if he could photograph the episode. Permission granted, he snapped thirty-seven breathtaking images of the oiler's demise.[7] As he took pictures in rapid succession, he saw the explosion when the 5-inch/38 gun magazine on the *Miss* blew up at 0605, and he captured it on film. At the same moment, submerged deep in the waters off Ulithi, submarine *I-36* recorded the explosion by hydrophone monitoring, recorded as occurring at exactly 0605.

Joseph Rosenthal, an Associated Press photographer on board the carrier *Ticonderoga*, captured on film the death throes of *Mississinewa*. His pictures would make the front pages of American newspapers a month later when the Navy cleared them for release.[8] Later in the Pacific War Rosenthal became a photographic legend when he took one of the most famous war photos of all time—the classic shot of U.S. Marines raising the American flag on Iwo Jima in 1945.

Before dawn, sailors aboard the cruiser *Santa Fe* had hoisted a Kingfisher floatplane from the deck at 0525 in preparation for the daily antisubmarine patrol above Ulithi. Lieutenant Blase Zamucen was the pilot, with aviation radioman third class Russell Evinrude as his passenger. [9] Daylight would come within minutes. The light cruiser went to readiness III, sunrise phase condition, as the aircrew taxied out into open water and took off. Only minutes after the Kingfisher took off, the radio buzzed on the bridge of *Santa Fe* as it relayed the news of a periscope sighting.

The floatplane had been in the air fifteen minutes when *Mississinewa* exploded. Zamucen would perform extraordinary acts of heroism that day, but for many it would be years before they learned the name of the man who saved them from the burning oil slick surrounding the crippled oiler.

CHAPTER 15

Escape

When the Kaitens are released to begin their attacks, the targeted ships are far, far away. The pilots try desperately to overtake them. They fail. They're alone in the middle of the Pacific Ocean. It's possible to open the hatch and climb out. But what would you do in the middle of the Pacific? I believe they thought it better just to blow themselves up.

—Naoji Kozu[1]

Southeast of Ulithi, the Japanese submariners aboard *I-36* waited patiently for word about the success of Ensign Imanishi's *kaiten* launched earlier in the direction of Mas Island. Three of *I-36*'s *kaiten* never launched at all. After Imanishi's departure in the first *kaiten*, pilots Yoshimoto and Toyozumi had attempted to launch, but their craft were found to be jammed in the V-shaped wooden cradles on deck and could not be released. Angry and shamed at the failure, they screamed and swore, their sounds heard loudly by the men in the mother submarine; they crawled out of their disabled *kaiten* and reentered the submarine through the access tubes that connected the *kaiten* escape hatch to the submarine's interior. Both men were sobbing, deeply distraught at their lost opportunity.[2]

The fourth *kaiten*, where sat the cramped pilot Kudo, also failed to launch, apparently for the same malfunction. Since his craft had not been fitted with an inside access tube, the unlucky pilot was forced to remain in his *kaiten* until the captain deemed it safe to surface; only at that time could he be released and taken inside the mother submarine. With destroyers circling everywhere, it was terribly risky to surface, and he waited for some hours in his tight quarters. Captain Teramoto risked detection later when he surfaced to retrieve Ensign Kudo. He found the pilot bitterly disappointed and feeling shamed, like the other two pilots who were already freed from their *kaiten* and back inside the submarine. He joined them, crushed at the foiled crusade, his dreams of glory for the empire destroyed.

Commander Teramoto dived *I-36* to periscope depth and ordered the sonar operator to listen for explosions. They recorded one explosion at 0545 and another at 0605; both appeared to come from south of Mog Mog Island. "Ensign Imanishi scored a hit," they concluded exultantly. The excited crew quietly exchanged congratulations, but the celebration was short-lived. A deafening noise indicated that a depth charge was close, the first of more than a hundred that rained down on their submarine. Teramoto dived deep to escape.

The mood grew tense as the sound operator estimated the distance from the succession of exploding depth charges. None were yet very close to *I-36*, but that was little consolation to the Japanese, as the next round of depth charges could crush the submarine's fragile hull, its one weakness.

———

At 0555 Commodore Worrall R. Carter, the commander of Service Squadron Ten, directed rescue operations by voice radio from his office aboard the destroyer tender *Prairie*. The fire rooms and engine rooms aboard every ship at Ulithi frantically worked up steam to evacuate the harbor. Oilers and station tankers close to the stricken *Mississinewa* began to weigh anchor as smoke, flame and exploding ammunition threatened their ships.

As the senior officer at Ulithi, Carter was responsible for the safety of fleet units and vessels. Assuming, as most commanding officers did, that they had been attacked by a midget submarine, the fear of more lurking in Ulithi Lagoon was the uppermost concern in Carter's mind. It would be a few days or weeks before the U.S. Navy fully understood what type of craft had actually brought down the *Mississinewa*; the discovery of the new Japanese *kaiten* weapon was made later. It would be longer still before that discovery was widely acknowledged, even in military circles.

In the minutes after the *Miss* erupted in flames, U.S. Navy destroyers and destroyer escorts made a frenzied search for midget submarines in the lagoon, weaving through the Third Fleet anchorage as they dropped depth charges.[3] Although they dropped them one at a time rather than in a pattern, to avoid damaging ships' hulls, nevertheless damage occurred to various ships, and the blasts repeatedly shocked and jarred small boats attempting to rescue survivors, who were further traumatized by the frequent shock vibrations the charges created in the depths of the lagoon.

Officers and sailors now on high alert at Ulithi knew the burning *Mississinewa* was the result of enemy action. Obviously it was an attack by Japan, who had feared the United States would gain the upper hand with the strategic value of Ulithi as an advance base. They did not know that the Imperial Navy had fielded a top-secret suicide weapon unlike any previous torpedo or submarine, although within a few days it would become clear that *kaiten* manned torpedoes had caused the attack at Ulithi.

While Carter and others speculated on the dangers to come, fire swept down the starboard side of *Mississinewa* and bunker oil spread out from the hull in a layer six inches thick. Floating on top of the heavy fuel was hundred-octane AV gas, acting as a wick and igniting the fuel.

Billowing greasy smoke obscured the tanker from observers. Spreading flames engulfed the starboard side at the waterline, threatening to curl around the fantail.

A slight breeze shifted the burning ship, slowing the spreading oil and flames on the port side, and the aft port quarter suddenly offered escaping sailors a moment to reach open water. Flames rose higher than the masthead. A column of smoke rose and rolled out like a mushroom in the sky.

Captain Philip Beck had dozed in his bunk just before 0530 reveille, the last few moments of peace on his last morning as skipper of the *Mighty Miss*. Jolted awake by the first heavy explosion, Beck thought the impact came from the forward port side. Then the centerline tank explosion threw him against his cabin's aft bulkhead; he knew in a flash the ship was in terrible trouble.

Blowtorches of flame shot through the cabin portholes, forcing him to crawl along the deck to elude the tongues of fire; he crawled through choking heat to reach the passageway, where he found a sailor lying unconscious or dead. He dragged the man along the deck and down the ladder to the boat deck amidships. He found two enlisted men heading aft, away from the flames, and ordered them to put a life jacket on the unconscious man and throw him over the stern; it was his only chance for life. Beck then gave the word no captain wants to give: Abandon ship! He ordered the men to pass the word, as the PA system was inoperable.

To prevent more munitions explosions, he ordered chief gunner's mate Stewart Cass to flood the aft magazines. Cass attempted to reach the valves back in the butcher shop, but the heavy smoke forced him to retreat. Again he tried, burning his hands as he fought to open the wheel on the water valve, and again he had to retreat and report his failure to the captain. A magazine explosion would have dire consequences for *Mississinewa* and Beck knew it; he decided to hose down the ready ammunition boxes. He helped three men reel out a fire hose

into the passageway, but the line had no water pressure. As the four
exhausted officers lay on the deck to catch their breath, the magazine
blew up. They hugged the deck and somehow survived.

The ship was doomed, burning furiously from amidships forward
and moderately from amidships aft. The bow was already under water.
Everything that could burn was on fire: hoses, lines, gun covers, lube
oil, cargo, deck gear.

Trying to avoid the flames, Beck made his way to the officers' quarters, yelling, "Abandon ship over the stern," but he saw no sign of life.
Clad only in his cotton pajama bottoms, he tore them off as the gar-
ment began to burn. Beck tried to open the main steam-smothering
valve to the cargo tanks in order to stem the raging fires, but debris,
fire, and the dangerous vapors escaping from broken steam lines prevented him from reaching the valve. He headed aft and reached the aft
crew quarters' starboard side hatch. Donning a life jacket, he headed
up to the stern port boat deck. The heat was unbearable.

The three men he'd left behind on the deck reappeared. Lieutenant
Stutzman, injured but still on his feet, joined Beck in the passageway.
Chief machinist's mate George Douning and Cass appeared with two
enlisted men. Doors and portholes to the port passageway were still
open; fortuitously Beck ordered the men to close them. They were just
in time. A massive explosion tore through the ship seconds later, evidently the aft 5-inch/38 ammunition magazine. Beck immediately
wondered if the center bunker, half-full of Navy special fuel oil, had
also exploded. The situation was grim, the scene surreal, as fire raged
and antiaircraft rounds blasted sightlessly in the heat. Beck, seeing that
the fire was out of control, told his companions to grab the two CO_2 fire
extinguishers to cool the deck, and they all raced for the poop deck,
where they would abandon the ship.

From their vantage point at the stern, they witnessed countless
scenes of horror and heroism being played out in the water.

Only one man on the ship's bow survived. At 0545 that morning
Eugene Cooley had awakened the moment his skivvies caught fire and

scorched his skin. He heard a dog's frantic barking coming from under the starboard 3-inch/50 mount and saw the ship's mascot, Salvo. A wave of flame swept over the starboard mount, causing Cooley to forget about saving the dog and find an escape route. The roar of flames behind him convinced the New York boy to abandon ship. Without hesitation, he dived headfirst from the bow into the flaming water. The cool salt water took away some of his fear, allowing him to remember basic water skills. He splashed the flames away, gulped for air, and dived deep, splashing again each time as he rose to the surface for a breath. At last he cleared the flames several yards from the bow, surfacing for the last time amid oil and roiling smoke. Cooley flipped over on his back, choking as his lungs ingested smoke, and nearly blind from oil that burned his eyes. *Mississinewa* had disappeared behind a black curtain. He distanced himself from the flare-ups caused by fresh AV gas feeding the fire and heard a voice through the din; a small boat from *Mascoma* suddenly appeared, and two pairs of hands hauled the exhausted boy aboard.[4]

At reveille Rocky DeMarco had been kicked awake by the chief, but before he could protest both men were slammed to the deck as the *Miss* blew up. They careened uncontrollably toward the edge of the cargo deck as the ship lurched. Arms and legs flailing, both men grasped for a stanchion rail to avoid falling to the well deck below. "Go to your fire station, sailor," screamed the chief. Headed for the bow, DeMarco collided with Lieutenant Stutzman, the Second Division officer, who was heading aft. "Where are you going, sailor? Get aft now," Stutzman yelled.

DeMarco reversed direction and found an open spot at the fantail rail. Men were jumping into the water without looking, landing on swimmers. Deadly flames closed in on swimmers clustered near the fantail, as burning oil crept farther aft along the starboard side. DeMarco took his chances and jumped, braving a swim under burning oil before clearing the flames. Exhausted, he floated for a moment to catch his breath before swimming away from the burning hull.

A voice hailed him through the smoke. Clinging oil made DeMarco nearly blind, but he made out the blurred image of an approaching boat. Someone tied a line around his arm to keep him afloat while other survivors critically in need of help were pulled into the boat first. A sailor noticed burns on DeMarco's back and yelled for help. Boat occupants yanked on his arms and legs until he fell into a heap in the bottom of the rescue craft. Two grievously burned shipmates moaned next to him. Oblivious to his burns, he felt a sense of relief surge through him.

In his haste to exit the crew's compartment, Frank Wilcox had slashed his bare feet on broken lantern glass littering the ladder steps and deck. Flames seared the left side of his face. Rushing up the ladder, he felt an explosion that drove red-hot shrapnel into his back just as he neared the safety of the poop deck. He staggered to the fantail rail, finding seaman Peter Moran frozen in fear, his knuckles white as he grasped the stanchion pipe.

"I can't swim. I can't swim," the frightened man wailed in panic. Wilcox reassured Moran, "I'll help. We have a better chance in the water. Look. The whaleboat's only fifty feet out from the stern." Wilcox struggled to loosen Moran's grip but to no avail. Moran's buddies, already treading water below, screamed and pleaded for him to jump. "You can make it, Pete," they kept saying. But no amount of begging could overcome Moran's fear of the water. The scene was repeated seconds later, as fire control man Jack Atkins struggled with another terrified sailor who refused to go over the side.[5]

Wilcox jumped, knowing full well that a dog paddle was the limit of his swimming skills. Navigator Rowe's constant warnings about the danger of barracudas were quickly forgotten when Wilcox noticed a man flailing in the water. Grabbing a rope fender, he tossed it toward the drowning sailor only to see the sailor's head slip beneath the water and disappear. A small boat came alongside, and rescuers hauled Wilcox in. Remembering Moran, Wilcox looked up at the fantail, but the panicked deckhand had disappeared. He was later recorded as missing in action, presumed dead.

The *kaiten* explosion had slammed John Mair to the deck. Dressed only in skivvies, the Wisconsin sailor leapt to his feet and felt the ship shudder from stem to stern. Flames engulfed the bow. Drops of hot oil fell like rain, and Mair ducked under the raised cargo deck for shelter. Wondering what had exploded, his first thought was "Some fool's been smoking over the AV gas tanks again." Aboard an oiler, fire was the constant threat, and smoking near the tanks was always a bad idea. Why didn't matter now; he had to escape the encroaching heat and flames. He scrambled to his footlocker in the aft crew's quarters and slipped into his dungarees and shoes. He thought about his life jacket, stashed inside the engine room hatch only a few paces away. He groped for it on top of the ventilator, but it was gone—someone else had already grabbed it.

"Abandon ship. Abandon ship," rang the command, as panic-stricken sailors pushed and shoved one another at the rear compartment ladder, seeking safety. Men gathered on the poop deck above to await their turn jumping off next to the 5-inch/38 mount. Mair looked at the water and wondered if he'd drown without a life jacket. Hot oil and debris pelted his naked back. He wheeled about toward the bow; peering through a gap in the smoke and flames, he saw the entire forward section of the ship ablaze. Near the starboard rail, he was repelled by burning waves closing in on the stern. He was encouraged to see that the blazing water cleared amidships on the port side, but he doubted that chance would last long.

Sailors who had managed to escape the stricken oiler moments before were already manning two work party boats tied to the fantail. Mair jumped twenty feet to the water and swam to the nearest boat. Once aboard, he and the others hauled exhausted, frightened shipmates out of the water as fast as they could. Fireman Harold "Bootie" Boutiette struggled to stay afloat after slipping below the surface of the water. Mair mustered the strength to manhandle the Massachusetts man over the gunwale, and the pair collapsed in a pile. "Thanks" was all Bootie could mutter.

Bob Vulgamore fell out of his hammock at the explosion, slashing his ankle on a large manifold wheel underneath him. He hobbled aft, joined by other sailors escaping the searing heat. The Ohio sailor peered over the rail, astonished to see fire along the entire length of the ship. He scaled the ladder to the poop deck and eyed the distance to the water; when he saw fire curling around the fantail from the starboard side, he knew it was time to jump. He landed in the water and swam a good distance, then flipped onto his back. Something bumped him, and he discovered it was a rolled-up life jacket. He pondered on the random chance as he unrolled the life-saver and wriggled into it, then swam toward a wispy break in the smoke. The roar of an airplane engine filled his ears, and a Kingfisher floatplane taxied on the water past him. After being pulled into a passing boat, he shed the life preserver, tossing it back into the water for some other needy swimmer.

One man swam frenziedly through the flames, but his wet clothes held him back. It was coxswain Vincent Carelli, the popular New Yorker who ran the mess hall casino. The colorful figure was known for his winning skills in poker, and he'd lightened the wallets of dozens of men as he laid out a royal flush or a straight. As the fire raged around him in the water, he slipped his trousers off to make his way, and realized a few moments after they sank that he'd carried his $8,000 winnings in his pocket. All those carefully folded bills would be eaten by fish or scattered on the harbor bottom. He reached the side of the captain's gig.

Executive Officer Lewis pulled Carelli into the gig and ordered him to steer away from the stricken ship, saying they couldn't save any more. He met with instant resistance, as Carelli retorted, "Go to hell, sir! I'm not leaving until every man we can find is in this boat."[6]

Metalsmith Al Bell and carpenter's mate Bob Maggiani headed for the aft crew's quarters to get dressed after the explosion knocked them off their cots. Bell had worked on Lieutenant Fuller's cargo detail the night before, shifting AV gas between tanks; he knew that port and starboard number 1 tanks were not full of seawater as they should have been. He also knew that centerline tank number 3 was empty and held volatile AV gas fumes; as that thought struck him, the fire hit those fumes, causing a second massive explosion in the bow that rocked the oiler again. He was sure the ship was breaking apart. "It's the AV gas, Mag. We didn't purge all of the tanks last night," yelled Bell. "Let's get the hell out of here. The ship is doomed." Two years earlier Bell had abandoned the carrier *Wasp* near Guadalcanal; he hoped he would make it this time, too. The pair leapt over the port rail and swam to the boat steered by coxswain Carelli.

Radar striker Ed Kinsler was waiting for a chance to get through the flames and leave the *Miss*, when he had the fatalistic thought: "My day to die has come." The notion spurred him into action, and he tore off his clothes just as a breeze opened up a swath of water off the port quarter. A former lifeguard, he made powerful strokes that churned the water as he swam off. When he turned to look back at the stern, he saw a scene of horror. Flames and smoke enveloped the ship. Just then—a clock on a harbor ship somewhere recorded 0605—the fire reached the aft 5-inch/38 magazine. The resulting blast lifted the *Miss* out of the water. A gargantuan piece of shell plating hurtled skyward. "So long, world," Kinsler thought as he watched the hot metal fall toward him. The bulkhead missed him by only a few yards and splashed into the ocean with a loud hiss. Weakened by shock and fear, he was barely able to tread water and could hardly talk to the rescuers who found him; he gripped the gunwale with frozen fingers, and they couldn't pry him loose, so they grabbed him by the hair, dunking him a couple of times to gain enough momentum to pull him up into the boat. Throwing up oil and salt water, he sobbed and thanked God as he sat down.

Even at the moment of doom, storekeeper Jack Maher worried about the ship's mascot, Salvo, and tried to find him. His buddy William Ruwell grabbed him by the arm, shouting, "Forget the dog! We're getting off while we can." Maher shook loose from Ruwell's grasp and went to look for the dog. Ruwell reached the poop deck to find John

Costello shaking with fright. He couldn't swim, but Ruwell urged him to jump, saying he'd stay with him in the water. It was no use. Costello stared at him, clutched the crucifix around his neck, raced for the galley and dogged down the door behind him. Ruwell hesitated for a second, but the next explosion blew a new round of hot oil into the sky, burning the top of his head and searing his arms. He raced for the poop deck.[7]

Three small boats beckoned. Ruwell did a swan dive into the warm water. In moments he found a new terror—a giant dome surfaced near him and he flinched, believing it was a Japanese mine. A pair of green eyes looked at him, and he realized it was a giant sea turtle paddling through the mayhem, disturbed by the unusual water activity caused by the explosions and depth charges. Reaching a boat, Ruwell got in and helped twenty-one other men into the craft over the next few minutes.

Loaded and ready to depart, the helmsman started the engine, but the mooring lines were tangled in the prop. Knife in hand, he dived overboard and cut the entangled lines. The boat unloaded its survivors to a waiting ship and returned to the scene of the carnage; Ruwell remained with the helmsman, and the two retrieved a dozen more oil-covered sailors from the water, all suffering from burns and various injuries. The helmsman headed for the tanker *Pamanset* to get immediate medical care for the injured.

Back on the ship, seaman Herb Daitch ran across Jack Maher, who was still looking for the ship's dog. Maher headed for the hatch; "I've got to find Salvo. I've got to get the dog," he kept saying. Men fled past Daitch to reach the ladder, but he stopped to grab Maher by the arm. "Forget the dog," Daitch begged, but Maher shook loose and headed in the opposite direction. Daitch was the last one to see him alive.

————————

Lieutenant Blase Zamucen and radioman Russell Evinrude had been flying over Ulithi Lagoon in *Santa Fe*'s Kingfisher OS2U floatplane, when they saw the explosion aboard *Mississinewa*. Dropping the plane for a closer look, Zamucen saw oil spread out from the tanker and catch fire. He and Evinrude watched as men began jumping off the blazing ship; both aviators realized the sailors wouldn't have much of a chance against the flames. Zamucen made a quick decision to land his tiny plane on the lagoon's surface and taxi to the edge of *Mississinewa*'s port-side flames.

It was a heroic move. He dropped down, kicked the rudder and spun the plane's tail toward the flaming oil, revving the rotary engine to fan flames away from sailors struggling to stay afloat. Disregarding his own safety, Russell Evinrude climbed out of the rear seat and secured a line to the plane. Straddling the plane's fuselage, he tossed the long line out into the water and urged oil-covered sailors to grab hold.

At that moment John Bayak was close to drowning, seeing visions of his dead parents. His oxygen-depleted lungs burned as he rose to the surface, gasping and choking. Adrenaline surged through his body, but he was completely exhausted, certain the flaming port-side oil slick spreading swiftly would overtake him. Just then Zamucen taxied the floatplane to the edge of the oil slick and blew the flames back from Bayak and others; the new path through the waves led them to a lifeboat. Oil-covered hands reached down and pulled the pharmacist's mate into a boat. He started administering first aid to the wounded he found there. Only later did he learn that his best friend, Gaston Cote had died where he slept—in Bayak's assigned bunk under the bridge.

The detonation had awakened medical officer John Bierley, who'd been asleep in his port-side bridge cabin. "Doc, let's get the hell out of here," screamed supply officer Herbert Allen from the bunk next to him. Bierley struggled to his feet as the ship yawed to port. He had reached for his uniform pants when fingers of white-hot flame entered the cabin through the porthole, scorching him on his neck, head and hands. He forgot about dressing and followed Allen into the passageway. The centerline AV gas tank sent a wave of flame down the narrow passageway, and the doctor covered his eyes with his hands just in time to protect them. Stepping on hot debris, he injured his left foot in the passageway. Lieutenant Stutzman emerged from a cabin and saw that the pajama-clad doctor was not wearing a life preserver.

Stutzman offered a life jacket and Bierley took it. The officers reached the boat deck chased by falling debris, oil and flames. The doc jumped over the port side from the boat deck, further injuring his foot as he collided with floating debris. His pajama pants slipped off and he felt salt water stinging his burns. A voice hailed from an approaching boat. He turned back in the water to look for two officers, Wilson and Allen, he'd seen jump into the water, and he saw the flames overtake them. The two disappeared below the surface and did not reappear.

The 0545 explosion knocked Joe Morris unconscious. He awoke in a coil of six-inch fueling hose as the *Mississinewa* quivered and shook. A mushrooming fireball engulfed the bridge, and he blacked out again as the centerline tank detonated. The storage locker with life jackets was an inferno. Facing a water entry without a life jacket, he weighed his chances of staying or swimming, but secondary explosions shook the ship, and swimming won out. He plunged over the port side with two other sailors and dog-paddled wildly, slipping beneath the surface every time he slowed his arms to rest. He spotted the floatplane and hope gave him added strength.

Evinrude screamed over the noise of explosions and the plane's motor, "Grab the line behind you. Grab the line." Exhausted, Morris somehow found the strength to grab the line, along with two other men. Zamucen revved the engine and edged the tiny plane away from the flames, taxiing toward the small boats astern. Evinrude pointed to the rescue boats, screaming above the din of explosions, exhorting each man, "Let go!" as they neared a rescue boat. Morris dropped off the line and watched Zamucen and Evinrude go back to the flaming oil slick. The aviators repeated their daring rescue four more times until they had rescued twenty *Mississinewa* sailors.

Joe Contendo was taking an early morning shower when the death-blow to the oiler knocked him to his knees. The starboard hatch leading to the forward well deck blew off its hinges, hurtling across the compartment and demolishing an unoccupied bunk. Within seconds flames swept through the sleeping space, immolating three sailors still in their racks. Naked and covered with soap, Contendo lunged for the ladder to exit the compartment. He saw fire igniting *Mississinewa*'s number 3 centerline AV gas tank; sheets of flame gusted through the port-side hatch and nearly knocked him off the ladder.

Oil and AV gas floated out from the ruptured hull and burst into flame. A slight breeze slowed the flames on the port side. Emerging on the boat deck one level up from the crew's quarters, Contendo looked toward the bow and saw a grisly sight. Several sailors sleeping on top of the forward AV gas tanks had been blown upward into the catwalk and a maze of pipes; their bodies were unrecognizable, only a mass of mangled, charred flesh. Contendo began to doubt his own chances of survival, even though he'd so far eluded death.

Contendo joined others already in the water and swam away from the ship's hull. The heat from the burning oil was so intense that the Rochester, New York, boy was certain the flames would overtake him. He saw a large group of men clinging to a floater net fifty feet from him; the spreading flames crept perilously close to the survivors. Suddenly a spontaneous flare-up engulfed the floater net, killing all the sailors clinging to it. The terrifying sight inspired Contendo to swim as hard as he could to reach open water. A boat searching the port side for survivors finally reached amidships and hoisted the young deckhand to safety.

Few men from the forward crew's quarters survived the devastation wreaked by the number 3 centerline tank explosions. Fire swept through their compartment with amazing ferocity, blocking all escape routes. Earl Givens awoke as the boatswain's mate made his way through the compartment at 0530. "Anybody not up in five minutes pulls extra duty." Just minutes later, the wing tank explosion had thrown Givens out of his bunk. A hot sheet of orange flame blew through the starboard hatch, and he tried to escape out the forward port-side hatch leading to the well deck, but flames drove him back. Givens, clad only in skivvies, followed others up the ladder; at that moment the ship shuddered and rocked as the centerline tank fumes ignited, sending another wave of flame through the port hatch and blistering his back. He reached the boat deck to find Bill Dennehy gripping the stanchion rail and frozen with fear. "Let's get off! It's going down," screamed Givens, pounding his fists on Dennehy's hands to loosen his grip. The pair briefly struggled; Givens got the upper hand and pushed Dennehy over the rail. They lost track of each other after they splashed into the sea.

Dennehy landed in the fast-spreading oil and fought for his life. He splashed away the flames, surfacing twice, gasping for air. He had no idea where he was, as smoke obscured his vision. Surfacing a third time, he cleared the edge of the flames where *Lackawanna*'s boat found him treading water. Givens followed Dennehy into the water, rising to the surface amid floating flames. The Alabama man was a strong swimmer and managed to surface for air amid the flaming oil three times before finally reaching open water. He flipped over on his back and floated for several minutes to rest. The aft tanks blew upward with a roar, raining down debris; the burning oil was spreading toward him. A boat came alongside. Deckhand John Girt pulled the exhausted seventeen-year-old into the boat.

***

Raleigh Peppers was the first to leave the steward's mates' cabin on the port side as fire swept through the forward berthing. The twenty-year-old steward from Tennessee had grabbed hold of the ladder rail three feet from his sleeping quarters, when fear froze him in place. A sailor behind him pounded on his arms until Peppers released his grip. The fleeing man pushed the steward aside. Peppers remembered that his pal, James Reeder, the wardroom cook, was still in their cabin, and he turned toward the hatch to warn him. He collided with racing men as shouts and screams filled the air; they blocked his path and made it impossible for him to get down the passageway to warn Reeder. "Damn," he cursed. Fleeing sailors pushed and shoved; pandemonium reigned. Peppers waited agonizing seconds before his turn came to scramble up the compartment ladder. He made his way aft after reaching the boat deck and jumped over the port rail, all the while hoping Reeder would make it.

Immediately after the blast, First Lieutenant William Kuhn had retreated with the captain to the starboard side while Beck surveyed the flames consuming the forward part of his ship. The two separated as they ran for the safety of the stern. Kuhn reached the fantail, looked up and saw men throwing floater nets into the water from the poop deck above him. Unable to swim, he wrapped a life belt around his belly, went over the rail and surfaced quickly, looking for a net. Struggling to stay afloat, he grabbed the foot of machinist's mate Stanley Johnson at the urging of the enlisted man. Johnson swam with his arms while Kuhn flayed the water furiously with his legs. Together both men were able to reach a boat.

Up on the deck, boatswain's mate Clarence Walsh struggled with the frozen front davit of *Mississinewa*'s twenty-six-foot motor whale-boat. "Help me here. Help me, sailor," he pleaded as frightened sailors ran past him, ignoring his plight. No one stopped to help, so frightened were they. Walsh continued to call for help as Ensign William Brown frantically worked to get the crank to function on the stern davit. As the flames grew nearer and the smoke thickened, Walsh realized that men could become trapped in the aft crew's quarters. He abandoned the effort to free the front davit of the whaleboat and ran for the port-side hatch to order the men to abandon ship. In his confusion, he forgot to tell Brown he was leaving. He found a few men in the port compartment and told them to get out. After that, he headed for the port quarter fantail and found a group of twenty sailors there. Walsh ordered them to abandon ship, waiting until the fantail was clear of men before he jumped over the side into the water.

After Walsh swam out five hundred feet, he saw *Santa Fe*'s floatplane taxiing along the edge of the flaming oil. Evinrude, the floatplane observer, spotted Walsh in the water and directed pilot Zamucen to drag the long line behind the plane, placing it near the boatswain's mate. Walsh hung on as the pilot deftly maneuvered, dragging the line near a small boat from *Tallulah*. Once aboard *Tallulah*, the chief pharmacist's mate gave the bo'swain a shot of morphine for his burns. A trip to *Tallulah*'s sick bay came next, and Walsh was onboard the hospital ship *Samaritan* within the hour.

From the first moments after the initial blast, Ensign Pat Canavan, the First Division officer, was concerned for the welfare of his deckhands. "An AV gas accident? Where were the men working?" Merchant Marine training took over, as he recalled his academy instructions in event of a fire aboard ship: "Don't enter a passageway to escape until fully dressed. Clothing is your protection from fire." Canavan dressed and strapped on his sidearm. He crawled over two men slumped in the passageway as he exited the cabin.

Robert Rowe was dressing when the number 3 centerline tank blew, igniting with a roar. The force slammed him to the cabin floor as white-hot flames entered the porthole opening, enveloping him. As he exited his cabin, Canavan met Rowe and saw he was horribly burned. Canavan continued aft. Slippery oil covered the ladder that led from the bridge to the well deck. Reaching the cargo deck, he saw ten sailors, some of them moving, some eerily still despite the frenzy around them. He supposed they were dead. Looking over the water, he saw oil spreading quickly down the starboard side. He decided to board the whaleboat that crewmembers were launching from the port side. One end of the boat hung askew over the side of the ship, knocked off its davit. Cana-van slipped the hand crank he found on the deck into the remaining davit holding the boat in place. The crank didn't fit. He didn't know that his roommate, Walsh, had struggled with the same hand crank a couple of moments earlier. An enlisted sailor staggered toward him, and Canavan recognized a lad who worked in the ship's laundry. Fire had burned away almost an inch of the sailor's flesh, revealing only charred muscle. Reaching the number 5 gun on the fantail, Canavan could clearly see an escape route within a section of water off the port quarter. He swung over the rail and plummeted toward the water below.

The detonation of the *kaiten* warhead catapulted radar strikers P. T. Upchurch and J. P. Hammond upward, into the base of the 20mm mount on the flying bridge, their favorite spot for avoiding the nightly rain showers. "Damn," cursed Hammond, suffering a deep gash to his head. Flaming debris rained down around them as the two made their way toward the radio room on the bridge. In the confusion, the friends lost track of each other. Hammond made it off the ship and was pulled to safety by Zamucen. He was placed on board an amphibious landing craft anchored close to the smoldering *Mississinewa*, all the while bleeding profusely from his head wound.

The events of the night before came back to haunt some sailors. Sea-man Harold Ritchie, carpenter's mate Bob Maggiani and ship fitter Fred Cooper were among the sailors who had been helping transfer cargo to the various tanks forward of the bridge. The men went to sleep knowing the empty tanks had not been purged, but with Captain Beck's orders to end work and watch the movie, they figured it was all right to disregard the protocol—nothing was likely to happen in port. Ritchie, exhausted after helping on Fuller's work detail, planned to turn in soon after the movie ended. He sauntered across the cargo deck with his mattress, heading for his usual sleeping spot; it happened to be on top of the aviation gasoline tanks forward of the bridge, where cool breezes swept across the deck at night. As he was headed for the tanks, he heard a voice. "Hey, Ritchie," gunner's mate Jimmie Kesner beckoned, "come on over here a minute." The two talked for a bit, and Ritchie finally threw his mattress down on the cargo deck next to Kesner's and curled up and went to sleep. His decision to forgo the aviation tanks saved his life.

Ritchie awoke the next morning in time to see ships of Cruiser Division Five and Destroyer Division Seven steam south past *Mississinewa* and exit Mugai Channel. Breakfast would start being served by 0545, and Ritchie was obligated to take his turn serving in the mess hall. He had just slipped on his trousers and his left sock when the *kaiten* struck. As debris started falling from the skies, he ducked inside the nearest hatch and headed for the chief's quarters on the port side. Looking down from the stern, he saw at least twenty men already flailing in the water and two *Mississinewa* boats still tied up on the fantail. Ritchie had not heard an abandon ship order but had always thought a torpedoing would be catastrophic for the *Miss*. The instinct for survival took over—he knew the only safe place was away from the ship. He grasped the line and went down.

Treading water several feet from the stern, he looked up to see men still at the rail, including panic-stricken Peter Moran. A few scrambled down a Jacob's ladder; others jumped from the poop deck near the stern-mounted 5-inch/38 gun. Explosions and debris flew hundreds of feet in the air as the fires spreading aft ignited more ready ammunition, lube oil drums and flammable equipment. *Mississinewa*'s own forty-foot launch picked up Ritchie, uninjured.

At the time of the big bang, gunner's mate Frank Kennedy was standing at the door of the post office with the key inserted in the lock when seaman Jim Kirk, the ship's tailor, ran up behind him screaming in pain. "Frank, get my clothes off. Help me." Kennedy whirled around to see Kirk's clothes afire, and he immediately reacted by ripping the burning garments off the boy. Kirk was grievously injured. "Wait just a minute," Kennedy replied. "I'll help you." He went inside the post office and opened the safe, removing the Register of Money Orders Book and $215 in postal funds. He put the valuables in a canvas bag and turned to help Kirk. The mess hall filled with smoke as burning mattresses, blown off the cargo deck and into the mess hall, littered the inside. Looking around frantically, the mailman realized that Kirk was gone. The gunner's mate noted that the breeze was coming down the port side, so he headed toward the chief's quarters, where he ran into Chief Lester Rankin. "Do we abandon ship, sir?" he yelled over the din of explosions. "Over the side, sailor," Rankin yelled back. Kennedy mounted the rail and jumped, getting picked up swiftly by Willie Potter's launch from *Lackawanna*. Kennedy saw that seaman Kirk was already in the boat, but the boy was in agony from his extensive burns.

Ray Fulleman had just walked from the cargo deck, where he slept, to his bunk just inside the aft crew's quarters when the blast rolled the tanker to port. Looking in the direction of the blast, Fulleman saw only red sky through the hatchway. Like other sailors, he thought an AV gas tank might have exploded. Life jacket on, he darted through the hatch leading from the crew's quarters, to reach his battle station in the fire room, where he found Howard Bochow and Red Foster on duty. Fulleman knew that more than one boiler on line was required to build enough steam pressure for the ship's steam smothering system. He could see that Foster was having trouble keeping steam pressure up in the auxiliary on-line boiler. Fulleman hurried down to the boilerplates and had started to light off another boiler just as Edmund Smith arrived.

Trying to start the second boiler in the shortest possible time, Fulleman threw in the largest burner nozzle. Smitty, the chief water tender, observing this, told him to use the smaller nozzle. "What do you want to do? Break some of the brickwork [in the boiler]?" he asked. Not knowing the severity of the explosions, the fire room chief hoped to save the ship for future use after the fire was contained. The second boiler did little to help as the auxiliary steam line continued to lose pressure.

Smitty lost phone contact with the engine room as the fire room sailors struggled to feed water in the two boilers. By this time, the worried fire room sailors had counted many explosions above deck. Worried that they might get caught deep within the bowels of the ship if it sank, Smitty sent Bochow to check on what was happening above. Being trapped down belowdecks in a burning ship was a fate that none of them wanted to face.

"You'd better get out. Everybody's gone." Fred Schaufus shouted his warning through the fire room hatch as he made his way aft. Fulleman, now at the check valves near the hatch, called down to the others in the fire room to heed Schaufus's warning. Ironically, dangerous as the situation was, Navy training took over as the experienced water tenders took time to secure the boilers, blowers and pumps, but left the stops open so *Mississinewa* generators would keep supplying electricity to the ship's lights. According to the control panel clock, fifteen minutes had elapsed in the fire room since the initial explosion.

Through the starboard hatch, acrid black smoke poured into the fire room, requiring the sailors to slam the hatch shut and reverse their escape route. "Port-side hatch, quickly." The men went up a level in the fire room and exited by way of the chief's quarters. Smitty told Fulleman to check that Bochow had gotten out of the fire room. Smitty and Foster headed aft down the passageway toward the stern, while Fulleman, searching for Bochow, turned back to the fire room hatch. Finding the fire room hopelessly full of smoke, he called in three times, "Bochow, you down there?" No response. Fulleman realized it was futile and turned to join Smitty and Foster. As he turned to head down the smoky passageway to the stern, someone yelled, "Hey, you can't go back there. The ammunition is blowing up."

Fulleman moved forward in the passageway, but smoke made that route impossible. Standing there a few seconds, the thought flashed through his mind, "Oh, Jesus. My Mom's going to get a telegram that

I'm dead." A flash of white going through the smoke at the forward end of the passageway caught his eye; it was a machinist's mate in skivvies. Following the racing sailor, Fulleman found his way down a ladder to the port-side well deck.

A solid wall of fire encircled the ship except for a V-shaped opening of water free of flames the breeze had somehow provided off the port quarter. Fulleman slid down the side of the hull from the deck that was now only four feet above the water. Heavy bunker oil floated in a thick layer on the water. Pushing himself away from the hull, he began to swim using a sidestroke. The fire on the starboard side encircled the stern and raced to meet the port-side flames. Taking advantage of the side-stroke to watch the fire, Fulleman planned to slip out of his life jacket and swim under the flaming oil.

With each stroke, he watched the shiny silver ring on his finger slice through the thick layer of oil. Like other sailors standing long, monotonous watches, he'd made the ring out of a silver quarter. It calmed him to focus on something so immediate. A few yards out from the ship he looked back, noticing a dozen men still aboard gathered around the smokestack. Fifty-five-gallon drums of lube oil stacked on the cargo deck began to explode, hurtling into the air like Roman candles. Fulleman watched as each drum exploded, flipped through the air and landed in the water among the survivors. The words of the Hail Mary echoed in his ears.

Fulleman watched from the water as destroyers and destroyer escorts began to circle *Mississinewa*. He finally realized that the explosion must have been the result of an enemy attack, since the destroyers looked as if they were preparing to drop depth charges. A new fear gripped him as he realized that the concussion from depth charges could blow a man's guts out.

A rescue boat came toward him, maneuvered by coxswain Carelli, who had recognized Fulleman. Grabbing his clothing, several men pulled Fulleman into the boat. His entire body was covered with thick, gooey oil except the side of his head that had been above water when he sidestroked away from the hull.

He found that the forty-foot launch had already picked up fire room sailors Bochow and Foster. The three were safe, thanks to the warning by Schaufus. Still, there was no sign of Smitty. Fulleman hoped he'd made it to another boat. Throughout the day the fire room sailors looked for him in vain. They never saw Smitty again.

Stanley Johnson, a machinist's mate, actually witnessed Smitty's violent end. Johnson had gone over the side with first officer William Kuhn, the pair struggling to stay afloat. Kuhn, a nonswimmer, hung on to Johnson's leg. Water tender Smith was afloat in the water fifteen feet to Johnson's right and appeared to be all right. Suddenly a fifty-five-gallon drum exploded on the cargo deck. In a matter of seconds it skyrocketed up in the air and arced downward to hit Smitty squarely on the head. The chief water tender disappeared. Johnson, only an average swimmer, could do nothing to help. If he slowed his flailing arms and legs, he knew Kuhn's weight would inadvertently drag him under. Smitty was nowhere to be seen, and Johnson felt sure he had died instantly.

Uncertainty surrounded the whereabouts of fire room sailor Robert Kimbel, who couldn't be found even in the days afterward. The exact fate of the Pennsylvania sailor would forever remain a mystery.

The day had started differently for other black gang sailors. "Get your butt out of here," a sleepy machinist's mate first class Gus Liveakos growled at the master at arms. It was 0530 reveille.

"I worked all night," complained Liveakos. The master at arms carried on, making his way forward, to rouse more sleepy sailors. The explosion, moments later, quickly brought Liveakos fully awake. The machinist's mate headed for the engine room. Johnson and Schaufus were still struggling to get the generators on line, with little success.

Dressed only in skivvies and a T-shirt, Liveakos emerged topside to find the crew abandoning ship.

He jumped over the port rail. A voice begged for help. "I can't swim. Come help me," machinist's mate Francis Crotty pleaded. The boat reached Liveakos, but he pointed to Crotty in the water near the flames and waved the boat on. A survivor in the boat threw a line to Crotty to keep him afloat. The line got tangled in debris and prevented the boat from coming closer to the struggling sailor. Coxswain Earl Tuttle jumped overboard, cut the line and pulled Crotty aboard. The boatload of survivors then plucked Liveakos from the water. The rescued machinist's mate located the next man—forty-two-year-old machinist's mate second class Marion "Pop" Clayton grabbed the side of the boat. Liveakos tried to pull him out of the water by himself but was too exhausted to get Clayton over the gunwale.

"You son of a bitch! Get in the damn boat," snarled Liveakos. The others helped Clayton aboard, and he immediately took a swing at Liveakos, missed and fell exhausted into the bottom of the boat.

Liveakos, having abandoned ship wearing only a T-shirt and skivvies, later offered his T-shirt to an officer who had been pulled into the boat completely naked.

"You'll only be half-naked now, sir," Liveakos told the officer, hoping the man would feel a little better.

John D'Anna, ship's cook striker, was wearing his skivvy shirt, white cook apron and dungarees when he jumped over the port-side rail, but was left with only skivvy shorts when he was plucked from the water.

Once pulled from the water and sitting in a whale boat, D'Anna could not help but notice the new demeanor of Executive Officer Robert Lewis, also in the boat. Lewis remained unusually silent, neither giving orders to the boat crew nor directing rescue efforts, evidently too shocked by events to function. It was coxswain Vince Carelli who finally yelled, "Let's get out of here before the ammo blows," coaxing the balky whaleboat motor to life on his second attempt to start it.

Bill Gimmeson, a seventeen-year-old seaman second, was afraid to leave the ship without an officer's order. He spotted an officer near the stern rail struggling to get air into an inflatable life belt. Gimmeson helped him, but to his horror the officer jumped over the rail without looking, landing in flaming oil. Gimmeson, frightened and panicky, jumped into the water, swam as fast as he could and passed the officer, who called for help as he flailed the water. Ignoring the man's cries for help, Gimmeson reached a floater net and clung to it, waiting for a rescue boat. The image of the drowning officer haunted him.

Assistant communications officer Lieutenant Charles Scott heard the screams of sailors being enveloped in flames near the bridge. Flaming gas and oil were spreading across the water. He saw more than a dozen sailors in the water, swimming to escape flaming oil spreading out from ruptured starboard number 3 wing tank. Clad only in skivvies, Scott donned his uniform, ball cap and slippers before slipping on his life jacket. He ran to his GQ station on the starboard 3-inch gun, but a wall of flame blocked his attempt to reach the weapon. He expected to see a formation of enemy planes overhead. Scott observed that the entire starboard side of the ship was engulfed in flames. Looking around and seeing no one else, he wondered if he should abandon ship, too. He retreated to the deck below, exiting the forward hatch to see what was happening. Flames enveloped the ship forward of the bridge. Scott leapt to a ladder attached to a deck winch, scurried down the ladder and reached the well deck below.

Peering over the port side, Scott could see blazing oil creeping along the hull heading aft. "Jump, Scotty, jump!" Bill Brown was behind him, urging his shipmate to escape. Scott dived over the port-side rail into water clear of flames. Remembering abandon-ship procedures, he kicked off his trousers and slippers but decided not to inflate his life jacket until safely away from the ship. In the water, Bill Brown quickly overtook his fellow officer, who was content with leisurely strokes distancing himself from the hull. An engineering sailor approached Scott and motioned he was too tired to swim further. "Grab a kapok jacket," urged Scott. Several jackets swirled in the oily waters nearby, tossed aside by sailors already rescued.

───────────

Lieutenant James Fuller donned his helmet, pistol, shoes and pants after the explosion, expecting a call to general quarters. He made his way out of the officers' passageway aft, narrowly avoiding Douning, and saw the bridge engulfed in flames. He retreated to his cabin for a shirt. "It's our gasoline," Fuller shouted to the other officers. He thought a foolish accident had caused the explosion. The main deck was now covered with flames, so Fuller and the others made their way aft through the smoke. He sighted a swath of clear water off the port quarter and saw two floater nets on the surface.

"Maybe I could make it to a net," he thought. Fuller spotted the motor whaleboat still in its davits and had begun to crank the stern of the whaleboat from its davit when the 5-inch/38 magazine exploded, knocking him senseless. The blast threw the bow of the whaleboat over the side of the ship. Stunned, Fuller lifted himself off the deck. Through the smoke he could see small rescue boats making their way toward the stern.

Getting into the water, Fuller landed next to badly burned Jim Kirk, who was clinging to a life jacket. Kirk, unable to swim, was barely afloat, so Fuller took him in tow, pulling Kirk as he swam, avoiding the fire on the water near them. Fuller struggled to pull Kirk for several minutes but swam on alone after he realized they weren't making headway. He hoped a boat would come soon.

Ensign Donald Metcalf had been aboard *Mississinewa* only thirty-six hours when he heard the clanging of metal that followed the explosion. Ten seconds passed before the flames in the officers' passageway on the bridge subsided and Metcalf could make his way aft. Hot oil rained on him as he groped his way along the oil-slicked centerline catwalk above the well deck. Another sailor slipped and stumbled ahead of Metcalf, who helped the man to his feet and continued. He reached the fantail to find a dozen men gathered around, each man waiting his turn to escape by sliding down ropes clogged with sailors. Flames suddenly whipped around the starboard fantail and enveloped the ropes. The men clinging to them clawed furiously back up, seeking the fantail deck. Metcalf was horrified. The water was on fire and the ship was burning furiously. There seemed no place to go to escape the flames.

Kirk, barely alive, was picked up by coxswain Potter's boat and brought on board *Lackawanna* in a stretcher basket. Fuller, who had left Kirk, continued to swim and came upon the badly burned ship's navigator, Lieutenant Robert Rowe. "Can I help you?" the young cargo officer asked the thirty-four-year-old Rowe. "Hail a boat," Rowe answered weakly. Sailors, manning a small boat from *Mascoma* helped the badly injured Rowe out of the water and immediately headed for their ship. Another boat came along a few moments later and pulled Fuller from the water to safety.

Outside the crew's quarters was a scene of commotion. Terrified sailors pushed and shoved one another trying to scale the rear ladder to the boat deck as fire swept over the deck. Some men huddled together trying to spot open water through the smoke. One sailor, John Girt, deciding to wait no longer, climbed two ladders and reached the catwalk that connected the bridge to the aft boat deck level near the stack. He had just ventured onto the catwalk when the centerline tank explosion covered him with hot oil, searing his exposed skin. Girt reached the fantail, kicked off his shoes and jumped over the side, plunging so deep that his lungs ran out of air before he surfaced. Rescuers spotted him, gasping and choking,

Moments later, the men of the gig pulled badly burned steward's mate Harry Caison from the oily water. On the first attempt to pull him in, the flesh sloughed off his burned arms and the boatmen accidentally dropped him back into the water. The injured man's skin was mostly gone, leaving only pink flesh underneath; his milky white eyes barely clung to life. The smell of death was everywhere in the boat. Burned hair and flesh mingled with the heavy smells of oil and charred paint.

Back in Missouri, Marjorie Roberts woke suddenly in her hospital bed and cried out, "Oh God, something has happened to my husband!" She struggled to climb out of the anesthesia fog after her baby's birth. Crying hysterically, she was overwhelmed with fear. A nurse tried to reassure her: "You just got a letter from him yesterday and everything's all right." But the letter from her husband had been written a week earlier, and Marjorie knew that events happen in a flash. She felt with dread certainty that he was gone. Word would come to her eventually from the high command that would prove her telepathic sense was correct. Little Judy Roberts was born on November 19, 1944. On the other side of the international date line in Ulithi, it was November 20. Machinist's mate second class Orlando Roberts died on the *Mississinewa* as his wife gave birth in Missouri.

Another telepathic event happened in New York with the Martino family. Seaman Joseph Martino had awakened before reveille and was nursing a cup of strong coffee in *Mississinewa*'s mess hall. He missed his six children back in Yonkers, as he always did, and he was thinking of his littlest child, Bea, three years old, when the explosion knocked him to the deck and shattered his coffee cup. Seeing the bridge covered in flames, he joined the stream of sailors running for the fantail and jumped off into the perilous seas. Weeks later he learned that at the hour of his crisis in Ulithi, Beatrice had woken from her afternoon nap crying inconsolably, "Daddy's in the water. There's fire." Nothing could calm the girl, who wailed over and over. Ten thousand miles away, Joe Martino struggled to survive in the fiery waters at the exact time Bea was crying for him. Fate was kind: Martino would live to see his little girl again.

Scene after horror scene unfolded as the morning spun forth in timeless reels. At the rail a frightened young sailor stared down in wide-eyed terror at burned bodies floating in the oily water. While others raced about, he stood paralyzed, muttering, "My God!" over and over.

———

Captain Beck stood on the fantail of his sinking ship, accompanied by Stutzman, Douning, Cass and enlisted sailors Herrington and McMillan. Concluding that they were the last men left aboard, Beck gave the order to abandon ship. The fifty-year-old skipper jumped over the fantail with Stutzman, followed by the enlisted men. A rescue boat from the *Cache* reached the men and pulled them aboard. All survived except Herrington, who died of his injuries.

Beck watched as the ship under his command sank beneath the water, enveloped in a fire burning all around in billowing gusts of thick black smoke. The scene played out under a strange cacophony of after explosions from barrels of oil and stored munitions, a crazy rhythm of death in stark contrast to the azure waters of the tropical oasis. The captain sat in the boat with other survivors. Shocked and in pain, burned and suffering, they all struggled to make sense of the sight unfolding before their eyes. The mammoth ship was sinking bow first, still wrapped in flames until the final waves snuffed them out. With a hiss as the fires died, the oiler disappeared from view.

Years later it would become known that the ship's port side caught first on the bottom as it turned and the hull continued to roll, leaving the wreck upside down in its watery grave. It would not be seen again for fifty-seven years.

The *Mississinewa* survivors were burned, bloodied and blackened with oil, but at least they would live to see another day.

CHAPTER 16

Rescue

I felt sick seeing these men screaming from pain and covered with oil.

—Lieutenant Milford Romanoff, officer of the deck,
USS *Lackawanna*

In *Lackawanna*'s gig, Jim Factor approached *Mississinewa* on his second rescue trip of the day. The oiler burned out of control. Three men escaping the ship reached the fantail through the smoke and flames; Factor watched them reach the poop deck and climb down a ladder toward the water. The fire's intense heat threatened the rescue efforts, but doggedly he edged the small boat forward, a hundred feet from the burning ship.

Factor worked the gig into the swirling smoke and flame. Three survivors had plunged from the ladder into the oily water near flames that threatened to engulf them. Burning oil was closing in fast on the men; with no time to board the small boat, they grabbed hold of the gunwales and hung on. At full speed Factor backed the gig out of harm's way as the oil-covered trio clung to the boat. He paused outside the edge of the flames to scan the water for more men. Certain that the three sailors were the last men still left in the water, *Lackawanna* rescuers took the survivors aboard the gig and headed for their ship.

Bow hook Bill Depoy gestured to coxswain Willie Potter, as he spotted *Mississinewa* sailors struggling in the water. Potter edged the launch closer to where Depoy was pointing, until he could make out an oil-covered head. He gave engineer Earl Ertel three bells, the signal to stop. Depoy reached over the side, grabbing men's belts, clothing or hair to pull the slippery, oil-soaked sailors into the launch. Sick to his stomach at the sight of skin sloughing off burned and naked sailors, he redoubled his rescue effort. Smoke, fire and after explosions created a chaotic nightmare of noise and color. A hot chunk of metal bulkhead whistled through the air and embedded itself in the bottom of *Lacka-wanna's* launch, the white-hot debris narrowly missing Potter at the helm.

Potter peered through wispy gaps in the smoke for a glimpse of the poop deck, where survivors were still abandoning ship. He saw chief machinist's mate George Douning signal the launch with a rag, and he could tell the fire would soon engulf the sailors waiting there for help. He darted in and within minutes got them into the launch, all the while getting jolted and jarred by explosions that never stopped. Staccato shocks blasted every time the flames reached ready ammunition, lube oil drums and fuel, and the ship was ripping apart even as it sank.

The *Lackawanna* men collected twenty survivors and circled the area for a few minutes searching for more. Helmsman Potter glanced at two badly burned men in the boat, Clemence Carlson and Jim Kirk, and knew they stood little chance of survival. Nearly skinless and with charred muscles visible, the boys lay dying.

As the gig returned, sailors on the *Lackawanna* stood by, ready to help unload the survivors despite the burning oil pocking their own skin. Romanoff organized immediate medical care. Potter deftly maneuvered *Lackawanna's* launch alongside the ship with his burned passengers. Potter, once considered something of a joker by the deck force, had displayed such cool courage under fire that his shipmates would never forget it.

As the launch was lashed to the port boom, *Lackawanna* sailors lined the fantail, gazing at the pitiful sight of the terribly injured men.

Men lowered a stretcher basket to the launch, and seaman second class Kirk, badly burned, was carefully strapped into the Bailey basket. Horribly disfigured from his burns, he'd lost much of his skin, giving him the appearance of an albino.[1]

Life was slipping away from Kirk, but as the critically injured eighteen-year-old reached Lieutenant Romanoff's side he raised his burned arm in a salute. "Permission to come aboard, sir?" came from his lips in a ragged whisper, his eyes struggling to focus on Romanoff. A pharmacist's mate examined him and Kirk asked for a drink. His charred buttocks were nearly gone, exposing most of his pelvic bone. The gut-wrenching sight was too much to bear even for the old salts; several *Lackawanna* sailors looked away with tears in their eyes.

Lieutenant P. W. Bransford, the senior medical officer, quickly organized help for the fifty-nine oil-covered survivors. Dr. Bransford had just taught a short first-aid burn course that *Lackawanna* sailors had to complete, where they learned how to clean a burn, sprinkle it with sulpha powder and cover the injury with petroleum jelly. Ed Miremont and others put that training to use, removing black oil from injured survivors.

Tempers flared in the aftermath of the blast. Lieutenant Basil Bininger, the supply officer, seethed with anger as *Lackawanna*'s skipper refused his request to radio other ships for clothes. "Why the hell not, sir?" Bininger said. "These men need clothing and personal supplies." "The Japs will intercept our TBS message and attack us," Homan responded with anger as he stood toe to toe with Bininger. "I'm not taking any chances that would endanger the ship. Romanoff already disobeyed my order to call back our boats from the fire scene—now *you're* questioning my decision." Bininger stormed off the bridge and ordered *Lackawanna* sailors to pass the word to donate any clothing they could spare to help the survivors that continued to arrive on the fantail. Officers Romanoff and Bininger disregarded Homan's threats of discipline and continued to help survivors.

Some survivors needed no medical aid, but every one of them was covered with oil and needed cleaning up. Water tender Fulleman, like other *Miss* sailors, stood in a large washtub as two *Lackawanna* sailors wiped heavy bunker oil off his body. He was finally led to a hot shower, and a *Lackawanna* sailor offered him fresh clothes; a little later a pharmacist's mate distributed small bottles of brandy to *Miss* sailors. The liquid burned going down, and several survivors got sick from ingesting the mix of salt water, oil and brandy.

Ray Fulleman had been fully dressed when he abandoned ship, including his work gloves stuffed in the back pocket of his dungarees. After the shower he scooped up his oily dungarees and headed below. The firemen on duty offered him a cup of coffee and the twenty-year-old cleaned his clothes in hot soapy water and hung them to dry in the fire room's heat. He wiped the oil off the paper currency still in his wallet. Returning topside in his borrowed clothes, he couldn't take his eyes off the *Mississinewa*, the ship he'd called home. He watched it burn for the next two hours until it finally rolled over to port and sank bow first. "The saddest day of my life," he told a buddy as he watched the *Miss* slip beneath the surface.

Ensign Tom Wicker, *Lackawanna*'s assistant gunnery officer, was moved by the courage exhibited by the survivors and his ship's own small boat crews. Wicker watched through binoculars from the bridge as crewmates Jim Factor, a fireman, and coxswain Willie Potter maneuvered their small boats near flames and smoke to reach men in the water. He walked to the fantail to meet the arriving men and later reported: "The men of the *Mississinewa* demonstrated a great deal of courage. They were laid out on the deck of the ship, many with burns and injuries. Our men would ask, 'Is there anything we can do for you?' 'Yes. Do you have a smoke?' was often the reply. The men, once aboard, complained little of their pain and suffering after medical treatment."

By 0830 *Mississinewa* had completely rolled to port and slipped beneath the waves, leaving only the screws visible above the oily water. Floating pockets of flaming oil and aviation gasoline still burned on the surface of Ulithi Harbor where the bow had been. *Lackawanna*'s water tender Harold Williams stood at the starboard rail of his ship watching the death throes of the *Mighty Miss*. "Thank God it wasn't us," he muttered as he turned away from the awful sight.

———————————

Sailors aboard *LCI-79* had responded to their 0550 general quarters alarm and begun taking on *Mississinewa* survivors minutes later. The oiler's gig was the first small boat to approach *LCI-79*. In the bottom of the boat lay steward's mate Harry Caison, his pink flesh exposed; little remained of the black man's skin. His eyes were milky white and he was in shock; most sailors thought he stood little chance of surviving, but he was transferred to hospital ship *Solace* and recovered from his severe burns.

"There's a man in the water trying to reach us." A deckhand hollered to shipmates for help. "Hurry, get him out of the water before he goes under." The man was Ensign Donald Metcalf, who had been aboard *Mississinewa* for only thirty-six hours when the ship exploded. He narrowly escaped some bulkhead debris that landed in the water ten yards away. A strong swimmer, the ensign headed for *LCI-79*, where the sailors pulled him, naked and exhausted, from the water.

LCI-79 took aboard more *Mississinewa* survivors than any other vessel anchored at Ulithi, rescuing eighty-seven men within twenty minutes of the first *kaiten* explosion. Thirty-one survivors were removed to the hospital ship *Solace* within fifty minutes of their rescue. The remaining fifty-six survivors stood at the rail of *LCI-79* and watched the stricken *Miss* burn furiously, even as their shipmates still aboard continued to jump off the fantail. "I guess I won't have to chip paint off the engine room bulkhead anymore," John Mair consoled himself.[2] Bill Brzykcy stood at the rail wearing only skivvies and dog tags. Like most of his shipmates, his cheeks were wet with tears.

Harold Ritchie hadn't forgotten about Ed Coria, who as far as anyone knew was still sitting in the brig waiting for his trial. Ritchie and a number of other sailors worried about whether he was still locked up or dead, but there was no way to go back into the ship and look for him. They would learn later that his incarceration had ended early, and he had made it safely off the ship.

The crew of USS *Samaritan* had observed the *Mississinewa* fire by 0550 and immediately stoked all boilers in preparation for getting under way. Commodore Carter, Commander of Service Squadron Ten, at 0745 gave orders to proceed to the *Mississinewa* in berth 131. Steaming at 13.2 knots, *Samaritan* arrived at berth 131 by 0824, just as *Miss* was slipping beneath the oil-covered lagoon. Patient transfers from nearby oilers started immediately, and by 1034 twenty-four were aboard the hospital ship.[3] Within a minute of picking up the last *Mississinewa* survivors *Samaritan* was under way and by 1120 was anchored in the southeast corner of the seaplane anchorage.

Mississinewa's chief medical officer, Dr. John Bierley, had been aboard *Samaritan* for almost an hour and received treatment for burns on his back, neck and left foot. "When are you going to let me go help my crewmates?" he begged. Bierley, a surgeon, was increasingly frustrated and continued his persistent requests to see *Mississinewa* patients. An annoyed *Samaritan* medical officer snapped, "Doc, you're aboard as a patient. Now shut up and stay in sick bay." Bierley lay back in his hospital bed.

Samaritan's Boat No. 2 picked up *Mississinewa* bos'n Clarence Walsh from USS *Tallulah* and delivered him to the hospital ship for medical treatment. Walsh was the only survivor picked up by *Tallulah* sailors. Seamen Kirk and Carlson, mortally injured, were transferred to *Samaritan* at 0825. Both *Mississinewa* sailors died within the hour. Machinist mate Stanley Johnson from the *Miss* accompanied Kirk in order to verify what had happened; he confirmed Kirk's identity after his death. Kirk succumbed to his burns by 0930; Clemence Carlson died shortly after. *Samaritan* sailors took the bodies of both men to Asor Island for burial at the U.S. Naval Base Cemetery.

———————

Oily *Mississinewa* sailors were now to be transferred to the *Tappahannock* from the crowded decks of *LCI-79*. After the ship tied up alongside *Tappahannock* at 0917, thirty-six uninjured crewmembers climbed a ladder to the deck and headed for the fantail, trying to distance themselves from the forward AV gas tanks. "We're lucky to be here," electrician's mate striker Joe Morris commented to the survivor next to him. "Maybe you were lucky. I'm not so lucky," came the response as the man gasped for air. Morris learned later that the intense heat had seared the man's lungs. Morris, clad only in skivvies and covered with oil scum, was miserable from the pain of his burned feet. The chief medical officer handed him a bottle of brandy, but as he reached out to take it, it slipped through his shaking fingers and shattered on the deck. The doc handed him another and went on down the line.

It appeared to the survivors that none of their officers had come on board with them. At last, Ensign William Brown arrived on November 22 to take charge of the survivors still aboard *Tappahannock*, whose deck log for November 20, 1944, shows thirty-six *Mississinewa* survivors transferred from *LCI-79*.

———————

Cache, anchored only six hundred yards from the port beam of *Mississinewa*, dispatched a rescue boat at 0558. Captain Beck was plucked from the water by *Cache*'s boat and arrived on board at 0648. *Mississinewa*'s commanding officer watched his ship settle lower in the water. The once-proud oiler was wreathed in smoke and burning furiously.

"I saw my ship completely enveloped in flames over one hundred feet high," he said later. "Tugs arrived at the scene and were pumping furiously on the flames, but to no avail. At about 1000 the ship slowly turned over and disappeared from sight. I cannot report on anything such as Gunnery Department, Engineering Department, Medical Department . . . as the entire episode took place so fast and furiously that there was no time for anything except to abandon ship as quickly as possible."[4]

John Paine, a motor machinist's mate on the *Cache*, had returned for a second run to the fire scene. As Paine's gig made its way again toward the sinking tanker, the *Cache*'s doctor and pharmacists' mates moved quickly to aid the first group of wounded. The gig approached the edge of the flames, and Paine reached over the gunwale to pull an oil-covered survivor into the boat. He was horrified to see the burned skin on the injured man's back roll up like a window shade. The injured sailor passed out from the agony of his burns and was transferred minutes later by stretcher to *Cache*'s well deck.

Cache's motor launch and whaleboat returned to the ship after rescuing three *Mississinewa* officers and thirty-eight enlisted men. *Cache*'s medical officer dispensed bourbon to the *Miss* survivors, with available hands assisting with first aid. Radar striker Ed Kinsler arrived on deck in time for a shot of bourbon. He promptly became violently ill.

Most of the *Miss* crew were in need of decent clothes. The crew of *Cache* dipped into their lockers and donated clean clothes and shoes to the grateful survivors. *Cache*'s galley crew hurried to the well deck with ice water, food and fresh coffee. General quarters had postponed breakfast, leaving plenty of fresh food to feed the survivors. The captain ordered twelve injured survivors in need of medical care to transfer to *Samaritan* at 0840; two more were taken at 1245 at the request of *Cache*'s medical officer.

Captain Beck acknowledged the rescue efforts of the *Cache* sailors in his report to the ship's commanding officer, commending the "boats' crews and persons in charge [who] did an outstanding job in the rescue of survivors. In several cases, the boats had to go to the edge of the flames to pick up survivors from the water. Many of the men had blistered faces from the intense heat and they deserve great credit for a job well done."

Lieutenant Scott, arriving aboard *Cache*, accepted an offer of clean skivvies, socks, tennis shoes and jeans. He then consoled Ed Kinsler, who was crying at the rail as *Mississinewa* burned in the distance. "I couldn't find Pops," Kinsler said in tears, referring to the older radar-man he had befriended. He learned later that Pops had survived.

The Communications Division had not come though the inferno unscathed. Originally numbering thirty officers and men, they had lost two officers, Wally Wilson and Robert Rowe, and two yeomen. Six signalmen and six radarmen, including Pops, had survived, as did nine radiomen and three quartermasters. Supply officer Herb Allen was never found, nor was assistant engineer Bill Atkinson.

As the shock of the morning's horrific events settled in, everyone was numb. Charley Scott and Mac McCollister had lunch in the *Cache's* wardroom in silence; no one wanted to talk about the ship or the unspeakable sights they'd seen. Captain Beck requested to see the surviving *Mississinewa* officers who had been taken aboard other oilers, in order to hear their stories. Jim Fuller had checked several cabins aft to make certain his fellow officers had escaped; he told of ransacking drawers in the cabin of chief engineer Ernest Gilbert in an effort to find a cloth to wave at rescue boats. The cargo officer reported that the cabins were riddled with holes from shrapnel when the ready ammunition boxes exploded.

Gunner's mate Vonzo Smith was seated in the bow of *Mississinewa's* gig as it approached *Prairie* after having unloaded survivors to *LCI-79*. Smith and nine other men were directed to take the small boat to *Prairie*, where the survivors were treated to a breakfast of bacon and fresh eggs. Later that morning all ten men reported aboard *Cache* wearing fresh clothes provided by *Prairie* sailors. *Cache* retained the motor launch brought by Smith to their ship. John Paine, the sailor who had helped in the morning's rescue effort, later saw *Mississinewa's* launch receive a fresh coat of paint and the number 67, replacing the numeral 59 on the hull. The launch was the only noteworthy piece of equipment that survived the sinking.

Aboard the *Mascoma* at 0550 that morning, Captain Henry Timmers had ordered general quarters and sent the ship's motor launch and whaleboat shoving off five minutes later. Rescuers began plucking *Miss* survivors from the water near the edge of encroaching flames. Timmers shifted berths to get farther away as flaming debris rained down on his vessel.

The survivors were covered from head to toe with oil. Few had enough strength left to climb the cargo net; unloading them was a struggle because *Mascoma* was riding high in the water. Sailors offered helping hands and finally got everyone aboard, three officers and nineteen enlisted men.

An older officer, navigator Lieutenant Robert Rowe, was badly burned.[5] The man was unconscious and in critical condition; the medical officer transferred him as soon as possible to *Samaritan* in hopes he could survive his burns. Rowe succumbed without regaining consciousness. He was the most senior officer from the *Mississinewa* to die.

Lieutenant John Bierley, the medical officer from the *Miss*, was injured, but not seriously. "Close your eyes, Doc." The *Mascoma*'s medical officer admonished his counterpart. The medical officer sprayed a blend of antibiotics and oils on Bierley's face to ease the pain from his burns. Bierley knew the burns weren't life-threatening, but he was agonizing over fellow officer Rowe's critical condition. Bierley was relieved to see that the four other men there had minor burns and injuries. Few enlisted men had been injured.

Mascoma crews on the small boats displayed extraordinary courage by risking their lives, edging their boats in close to the intense heat and flames surrounding *Mississinewa*. Six *Mascoma* boat crew members were awarded the Navy and Marine Medal for their rescue efforts.

USS *Pamanset* had been anchored one and a quarter miles from *Mississinewa* when the tanker erupted in flames. *Pamanset* sailors heard the blast from the *Miss* AV gas centerline tank number 3 a minute after the *kaiten* explosion, and knew the ship was in serious trouble. *Pamanset* sounded general quarters at 0555. A motor whaleboat was en route to the scene of the blaze by 0602. *Pamanset*'s whaleboat crew pulled Lieutenant Howard Halper and twenty survivors from the water and returned to their tanker by 0625. Several men with minor injuries were treated, including radar striker J. P. Hammond, whose head laceration from his collision with the flying bridge gun tub was stitched in *Pamanset*'s sick bay.

"Come on, come with me." An officer motioned to Robert Vulgamore, who was naked and covered with oil and scum. The officer took Vulgamore to his cabin and pulled out a pair of boxer shorts, saying, "Here, these just might fit you."

"Sir, that's right nice of y'all," the fireman said in his southern Ohio drawl. "I think I'll wait until I can get a shower before I put these on." The shower was going to have to wait. *Mississinewa* survivors were lined up on the fantail. The ship's medical officer went down the line and handed each man a small bottle of Seagram's Seven whiskey and ordered the men to drink it. Vulgamore downed the liquid and felt a warm burning sensation as it trickled down his throat. He looked at the young sailor next to him staring at his bottle.

"I can't drink that," the youngster protested to Vulgamore.

"Well, you're supposed to. That's what the man said," Vulgamore told the boy. "It might be good for you. That's why they give it to you."

"I'm not going to drink it. Here, you take it," insisted the boy. The young survivor pressed the bottle into Vulgamore's hand in exchange for the empty bottle. The gold liquid didn't last long, and Vulgamore was once more standing with an empty Seagram's Seven bottle when the pharmacist's mates came to gather them.

The men gradually left the fantail to shower, while sailors collected donated clothes for the survivors. The *Pamanset* sailors pulled out life jackets until every one of the survivors had been outfitted. When the Ohio fireman returned to the deck, showered and dressed in fresh clothes, he saw that the *Mississinewa* had disappeared from view. He watched as fleet tugs worked feverishly to extinguish the flames from burning NSFO and AV gas. Smoke still billowed into the sky already darkened with wispy patches of gray and black.

"We don't have bunks for you guys," *Pamanset* sailors apologized. "You can sleep on the deck or in a companionway, wherever you wish." But the *Mississinewa* survivors clustered on the fantail refusing to move, as it was the farthest area away from the bow AV gas tanks.

Seaman Sy Golden realized he was injured only when *Pamanset* sailors cleaned oily residue off his back and found it was covered with burns. The soles of his feet were burned as well, after his shoeless escape from the *Miss*. The adrenaline rush from his escape eventually gave way to pain from his burns. Golden had difficulty walking for several days after, as he hobbled around on his injured feet.

Storekeeper William Ruwell had been the first man to climb the Jacob's ladder from coxswain Tuttle's boat, and he promptly collapsed on the deck from exhaustion. A pharmacist's mate urged him to drink a small bottle of Old Grand-Dad whiskey. "It'll steady your nervous shakes." The calming effect kicked in a few minutes later, and then Ruwell began to notice the slimy ooze that covered his entire body. A *Pamanset* sailor handed him a towel, a yellow bar of soap, a set of dungarees and a pair of white canvas shoes. The soap and hot water did the trick, except for the oil around his eyes that resisted all efforts.

Mississinewa was aflame from bow to stern when Ruwell returned to the well deck; slowly it turned to port until the bronze screws were clearly visible, and within moments it slipped beneath the sea. Ruwell's heart sank. He had never been more depressed. Thoughts of John Costello and shipmates who had perished overwhelmed him as he prayed, "God, guide them through the valley of the shadow of death." He felt he could do little more.

Breakfast was served the next morning, but Ruwell couldn't eat. He managed to down little more than a cup of coffee. Finding a secluded niche on the deck, he curled up and went to sleep. A *Pamanset* sailor woke him, asking his name, rate, service number and hometown, as a list of survivors was tallied; the man suggested Ruwell go to sick bay to treat his burns. He arrived to find a long line of survivors who'd suffered minor burns and sick stomachs from ingesting salt water and oil. The doctor issued a tube of ointment to Ruwell and asked him to apply it freely and often. Ruwell ate a little at lunch and his appetite began to return by Tuesday's dinner.

The transporting of *Miss* survivors to the heavy cruiser *Wichita* would take place on Thursday. An LCM pulled alongside *Pamanset* to transport survivors across the lagoon. Several men had difficulty going down the Jacob's ladder, and *Pamanset* sailors rushed to help everyone aboard. The ride across the harbor was difficult for many *Miss* sailors, as they wondered about the fate of shipmates.

As dusk was falling on November 20, the destroyer skippers grew nervous about the recurrent risk of submarines and began dropping a fresh round of depth charges. *Mississinewa* ship's cook Cookie Cuevas experienced a new round of terror, as did the other survivors. Just as they finally had begun to relax and leave the fantail, they heard the depth charges and rushed to the stern rail, wondering if they would have to abandon ship again.

The effects of the depth charge explosions were amplified with *Pamanset* lightly loaded, and the terrified survivors continued to crowd the fantail rail. The captain left the bridge and spoke to them, trying to calm the fears of the shaken men. He issued orders to his crew: "Put cots on the deck for these sailors. I want a watch set and an eye kept on the *AO-59* guys. If they move at all, notify a pharmacist's mate immediately."

The hospital ship USS *Solace* had a few nicknames among the sailors: "Workhorse of the Pacific," "Can Do," "Ice Cream Ship" and "the Gallant Lady." The *Solace* was the first hospital ship to take on survivors from *Mississinewa*, when at 0647 a small boat sent from *LCI-79* anchored close to the burning tanker. Six men showed serious burns, fifteen others had lesser ones. The survivors described their harrowing escapes to the *Solace* crew as men gathered to listen.[6]

Chief Timberlake, the medical department co-coordinator for patient services, stood on the quarterdeck with the physician, Dr. Beck. Stretcher-bearers and patient embarkation personnel surrounded the two men. Timberlake passed on to *Solace* sailors a story told by a *Mississinewa* patient who had escaped the burning water by diving under the surface, swimming as far as he could, surfacing with flailing arms to splash burning surface oil away, and gulping deep breaths of air. A good swimmer, the patient said that although his method worked well, he found the fire was burning up surface oxygen, and he was about to give up. Out of nowhere, a Navy Kingfisher floatplane maneuvered near the fire's perimeter, trailing a knotted line that survivors could grab. The force of the floatplane's propeller wash blew flames away from men in the water, while the plane's gunner directed the pilot to them. Captain Beck credited the pilot of the floatplane with saving many of his men.

"The pilot of that plane," Captain Beck said, "had more nerve than I like to think of. He saw our plight and put his plane down on the water. Then he would taxi up to the rim of the flames, throw out a thin line with a floater attached to it for those struggling men to grab a hold, and tow them to safety. He kept on going back until he had rescued at least 20 men who otherwise probably would have burned to death. I wish I could find out who that pilot was—he just disappeared after his rescue work was done."[7]

The courageous pilot was later identified as Lieutenant (j.g.) Blase Zamucen, known as "Zoom Zoom" by his fellow fliers. Three months after his heroic rescues, Zamucen and his radioman Russell Evinrude were awarded the Navy and Marine Corps Medal. Zamucen's citation read:

In the name of the President of the United States, the Commander

FIRST Carrier Task Force, Pacific, presents the Navy and Marine Corps Medal to:

Lieutenant (Junior Grade)
Blase Christopher Zamucen Usnr

For distinguishing himself by heroism in the rescue of survivors of a burning, torpedoed ship. While piloting a cruiser based airplane, he saw the ship torpedoed. He instantly turned his plane and flew low over the then blazing ship and seeing survivors struggling in the burning oil near the ship, with no boats in the vicinity, immediately landed his plane to affect rescue. He taxied the plane to within 20 feet of the blazing oil in spite of the intense heat, smoke, and exploding ammunition and threw a buoyed line to the men struggling in the oil near the flames. Upon towing one group clear of the increasing ring of flames he again approached close to the flames and towed a second group to safety. After the second trip, boats approached the fire and he resumed his station on antisubmarine patrol. His utter disregard of his own safety was at all times in keeping with the highest traditions of the United States Navy.

M. A. Mitscher,
Vice Admiral, U.S. Navy

Mississinewa pharmacist's mate Kelly McCracken volunteered to come aboard *Solace* to assist with *AO-59* patients and help identify deceased shipmates. The charred remains of *Mississinewa* sailors were brought to the autopsy room, where Commander Archie Ecklund, a pathologist, was waiting with two embalmers. Ecklund prepared death certificates with help from McCracken. Dr. Lloyd Dahl and his dental corpsmen also assisted. One body was so badly burned it was impossible to take fingerprints; the victim's watch and wedding ring were little more than blobs of metal fused onto his bones. Within two days, McCracken was able to tentatively identify all the remains except for the horribly charred corpse; it was believed the unidentified body was Joseph DeSantis, owner of *Mississinewa*'s mascot, the little terrier Salvo.

———————

By Monday afternoon, November 20, *Mississinewa* survivors were scattered in groups aboard ships throughout Ulithi's anchorage. The survivors spent the rest of the day asking the whereabouts of shipmates. Little was known about other crewmates in the hours after the tragedy, and sailors sought any tidbit of information regarding missing friends. A better understanding of the personnel losses was not known until three days later, when remaining survivors were transferred to the heavy cruiser USS *Wichita* for transportation back to the United States.

CHAPTER 17

The Shadow of Death

The islands in the Inland Sea were beautiful as we passed through. It probably sounds affected to say it, but we felt, "These islands. These waters. This coast. They're ours to defend." We thought, "Is there any more blessed place to die?" I don't think anyone who wasn't a Kaiten pilot can understand that feeling.

—Yutaka Yokota, departing on a *kaiten* suicide mission[1]

Arriving at berth 131 where the burning oiler was engulfed in smoke, Lieutenant Aubrey H. Gunn, commanding officer of fleet tug USS *Arapaho* (ATF-68), was unable to identify which tanker was on fire. The *Mississinewa* was enshrouded in a black blanket broken by flames billowing skyward the entire length of the ship. Gunn cautioned his navigator to warn the helmsman to watch out for the small boats darting in and out of the roiling smoke on the water looking for survivors. The *Arapaho* lay to at 0630 and prepared its fire pumps.

Gunn had just ordered the pumps brought on line when *Mississinewa*'s stern 5-inch/38 magazine blew up with a roar, hurling hot metal debris into the air. *Arapaho* sailors were horrified to hear the screams of a *Mississinewa* sailor trapped near the oiler's stern that was now completely on fire. The crew of *Arapaho* turned to with grim determination as the whistle of exploding lube oil drums heading skyward from the cargo deck rocketed through the air with eerie sounds and fell into the seas with loud hisses. The tug pushed its bow against *Mississinewa*'s port side amidships and slowly scraped down the port side of the oiler's hull while firefighters directed hoses on the port-side flames smothering the stern.

Seeing the action from the nearby tug *Munsee*, photographer Sid Harris gripped his 35mm camera. "We headed in with our bow against the starboard stern quarter, water spurting from about 20 hoses," he said. "The sea around the ship was boiling with flaring up oil. Shells and drums of gasoline were exploding in a cacophony of sound, adding a garish rhythm to the nightmare, blacking out the brilliant morning sun with ominous shadows. A crackling blast of heat almost beat us back, but we came in as close as possible and played out streams of water on the fiercely blazing ship. Ammunition exploding practically under our noses had me worried. With my ears ringing from the concussion of the magazine explosion, I developed enough common sense to place my steel helmet on my head—somewhat dubious physical protection, but it did provide mental relief."[2]

The ready ammunition boxes on the *Miss* received the first streams of water. *Munsee*, still alongside the starboard stern, was made fast to the tanker. *Mississinewa* was now linked with the rescuer, and all hands aboard *Munsee* valiantly fought the inferno at close quarters. The heat was terrific and the clouds of black smoke hampered the firefighting. Aviation gasoline floating on the heavy bunker crude created a billowing inferno around the punctured hull. The fire boiled upward and engulfed the bow of the 205-foot-long tug. Captain Pingley ordered the bowline cast off, and *Munsee* separated from the hull. The tug's engines backed her into the flames near the tanker's stern. Fire hoses had to be directed to the flames now surrounding the bow of *Munsee*.

Harris described the firefighting at the stern of *Mississinewa*:

"We backed off and came around on the exposed side of the tanker, bringing our bow against their starboard quarter and poured water into the blasted, burning hulk. Other tugs had come up and they also nosed in along the starboard side and deluged the flames. Suddenly, blazing oil began pouring around the bow of the tanker and flaming up on the tugs alongside. As the seething mass pushed along the side of the burning ship, one by one, the tugs were forced to back off to keep from becoming part of the holocaust. We [*Munsee*]were the last to go. After dispersing the flames, we came in again amidships, tying up against the AO-59. There was another gush of oil and we were sur-rounded by the viscous, boiling, burning fluid. This fiery river was cut in two with streams of water and extinguished by the other ships as we concentrated on the tanker. From time to time, the black suffocating smoke would swoop down obliterating even the fire and we could only hope we were plying our water on the flames. Soot and oil and salt spray drenched us all; we were covered from head to toe with the sticky mess."[3]

From his vantage point aboard USS *Lipan*, crewmember Fred Kimball noticed that the anchor chain on *Mississinewa* was almost white-hot under the water. Drums of lube oil exploded and whistled off into the sky from the oiler's cargo deck. Kimball smelled paint burning on his tug and saw it curl off from the intense heat. Smoke rose two hundred feet in the air.

Suddenly flames leapt out from *Mississinewa*'s bow and swept over the forecastle of the salvage ship USS *Extractor*. Two sailors were severely burned.

Lieutenant O. K. Coffin, a firefighting officer aboard the fleet tug *Menominee*, was officer of the deck, and he notified his captain, James Young, of the *Miss* explosion and the large oil fire. At that moment all they knew was that one of the tankers in Service Squadron Ten's anchorage area had been struck. Gunner's mate Ed Loebs raced to the aft 40mm gun mount aboard *Menominee* as GQ sounded. All four engines made the tug throb as ATF-73 reached flank speed.[4] Captain Young nudged the tug against the bow of *Mississinewa* but had to back away from the heat and flames. The fire control officer directed a *Menominee* crewman to aim a fog spray on sailors manning the fire-fighting hoses as the heat became almost unbearable. Loebs became alarmed when ready ammunition began to explode, with wayward shells streaking close to *Menominee*.

Loebs could see the port-side 3-inch/50 gun aboard *Mississinewa* glowing white-hot; he thought the gun would melt down. *Menominee*'s executive officer, Lt. (j.g.) C. R. Nance, made his way about his vessel noting the cool proficiency of the crew in such dangerous circumstances; the deckhands sprayed tons of water on the burning ship. As Loebs watched, the oiler listed heavily to port. An eerie feeling came over the young gunner's mate as the bottom of the hull came into view. The end was near for *Mississinewa*.

Fire consultant officer D. S. Gray reported to Commodore Oliver O. Kessing at the scene of the *Mississinewa* fire and offered his services for firefighting.[5] Gray was directed to report to Captain Young aboard *Menominee* at 0710 and noted that the tug's firefighting officer had the streams of water well placed on the burning tanker and crew effectively organized. The two officers, Coffin and Gray, decided the proper technique for fighting the blaze called for heavy streams of water to drive the fire ahead, thus permitting the placement of firefighting teams with hoses on *Mississinewa*'s stern to battle the fire forward.

Pingley ordered his men to report the draft of the tanker to him at regular intervals to ensure time to save his men if the tanker suddenly settled enough to sink. Three hoses were passed to men standing on *Mississinewa*'s blackened and twisted decks. The 2.5-inch Navy fog nozzles were effective in fighting the flames, successfully extinguishing the threat on *Mississinewa*'s stern. The three *Munsee* teams managed to knock the fire forward using straight streams from hoses set at seventy-five pounds of pressure. Soon only the port side and the oil on the water around the settling tanker were on fire, and the tugs standing by concentrated steady streams of water on the remaining surface fires.

At the time of boarding *Mississinewa*, the starboard side forward to the bridge was free of fire. Oil was burning on the main deck on the port side; compartments aft on the poop deck were on fire. Ammunition burned and exploded in the port-side ammunition stowage and clipping room on the main deck amidships. Gray reported later that the ammunition continued to be a hazard to firefighting operations. The port side was burning and oil was on fire along the hull forward of the poop deck. The first hose stream was directed to the port clipping room that was engulfed in flames. Gray reported that the coolness and efficiency of the enlisted men who beat back the flames with their fog nozzles were noteworthy.

Gray directed heavy streams of water to wash oil off the tanker and into the water, thus removing a source for ignition, and tugs nearby moved in to smother the flames on the water. Foam couldn't be used to fight the fire—it was impossible to blanket such a large area. After thirty minutes Lieutenant Gray noticed that *Mississinewa* was settling by the bow. The forward team from *Munsee* was standing on the deck in water that reached to their knees, even in some places to their hips.

By 0815 the fires were completely extinguished from all parts of the oiler still afloat. Sailors secured the hose lines and withdrew their equipment to *Munsee*. *Mississinewa* was sinking; the bow slipped below the surface of the water, and seawater lapped at the main surface of the well deck. Captain Pingley, anxious to get his men off before the ship sank, had been checking the rise of the oiler's stern.

By 0815 it was obvious that the explosion, the shifting oil and the tons of seawater poured on the fire-ravaged *Mississinewa* had sealed the oiler's fate. Captain Pingley ordered all firefighters off the sinking ship. All hoses were salvaged except one that was abandoned when the stern rose alarmingly. All could see that *Mississinewa* was about to slip under the surface of Ulithi Lagoon.

Sailors aboard *Munsee* shouted warnings to the remaining firefighters as they leapt to the deck of their tug. Crewmen rushed to cut the lines tied to *Mississinewa* as the burned-out hulk began to roll to port, luckily away from the small tug. One *Munsee* firefighter leapt from the tanker's deck as she rolled, and he fell into the oily water between the sinking ship and *Munsee*; his shipmates plucked him out of the filthy water.

At 0825 the fire-blackened hulk of *Mississinewa* continued to roll to port and began to sink bow first. Minutes later the only visible features were the twin screws, rudder and a small portion of the stern. Exhausted firefighters stood on the *Munsee*'s fantail witnessing the death throes of a ship they had hoped to save.

Sid Harris wrote a few days later:

> The fire was under control when the torpedoed ship lurched slightly. It was sufficient warning. All men on board rushed for the rail and safety of our ship. They just made it. As we cut lines and hoses and endeavored to get clear, the tanker rolled over on its port side and slowly began sinking, bow first. The shifting of oil through the hole blown by the torpedo [*kaiten*] and the cumulative effect of the tons of water poured aboard while fighting the blaze had overwhelmed the gallant ship.
>
> We headed for our anchorage, to clean up our ship and ourselves. Our last view of the tanker was of its stern, upside down and tenaciously afloat; its twin screws supplicatingly stretched toward the heavens as though they were striving to hold the ship above water—or were they a lonely beacon marking the site of its grave?[6]

Captain Pingley wrote *Munsee*'s Action Report six days after the valiant effort to save USS *Mississinewa*:

> At 0543, the quartermaster on watch called me and reported a fire on board a tanker in the vicinity of berth 130. Preparations to get underway were made. On the approach to the tanker which was identified as the USS *Mississinewa*, that vessel appeared to be enveloped in flames. On closer approach this ship commenced to cover with fuel oil descending from large billows of smoke. Fire pumps and hose were

made ready on the run down, a distance of approximately two miles. Maneuvered to get alongside the tanker's starboard quarter. Several explosions were observed, one, surmised to be a magazine on the starboard side aft, several pieces of metal dropped close aboard. The heat alongside was terrific and clouds of heavy black smoke which enveloped this ship created a disagreeable situation. Ship's ventilation system was secured while alongside. Though it was reported that the tanker was settling by the bow, it was assumed that the tanker would continue to float and preparations were made to board her with foam and foam generators and chemical fire extinguishers.

No survivors were picked up by this vessel. It is doubted if a living person was on board the tanker when this ship went alongside. Crew's space aft was a raging inferno, though this space was brought under control, no signs of living persons existed.[7]

Admiral Halsey formally commended Captain Pingley for his outstanding efforts to save *Mississinewa*.

For outstanding performance of duty as Commanding Officer of a United States Tugboat in fighting a fire aboard a United States Ship on 20 November 1944. Despite adverse conditions and terrific heat, he brought his ship alongside the burning vessel in an effort to fight the fire. He remained in this position, although surrounded by burning oil and in constant danger from exploding ammunition, until all hope of saving her was abandoned and she commenced to sink. His conduct was at all times in keeping with the highest traditions of the naval service.

Fleet tugs and smaller vessels remained on the scene of the fire for the next three hours, until the ship disappeared.

The time was 0905 when the *Mighty Miss* fell beneath the waves of Ulithi Harbor. As the last vestiges disappeared in the murky water, USS *Extractor* placed a buoy marker—a red barrel with an attached red flag—over the exact location where the tanker's stern was last seen. Total time from the initial explosion to final demise was three hours and eighteen minutes.

———————

Even as the *Mississinewa* twisted and sank to the bottom two hundred feet down, the drama continued in the harbor. Destroyers still circled, many skippers convinced there were still enemy submarines in the harbor. The waters were polluted with oil and debris. Tugs and hospital ships still dealt with the wounded and the dead.

While many support craft recovered bodies that day, the fleet tug *Arapaho* was one of the busiest, according to Marshall Doak, the chief pharmacist's mate.

"We heard the explosion," he recalled years later. "I guess we were about a thousand yards from it. We got right under way. The water was covered with smoke and fire, and we didn't find any live people, only bodies. The ships that got there before us were picking up survivors, we were picking up the dead. We took the bodies from the water—we were only about four or five feet clear of the *Miss* and the firefighting was happening on the port side—and so we brought them up on the starboard side. They were examined and fingerprinted."[9]

Doak was used to body recoveries, having taken part in the landings in the Pacific at Eniwetok, Tarawa and other now-historic islands. His years of extensive medical and dental training helped with the grim task he was now facing.

"We used Form N," he said, "a red form that held their fingerprints and a physical description of the bodies, their injuries and any identification, like dog tags. I had six to eight bodies to deal with right away, I got more later. If they had dog tags, we'd state the name, otherwise it was 'Name Unknown.'" Eventually the bodies and the accompanying Forms N were sent to the hospital ship *Solace*, where *Miss* crew members made a final effort to identify their mates.

"The bodies were quite intact," Doak noted. "They all had their limbs and heads intact. Mostly the cause of death was asphyxiation. They'd succumbed to the explosion and lack of oxygen under the water. We were working furiously, and our ship was only ten or fifteen feet from the *Miss* when she went down, but I never even noticed, I was so busy tending to the dead." Doak worked feverishly to identify the dead sailors. He knew how much the families back in the States would want resolution.

"I signed my name to Form N. And since there was no chaplain on board, I became the chaplain, too," he said with a hint of something like pride. He said he felt privileged to send off the dead in a respectful manner, and he took time to honor them.

"If someone was wearing a St. Christopher's medal, I'd dip my fingers in water and make the sign of the cross on their forehead. I said a prayer over every man. I'd say 'God bless this man, God bless his soul, God bless his family and his loved ones. Help them to understand what happened here today.'"[10]

It was a long day, and when Doak was done documenting the wounds and finding what identifying marks or dog tags he could, the bodies went to the *Solace* for further identification by *Miss* crew members. Among the bodies that *Arapaho* sailors had recovered was *Mississinewa* sailor James Moffatt, a fireman first class, found floating in berth 131.[11] Like the others', his remains were delivered to the hospital ship.

Except for Moffatt, no word of the body recoveries was recorded in the *Arapaho* logbook. "At no time did any officer ever come near me to see what I was doing or ask the results," Doak said. "There was too much going on with the firefighting and survivor rescue." The only official record was the Action Report of *Arapaho*'s Captain Gunn, wherein he noted the damage caused by the explosion.

> From the torn up superstructure, our strong belief is that the ship received a hit just forward of the bridge. The ship appeared to be lower amidships than either forward or aft, leading to the belief that possibly

it had almost broken in half. It is problematical whether the ship could have been partially salvaged and towed clear if the fire had been allowed to burn itself out without water being thrown on the fire. However, the ship was gutted from stem to stern by terrific fire in it.

But just after the *Miss* went down, another drama took place with *Arapaho*'s crew. It was an event the significance of which would not be understood by the sailors for many years afterward. The tug crew, tasked now with cleanup, was making another round in that part of the harbor, looking for flotsam; the bodies had all been recovered, so they thought, and the new duty was to clean up the waters. The tug had put a boat over the side with a detail at 0915, as the men were ordered to sink the drums and boxes that bobbed and floated over the oily grave of *Mississinewa*. Among the men sent out to shoot and sink debris was pharmacist's mate Doak, who was known to be an excellent shot. Although he was nearly exhausted from the last two hours of identifying bodies from the ill-fated oiler, he took up his rifle and went out in the small boat.

"We were ordered to sink all the flotsam bobbing in the water," he said. "We got our guns and went out shooting, but there was something out there we couldn't sink. I asked them to get closer so I could have a better look. It was another body! It was floating vertical, standing up in the water column. We retrieved it and brought it on board."

The discovery was as mysterious as it was gruesome. It would haunt Marshall Doak for the rest of his life.

"The body was not Caucasian," he said firmly. "We didn't know at that time there might have been a Japanese submarine in the area, but I could see he was very different. He was wearing strange clothing, a jacket or a uniform that looked like a tunic, strange pants, and his shoes were different. I'd never seen any uniform from any country that looked like that. His head was partly gone—from the ears up it was cut off . . . it looked like someone had taken a razor to his face and just sheared it off, so you couldn't see his facial features above the chin. I was very puzzled. In all my body recoveries I had never seen an injury like this."[12]

The *Arapaho* men brought the dead man aboard. He was finger-printed and searched for dog tags or any identifying marks. Nothing of note was found except his strange clothing and his unusual injuries. Doak recalled later that he was wearing dark-colored long pants that were not a U.S. Navy uniform.

"I prayed over him the way I did for everybody," he added. "God bless this man, God bless his soul. God bless his family and loved ones. Help them to understand what happened here today."

The *Solace* sent a boat over to the *Arapaho* to collect the victims' bodies for further identification and ultimate notification of next of kin. The one body labeled "Unknown" was put on board with the others. No record of the unusual finding was recorded in the ship's log. "There was just so much going on that day that a lot of things didn't get recorded," Doak said by way of explanation. "And then the *Miss* went down."

Although the intelligence was not shared immediately, within a few days of the sinking, the U.S. Navy suspected that Ulithi had been penetrated by an organized *kaiten* attack, as they found evidence of one or more *kaiten* on the reef at Pugelug, and the *kaiten* was mentioned in the Action Reports of the *Case* and *Rall*. The Imperial Japanese Navy, on learning that a ship in the anchorage had gone down, surmised it was Sekio Nishina who hit the *Mississinewa*. It would be fifty-seven years before divers would find the shipwreck and isolate the deathblow that claimed it; that information would point to Nishina, who first entered the lagoon and headed for the *Miss*. But Marshall Doak wouldn't piece it all together until sixty years had gone by, and then he realized that the man with the Japanese clothes and strange injuries was almost certainly Sekio Nishina.

CHAPTER 18

Mission Failure

[For the Japanese] . . . the experience of loss was an almost inexplicably bewildering one . . . Unlike Allied memories of a desperately hard-fought progress through the Pacific to ultimate victory, Japanese narratives of the Pacific War often descend precipitately from brief tales of victory and joy . . . into a shapeless nightmare of plotless slaughter.

—Cook and Cook *Japan at War, An Oral History*[1]

Two Japanese submariners, Minoru Yamada and Toshiharu Konada, attempted years later to understand and explain what went wrong with the *kaiten* launches at Ulithi. Yamada, once the navigator of fleet submarine *I-53*, had studied the U.S. Navy action reports shared long after the war. So, too, had Konada, a *kaiten* pilot himself, examined the documents. With the new documents and history's hindsight, they reconstructed the events.[2]

Hours before Sekio Nishina's launch, Captain Orita had brought *I-47* to a station somewhere off the eastern reef of Ulithi Lagoon. Hovering a few feet below the surface, the first of Japan's *kaiten* had launched from *I-47* between 0415 and 0430; the precise launch time remains uncertain.[3] The other three pilots launched five minutes apart.

The *kaiten* course was to penetrate into the lagoon through Zau

Channel and attack targets of opportunity. However, visibility was limited by the miniscule periscopes, crude navigational instruments, and landmasses that were not only unremarkable but also very hard to distinguish in the darkness. One or more of the pilots may have become confused and headed instead for Zowatabu Channel, the narrow entrance between Pugelug and Feitabul islands two and a half miles south of the intended passage.

Low tide had occurred at 0325 (as noted in Commodore Carter's Action Report submitted to Admiral Nimitz on December 8, 1944). The low tide left the *kaiten* less than nine feet of water in which to make it through the opening—the wrong opening, as it turned out—in the reef; it was not Zau Channel but far to the south. Yamada re-creates what may have happened that fateful morning:

It is likely a *kaiten* pilot from *I-47* became disoriented and lost after his launch shortly after 0400. In the darkness, the pilot may have attempted to locate and penetrate Zowatabu Channel and become stranded on the reef at low tide. *Kaiten* had their 3,418-pound warheads secured in a safe setting until the pilot armed them. The safety device also provided the ability to detonate the warhead if the pilot so chose. The Japanese call this ritual suicide by *kaiten* pilots "self-determination." Once stranded on the reef, the pilot may have self-detonated the *kaiten* rather than be taken prisoner or face a less than honorable death by suffocation or drowning inside the *kaiten*.

Debris from a *kaiten* was found washed ashore on a reef south of Pugelug Island sometime after November 20. The pilot's cabin amidships and the forward section carrying the warhead were gone, but the rear section with the propulsion system for the manned torpedo remained intact.

The remains provided the first evidence of a new Japanese suicide weapon. However, the war in the Pacific was changing so rapidly that submarines at the soon-to-be-obsolete anchorage of Ulithi were not a priority; it was not until January 22, 1945, that warnings of the new threat were sent to the following commanders: Forward Area, Pacific;

the Marianas Patrol and Escort Group; and the Western Carolines Patrol and Escort Group.

With the predawn explosion, *Sumner*'s lookouts had witnessed a very ignominious beginning to the *kaiten* launches, although later that morning one would prove successful. Because of its complexity, the weapon never met expectations or achieved the success of its airborne cousin, the *kamikaze* plane.

The sailors on the deck of *Case* got a good look at Japan's new secret weapon. The *Case* Action Report describes the impressions of topside personnel.

> This submarine was definitely identified as of the midget type. Average of observer's estimates of length was sixty to seventy feet. At time of surfacing, bow was inclined about five degrees upward and two torpedoes were clearly visible, one above the other, protruding slightly from bow. When submarine passed down starboard side at about 0534, screws were visible and appeared to be surrounded by some type of cage guard. Conning tower was low, estimated to be two to 3 feet and a single periscope supported by an inverted U-shaped bracket extended approximately six feet above. With binoculars, it was possible at close ranges existing to tell direction of periscope train. Body of submarine was dirty brown in color, which may have been rust.

Case's executive officer attached two drawings he had made of the action. Drawing number 1 showed the nearby islands, the location of antisubmarine nets and the track of Cruiser Division Five during the attack; a map scale was drawn at the bottom. The second drawing showed the track of the cruisers, as well as *Case* and the Japanese *kaiten. Case*'s exec pinpointed the attack in his report.

This *kaiten* was most certainly launched from *I-47* and probably was piloted by either Sato or Fukuda. Sato was to penetrate Zau Channel and head west for his attack. Fukuda, last to launch at approximately 0430, was about twelve miles from the target area. If traveling at the suggested speed of twelve knots, he should have arrived near the entrance to Zau or Mugai channel about 0530. Fukuda was directed to hit a target outside the entrance to Zau Channel as a diversion. Seeing the ships exiting Mugai Channel, a little over one nautical mile northeast of Zau Channel, Fukuda may have continued north. His arrival, a few minutes before sunrise, would have coincided with the periscope being spotted by *Vigilance* at 0523.

The *kaiten* rammed by *Case* could not have been Ensign Imanishi, who launched from *I-36*. Imanishi was directed on a course of 285 degrees at a speed of twelve knots and would have arrived just west of Mas Island about 0550, much too late and to the north of the ramming event to be the *kaiten* spotted by *Vigilance* at 0532. It is highly unlikely Imanishi piloted the *kaiten* sunk two miles directly south of the center of Mugai Channel; Fukuda was most likely in the *kaiten* destroyed by *Case*.

In a 2001 essay Yamada indicated that this *kaiten* pilot must have neglected to arm his warhead, instead leaving the weapon in the "safe" position. Yamada believed that *Case* would almost certainly have been sunk if the warhead had been armed. If the *kaiten* pilot was Fukuda, he had been sealed in the *kaiten* for two and a half hours; if the pilot was Sato, he had been sealed inside his craft for four and a half hours. Yamada concluded that either pilot would have been adversely affected by the long waiting period and probably neglected to arm his weapon.

U.S. Navy ships anchored within Ulithi Lagoon had all picked up the TBS radio warnings from Cruiser Division Five and Destroyer Squadron Four outside the reef as they chased down and sank the submersible. For most of the vessels, general quarters had been sounded by 0550, and engineering sailors had moved quickly to raise the steam pressure in ships' boilers in order to get under way, should it be deemed necessary.

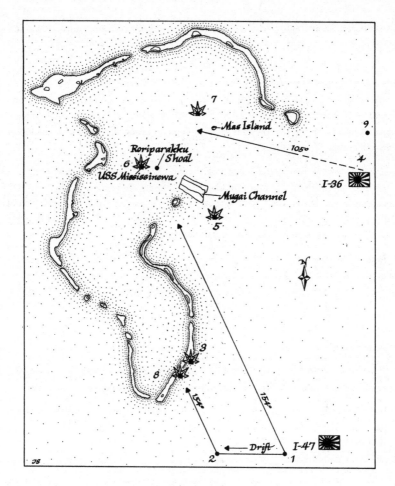

Kikusui Attack

1. Time: 0400: *Kaiten* launch position as reported by Lt. Cmdr. Zenji Orita to IJN Sixth Fleet. *I-47* was reported to be 13.8 miles southeast of the 100-foot-tall bright beacon on Mangyang Island. Orita reported a course of 154 degrees northwest for the attack. It is not known if *I-47* navigator Lt. Shunichi Shigemoto compensated for the .9 knot equilateral current that pushed *I-47* farther west between 0100 and the 0400 launch time. Nishina and the three *kaiten* pilots from I-47 were instructed to follow a course of 154 degrees penetrating Zau Channel between Lolang and Mangejang islands. This attack plan would place all four *kaiten* in the center of Ulithi lagoon, where they would spread out and attack the best target possible. In 2001, former I-53 navigator Lt. Minoru Yamada wrote a 48-page essay on the *Kikusui* mission as he and author Mike Mair shared research. Mair revealed that the U.S. Navy reported two explosions on a shallow reef covered by only 9 feet of water during low tide south of Pugelug Island. The U.S. Navy recovered the remains of one Type I *kaiten* on this reef after the November 20 attack. The

Kikusui mission was compromised from the outset; five Japanese pilots died around Ulithi, including two *kaiten* that blew up on the shallow reef south of Pugelug Island.

2. Time: 0400–0430: Former I-53 navigator Minoru Yamada wrote that in his opinion, *I-47* drifted farther west than had been planned, due to the possible navigational error by *I-47*'s navigator Shigemoto. Note that a course of 154 degrees from the western launch position as plotted by Yamada in 2000 places two *kaiten* pilots on a course that ends in their destruction on the shallow reef south of Pugelug Island. Low tide at 0325 left only nine feet of water above the reef.

3. Time: 0418: USS *Sumner* (ARS-5) reports an explosion on the shallow reef a half a mile south of Pugelug Island. Lt. Commander Irving Johnson, *Sumner*'s captain, reported to Commodore Carter aboard Service Squadron Ten's flagship USS *Prairie* that violent shock waves from the explosion shook his ship. Since explosions from undetected Japanese mines were commonplace, the incident was dismissed.

4. Time: 0454: Ens. Imanishi, launched on a course of 105 degrees from I-36 some 9.5 miles southeast of Mas Island skidded over the antisubmarine net to the west of Mas where he was spotted by alert lookouts aboard the light cruiser USS *Mobile* (CL-63).

5. Time: 0538: USS *Case* (DD-370) rams a *kaiten*, perhaps Sub. Lt. Fukuda, two miles outside the entrance to Mugai Channel, which raises the alarm within the lagoon that a Japanese attack was in progress.

6. Time: 0545–0547: Sub. Lt. Sekio Nishina successfully penetrates Zau Channel and sinks USS *Mississinewa* (AO-59) near the entrance to Mugai Channel.

7. Time: 0653: Ens. Taichi Imanishi was spotted by alert lookouts and was quickly dispatched with depth charges by destroyer escort USS *Rall* (DE-304) between light cruisers USS *Mobile* (CL-63) and USS *Biloxi* (CL-80). Imanishi's body was recovered by LCI-602 in Berth 23 on 23 November 1944.

8. Time: 1132 USS *Sumner* (ARS-5) and USS *Reno* (CL-96) report a large explosion accompanied by an enormous column of water on the shallow reef south of Pugelug Island. Former I-53 navigator Minoru Yamada wrote in his essay that he believed a *kaiten* from *I-47* was stranded on the reef during the early morning after the 0325 low tide. Stranded for eight hours or more, the conditions inside the *kaiten* must have been horrendous in the intense equilateral heat. Kaiten pilots were instructed to use "self determination" and blow up their *kaiten* if discovered by the enemy or if they could not complete their mission. This *kaiten* was not found and may have slipped into deeper water.

9. Time: 2204 Lt. Commander Teramoto surfaces I-36 15 miles east of Falalop Island and jettisons three useless *kaiten*. Two TBM Avengers flying patrol reported a submarine, unable to submerge, fifteen miles east of Falalop Island, bearing 100 degrees. The planes had spotted *I-36* or the useless suicide torpedoes wallowing on the surface. The planes attacked and reported a submarine sunk. *I-36* escaped and sped away on the surface at a speed of 20 knots arriving safely in Japan.

MAP BY JACK SCOTT.

Nishina had been instructed to navigate straight north and penetrate the anchorage as far as he could after entering Zau Channel. The launch time and directed speed of twelve knots would place him at the Zau Channel at approximately 0515, just minutes before the sun rose. He took less than twenty minutes to locate his target after entering Zau Channel; his instructions had been to proceed due north after penetrating the channel, which would have placed him in the midst of Commodore Carter's Service Squadron Ten fleet oilers.

Historians have speculated on why Nishina did not sink an aircraft carrier or battleship. The most likely reason is, simply, that those capital ships were anchored farther to the north, near Mog Mog Island; they were actually located in the target area assigned to Ensign Imanishi. Nishina found himself among the oilers and station tankers of Commodore Carter's Service Squadron Ten. Depth charges were going off all around Nishina, and he must have felt pressed to pick a nearby target. *Mississinewa* was fully loaded, sitting low in the water with its starboard beam squarely facing him as he took his final approach.

The commanding officer of the oiler *Cache* reported seeing what was to be the second suicide sub observed that morning. At approximately 0548, a periscope was sighted four hundred yards from the floating beacon on Roriparakku Shoal; it was on a bearing approximately 310° True. A *kaiten* launched from *I-47* and entering the lagoon through Zau Channel on a heading of 310° would have passed the coral head at the observed distance. Siting the first large, available vessel only a few hundred yards away, the *kaiten* chose its target—*Mississinewa*. *Cache*'s captain could now only watch as the *kaiten* turned and increased its speed to maximize the anticipated damage.

Sometime between 0545 and 0547, as recorded in the deck log of every ship anchored at Ulithi on November 20, 1944, *Mississinewa* exploded, and it soon became clear that it was a strike by an enemy vessel or torpedo. What was not recorded then was that the *Miss* was the first ship ever successfully attacked by the special attack weapon called a *kaiten*, the Japanese human torpedo meant to shake heaven.

Captain Zenji Orita, commanding officer of submarine *I-47* and overall commander of this mission, watched the drama unfold from the mother sub's conning tower. Floating on the surface twelve miles southwest of the lagoon, Orita had taken a great risk by remaining exposed, but he wanted to witness and record the results of the *Kikusui* pilot's attack. Orita felt that an accurate report to Admiral Miwa at Sixth Fleet headquarters would help justify the four lives he had just consigned to their doom.

"5:45, Captain," the signal officer said, as he stood on the bridge next to Orita. "There," shouted Orita as a great reddish-orange light flared in the center of the American anchorage. A column of fire shot up, and a black cloud quickly spread over the sky. Clearly Nishina had struck a target with his *kaiten*. "A direct hit!" the signal officer shouted down into *I-47*'s interior below from the bridge. Although the distressed ship was an oiler, at twelve miles they could not identify it, and in a briefing two weeks later in Japan the hit would be reported as an aircraft carrier. The submariners burst out cheering.

Orita checked his watch and noted that the time was 0547 as he heard the cheers of the men below deck. He shouted, "Congratulations, Nishina!" Orita saw another flash and another column of fire at 0551, several minutes after daybreak, and the crew went wild, shouting and laughing. The captain of *I-47* had just witnessed AV gas fumes explode in *Mississinewa*'s number 3 centerline tank. Orita wanted to stay on the surface to watch the results—a risky gamble, but he wanted to be sure of the *kaiten* pilot's success. The lookout's warning changed Orita's plans. "Destroyers, Captain. Right, five degrees. Range, two miles. Approaching."

Orita responded crisply: "Emergency dive. Take her down to one hundred and seventy feet. Down angle fifteen degrees." Coming to periscope depth thirty minutes later, Orita watched the American destroyer heading back toward the anchorage entrance. The danger to *I-47* had temporarily passed, but Orita remained submerged the rest of the day.

A mild shock was felt at approximately 0637—"a small explosion inside the lagoon," said the sound operator to Captain Orita. It was the precise moment that destroyer escorts *Gilligan* and *Cotton* had begun depth-charging a suspected *kaiten* spotted between the light cruisers *Mobile* and *Biloxi.*

At 0640 Orita ordered all hands to maintain silence and spend a minute in prayer for their departed comrades. Having avoided detection earlier, Orita now made a decision to depart the area as quickly as possible to avoid any further confrontation with the U.S. forces. *I-47,* having launched Japan's first successful *kaiten,* swung north and headed for the Leyte area. Orita slowly navigated away from Ulithi. Years later he said, "Throughout *I-47* men were alternately cheering and crying, happy for the successful warriors, yet saddened by their deaths."[4]

Ten minutes after the *Mississinewa* blew, the second Japanese mother submarine, *I-36,* released its only serviceable *kaiten* at 0454 off the northeastern entrance to Ulithi. Not wanting to risk detection, Captain Teramoto remained submerged and listened for explosions. His sound equipment had picked up one at 0545 and then another at 0605, after Imanishi's launch. The first detonation, coinciding with U.S. Navy Action Reports, was a *kaiten,* irrefutably Nishina striking *Mississinewa.* The second explosion was the oiler's ammunition magazine, blowing up from the fires spreading aft.

As the horror scene unfolded within the harbor and the destroyers feverishly depth-charged inside and outside the atoll, all ships stationed in Ulithi Lagoon were preparing for more submarine attacks. TBS radio had warned the ships of the *Case*'s ramming of a midget submarine while *Mississinewa* burned ferociously in the center of Mugai Channel. Black plumes of smoke billowing skyward served as evidence of a *kaiten*'s recent success.

At 0600 *Mobile* lookouts spotted a puff of white smoke on the water above the torpedo net on its port quarter, on a bearing 120 degrees true and at a distance of twenty-five hundred yards. The puff of smoke, most likely spray kicked up by the broaching *kaiten* scraping on the reef or net, probably revealed Imanishi's presence. A second lookout spotted a periscope in the same direction and location; it was moving toward *Mobile*'s port quarter at a speed of two to four knots.

The bearing and course of the *kaiten* would suggest that Ensign Imanishi, launched from *I-36*, had successfully navigated above the submarine net west of Mas Island and entered the lagoon. After its return to Japan, *I-36* reported that Imanishi's *kaiten* launched at 0454 from a point 105 degrees and 9.5 nautical miles from Mas Island. With a speed of twelve knots, the *kaiten* would have taken forty-eight minutes to reach the reef, putting Imanishi there at approximately 0542. All the evidence—the attack course, timing of the sighting one hour after Imanishi's launch and the location of Task Force 38—coincide with Imanishi's directed attack plan and would confirm his station at the helm of this *kaiten*.

Mobile opened fire on the approaching *kaiten*. The submerged target changed course fifteen degrees to starboard, and the periscope disappeared at an estimated range of twelve hundred yards from *Mobile*. The 40mm fire from *Mobile* had been very accurate, and the course change by the *kaiten* was clearly an attempt to avoid the barrage.

Ten seconds after *Mobile* ceased firing, a small wake was sighted again, originating from the *kaiten*'s position prior to the fifteen-degree course change. Headed directly for the port beam of *Mobile*, the minisub was rapidly accelerating at a shallow depth. Closing to within fifty yards of *Mobile*, it disappeared. The deck log entry implies the submarine dived to a greater depth. Eyewitnesses reported that the torpedo, or submarine, passed under the keel of *Mobile*. Whatever happened, the incident was immediately relayed to the task group commander, who ordered destroyers in the area to get under way and commence patrolling in the vicinity of *Mobile*.

Did Imanishi attempt to attack *Mobile* and misjudge the depth, passing completely under the keel, or was the disappearance of the wake an effort to bypass the light cruiser for a more tempting target? The latter would have been a risky decision, as the water depth under *Mobile*'s keel was only 107 feet.

Eight minutes had passed since *Mobile* lookouts had spotted the periscope. At 0608 a peculiar twenty-five-foot swirl of water was observed between *Mobile* and *Biloxi*. *Mobile* believed a submarine was causing the water disturbance and directed destroyers to investigate. The swirl continued, and at 0640 the first destroyer and destroyer escort arrived in the area between *Mobile* and *Biloxi*. *Gilligan* and *Cotton* began making depth-charge runs between *Mobile* and *Biloxi* on a bearing of 120 degrees, one to three thousand yards from *Mobile*'s position.

Gilligan dropped thirteen depth charges in quick succession. *Gilligan* sailors spotted a small slick of light oil, then a large slick of heavy oil. Two large air slugs, definitely not depth-charge explosions, were seen. Lieutenant Comdmander C. E. Bull, *Gilligan*'s captain, reported that the oil probably came from the fuel section of the *kaiten*. However, *Mobile* personnel had not observed any positive evidence of damage to a submerged submarine or identifiable debris as a result of *Gilligan*'s action.

USS *Rall* had sounded general quarters, and all hands prepared to get under way at 0612. The watch petty officer reported to the officer of the deck that he had seen an explosion aboard one of the auxiliary oilers anchored near the Mugai Channel entrance at about 0550. The TBS watch reported hearing messages that several submarines had been sighted in the channel and a midget submarine had been rammed and sunk by destroyer *Case* near the harbor entrance.

Rall was under way by 0625 on a course of 150 degrees to join the search around *Mobile*. As the destroyer escort approached, *Mobile* notified *Rall* by signal lamp and TBS radio that a swirl had been sighted in the water between it and *Biloxi*. *Rall* was directed south and astern of *Biloxi*; coming about, it headed for the water between the two light cruisers. At 0643 it sighted a swirl two or three yards in diameter about three hundred yards from the port side of *Mobile*. Rising bubbles seemed to further agitate and enhance the water movement.

Many years later Toshiharu Konada, chairman of the All Japan Kaiten Pilots Association (*Kaiten-kai*), explained the swirl and bubbles: During training he had seen *kaiten* pilots dive too deep and get stuck in the mud; the swirls occurred as they tried to extract themselves. Was the *kaiten* on the bottom?

USS *Rall* reported the swirl in the water at 0643[5]; the *kaiten* had received heavy and accurate fire from the guns of USS *Mobile* at 0608, which may well may have damaged it, probably causing it to fill with seawater and sink. Another possibility is that the *kaiten* had dived into the seabed at high speed, its control unit broken, and gotten stuck in the sea bottom with propellers turning, which could have caused the telltale swirl on the surface of the water.

A depth charge set to detonate at fifty feet was dropped at 0647 as *Rall*'s stern passed through the swirl. *Mobile* reported that the charge had overshot the swirl by fifty feet. *Rall* reversed course and, six minutes later, as the bow passed through the swirl, dropped two more depth charges set to detonate at seventy-five feet.

The ships *Mobile*, *Halloran* and *Cotton* all reported two men swimming in the center of the turbulent water immediately following the second depth charge. *Halloran* was dispatched to pick up the swimmers, as it was now closer than *Rall*, whose momentum from the successful high-speed depth-charge run had carried it out of the area. They observed one Japanese male actively swimming, while another man appeared lifeless. Before recovery could be made, one body was seen to pass by the fantail of *Halloran* and disappear. No further mention was made of the other body, but both Japanese swimmers apparently drowned. Unable to find the two swimmers, *Halloran* retired from the area. Because the Type I *kaiten* had only a single pilot, credible accounts that two Japanese surfaced after the *Rall* depth-charging seem unbelievable, yet eyewitnesses on three U.S. Navy ships claimed they saw two Japanese swimmers.

Mobile sent out a small boat to buoy the spot of the depth-charge attacks immediately after the destroyer escorts had left. The small boat crew recovered a block of wood, a wooden seat with Japanese markings and a small, brightly colored pillow with Japanese writing on it, but no bodies.[6]

The reported appearance of two Japanese bodies in the water after this attack remains a mystery. One possible explanation is that the only type of Japanese midget submarine *Ko-hyoteki* that was known to the U.S. Navy carried two crewmen. Possibly American sailors expected to see two Japanese bodies. The U.S. Navy was unaware of the development of the one-man *kaiten* until its first operational mission that morning.

On the morning of November 23, a body was recovered in berth 23 by *LCI-602*. The body, clad only in a pair of shorts, was badly decomposed and bloated. Hospital ship *Solace* identified the body as that of a Japanese male. *Solace* further reported that the shorts had Japanese characters imprinted on the cloth. The shorts were turned over to the commander of the Third Fleet for examination.

Minoru Yamada (*I-53* navigator) and Toshiharu Konada (*Kaiten-kai* president) both stated years afterward that the presence of two *kaiten* in the northeast area of Ulithi is unlikely, given the Japanese attack plan. Imanishi had definitely been in that area and was most likely one of the victims. Evidence would suggest that both *Gilligan* and *Rall* were attacking the same *kaiten* and that *Rall* successfully sank the damaged suicide submarine piloted by Ensign Imanishi.

This account was taken from USS *Rall*'s Action Report and clearly indicates that *Rall* actually dropped the depth charges that resulted in the destruction of the Japanese attacker. Many other accounts of the attack credit light cruiser *Mobile* with sinking the *kaiten* because it coordinated the attack by destroyer escorts. The whereabouts of Ensign Sato, who launched from *I-47* and presumably headed east after entering Zau Channel, remains a mystery.

———

At this point U.S. forces had no idea how many vessels or even what type for certain might be participating in the attack. The lagoon was whipped into a foaming cauldron of wakes and waves as ships and planes searched inside and outside the reef for more submarines. Many U.S. ships attacked phantom targets, and no evidence of other "kills" was ever confirmed.

Four hours after the *Miss* explosion, Captain D. A. Spencer, skipper of the heavy cruiser *Wichita*, returned from Leyte and Luzon with a broken tail shaft and two damaged screws.[7] He delayed entry into Ulithi after receiving word at 0901 that enemy midget submarines might be present in the anchorage. While waiting east of the entrance at 0950, one of *Wichita*'s floatplanes reported a submarine conning tower awash in the vicinity of Mugai Channel. They attacked the reported submarine with bombs and machine-gun fire. A short time later, the destroyer *Ingraham* was detached from the cruiser group to investigate, but no evidence of a submarine was found.

At 1015 *Gilligan* was recalled by TBS to the area around cruisers *Mobile* and *Biloxi*. The *Biloxi* notified it by radio that suspicious small air bubbles were appearing on her port side. Captain C. E. Bull wrote in the *Gilligan*'s Action Report that *Weaver* had depth-charged the area prior to his arrival and he observed small bubbles three hundred yards from the port beam of the *Biloxi*, in berth 16, not likely to be coming from a submerged midget submarine. Nothing further came of this sighting.

News of the *kaiten* strike on the oiler *Mississinewa* alerted ships moored to the southwest of the burning tanker. Light cruiser *Reno* was anchored in berth 630 in the extreme southwest area of Ulithi Lagoon, putting the cruiser about two thousand yards southwest of Zowatabu Channel. The repair ship *Vestal* was moored on the starboard side of *Reno* and *Zuni*, while *LCT-1052* was moored to port. Other ships anchored nearby included *Camel*, *Montgomery*, the disabled cruiser *Houston*, and *Hector*, lying alongside the crippled cruiser. *Gladiator* was in the vicinity of the dry dock, in berth 632, and *ATR-80* was southwest of the dry dock. *Sumner* was anchored in berth 645.

Reno's captain instructed smaller vessels to set up a patrol in order to screen for midget submarines. The skipper of *Reno* dryly noted in his report to Service Squadron Ten that he had meager protection for his cruiser.[8] *Gladiator* was instructed to patrol the area to the north of *Reno*. *Zuni* would patrol an east-west line in the lagoon at longitude 139 degrees 9 minutes. *ATR-50* was to patrol the inside approaches to Zowatabu Channel. *ATR-80* patrolled a north-south line three miles long.

Communications during the day of November 20 indicate that the U.S. Navy quickly realized Ulithi was now a security problem. The commanding officer of *Houston* directed *Current* and all other available small boats to patrol the southern portion of the anchorage. Ensign M. R. Webb from *Reno* embarked on *LCM-78* and was ordered to patrol the inside approaches to Zowatabu Channel. Two motor launches from *Vestal* augmented the patrol. The small boats were equipped with small arms and signaling operators.

At 1050 an underwater explosion occurred on the inner northern edge of Zowatabu Channel. *LCM-78* was on a southward leg of its patrol when the explosion took place, twenty-five feet astern of the landing craft. The explosion did not damage the hull but wrecked *LCM-78*'s engine and caused numerous injuries among the crew.

East of Falalop Island, the three disappointed *kaiten* pilots aboard *I-36* requested Captain Teramoto to surface so they could attempt to repair their torpedoes for a follow-up strike. *I-36* had already braved detection once by surfacing to retrieve Ensign Kudo from his defective *kaiten* strapped to the deck. With the wide-ranging hunt going on above him, Teramoto elected to remain submerged for the rest of the day.

"Sound Contact. Bearing 140 degrees, 1,000 yards." Sonarman third class S. M. Rutledge aboard *Vigilance* had made his second submarine contact of the day at 0723; he lost it five minutes later, then reacquired the underwater target at 0742. At the moment of contact, an approaching convoy was only three thousand yards from the Mugai Channel. Fearing the convoy might be in jeopardy, *Vigilance*'s captain immediately ordered an attack on the sonar contact. Assuming the submarine would be targeting the convoy's ships, he blanketed the area with depth charges set to detonate at periscope level. After the run, *PC-1177* joined *Vigilance*, and they searched the area for the next hour, with no sonar or visual contact.

A Marine Corsair spotted a submerged submarine in the area at 0858. Ship's cook third class Ulus Keeling, manning his 20mm gun high above the water on *Lackawanna*'s flying bridge, watched the Marine aircraft dive toward the water outside the lagoon. Aboard *Tappahannock*, signalman third class Jim Pfeiffer watched the same aircraft swoop down to mark the submerged enemy target. Circling the submarine's position, the plane signaled *Vigilance* with a flashing light while dropping a flare over the location. Reaching the flare marker thirty-six minutes later, *Vigilance* saturated the area with nine depth charges, again set for a shallow depth based on information the Corsair pilot provided. No evidence of a hit occurred and no additional sonar contacts were acquired. These U.S. contacts correlate with *I-36*'s recollection of the day's events, and *I-36* was most likely the recipient of the futile attacks.

Yoshihisa Arizuka, the chief engineer aboard *I-36*, described the morning's attack:

We surfaced and accommodated the three pilots of *kaiten*. We navigated underwater and were caught by U.S. forces who had detected us by sonar. I think it was approximately 7:00 A.M. After that, we were chased until evening. Each crew member has a different memory of these days. Some crew members recall being frightened from over 100 depth charges dropped. I did not feel them as dangerous, as they were not close. *I-36* went northwest after launching Ensign Imanishi.⁹

He reported that all three *kaiten* pilots had been brought back into the hull of *I-36*. Captain Teramoto was now very concerned that the three, ashamed of their failure, might commit suicide, and he ordered a doctor to watch the young officers. Arizuka said later that their reputations had been redeemed—all three went on the next mission and were launched in *kaiten*. They did not die.

As the morning hours of November 20 ticked by, one suicide submarine remained unaccounted for. At 1132 Captain Irving Johnson aboard *Sumner* witnessed his second explosion of the day, when an enormous column of water erupted from the reef close to the location of the predawn detonation at 0418. *Reno* also reported seeing the same explosion.

The Action Report from USS *Sumner* describes both explosions witnessed on November 20.¹⁰ Was this the fate of *I-47*'s missing *kaiten*?

Launched between 0415 and 0430, this last *kaiten* would have been on a heading for Zau Channel, the same course as the pilots who launched before him. This pilot may have been confused by limited visibility. Attempting to cross the reef through shallow Zowatabu Channel at low tide, he may also have run aground. If he had not armed his warhead, as is quite possibly the case due to his long waiting period in the *kaiten*, he might have hoped the rising tide would refloat his vessel and he could finish his mission. However, if part of the sub remained above water during the day, the sealed mini-sub would have been exposed to the intense equatorial heat and turned into an intolerably hot oven. Conversely, if submerged, even the warm tropical water would have slowly sucked the warmth from the pilot's body. In either case, conditions inside would have been horrendous.

Unable to establish buoyancy, the pilot could have been trapped in the small craft for as long as eleven hours as his air ran out. With no opportunity for escape, the lone sailor must have reached the point of despondency. The impressive column of water rising from the self-detonated *kaiten* warhead obviously signaled his conclusion to the unsuccessful mission.

Minoru Yamada, a former navigator of *I-53*, described the overwhelming pressure of failure the unsuccessful pilot surely felt, given his sense of responsibility to the emperor. "[He] may have tried to observe secrecy and only self-detonate the warhead if the enemy came close to the *kaiten*. However, the condition was finally beyond all patience . . . and [he] decided to kill himself after the long wait since stranding."

Commodore Carter indicated that *Reno* was closer to the explosions and may have had a more accurate view of what happened. The first explosion at 1050 was described in *Reno*'s report, later confirmed by *YMS-324* as a magnetic mine set off by a patrolling LCM. The second explosion logged at 1130 and witnessed by *Sumner* was believed to be a *kaiten* blowing up on the reef two miles south of Pugelug Island.

The question remains: Was this the second *kaiten* in seven hours to self-destruct as it attempted to enter Zowatabu Channel that borders Pugelug? *LST-225* and the *Sumner* recovered the remains of a *kaiten* from the reef south of Pugelug Island; the date is undocumented. It is unknown if this *kaiten* propulsion unit, minus the pilot's cabin, resulted from the 0418 explosion or the 1130 explosion. If two *kaiten* had been stranded on the reef and their pilots self-destructed, perhaps one slipped into deep water and disappeared after high tide. The whereabouts of the debris from the final *kaiten* is a mystery.

Small boat patrols continued looking for telltale signs of enemy midget submarines until 2000 hours on November 20. Nothing further was observed within the lagoon, but outside the reef the action continued.

Two Avengers flying on patrol spotted a submarine fifteen miles east of Falalop Island they believed to be a *kaiten*. The sub appeared unable to submerge as the planes attacked. They claimed they sank the target at 2104; however, surface vessels combing the area with searchlights found no evidence of the sinking.

It is possible the submarine may have been *I-36*, surfacing after being submerged all day. U.S. planes sometimes recorded a kill only to learn later it was a surfaced submarine making an emergency dive. And in fact the mother sub *I-36* had been in the area; if so, it survived, because it returned safely to Japan. Chief engineer Yoshihisa Arizuka recalled that after the long, nerve-racking day spent avoiding detection, the sub *I-36* headed for the surface after dark to jettison its three useless *kaiten*. Surfacing close to the time when the Avengers attacked, the abandoned weapons may have provided targets for the prowling planes. From Arizuka's report, it is clear that *I-36* did not wait to determine the fate of the abandoned suicide subs.

"On the way to escape earlier, we heard the sounds of screws from destroyers," Arizuka reported. "Depth charges may have been dropped on us from both surface vessels and aircraft. At 2000 or 2100 hours, we heard the sounds of screws vanishing and we knew the enemy vessels had gone. We wondered if aircraft were there to discover us. Captain Teramoto faced a difficult time. *I-36* had the 13th electric radar, which could detect aircraft over the submarine but not directionality.

"Employing the radar, there were no aircraft sighted," he went on. "*I-36* surfaced, started its diesel engine and escaped from Ulithi at a speed of over 20 knots. It took five or six days to return to Ozushima in Tokuyama Bay. There we investigated the reason why three *kaiten* had not been able to launch."

After sending wireless reports to headquarters in the days after the attack, the mother subs *I-47* and *I-36* returned to Japan, as ordered by Sixth Fleet's Admiral Miwa. Both submarines arrived at the *kaiten* training base at Ozushima, Tokuyama Bay, where *I-36* delivered the three bitterly disappointed *kaiten* pilots to Ozushima in order to train for the next mission. Together *I-47* and *I-36* headed for Kure Naval Base and arrived on November 30.

On December 2 a special conference was held aboard *Tsukushi Maru*, the Sixth Fleet flagship, to discuss Orita's and Teramoto's reports on the *Kikusui* attack at Ulithi.[11] At the conference, attended by more than two hundred staff officers and specialists, the group debriefed the submarine captains and refined strategies for future missions.

Lieutenant Commander Bunichi Sakamoto, Sixth Fleet communications officer, summarized the results:

> Men on board I-47 had seen two fires. The crew of I-36 had heard explosions. Photographs of Ulithi were taken by a reconnaissance plane from Truk, on 23rd November, three days after the kaiten operation; from these, we can estimate that Lieutenant Nishina sank an aircraft carrier, as did Lieutenant Fukuda and Ensign Imanishi. Ensigns Sato and Watanabe sank a battleship apiece.[12]

The overly optimistic Japanese accounts of success, such as this report on the Ulithi attack that credited the sinking of an aircraft carrier, clouded the facts in a way that had plagued IJN war planning throughout the Pacific War. The U.S. Navy provided a detailed and accurate summary of the November 20, 1944, events.[13]

On the *Tsukushi Maru*, officers argued about whether the mission should be kept secret. Orita admitted that Nishina had wanted it so, but said he himself disagreed with the idea: "The enemy knows about it, I am sure. What value is there to keeping it secret?"

Orita hoped that if they made the mission public Japan would discard its strategy of attacking anchorages, for by now air and sea patrols as well as anchorage nets barred the way for *kaiten* to attack. But Orita knew most of the staff of the Sixth Fleet as well as the submarine school instructors were firm advocates of attacking enemy anchorages, and he was argued down before the formal portion of the meeting had even started.

More *kaiten* pilots would be lost in 1945, their deaths considered heroic and noble, in stark contrast to the disgrace and shame for those who failed to die.

Yutaka Yokota was one of many *kaiten* pilots who went on a mission but returned alive, in his case three times. Many *kaiten* were not launched due to damage or malfunction, or because there were no favorable targets, but preparation for each mission required the same stoic ready-to-die attitude. Yokota described his feeling before a launch:

"Kaiten pilots. Board. Prepare kaiten for battle," the sub's speaker blared. Our time had come. Once again we tied our hachimaki about our heads. Because we were men and vain, it would be a disgrace to lose composure. "We are now departing," we declared. "Please await our achievements."

You clambered up the ladder to the hatch leading to your kaiten. You didn't have much time, but you still looked back down and forced yourself to smile. "I'm going now," was all you said. You wanted to be praised after you died, just as much as you wanted it during your life. You wanted them to say, "Yokota was young, but he went with incredible bravery. He was dignified to the end."

At that moment, you're sitting in the cockpit. Compose yourself. Gather your thoughts. If you're harried, you'll fail. You have only one life. "You're going to your mother," I calmed myself like that. The crewman who took care of my kaiten was Warrant Officer Nao. As he closed the hatch from below, he stretched out his hand. "I pray for your success."[14]

On that mission, his second, Yokota sat in his craft after three other *kaiten* had gone; he waited twenty minutes, then was told no more targets were left. His launch was scrubbed. He later went on one more mission and was once more prepared to die, but he returned again, after a faulty fuel line caused his *kaiten* to break down. He wanted to crawl into a corner and die from his failure, he said later. His anguish was even greater when the war ended and he felt shamed at homecoming.

> I was really beaten up this time, called a disgrace to the kaiten corps for coming back alive. They envied me for having been chosen to go when they had not been selected.
>
> One day a maintenance mechanic told me that Japan had lost. What are you saying, you filthy bastard? I could not believe it. That night we were all assembled. The senior commander of the Special Attack Forces told us the news. He was in tears. I left the gathering, and went through the tunnel in the base toward the sea. I cried bitterly, "I'll never launch. The war is over. Furukawa, Yamaguchi, Yanagiya, come back. Please return."
>
> I cried and cried, not because Japan had lost the war. "Why did you die, leaving me behind? Please come back." My tears were not tears of resentment or indignation, nor were they in fear of Japan's future. They were shed for the loss of my fellow pilots.[15]

Japan had so many losses to grieve. Along with the families of the dead, the "mother" of the *kaiten* trainees, Asako Kurashige, was heartbroken for the brave young men who had gone to their deaths.

"We must never again repeat the anguish of war," she said years afterward. "However, we must convey to the young people of today the spirit of the young men who set out in defense of their country."

CHAPTER 19

December 1944

Any man who may be asked in this century what he did to make his life worthwhile . . . can respond with a good deal of pride and satisfaction, I served in the United States Navy.

—President John F. Kennedy,
August 1, 1963, to the U.S. Naval Academy incoming class

Miss survivors coming off other rescue ships were boarding the heavy cruiser *Wichita*. The vessel would be their home for the next month as it transported them first to Eniwetok, then to Hawaii and finally to California. The *Wichita* was a large ship, sixty-one feet longer than *Mississinewa*, and it had a much bigger complement; the crew of nearly one thousand sailors meant there was little room for the additional *Miss* passengers. Two hundred and nine *Mississinewa* enlisted personnel crowded the decks along with several *Houston* survivors who had arrived at Ulithi a month earlier. The tight spaces made it difficult, but the *Miss* sailors tried to avoid interfering with *Wichita*'s crew as they went about their duties.[1]

Hit by a dud torpedo, *Wichita* had limped into Ulithi late on the day the *Miss* was lost. Divers went over the side the next morning to inspect the damage to number 4 shaft and struts. The first group of *Miss* survivors, 145 enlisted men, boarded *Wichita* late in the afternoon on Wednesday, November 22, followed by a second group of 64 enlisted men.

———————————

Two *Mississinewa* sailors met as they boarded the cruiser, surprised to see each other. "I thought you were dead!" John Meirider said to Joe Morris. "Last time I saw you, you were barely above the surface of the water." Morris asked for news of Ed Mitchell, another electrician's mate; the last Morris had seen of him was the night before the attack, when he left to sleep on the bow near the aviation gasoline tanks. Meirider told him Mitchell was gone, and Morris registered the shock.[2] John Mair climbed out of *Tappahannock*'s boat and scanned the deck filling up with survivors. He spotted a missing friend, machinist's mate Alexander Day, who stood with a group of engineering sailors, and heard that most of his engine room watch survived.

Survivors sought out crewmates all over the main deck of the disabled cruiser and asked about buddies not seen since Monday's sinking. Good and bad news produced great relief or grief, and sadness seemed to overwhelm the dazed survivors, who were still processing the loss of the ship that had been their home. The Japanese attack still seemed incredible, yet the bedraggled, injured and shocked sailors had to come to grips with the aftermath. They were suffering with what is now called post-traumatic stress, but in those days it was called shock, and they tried to overcome it as best they could.

As always, scuttlebutt grouped sailors in clusters as they theorized about what had happened and where they were going next. On November 22 and 23 the *Miss* sailors didn't know what the future held, and scuttlebutt fostered the rumor that *Wichita* would take survivors to Pearl Harbor, place them in a rehabilitation station and ship them back to the Pacific. Other men had heard that the *Miss*'s complement would be split up and the men with skilled ratings sent back to sea immediately to fill crew shortages on other Third Fleet ships. The rumors were persistent and *Mississinewa* sailors grew uneasy. Shocked and traumatized, still unable to get the oil off their skin, burned and bruised, all they wanted was to go home.

Thursday, November 23, was Thanksgiving Day. *Wichita* cooks had spent two days preparing a feast for the crew and passengers: roast turkey, sage dressing, cranberry sauce, giblet gravy, creamed whipped potatoes, asparagus tips, baked corn, sweet mixed pickles, stuffed olives, mincemeat pie, fruitcake, hard candy mix, hot rolls, iced drinks and cigarettes. Hungry sailors offered silent prayers of gratitude before the feast began.

That day the *Mississinewa*'s newly arrived officers gathered the survivors for a head count and summoned three *Wichita* yeomen to interview them for personal accounts for a commodore's report. The horrors of the attack—the deaths, the flames, the burning oil and above all the terror—were relived with tears and pain. It made for somber interviews.

Ex–USS *Mississinewa* skipper Beck addressed what was left of his crew. He told the men that, because he had brought *Mississinewa* sailors to the Pacific as a group, he would make certain they returned to the United States together. The promise came as welcome news to survivors.[3]

Commodore W. R. Carter, commander of Service Squadron Ten, received all the eyewitness interviews and the first death tally. He sent a report to various Pacific commands on November 23 after receiving the head count of survivors aboard *Wichita*; hospital ships *Samaritan* and *Solace* also forwarded their lists of *Mississinewa* patients. The list was later revised to read as follows:

OFFICERS

Survivors	16
Missing	3
Dead	1
Total Attached	20

ENLISTED PERSONNEL

Survivors	220
Missing	45
Known Dead	13
Total Attached	278

Casualty figures were revised again three times before final notification went to the families of the sixty-three deceased; their status had changed from Missing to Presumed Dead to—finally—Killed in Action. Sixty-two men were killed or went missing on November 20 or immediately afterward, and the sixty-third man succumbed to related medical trauma two months later.

Commander Philip Beck received orders on November 22 to go to Pearl Harbor and bring survivor lists and all pertinent data. Beck was also ordered to ask *Mississinewa* survivors to identify the remains of any still unidentified dead crewmen.[4] Though the men tasked with this duty would forever remember it as the worst part of the ship's sinking, few could recollect the details later, their minds mercifully blocking out the memories.

Ensign Pat Canavan had the task of selecting the men to identify bodies; he accepted volunteers from the survivors.[5] Machinist's mate first class Gus Liveakos was one of the first to volunteer. Liveakos's friend, gunner's mate Vonzo Smith, volunteered to identify shipmates from the gunnery department; Coxswain Earl Tuttle did the same for deckhands.

A Catholic priest serving as a Navy chaplain gave strict instructions to the volunteers: A positive identification would be accepted *only* if a shipmate recognized the face of the deceased. Each volunteer was issued a surgical mask and led to a tent on Asor Island containing the recovered bodies of *Mississinewa* sailors. It took a considerable amount of time to examine the bodies, but the volunteers managed to positively identify eighteen men. Ten bodies had been burned beyond recognition. Sailors returning from the I.D. detail described burns so severe that they recognized some deceased shipmates only by their tattoos.

Ensign Canavan accompanied seventeen-year-old Ed Kinsler in a launch to Mangejang Island to identify bodies that might have washed ashore there. Before embarking in the launch Kinsler had begged to be relieved of the duty, but Canavan insisted that orders were orders. The pair reached the beach and came upon a dismembered arm. Kinsler promptly became sick and fell to his knees in the sand, vomiting and crying.

"I can't do this," the seaman said. "Shoot me if you have to, but I just can't go on." The previous two days of death, fire and destruction overwhelmed both men. The young ensign began to weep as well; they forced themselves to move on with the unspeakable task.[6]

The number of dead kept mounting, and it would finally reach sixty-two in the weeks after the sinking. The final fatality came two months later, when machinist's mate Pellegrino Porcaro, a volunteer for I.D. duty, died at the Cheyenne, Wyoming, naval hospital from acute sinusitis and secondary meningitis caused by fire and smoke damage. He was the last man from *Mississinewa* to die of medical problems resulting from the November 20 attack.

The identification of the deceased continued on November 24 and 25, and the sailors assigned to the detail came back aboard *Wichita* by November 26. As a reward for their service, Liveakos and the six other volunteers were flown to Johnston Island, where they were given a second Thanksgiving dinner.

At this time the survivors learned some good news: The fueling support provided by the *Mighty Miss* in its last weeks had paid off in military victory, when the Palaus were fully secured by the Marine First Division on November 25 after seventy days and nights of fighting from cave to cave. Operation Stalemate had succeeded in its mission, and the *Mississinewa* had contributed significantly. Palau's Kossol Passage provided an unsheltered anchorage for supply vessels 550 miles east of the Philippines, and it also provided a base for three squadrons of long-range patrol and search planes.

After the boilers were lit aboard *Wichita* on Sunday morning, the crippled cruiser got under way. As the cruiser exited the channel entrance near 0600, the *Mississinewa* sailors lined the rail, bidding farewell to Ulithi. Fleet carrier *Enterprise*, cruiser *Wichita* and screening destroyers *Carlson* and *Crouter* increased their speed to sixteen knots and commenced gunnery practice at 0743 with 5-inch batteries and 20mm machine guns firing at target sleeves towed by *Enterprise* planes.

The unannounced gunnery practice shattered the already frayed nerves of *Mississinewa* survivors, who scrambled for cover. Bill Brzykcy had been standing next to a gun turret when the gun crew cut loose with both barrels in one salvo and knocked him off his feet. The smell of cordite hung in the air.

The concussion of a 5-inch gun near Bob Vulgamore nearly blew him overboard, but he hung on to the rail as blast after blast assaulted his unprotected ears. Vulgamore had trouble with his ears all the way home and never recovered full hearing. Seaman Earl Givens was walking near the fantail, unaware of the gun crew at their 5-inch/38 stations above him. The 5-inch muzzle blast spun him around and slammed him up against a bulkhead. He staggered away, unable to hear for the next three hours. Three days later it happened again: The already shell-shocked survivors were reminded they were aboard a ship of the line as ninety-five rounds of 5-inch ammunition were expended during gunnery drills.

The crew still sought news of missing crewmates. John Bayak learned that his friend Gaston Cote had died. Cote had been sleeping in the crew's quarters under the bridge—in Bayak's assigned bunk—when the ship was hit. Fire room sailors Howard Bochow, Red Foster and Ray Fulleman asked if anyone had seen Edmund Smith, the water tender known as "Smitty," in the water. None of the black gang had. They'd find out later he was missing in action, presumed dead.

Mississinewa cooks Fernando Cuevas and John D'Anna learned that their good friend Frank Lutz, the chief commissary steward, had died of a heart attack in the water. Just a month before Dr. Bierley had given him a physical exam and pronounced him fit for duty, but either the shock or the strenuous efforts to escape the ship had proven too much for his heart. Two weeks before his death the cooks had celebrated Lutz's anniversary marking thirty years of Navy service with a special meal, and Lutz had applied for shore duty after learning he was eligible due to his advanced age. Cheated by fate, he died in the oily waters of Ulithi.

Fred Caplinger was one of the busiest survivors aboard the cruiser; he labored in the paymaster's office patching together payroll records to help the homeward-bound sailors. The *Mississinewa* payroll records had gone down with the ship, requiring Caplinger to rely solely on his own memory to decipher the truth from interviews with his shipmates to complete their payroll records. Caplinger also needed to compile records of immunization shots before the survivors could debark from the cruiser once they reached the States. The storekeeper visited sick bay frequently, interviewing shipmates wrapped up like mummies in burn bandages.

Wichita limped into Eniwetok's harbor on December 1, the trip from Ulithi having taken seven days. Deckhands topped off *Wichita*'s fuel bunkers, and the cruiser immediately started its next leg to Pearl Harbor, en route to the final destination: California. The slow-paced *Wichita* steamed in column, screened by *Pocomoke* and *Wilkes*.

Although the crew was headed home, war still blazed on in the Pacific, and at times the cruise was eventful. Shortly after noon on December 4 a scream pierced the air when *Wichita* sailor Charles Gust lost his balance on a port side gun director and fell thirty-five feet to the communications platform below. Hitting the platform headfirst, he fractured his skull and died instantly.

Except for that horrific accident, life aboard the homeward-bound cruiser was mostly tedious. While the *Wichita* sailors were a working crew, most *Miss* sailors, having no watches and no duty, hung out with friends from their former watch sections. Bob Vulgamore had a deck of cards and played endless games of Idiot's Delight. John Mair sat under a gun turret spit-polishing his regulation shoes; after three weeks of polishing his shoe leather every single day, he felt he could lay claim to the shiniest pair of black shoes in the Pacific.

Vince Carelli, still the incorrigible gambler, passed his time playing poker with his borrowed stake of $25. The New Yorker won easily and relished the opportunity to relieve *Wichita* sailors of their pay. He had a long way to go to make up for the $8,000 loss on November 20—all his mess hall winnings had sunk to the bottom of the lagoon when he slipped out of his dungarees to swim away from the sinking ship. He played anybody who would play, jacks or better to open, and began to recoup his lost money.

The *Wichita* left Pearl Harbor and passed Hospital Point by mid-afternoon on December 9, to continue the journey home. By nightfall the cruiser's speed had reached sixteen knots and the crew and the *Miss* passengers began to anticipate their arrival at San Pedro, but a Pacific typhoon was gathering strength and the crippled cruiser was approaching the path of the storm.

Even before the weather added to their misery, conditions for the last leg of the trip home felt pretty rough. Sleeping accommodations for the passengers were virtually nonexistent. A few lucky sailors found themselves assigned to bunks, but most survivors had to sleep on the open deck. Ray Fulleman and four buddies curled up on the steel deck under a 40mm gun mount. Ammunition-ready racks and the weapon's steel plating offered little protection from the cold wind. When men huddled together on the deck to sleep, the two outermost men suffered, almost freezing from the increasingly cold nights. Every so often the sailors would rotate positions and two new unlucky survivors assumed the outer sleeping positions. As the cruiser reached northern latitudes, the survivors were finally allowed to sleep on the mess hall deck. A few lucky men even enjoyed the luxury of mattresses.

The typhoon blew in and the seas lashed the ship savagely. Bill Brzykcy watched the tossing waves rise perilously close to his perch near the bow, forcing him to make his way aft. Safety lines were rigged on deck, and Brzykcy had to grab one to keep his footing as water poured across the deck and drained over the side of the heavy cruiser. He'd almost reached the safety of the mess hall when the ship rolled to starboard and knocked him off his feet. The deck nearly touched the sea as he hung on to the line with all his might, desperate to keep from being washed over the side.

The cruiser rolled back to port, and Brzykcy leapt for safety, disappearing down the mess hall hatch. There he viewed an incredible mess. Coffee cups, trays, silverware, shoes and clothes had been tossed back and forth across the lower deck that was awash in the seawater pouring down the hatchway. Brzykcy watched a fellow shipmate vomit into the debris.

The survivors bedded down for the night, but the typhoon kept a relentless grip on the ship. With only two screws working, the crew held little hope of outrunning the storm. Shortly after midnight the wind peaked and unleashed its full fury against the stricken vessel.

It was a nightmare. Survivors trying to sleep in the mess hall began to slide from wall to wall, bouncing off the bulkhead and pitching headlong into the opposite wall. Pots and pans crashed down, clattering noisily as utensils hit the deck. Bumps and cries of pain were heard as bodies of sleepless survivors thudded into one another or hit hard against bulkheads and tables. Bob Vulgamore reached up above his head for a handhold as he lay on his mattress under a mess hall table, which was attached to a bulkhead. He held on with a demon grip.

After three terrifying days, the battered and bruised seamen finally felt the ship stabilize on December 12. They learned later that *Wichita* had rolled forty-six degrees during the storm and even took water in the smokestack. The cruiser that had survived the Pacific fighting almost got sent to Davy Jones's locker by a rogue typhoon.

The last three days of the cruise dragged on as bored sailors waited for a glimpse of land. *Wichita*'s surface radar pinpointed San Miguel Island at 0350 on December 15, and Santa Rosa Island came into view three hours later. Finally the California coastline appeared on the hazy horizon. Sailors lined the rail, some hanging their heads to hide the tears welling up in their eyes. Heads were bowed and hearts were thumping as survivors got their first glimpse of America since their departure six months earlier.

The ship docked. Strangely, the skipper of *Wichita* released his own sailors to disembark but ordered the *Mississinewa* crew belowdecks. The survivors sequestered below heard a dockside band playing "Anchors Aweigh." One *Miss* sailor made his way topside, against orders, and quickly dropped back down the ladder from the hatchway to report. "This is great—there's a band playing and girls giving out donuts and coffee," he relayed to his fellow crewmates. A few men tried to go topside, but a *Wichita* officer stopped them at the hatch, yelling, "Where do you guys think you're going?" He ordered them back and they waited for a half hour, then rebelled.

Mississinewa sailors grumbled belowdecks as they chafed at the senseless restraint. The survivors were told they would report to the commandant of the Eleventh Naval District to await assignment. Strains of music from Xavier Cugat's Latin American band at dockside floated through the air, and *Wichita* crewmen taunted the survivors, "The old man doesn't want your ragtag bunch seen on deck." The survivors, seething with resentment, looked at one another. They wore the same mismatched clothes they'd worn for the last thirty days. Apparently the captain felt that if there were no uniforms, there'd be no topside view, no cheering crowd, no reception.

An hour after the cruiser docked the captain finally relented and permitted the motley crew to head topside. The *Wichita* sailors had already departed and the band was gone. Undaunted, more than two hundred bedraggled men from the *Miss* filed down the gangplank of the cruiser and finally felt the security of a stateside dock under their feet. They were home.

The greeters had already kissed their men and left the dock. For the *Miss* crew, there was no band, no girls and no welcome. They surveyed the dock, littered with cups, napkins and WELCOME HOME signs for the *Wichita* sailors. An officer gave the order to "Fall in," and the survivors lined up dockside for a quick lecture on secrecy: "You men are not to talk about the ship's sinking to anyone. The Japs may not know what they've sunk." They marched in loose formation to waiting buses and stake trucks to be transported to the San Pedro barracks. Because they had lost most of their personal items as they abandoned ship, their worldly goods consisted of a small ditty bag, with comb, soap and toothbrush, and the mismatched clothes on their backs.

They felt like orphans as they reached a remote barracks area on the base and were still kept confined. Finally an officer told them to line up and said they could call home, but once again they were given a strict warning: Tell no one about the sinking of the *Miss*.

"Don't tell anyone where you've been, what happened, or where you are now" was the stern message. "Simply tell your families you're okay and coming home soon." But the order didn't make sense, for right there in San Pedro they had seen an Associated Press story in the *Los Angeles Times* featuring a photo of the *Miss* burning and another story of Zamucen's daring floatplane rescue.[7] The newspaper stories had already alerted some of their families to the tragedy at Ulithi.

Years afterward the survivors recalled the impact that news had on their families and the general public. When these sailors got home, John Mair said, "everyone had seen Joe Rosenthal's photo on the front page of every newspaper in the U.S., so they told family and friends about their escapes."

Even so, while the survivors stayed on San Pedro, no mention was ever made of how the ship was sunk, either by the Navy or by the

Associated Press. The crew did not know what sank their ship—they assumed they had been torpedoed.

The diaspora of homecoming began to take shape as the men called home, got money, made arrangements to get back to Iowa, New York, New Jersey, Wisconsin. They spent a few days getting organized and at times ducked into the base canteen for donuts and coffee. One of those mornings John Mair wore the shiny shoes he had spit-polished, his only presentable feature, and followed two scruffy-looking shipmates into the canteen. A Red Cross volunteer looked at them with surprise and said they'd have to leave. "Hey, ma'am, this is all we've got to wear. We lost our ship!" came Mair's reply. Seeing the sailors were hungry, she relented. Back at the barracks a short time later, officers told the rest of the crew that the base canteen was off-limits until they were issued uniforms.

Many sailors had received back pay aboard the *Wichita*, thanks to the efforts of storekeeper Fred Caplinger to re-create pay records, but other *Miss* survivors were penniless. Pharmacist's mate Kelly McCracken loaned John Bayak a few dollars but asked for a payback. Bayak made good, but McCracken wondered later why he had even asked for repayment—after all they'd been through together, money seemed trivial.

When the sailors submitted their lists of items lost in the sinking, they knew no proof was needed to get reimbursement, and more than a few took advantage. "I lost a watch when the ship went down" was the story of many *Mississinewa* sailors that day. After getting compensation for a new watch, Fred Schaufus was one who walked away with a smile—like many other claimants, he'd never even owned a watch.

Some sailors needed money to get home for "survivors leave," and the base chaplain connected them with the Red Cross, which was offering loans, payable with interest to be sure, but loans that could pay for transportation home. A railroad representative made arrangements to get the men on the trains to head east. Eugene Cooley, the one survivor from the *Miss*'s bow, was one who accepted the Red Cross loan.

But the newspaper revelations of *Mississinewa*'s demise played havoc with families waiting for word on their sons, and families that had stopped hoping, convinced their sons were dead. One sailor who had to convince his family he was alive was the ship's cook, John D'Anna.

D'Anna called his home in Detroit and he heard his father's voice. "Dad, it's John. I'm in San Pedro. I'm coming home," he said. Incredulous, D'Anna's father dismissed it as a prank pulled by John's brother Sam, and he said angrily, "I'm going to beat you up. John's in the Pacific." John tried again. "It's really me, Dad! I'm in the States. I'm coming home." The phone went silent. The elder D'Anna was speechless; he handed the phone to his daughter, who conversed excitedly with her brother. Young D'Anna was penniless, so his father dashed off to the Western Union office to send $100 for a train ticket to Detroit.

The Mair family was equally stunned by their good fortune. "Jackie? Is it really you?" Ella Mair asked from Clinton, Wisconsin, hardly believing her ears as her son's voice came over the phone from California. "It's true, Ma. I'm coming home for thirty whole days." John Mair hung up the phone without saying why he was coming home or that his ship was gone.

Ray Fulleman had delayed calling home with the news of his arrival stateside, but when he saw the AP photograph in the newspaper, he feared his mother might see it. He called and found with great relief that the Wirephoto hadn't yet come out in his hometown paper. He left Los Angeles's Union Station for the first leg of his trip to New Jersey. Shivering in the freezing Chicago winter air as he waited for his connection, he found that his tailor-made dress blues of eight-ounce wool weren't thick enough for the frigid northern city. Pulling the collar of his pea coat right up to his squared-off sailor's hat, he tried to stop his uncontrollable shivering. He boarded the eastbound train and arrived on Christmas Day at New York's Grand Central Station, where he caught a subway headed for Penn Station. Finally arriving at Newark, New Jersey, he took a streetcar for downtown Verona, arriving at 11:00 P.M. He grabbed a cab to avoid walking four blocks in the blowing snow in his lightweight dress blues. A few minutes later he was reunited with his family, who stayed awake all night to celebrate the sailor's home-coming.

A few weeks earlier, another mother had been unaware of her son's danger. In late November, deep in the backwoods near Portland, Ore-gon, Mary Girt encountered the oil deliveryman, Blondie, at the fami-ly's logging mill and asked him to mail a letter to her son John, who was "somewhere in the Pacific aboard the *Mississinewa*." Blondie trav-eled back to town with the letter on the seat beside him, but for some reason he didn't mail it. The next day he got a nasty shock when he picked up the local paper and saw the AP photo of the *Miss* burning up. How could he possibly go back to the logging mill and face Mary, knowing her son's ship had been torpedoed? Just before Christmas he drove up the rutted logging trail with foreboding. He hadn't mailed Mary's letter, and he still didn't know John Girt's fate. But it was all right: he heard her happy voice saying, "John's all right—he called the Jewell Fire Station yesterday and he's coming home for Christmas."

In Bethlehem, Pennsylvania, John Bayak was thinking about mar-riage. Arriving home a month after the sinking, he sought out his girl-friend, Helen, seventeen years old. The couple knew that even though he'd survived the *Miss* attack, times were uncertain, as the war still raged. They decided to get married. A few weeks later seventy-five guests gathered at St. John the Baptist Church to witness their wed-ding vows.

For John Mair and the other sailors going home by train, there was little to do on the way except eat, sleep and gamble. Cards and dice came out of hiding, and the heated cries of "Full house!" and "Flush!" entertained other travelers. Mair played poker all the way to Chicago. Christmas night in his hometown in Wisconsin was cold that year—twenty degrees below zero—but it seemed warm and welcoming to the young man who'd seen so much death and danger in faraway Ulithi. For a month he'd be able to forget fueling warships at sea.

Even as the *Miss* men took their survivors leave, the War in the

Pacific carried on. On December 8, as Mair had sailed home on the *Wichita*, the US Air Force had started a seventy-two-day bombardment of Iwo Jima. In great secrecy, on December 17 the U.S. Army Air Force began preparations for dropping the atomic bomb on Japan by establishing the 509th Composite Group to operate the B-29s that would deliver the weapon.[8]

While *Miss* sailors were reuniting with their loved ones back in the States, the week of December 20–27, 1944, marked an engagement of great import in the European Theater of War. The Battle of the Bulge was focused on an intense encounter between American and German forces in a small town in Belgium called Bastogne, a crossroads in the Ardennes vital to the German campaign. American troops were encircled and under siege, and the situation appeared increasingly desperate. Most of the battle's twenty-seven hundred American casualties took place during the first three days. The coldest, snowiest weather that the rugged, mountainous forest had seen in memory took a serious toll on U.S. troops. On the 26th the besieged American forces were relieved by elements of General George Patton's Third Army. Bastogne was a game-changer for the European Theater, retaining control of the critical region and boosting morale among Allied troops.

That December after the *Miss* went down, dozens of Navy families struggled to understand why fate had taken their boys. The lucky ones celebrated the return of their heroes. Some sailors' tours were finished; some would go back to war, but for the moment they were home. The *Mississinewa* was left to sink into the mud of Ulithi, and the reason for the sinking was still closely held in intelligence circles. The U.S. Navy did not officially acknowledge the real story behind the front-page Associated Press news and photo making headlines around the country, so heavy was the veil of secrecy around Japan's suicide weapon, the *kaiten*.

CHAPTER 20

Setting Sun

There are different kinds of war. In those days a surrender meant a surrender and a treaty meant a treaty. In those days you came forth with a flag and it was over. In World War II, all the combatants were in uniform, other than the spies. Today it can be anybody who's your enemy. And now a war just keeps on going—there's no declaration of war, and sometimes it seems there's no end.

—Daniel Inouye (1924–2012),
late U.S. senator from Hawaii, WWII military hero[1]

As a result of the Japanese penetration of Ulithi Lagoon, and as U.S. naval officers began to comprehend the nature of the *kaiten*—a much smaller type of submarine than the larger fleet subs and therefore able to utilize smaller side entrances—the strategy and tactics of U.S. antisubmarine warfare would shift.

The initial response to the *Mississinewa* attack was an immediate and ferocious counterattack. U.S. Navy ships instantly began patrolling within Ulithi Lagoon, the Third Fleet anchorage, using the typical antisubmarine tactics used by destroyers and destroyer escorts. The weapon of choice was the ashcan depth charge rolled off the fantail depth-charge racks; hedgehogs could not be used due to the close proximity to other ships. Destroyers also patrolled outside the lagoon. But questions now arose as to how the submarines had successfully entered Ulithi in the first place.

On December 8 Commodore Worrall Carter, commander of Service Squadron Ten, sent his Action Report of the events of November 20 to Admiral Halsey, whose staff reviewed it. Halsey's chief of staff Robert B. Carney drew up a report on January 7, 1945, with his recommendations; his report was forwarded to Admiral Chester Nimitz, commander in chief, U.S. Pacific Fleet, at Pearl Harbor.

The report noted the Navy's regret at the loss of the oiler but acknowledged the crew's "cool courage in abandoning the ship." It first summarized the Ulithi findings: USS *Reno*'s commanding officer recommended netting all small channels at Ulithi; Carney recommended a better job of netting Mugai Channel, and ordered that no ships could anchor in direct line of the Mugai Channel entrance.

Carney's report also issued general orders for the Pacific Theater: All Pacific fleet anchorages must be completely netted, and baffles and gates must be used in the channels. A significant change was ordered for patrol boats: "PS- and SC-class vessels must be assigned to patrol the interior of anchorages in place of waiting for combatant ships to return for upkeep and repair." Previously, warships returning to port had been used for submarine defense; now the patrol boats were ordered to patrol the interior of harbors.

It took until Carney's recommendations on January 7, 1945, for Admiral Halsey to issue a warning to Pacific commands to net all anchorages and step up ASW measures to guard against *kaiten*. When he did so, ASW patrols outside fleet anchorages increased substantially.

Halsey admitted that the Pacific Fleet had been complacent and did not expect a Japanese attack on a major fleet anchorage. In fact, the attacks on anchorages did not end with the demise of the *Mississinewa*—a second *kaiten* attack occurred at the same anchorage in January 1945; no Allied ships were damaged. By February the Imperial Japanese Navy had reviewed its two missions to Ulithi and decided to attack U.S. supply lines and warship targets in the open sea with *kaiten*.

As the Allies in Europe marched toward the Rhine, greater U.S. deployments were arriving in the Pacific in early 1945. Allied war strategy and military might focused on the open sea, where the *kaiten* was never meant to operate. Although Japanese Navy officials finally persuaded the high command to use the *kaiten* to disrupt communications and shipping rather than to make anchorage attacks, the craft, difficult enough to maneuver in shallow water, was too erratic for the long distances at sea. The remaining *kaiten* missions were largely unproductive, as few I-class subs were left to carry *kaiten*, and an I-class submarine's speed, maneuverability and effectiveness was hampered by the weight and drag of four or six *kaiten* strapped to the deck.

Furthermore, the severe limitations on the activities of Japanese surface ships in the last months of the war, due to fuel shortages and other logistical problems, meant the surface ships never became fully operational in the role as *kaiten* parent craft. Despite the willingness to sacrifice their lives, the pilots and their suicide *kaitens* failed to change the course of the war, partly because of the changed tactical conditions and partly because of U.S. Navy intelligence.

After the Ulithi attack by the submariners of the *Kikusui* Mission, nine other expeditions were sent out before the war's end.[2] The second mission, called Kongo, sent out six submarines at the end of December 1944 to different locations: Ulithi, New Guinea, Palau, Guam and the Admiralties. They engaged with a transport ship in Palau, USS *LST-225*, but no sinking of Allied vessels was confirmed, although the Japanese claimed that the New Guinea strikes were fruitful. During that expedition to Ulithi, one of *I-38*'s *kaiten* approached the ammunition ship *Mazama* but prematurely detonated forty yards off the ship.[3] Other missions to Iwo Jima and Okinawa followed, with little success. The ninth *kaiten* mission, *Tamon*, was notable. *Tamon* left for the high seas between July 14 and August 8 with six parent submarines and their *kaiten*. During this mission the submarine *I-53*, with navigator Lieutenant Minoru Yamada, launched a *kaiten* piloted by Sub-Lieutenant Jun Katsuyama some two hundred to three hundred miles northeast of Cape Engana, Luzon.[4] The destroyer escort USS *Underhill* rammed Katsuyama's *kaiten*, which detonated and blew off the destroyer's bow, killing Lieutenant Commander Newcomb and 111 of his crew. *I-53* launched two more *kaiten* to attack patrol boats as a diversionary tactic that allowed the submarine to escape. During the same mission, Japanese submarine *I-58* fired off its *kaiten* and claimed hits on a destroyer, seaplane tender, tanker and two transports (unverified); *I-58* used its own conventional torpedoes to sink the cruiser *Indianapolis* on July 30.[5] A tenth *kaiten* mission followed on August 16, but the parent sub was recalled, its *kaiten* unfired, two days later after Japan surrendered.

Despite the vast amounts of money, training and human resources spent on the *kaiten*, it fell as one more lost hope when Hiroshima exploded under a mushroom cloud on August 6, 1945. Three days later another atomic bomb struck Nagasaki, prompting Japan's unconditional surrender.

When the agreement was signed three weeks later on the USS *Missouri* that marked the surrender of the Empire of Japan, the *kaiten* was relegated to a footnote of World War II history. Only in 1999 would the survivors of the *Mississinewa* learn what had sunk their ship, but the U. S. Navy knew in December 1944 that it had been a *kaiten*—the dives after the attack by the men of the survey ship *Sumner* had located the aft section of one *kaiten* on the reef, which was recovered and analyzed. The eventual recovery of that *kaiten* was reported in a 1947 *National Geographic* article.[6]

In 2001, after analyzing both American and Japanese military documents, Japanese historians and submariners determined that Nishina had indeed piloted the one successful *kaiten* on the *Kikusui* Mission that destroyed the *Mississinewa*.[7] Details on the fate of Sekio Nishina finally came to light on the American side when Marshall Doak stepped forward in 2010 to tell his story of recovering an unidentified body along with the dead sailors of the *Mighty Miss.*

In addition to identifying the dead men, he prayed over them. For the previously unidentified man, Sekio Nishina, the act held an ironic and unusual distinction: The prayers said over his body were uttered by an American sailor whose navy he had tried to destroy. Unknowingly, the pharmacist's mate thought at first he was blessing a *Mississinewa* sailor, although he soon suspected otherwise.

After examining the victim, Doak didn't believe the body was a U. S. Navy man. Judging from the unusual physical trauma, the clothes unlike any sailor's uniform, and the Asian characters on the clothing, he felt the clues pointed to a Japanese combatant. In 2007, with history's hindsight, the pieces fell into place. The pharmacist's mate who had seen so many dead sailors was aware of the many forms death chose, from fire to blunt trauma. He rethought the unidentified man's wounds. "The metal shroud of the submarine must have covered him," he said, "and that accounted for why his torso hadn't suffered great damage." But, as Doak noted, the trauma to his head was devastating, the injuries unlike any war wounds the pharmacist's mate had ever observed. "His face was sheared off from the chin to the ears, and above that the top of the head was gone."

Historians surmise that at the moment of impact, when Nishina's vessel hit the oiler, the hatch blew off with great explosive force from the detonated warhead and Nishina was violently ejected. The probable cause of death was trauma from his head scraping the hatch coaming, which delivered the fatal blow and took his life instantly.[8]

In 2001 an expedition to find the *Mississinewa*'s grave was led by diver Chip Lambert. The discovery of the ship's exact resting spot was big news in the island chain of the Carolines, and the story was carried by newspapers in Hawaii, stateside and abroad. Of all the questions about the *Miss* that were answered by Lambert's team, one of the most important concerned the deathblow to the oiler: Exactly where was the lethal hit on the hull? And what might have caused it? Torpedo? Submarine? *Kaiten*?

Lambert's findings provided important clues. The underwater evidence pointed to final confirmation of the identity of the *kaiten* pilot who struck the killer blow and died in the *Kikusui* Mission. The explosion in the hull had occurred in the starboard bow, where the damage was documented underwater. The precise spot fitted perfectly with the trajectory Nishina had followed on his launch from *I-47* and the positions noted for his periscope wake as he moved through the lagoon. With the data transmitted to *Kaiten-kai* and Toshiharu Konada in Japan for analysis, Japanese historians felt they could finally establish the provable link between Nishina and the *Mississinewa*.

In his own country the submarine pilot was revered as a hero who had performed an honorable mission in service to his country. And as he had known it must be, Nishina died by the very weapon he created. The significance was not lost on Doak six decades later.

"I realized that I must have recovered Sekio Nishina's body," he said in 2010. It was so many years after, yet he said the shock and sadness still felt fresh. So much had been lost on that day in 1944 when *Mississinewa* exploded in rockets of flame. Doak shook his head and said wonderingly, "I can hardly get over it. There he was, the last body brought on board ship for me to identify. And it turns out he was the inventor of the *kaiten* suicide sub—and he sank the *Mississinewa*."

———

By the time the flames had died down on the *Mighty Miss*, the spirits of the dead—all the dead, including Nishina—had been commended to eternity. Perhaps the prayers and honorable disposition of Nishina's body could be seen as the ultimate reconciliation, but sixty-three American men also lost their lives as a result of his suicide mission. When he chose his destiny, his fate became theirs, and as surely as he was a hero in Japan, the men of the *Mississinewa* gave their lives heroically for the country they held so dear.

EPILOGUE

*"It has been saved, but not for me. It must often be so ...
when things are in danger: someone has to give them up, lose
them so that others may keep them."*

—J.R.R. Tolkien,
"The Grey Havens," *The Return of the King*[1]

*Foreseeing our nation at the danger of destruction, there was
no way left other than that we ourselves work as the most
effective weapons. We could save parents, brothers and sisters
and friends, only by sacrificing ourselves.*

—Toshiharu Konada,
kaiten pilot (survived), chairman of *Kaiten-kai* [2]

Across the Atlantic, the most bitterly cold winter in Europe's living
memory added to the soldiers' misery as the Battle of the Bulge reached
a fierce crescendo. Tanks rolled through Luxembourg, and the Rhine
could no longer stop the Allied push. Hitler was running out of places
to hide, and Germany would soon be taken. Victory in Europe would
be declared on May 8, 1945.

The War in the Pacific continued, but Japan yielded island after island
as the Allies relentlessly pressed their advantage in the air, on sea, on
land. In the last eight months of the War in the Pacific, *kaiten* missions
launched open-ocean attacks in a changing strategy, with attempts to
disrupt communications. In the brief span of time between January
and August 1945, *kamikaze* planes by the thousands attacked Allied
ships. Neither the *kaiten* nor the *kamikaze* could prevail over the influx
of freshly trained troops and the efficient industrial production of the

United States. In short, there was no stopping the inexorable march toward an Allied victory. In August the United States dropped atomic bombs on Hiroshima and Nagasaki, and Japan surrendered.

The Japanese surrender was signed in Tokyo Bay on September 2, 1945, in a cabin on the battleship *Missouri*. The end of the war came ten months after the sinking of the *Mississinewa*.

Ulithi had been all but abandoned as an anchorage after Leyte Gulf was secured by the end of December 1944 and the Pacific Fleet moved its forward staging area there. Few U.S. civilians ever heard of Ulithi; by the time naval security cleared release of the name, the war front had moved westerly and there was no longer any reason to print stories about it. But for seven months, from September 1944 to March 1945, Ulithi Atoll was the largest and most active anchorage in the world.

After the war a buoy marked the death spot for sixty-three American men on the oiler *Mississinewa*; unbeknownst to the commemorators, it also marked the spot where perished the submariner from the Imperial Japanese Navy's mother submarine *I-47* whose *kaiten* sank the ship.

After its moment of fame, Ulithi fell back into obscurity, but it holds a place in history as the spot where the *Mississinewa* became the first American ship to fall prey to a deliberate attack by a Japanese suicide submarine. The *Underhill* is the only other American ship known to have been sunk in a *kaiten* encounter, resulting from the destroyer escort's act of ramming the craft. The Imperial Japanese Navy claimed many more successes than the record shows; Japanese naval officer Kennosuke Torisu believed that 1945 *kaiten* attacks at Okinawa were fruitful, although the Japanese never could confirm those attempts.[3]

The *kaiten* program could only be viewed as a calamitous failure. Before the war was over, eighty-nine *kaiten* pilots died in action, most of them lost at sea after failing to bring down an American vessel. A few died attacking anchorages, such as the submariners of the *Kikusui* Mission that sank the *Mississinewa*. A small number perished in open-ocean attacks on U.S. Navy ships. Two would die by suicide at the end of the war: Lieutenant Hiroshi Hashiguchi killed himself in his *kaiten* with a pistol, and Ensign Hidesuke Matsuo took his life with a hand grenade. Others listed as killed in battle or missing in action may have self-detonated their weapon when no target was found.

In the end the *kaiten* were credited with sinking the *Mississinewa* and the *Underhill*, although German naval military historian Jurgen Rohwer credits them with more. In any case, the results did not match the high expectations once set for the *kaiten*. Japan's secret weapon exacted a higher toll on its own men than it did on Americans. In addition to the eighty-nine *kaiten* pilots killed in action and the fifteen who died in training, eight Japanese submarines, carrying six hundred men, were lost while carrying *kaiten*. In exchange, the Japanese estimated they had sunk between forty and fifty enemy ships. In fact, they sank only three.[4] The successful pilots were honored at the shrine of the emperor and promoted two ranks forward. Even as anguished relatives shed copious tears for the loss of their beloved men, some questioned the philosophy that sent their sons to such a terrible death. After the surrender, the surge of overt patriotic attitude manifest during the war abated under the occupation of their country. *Kamikaze* and *kaiten* pilots who survived were treated as dishonorable failures for having missed achieving their mission, and others viewed them as a disgrace, an overreaching example of patriotic zealotry gone wrong. But Toshiharu Konada, who had once been willing to die in a *kaiten*, impassionedly protested this view, saying "We were *not* crazy! We were not robots, we were not monsters. Foreseeing our nation in danger of destruction, there was no way left other than that we ourselves work as the most effective weapons."[5]

The USS *Mississinewa* Reunion Group was founded in 1999; *Kaiten-kai*, the All Japan Kaiten Pilots Association, was founded in

1962, with Mr. Konada as the chairman. The veterans of both countries saw a need to encourage the sharing of war experiences and the resulting intense emotions those events generated. An ever-diminishing pool of aging men has come together in these groups on both sides of the Pacific Ocean to talk about the battles and campaigns of World War II and especially the day the *Mississinewa* blew up. It was a day that changed all their lives, perhaps more than anything else ever would, and they wanted to talk about it. They wanted to understand what happened, and they wanted to be understood.

Some of those men of Japan and America encountered one another, both at Pearl Harbor and in Tokyo for December 7 commemorative ceremonies, at the National War Memorial in Washington, D.C., and at Yasukuni Shrine near Tokyo. They have shaken hands, even apologized, sometimes with tears, always with fervor, knowing that it is governments that send men to war—sailors and soldiers are the sacrificial lambs.

Defending the *kaiten* pilots, Konada said that it was life, not death, that drove the *kaiten* men to volunteer for suicide.[6] "I must tell you this," he said on a September day in 2002 at Yasukuni Shrine. "The *Tokkō* [special attack, or suicide] pilot was not a robot, but a human with heart, mind and will. We were not forced to do special attacks but we ourselves voluntarily chose to do so, understanding the necessity. *Tokkō* was born out of our severe wish to save those we cherish most . . . It was a deed of love. It was the utmost charity to rescue many people's lives."

POSTSCRIPT

KAITEN PILOTS *KIKUSUI* MISSION

I-47 Submarine, *Kikusui* Mission to Ulithi

Captain Zenji Orita; survived the *Kikusui* Mission. After the war wrote *I-Boat Captain*, coauthored by Joseph Harrington

Sekio Nishina, coinventor of *kaiten*; died November 20, 1944, in suicide attack on USS *Mississinewa*

Sublieutenant Hitoshi Fukuda, Naval Engineering School graduate, Fifty-Third Class, died at Ulithi

Ensign Akira Sato, law student at Kyushu University, died at Ulithi

Ensign Shozo Watanabe, economics student at Keio University, died at Ulithi

I-36 Submarine *Kikusui* Mission to Ulithi

Captain Iwao Teramoto

Sublieutenant Kentaro Yoshimoto, not launched, survived

Ensign Taichi Imanishi, who had been an economics student at Keio University; died November 20, 1944, at Ulithi

Sublieutenant Kazuhisa Toyozum, not launched, survived

Ensign Yoshihiko Kondo, not launched, survived

I-37 Submarine, *Kikusui* Mission; Diversionary Maneuver at Palau; Submarine Attacked and Sunk with All Hands, Including Four *Kaiten* Pilots

Captain Nobuo Kamimoto

Lieutenant Yoshinori Kamibeppu, a Seventieth Naval Academy graduate

Sublieutenant Katsutomo Murakami, Fifty-Third Naval Engineering School graduate

Ensign Hideichi Utsunomiya, a former law student from the University of Tokyo

Ensign Kazuhiko Kondo

JAPANESE *KAITEN* AND *KAMIKAZE* CASUALTIES

kaiten: 89 pilots died in action; 15 died in training accidents; more than 600 submarine crews and officers died carrying *kaiten*

kamikaze: more than 1,321 Japanese aircraft crash-dived their planes into Allied warships during the war; it is estimated that about 3,000 Americans and Allies died because of these attacks, but the damage done failed to prevent the Allied capture of the Philippines, Iwo Jima and Okinawa

kaiten on exhibit: According to Lieutenant Commander Mitsuma Itakura, four Type I *kaiten* from Ozushima Base were removed by the U.S. Navy after the war. One of those surviving *kaiten* is on exhibit at Yasukuni Shrine; it was captured by U.S. forces in 1945 and is on loan from the U.S. Army Museum in Hawaii. This *kaiten* consisted only of a training head and body; it was discovered in 1978 in storage at the U.S. Army Museum on Oahu. Another of the four *kaiten* rests at the U.S. Navy Underwater Warfare Museum in Keyport, Washington. The Type I at Keyport has all of its original military equipment intact, and the weapon has been opened up between the ribs for viewing by the public. Another *kaiten* is displayed at Pearl Harbor, at the Pacific Submarine Memorial next to the moored submarine USS *Bowfin*.

WAR MEMORIALS—UNITED STATES AND JAPAN

National Memorial Cemetery of the Pacific (The Punch Bowl) Http://En.Wikipedia.Org/Wiki/National_Memorial_Cemetery_Of_The_Pacific)

The site where USS *Mississinewa* sailors were reburied in 1949; they had previously been interred on Asor Island at Ulithi from 1944 to 1949.

The World War II Valor in the Pacific National Monument

A United States national monument honoring several aspects of American engagement in World War II. It encompasses nine sites in three states totaling 6,310 acres (2,550 Ha). The USS *Arizona* Memorial and the battleship USS *Missouri* are two of nine historic sites comprising World War II valor in the Pacific National Monument.

The U.S. National World War II Memorial

A national memorial dedicated to Americans who served in the armed forces and as civilians during World War II. Consisting of fifty-six pillars and a pair of small triumphal arches surrounding a plaza and fountain, it is located on the National Mall in Washington, D.C., between the Lincoln Memorial and the Washington Monument. It opened to the public on April 29, 2004. The memorial is administered by the National Park Service under its National Mall and Memorial Parks Group. More than 4.4 million people visit the memorial each year.

Yasukuni Shrine (*Yasukuni Jinja*)

A Shinto shrine in central Tokyo that commemorates Japan's war dead. The shrine was founded in 1869 with the purpose of enshrining those who died in war for their country and sacrificed their lives to help build the foundation for a peaceful Japan.

ACKNOWLEDGMENTS

We have had the good fortune to receive guidance and help from a number of people who gave generously of their time and energy to make this a better book than it would otherwise have been. We thank them all, even those whose names do not appear here and whose contributions only the authors know.

The book would not exist at all but for the events of the War in the Pacific and the people on both sides who fought and died for their cause; we humbly honor them all. With respect and admiration we thank the survivors of the USS *Mississinewa* and the survivors of the Imperial Japanese Navy submarine and *kaiten* programs, who shared their memories and often their diaries, files and official records, and who helped bring the story to life. We thank the men of other U.S. Navy vessels who shared their recollections of Ulithi, the *Miss,* and their time in the Pacific, in particular the sailors of the USS *Lackawanna* (*AO-40*).

We are especially grateful to James P. Delgado, archaeologist and historian, noted author, director of the Maritime Heritage Program at NOAA's Office of National Marine Sanctuaries, and dear friend through the years, who so generously shared his files and materials gathered for his own research of the Japanese submarine program in World War II and, even more, shared his impressions on many important aspects. Special thanks from the heart also go to his wonderful wife, Ann Goodhart.

We are deeply grateful to two men whose generous work contributed immeasurably to our knowledge of the *kaiten* program and the *Kikusui* Mission. The first is Toshiharu Konada (1923-2006), a *kaiten* pilot and former Chairman of Kaiten-kai (The All Japan Kaiten Pilots Association). He was Mike Mair's mentor and friend and is sadly missed. The second is Minoru Yamada (1922-2012), navigator of submarine *I-53*, researcher and historian, who worked with Mair to determine the theories as to what went wrong with the *Kikusui* mission, the positions of the submarines, and how the attack unfolded at Ulithi, which was different from what Zenji Orita reported in 1944. Their gentle spirits live on; we wish them a peaceful sleep.

Tomoko Nishizaki provided unparalleled assistance with translation and research, for which we are deeply grateful. As film commissioner for the Hiroshima Film Commission (Hiroshima Convention and Visitors Bureau), Tomoko heard the story of the USS *Mississinewa* and took a significant part by translating interviews and documents for this book. Her considerable translation skills and her formidable command of naval and military terminology are surpassed only by her kindness and sensitivity to the subjects.

Michael Mair received enormous support from Japanese researchers. He particularly wants to thank Noburu Ogawa, the former Director of Kaiten Museum, who shipped all the Japanese photographs residing in the museum to Mike; Masami Ono, nephew of the *kaiten* pilot killed by the USS *Underhill*, for his research and translation, and also for serving as liaison between Mair and Mr. Konada; and Mitsuhara Uehara, author of *kaiten* books, who shared his research and clarified important points.

Special thanks go to Marshall Doak, Chief Pharmacist's Mate, U.S. Navy, a gallant patriot who lived through many historic events in the Pacific War. He shared his memories of the hours after the *Miss* went down and his recovery of Sekio Nishina's remains. His spirit of optimism is an inspiration.

Simon "Sid" Harris very kindly shared his original negatives of 37 photos of the *Miss* burning and sinking and also his memoir, an extensive narrative written a week after the sinking called *Death of a Tanker*.

Very special thanks are due to Tony Tareg, Lt. Governor of Yap, who now owns the *Miss* and Manyang Island where the *Miss* memorial is located.

We are grateful to people whose behind-the-scenes efforts helped in many ways: Genevieve Davis for her caring presence; Arthur Finkelstein for reading and printing support; Bob Fulleman, who prepared photographs for publication; Ron Fulleman, who located *Miss* survivors for interviews; Elizabeth Hadas for her brilliant comments and suggestions; Jane Kepp, whose editorial insights are always stellar, as is her friendship; Bob and Jackie Kimbel for researching in the National Archives and Records Administration; Chip and Pam Lambert, who located the *Miss* in Situ and who shared their logs and data; Art Latham, editor and friend; Larry E. Murphy, underwater archaeologist par excellence; and George Philip, scion of a four-generation navy family who so generously vetted the book's contents (any remaining mistakes are ours!).

We especially want to thank our agent, Sam Fleishman of Literary Artists Representatives, for his insightful guidance during the complex process of taking this book from concept to publication; he has worked tirelessly to advance the story, and through it all he has been a friend.

Finally, the very professional team at Caliber/Berkley has our admiration and gratitude for the encouragement and excellent support they have shown, most particularly our editor, Natalee Rosenstein, and editorial assistant Robin Barletta.

Michael Mair wants to thank his family for the love and support they provided through the years of preparation, research and writing: his wife Nancy, son Brian and daughter Tracy; and Mike's siblings, Scott Mair and Julie (Mair) Effinger.

Joy Waldron sends huge hurrahs to her son, Logan Roots, whose great mind and ready wit always provide a marvelous sounding board when it comes to writing a book. A special bouquet goes to Joy's mother, Agnes Cuddy Johnson, whose three brothers all survived the War in the Pacific. Without her love and inspiration the book might never have come to fruition. It is a great sadness that she missed seeing the finished edition, but her star now shines brightly in the heavens.

APPENDIX A

USS *Mississinewa* Crew List

Note: Sailors' ratings as of the date they came aboard ship.
*   Killed as a result of the sinking
*m   MIA, body never recovered, presumed dead
**   Killed due to an accident aboard ship
-w   Wounded

OFFICERS

BECK, Philip G., Commander -w
LEWIS, Robert E., Lieutenant -w
ROWE, Robert Lyford, Lieutenant *
GILBERT, Ernest Lavelle,
    Lieutenant
HALPER, Howard Padgett,
    Lieutenant -w
KUHN, William E., Lieutenant (j.g)
WILSON, Wallace Monroe, Lieutenant
    (j.g) *m
ATKINSON, William, Lieutenant
    (j.g) *m

FULLER, James Arthur, Lieutenant
    (j.g) -w
SCOTT, Charles S. Jr., Lieutenant (j.g)
STUTZMAN, Frederic Henry,
    Lieutenant (j.g) -w
BROWN, William A. Jr., Ensign
BIERLEY, John R., Lieutenant -w
ALLEN, Herbert Ray, Lieutenant
    (j.g) SC *m
MEIRIDER, John J., Chief Electrician
DOUNING, George A., Chief
    Machinist -w

WALSH, Clarence Earl, Bos'n -w
SKIBBE, Bernard C., Pay Clerk -w
McCOLLISTER, Charles F., Ensign

METCALF, Donald E., Ensign -w
CANAVAN, P. F., Ensign

ENLISTED MEN

ADKINSON, Charles Edgar, CEM(AA)
AIMETTI, Angelo, S2c
AKERMANN, Harry Aloysius, S2c *m
ALLREAD, Kenneth W., MM1c
APPLEGATE, William F., S2c -w
ASPINALL, Thomas, F1c -w
ATHERTON, Richard A., S1c
ATKINS, John E., FC3c
BAILEY, Waldo E., S1c
BARGE, John P., S2c
BASSINGTHWAITE, Howard J., S2c
BAUGHER, Clyde L., SC3c -w
BAUMERT, Donald C., S2c -w
BAYAK, John A., PhM3c
BAZZLE, Luther A., Jr., SC(B)3c -w
BEAUZY, Jack E., MM2c -w
BEAZLEY, Robert Montague, Y2c
BEILOUNY, Louis E., S1c
BELL, Alfred D., M1c
BLAZINA, Martin E., FC3c -w
BOCHOW, Howard A., F1c
BODTKE, Thomas Duff, GM3c *m
BOUTIETTE, Harold K., F1c(MM)
BRADY, Nicolas Thomas, BM2c -w
BRAUTIGAM, Robert W., RM3c
BROWN, Joseph, StM1c *m
BROWN, Robert, GM3c
BRUECKMAN, Peter J., F2c
BRZYKCY, Florian, M., F2c
BURKE, Norbert D., S1c(SK)
CAISON, Harry P., StM2c -w
CAPLINGER, Fred Lloyd, SK1c
CARELLI, Vincent William, Cox
CARLSON, Clemence Robert, S1c *
CASS, Stewart E., GM1c -w

CASTLE, Hardy Vernon, S2c -w
CHODZIN, Eugene, F1c *m
CHURCH, George A., F1c (MMR) -w
CIEMIEGA, Frank M., S2c
CLARK, Gordon L., EM1c
CLARK, John Calvin, GM2c -w
CLAYTON, Marion Francis, MM2c -w
CLELAND, James V., SC3c -w
COCHRAN, Martin T., F1c
COLLIER, William Henry, F2c
COMBS, Lloyd, F1c -w
CONNELLY, Charles T., Jr., S2c
CONNERY, James J., S2c
CONNORS, Robert George, S2c
CONRAD, Warren Calvin, WT1c -w
CONTENDO, Joseph S., S2c
COOK, Roland G., S2c
COOLEY, Eugene G., S2c
COOPER, Frederick W., Jr., SF1c
CORIA, Edward R., S2c -w
CORRADO, Alphonse, S2c -w
CORRARO, Michael R., S2c -w
CORREIA, Frank T., S2c -w
COSTA, Edward J., S2c -w
COSTELLO, John Aloysius, S1c *m
COTE, Gaston Joseph, S1c *m
CRANE, James Joseph, S2c
CRAWFORD, David H., S2c -w
CROSS, Frederick Thomas, S2c
CROTTY, Francis Patrick, MM2c
CUEVAS, Fernando, S2c
CUMMINGS, Leo S., S2c
CUNNINGHAM, James A., S2c -w
CURRAN, Edwin B., S2c -w
CURRAN, Patrick, S2c -w

CURRY, Hal C., S2c

CURTIS, Earl William, S2c *m

CUSCIONE, Anthony Joseph, S2c *

CYBULSKI, Frank J., S2c

DADURA, Andrew, S2c -w

D'AGOSTINO, Anthony Leonard,
    S1c *m

DAIR, Raymond Frederick, RM2c -w

DAITCH, Herbert, S2c

DALZELL, Edward A., S2c

DANIEL, Calvin Coolidge, StM1c *m

D'ANNA, John J., Jr., S2c

DARCY, Edward M., S2c **

DAUPHINE, James W., S2c

DAURIA, Enrico V., S2c -w

DAY, Alexander, MM2c -w

DE MARCO, Rocco, S2c

DE ROSA, Peter, S2c

DE SANTIS, Joseph Salvarie, S2c *

DE SCISCIO, Dominick Louis, S2c

DECHAMPLAIN, Aurele J., S2c

DECKER, George E., S2c(RM)

DECKER, Hiram James, CMM(PA)

DEEN, Jacob Berton, CQM(AA) -w

DEGNAN, Francis M., S2c -w

DELANEY, Paul M., MoMM2c

DELANEY, Robert M., S2c

DELET-KANIC, Lawrence, S2c

DELIO, John S., S2c

DELRE, Nicholas E., S2c

DEMKO, Amos James, S2c *

DEMMI, Joseph, S2c *m

DENNEHY, William F., S2c -w

DENNIS, David Edward, S2c *

DEUSE, James Smith, Jr., S2c

DEVEAU, Joseph Darie, S1c *m

DI FONDI, Eugene Anthony, S2c -w

DI FRESCO, Mathew, S2c *

DI MAURO, Leonard S., S2c

DI NUBILA, Danny, S2c

DI SARLI, Armond A., S2c

DIETZ, Francis Anthony, GM2c *m

DILLON, William Bernard, S2c -w

DINEEN, Bernard A., S2c -w

DIXON, Clyde Earnest, SM2c

DOBLIX, Stanley J., S2c

DOLAN, Robert G., S2c

DREXLER, Howard J., F1c

DUNCAN, Robert J., SK2c -w

DUTTON, Dick Otto, RM1c (T)

EARL, Malcolm Dewitt, F1c

ELKINS, James W., F1c

ELLIS, Albert N., F1c

EPPINGER, Melvin Newton,
    F1c(MM) -w

FORD, Carl W., Sr., F2c

FOSTER, Lawrence E., WT1c -w

FRITZ, Lloyd George, GM3c

FULLEMAN, Raymond George, WT3c

GALLAGHER, Emmet T., RM1c

GENGENBACH, William Robert,
    CMM (AA) -w

GILLESPIE, James Bernard, S1c *m

GIMMESON, William Andrew, S2c -w

GIRARD, George Joseph, S2c *m

GIRGA, Andrew T., SC2c -w

GIRT, John V., S2c

GIVENS, Earl T., S2c -w

GLASER, Lawrence H., SM1c -w

GLASS, Bethel Lee, S2c *m

GLASSBURG, Asa W., S2c *m

GLAVIANO, Sam Joseph, S2c -w

GLAZER, Herman B., S2c -w

GLEAN, Duire, StM1c *m

GLEASON, James John, S2c *m

GLEASON, James M., Jr., S2c -w

GLENDENING Ray, S2c *m

GLENN, James A., S2c

GLENN, William Allan, S2c

GOIST, David M., Jr., S2c

GOLDEN, Seymour Harold, S2c -w

GOLDSBERRY, Billy L., S2c

GOLDSMITH, Kenneth, S2c *

GOLDSTEIN, Irving, S2c *

GONCALVES, Frank E., S2c

GONZALES, Tranquilino Jr., S2c -w

GOODWIN, Harrison G., S2c -w

GORGEN, Arthur H., S2c

GORISEK, Ludwig V., S2c

GREEN, David Fowler, Y1c *

GROUNDWATER, John William,
    Jr., F1c *m

GUERRIERO, John Michael, Jr., S2c -w

HAMMOND, James Postles, Jr., S2c -w

HARDIN, Joseph Virgil, MM2c *

HASKINS, Junior C., S1c -w

HERRINGTON, William Thomas,
    F1c *m

HERRINGDINE, Charlie E., S2c

HINTON, Vernon R., S2c

HOELL, Andrew Potts, RM2c -w

HOPPER, Isaac D., EM3c

HORRIGAN, John Joseph, S1c -w

HORVATH, Frank J., S2c

HOWENSTINE, Milan A., SF3c

HUBBARD, Miles Eugene, F1c *

HURD, William J., S2c

HURLEY, James W., F1c

HUSS, George W., RM3c

IGLESIAS, Louis, F1c

JANAS, William P., F2c

JARAMILLO, Arthur B., S3c

JARRETT, Claude Earl, S1c *

JAYNES, Thomas H., Jr., Y3c

JESSIE, Lucius James, StM1c *m

JOHNSON, Andrew J., MM1c

JOHNSON, Charles Frederic, S2c *m

JOHNSON, Robert Andrew,
    Jr., SK3c *m

JOHNSON, Stanley C., F1c(MM)

JOHNSTON, Harry F., CM2c -w

JONAS, Russell Lee, F2c

JONES, Robert F., F1c

JOSEPH, Kenneth Marsden, EM3c

KASALA, Edward J., FC3c

KATRENIC, Steve, S2c -w

KEEFE, Arthur A., SC2c

KENNEDY, Frank Joseph, GM2c

KESNER, Jimmie L., GM2c -w

KESSINGER, Robert James, S2c *m

KIMBEL, Robert Franklin, WT3c *m

KINSLER, Edward P., S2c

KINZER, Paul Martin, S2c

KIRBY, Lloyd Jay, S2c

KIRK, James Lovell, S2c *

KLINDERA, Robert O., WT2c -w

KLUG, Kenneth Charles, SF3c

KOPP, Nathan Jack, S2c -w

LAMOCK, Marcel Joseph, Bkr2c *m

LARDNER, Chester A., SF3c

LESTER, Everett W., SC3c -w

LETZGUS, George Howard, EM2c -w

LEWIS, James C., MM2c

LIPSKY, John, S1c

LIUPAKKA, Peter, Cox *m

LIVEAKOS, Gus, MM1c

LOEWEN, Philip S., QM2c -w

LUTZ, Frank Thomas, CCS(PA) *

LYDAY, Paul, F1c

MAGETT, Roosevelt, StM1C *m

MAGGIANI, Robert H., CM2c

MAHER, John Joseph, Jr., Sk1c *

MAIR, John A., Jr., F2c

MANION, William P., Jr., S2c

MANN, Lester Helm, S2c -w

MANTOVANI, Guido E., Cox -w

MARTINO, Joseph Francis, S1c

MARTISH, Walter W., F2c

MASSEO, Nicholas Joseph, S1c

McADOO, Francis K., F1c

McCAFFREY, Robert, S2c(RM) -w

McCONE, G. H., PM2c

McCRACKEN, Kelly T., Jr., PhM1c

McFADDEN, Leo G., S1c

McGARITY, James B., S2c -w

McGOVERN, Francis J., MM2c

McLAUGHLIN, Louis Keith, S2c

McMILLAN, David L., F2c -w

MILLER, Miah, CMM(AA)

MILLS, Richard, MM3c

MITCHELL, Edward Andrew,
   Jr., EM1c *m

MOAD, William M.Y2c

MOFFATT, James William, F1c *

MOLNAR, George H., BM1c -w

MORAN, Peter Michael, S1c *m

MORGAN, Tracey Prator, F2c

MORIN, Louis, S2c

MORRIS, Joe G., F1c

MURPHY, John J., III, CBM(AA)

OCKERMAN, Elmer D., SK1c

O'CONNELL, Daniel P., S2c

OVERFIELD, Paul L., S1c

PALUMBO, Alexander W., S1c

PAYNE, Hal Thomas, MM1c *m

PEAK, Calvin Ray, S1c -w

PEPPERS, Raleigh A., ST3c

PERNA, Leonard M., S1c -w

PESCE, Carmen J., Jr., S1c

PHELAN, Thomas J., Jr., S1c -w

PHILLIPS, Eddie Nathan, SM3c

PORCARO, Pellegrino, MM3c *

PORTER, John W., F1c

PYATT, Hickory E., F1c

PYLE, Charlie L., CSK(PA)

RANKIN, Lester Boyd, CY(PA)

REEDER, James, CK2c

RICHARDS, John Oscar Jr., CRM(PA)

RITCHIE, Harold S., S1c

ROBERTS, Orlando Franklin,
   MoMM2c *m

ROSELL, Irving Harold, S1c

ROSSENSHEIN, Oscar, F1c (MM) *m

RUWELL, William Frederick, SK2c

SARACINO, Oswaldo Joseph, B1c

SAVARD, Joseph E., WT2c

SAVOIE, Charles F., B2c

SCHAUFUS, Frederick G., MM2c

SCHICK, Frederick J., BM1c

SCHRODTER, Herman P., S1c

SCOTT, Charles S. Jr., Lieutenant (j.g.)

SHARKEY, John A., SC1c

SIDEBOTTOM, John, MM3C

SMALINSKI, Raymond, S F3c

SMITH, Charles E., Cox

SMITH, Edmund C., CWT *m

SMITH, Edward E., F2c -w

SMITH, Gerald Thomas, S1c *

SMITH, Vonzo, GM1c

SMITHERS, William Vincent, S2c

SOY, Leo John, RM3c -w

STACK, Thomas R., RT3c

SZCUC, Edmond Stephen, S2c

THEMM, Richard Robert, S1c -w

THOMAS, Alvin R., Cox

THOMAS, Clyde Leslie, S1c *m

THOMPSON, John L., S2c

THOMPSON, Philip J., QM2c

THOMPSON, Samuel Benson, S1c

TIMONEY, Leland E., S1c -w

TRADER, Edward T., Stm2c -w

TUTTLE, Earl A., Cox

UPCHURCH, Paul T., S2c

VAN ORDEN, Earle Raymond, S1c -w

VENN, Charles Albert, CM1c *m

VENTRILLO, James M., S1c

VIGLIOTTA, Edward Michael, S1c *m

VOLTZ, Kenneth R., S1c (FCR) -w

VULGAMORE, Robert Allen, F1c -w

WALLER, Harold E., M2c (T) -w

WALSHON, Bernie Abraham, S1c

WALTERS, William Calhoon,
   EM3c *m

WARD, Carnel L., CK2c

WARREN, Nathaniel, ST3c

WASHICHEK, Philip V., AerM2c

WETTERHALL, Robert R., GM3c

WHEELER, Frank Richard, S1c *

WHITE, William E., MM3c -w

WHITTEN, Winston, W., MM1c

WILCOX, Frank J., Jr., S2c -w

WILCOX, Keith Hinton, S2c

WILLIAMS, Warren A., MM1c

WINTER, Robert H., QM3c -w

WOODHOUSE, William Thomas, F1c *

YEIDA, Henry Lincoln, S1c

YOUNG, Arthur Judson, PhM2c -w

ZELINSKI, Stanley J., F1c

APPENDIX B

Official Navy Documents

ACTION REPORT OF CAPTAIN PHILIP BECK

Narrative by: Captain Philip G. Beck, USNR
USS *Mississinewa*
Recorded: 12 December 1944

This is Captain Beck, commanding officer of the ex-USS *Mississinewa*, AO-59, one of the largest fleet oilers. The *Mississinewa* was built by the Bethlehem Steel Co. at Sparrows Point, Maryland and launched the 28th of March 1944. Our sponsor was Miss Margaret Pence, daughter of Captain Pence, U.S. Navy. Admiral Gygax commissioned the ship at the builder's yard, May 18, 1944.

We sailed from Baltimore on the 23rd of May and arrived at Norfolk, Virginia on the 24th of May. On the 25th of May we left Norfolk for our shakedown cruise in Chesapeake Bay, arriving back in Norfolk on June the 5th. After drydocking and fitting out we sailed from Norfolk on June 16 for Aruba, Netherlands West Indies. On arrival at Aruba we loaded at once and proceeded to Pearl Harbor via Panama Canal. On July 10 we arrived in Pearl Harbor and sailed from there on July 15th for Eniwetok, Marshall Islands and arrived there July 24.

We remained in Eniwetok fueling various fleet units until August 20th when we sailed for Seeadler Harbor, Manus Island, in the Admiralty Group and arrived there on August 25th.

On September 1, we sailed to rendezvous with units of Task Force 38 under the command of Admiral Halsey, to fuel and service them. Our real mission had now really started and we were continually on the move. We took part in the Palau campaign and the Formosa raids and finally the Leyte campaign.

The ship had arrived at Ulithi Atoll Anchorage, Western Caroline Islands, Palau Group, on the 15th of November 1944 and anchored in 23 fathoms of water in berth 131 on the new chart. There was on board at arrival 404,000 gallons of aviation gasoline in No. 2 center tank and 9,000 barrels of diesel oil in No. 6 center tank. . . .

On the morning of the 20th of November 1944, reveille was held at 0530 as usual. I was in my bunk, just about ready to get up, at about 0545, when there was a heavy explosion, which appeared to be on the port side forward, followed immediately by a second very heavy explosion. I was thrown out of my bunk against the after bulkhead of my cabin and landed lying on deck. Somehow or other I knew we had been torpedoed. On looking up I saw flames shooting in through all the portholes similar to a giant blowtorch. To get up meant burning to death, so I crawled out into the passageway and stood up. It was very hot. There was a man lying on deck in the passageway apparently unconscious or dead. I dragged this man out on deck and down the ladder to the midship boat deck. There were two enlisted men running aft. I told them to take this man aft with them, put a life jacket on him, and throw him over the stern and to pass the word for all hands to abandon ship over the stern.

I noticed at this time that the ship was burning furiously from midships forward and moderately from midships aft and had started to sink by the head. Everything that would burn was on fire; hoses, lines, gun covers, lube oil, cargo deck. There was not a soul in sight but I shouted in to the officers' quarters midships to abandon ship over the stern.

I had on only pajama trousers and these were on fire, so I discarded them and ran aft with the idea in mind to open the main steam-smothering valve to the cargo tanks. When I got aft, I found it impossible to get to this valve due to fire, wreckage, and burst steam lines with live steam pouring from them.

I continued aft through the after crew's quarters where I picked up a life jacket and put it on and made my way up two decks to the port after passageway on the after boat deck. The heat was terrific. There were continual explosions apparently from the ready ammunition. This port after passageway was the only livable place on the ship. The flames were closing in fast. Here I met Lieutenant (j.g.) Stutzman, badly injured, but still on his feet, chief Machinist Douning, chief gunner's mate Cass, and two enlisted men who appeared uninjured.

The forward door to this passageway was open, as were the portholes in the four rooms leading off the passageway. I ordered all these men to assist me in closing the door and ports so that we could gain a little time to save ourselves if possible. We had no sooner closed the door and ports when there was a very heavy explosion aft which tore everything apart, including the doors and ports. This explosion was apparently the after magazine or the center burner tank, which was about half full. Twenty mms were going off and there was fire all around the 5-inch ready ammunition.

The engine room had been abandoned and there was no pressure on the fire main. Even if there had been, it would have been of no use except to cool off our way to the poop deck. There were two 15-pound CO_2 fire extinguishers in the passageway. We used these to cool things off so we could get to the poop deck and jump overboard.

I ordered the men with me to jump. We all jumped about the same time, except chief machinist Douning and Cass, the chief gunner's mate, who went down a ladder hanging over the stern.

There was a channel about 15 feet wide, which was not covered with burning oil, and through this channel, we made our escape. Boats from the USS *Cache* and the USS *Lackawanna* picked us up. I was taken aboard the *Cache* with several other men, where we received medical attention, food and clothes. Most of us were naked or had our clothes burned off.

As stated in this report, I knew somehow or other that we had been torpedoed on the port side forward. This proved correct after speaking to eyewitnesses on board the *Cache*, including her commanding officer that had made a separate report concerning the foregoing. The *Cache* was anchored about 600 yards on our port beam.

I cannot report on anything such as Gunnery Department, Engineering Department, Medical Department, as the entire episode took place so fast and furiously that there was no time for anything except to abandon ship as quickly as possible.

The five men mentioned herein and myself were the last to leave the ship. Insofar as anyone can account for time under such conditions, it is my opinion that we left the ship about 15 minutes after the first two explosions.

From the deck of the *Cache*, I saw my ship completely enveloped in flames over 100 feet high. Tugs arrived at the scene and were pumping furiously on the flames, but to no avail. At about 1000, the ship slowly turned over and disappeared from sight.

Considering the suddenness of the explosions and the intense fire it is nothing less than a miracle that more lives were not lost. Out of a total complement of 298 there were three officers and 57 enlisted personnel lost. Many of these would have survived had the forward doors and ports of the entire midship house been closed. The flames from the initial explosions entered the midship living quarters followed by a flood of burning gasoline and oil. All those men in the midship crew quarters were immediately burned to death. In the officers' quarters, just above, all officers came through except two. Of those who came through, one was critically burned and three severely burned. Of these last three, one was last seen on the poop deck. It is presumed he drowned after jumping from the ship. The one critically burned ran out immediately following the explosions, yet another officer in the same room waited a few seconds until the flames from the concussion had subsided and came through with minor blisters. . . . These three officers came through with no injuries whatsoever.

Asked by the interrogator if he had information on what happened to his ship, Captain Beck replied,

I will try and describe exactly what happened. I found these facts out afterwards, of course.

At about 0540 the morning of November 20th, a task force was leaving Ulithi Harbor. They sighted a periscope and the destroyer *CASSIN* rammed a sub out there. It was a Jap midget sub. At the same time the *CASSIN* dropped depth charges. At 0547 my ship was torpedoed and blew up as previously stated. This torpedo came from a midget submarine inside the harbor. He no doubt came in while the net was open for the task force to go out. The submarine was seen by eyewitnesses to make a full left turn and proceed up the fairway after my ship had been torpedoed. This same submarine fired a torpedo at the cruiser *MOBILE* and missed. In the meantime the alarm had gone off throughout the harbor and destroyers closed in on the submarine and depth-charged him and blew him up.

There was a third submarine destroyed about 5 miles to the eastward of the entrance by one of our bombing planes. The same day seven Japanese bodies were picked up. One of these bodies was that of an Imperial Marine, a large man about 6 foot 2 tall. It was assumed that these Marines were to be landed on some of the atolls around there for demolition purposes. On the 23rd of November, an eighth body, also a Japanese, was picked up.

DECLASSIFIED. CONFIDENTIAL. ACTION REPORT USS *RALL DE-304*

20 November 1944. Two Asw-Form Reports of Action on 20 November 1944 in Ulithi Harbor at 0647 and 0653, Resulting in Sinking of Japanese Midget Submarine.

1.   This ship . . . in anchorage berth 560. Many heavy units of the fleet were at anchor close by. At approx. 0550 the gangway watch petty officer observed and reported to the OOD an explosion onboard one of the ships anchored near the southern end of the anchorage and near the Mugai Channel entrance. The TBS watch reported having heard messages advising that several submarines had been sighted I the entrance channel and that one had been rammed there. At 0612 all hands were ordered to battle stations and preparations were made to get underway. At 0625 underway. Course was set at about 150 degrees T avoiding ships at anchor . . . as this ship stood across the anchorage. AS this ship approached the USS Mobile and USS Biloxi, anchored in berths 15 and 16 respectively, the USS Mobile reported by light and by TBS that she had sighted a swirl in the water between the Biloxi and her. The RALL then came about and headed through the space between the two anchorage Berths. AT 0643 a swirl about two or three yards in diameter was sighted about 300 yards on the port side of the Mobile and the ship headed for it. When first sighted this swirl in the water was about two hundred yards distant and dead ahead. The swirl was caused by a circular motion of the water and was agitated by rising air bubbles. No sound contact was made. At 0647, as the stern of the ship passed through the swirl, one charge set at 50 feet was dropped. The Mobile reported, by TBS, that the charge landed about fifty feet past the swirl. The ship was brought around to port and

headed back through the swirl again. The swirl in the water was still visible on this second run. As the bow passed through it one charge was dropped at 0653 and five seconds later a second charge was dropped. Both charges were set at 75 feet. Speed during both of those attacks was ten knots and sonar contact was not made on either. Immediately following the second attack two men were sighted swimming in the center of the turbulent water thrown up by the exploding charges and were reported by the Mobile via TBS. This ship stood around the stern of the Mobile to head back through the area but the USS Halloran de-305, being closer to the area of the attack stood in to pick up the survivors in the water. This vessel then cruised slowly through the area several hundred yards off the bows of the Mobile and Biloxi observing the activities of the Halloran and continuing sonar search until ordered by CTU 57.6.2 to join the inner harbor patrol in charge of ComDesRon One. After the Halloran had returned from the area the Mobile sent a small boat out to search the area and buoy the spot of the attacks. At 1050 the Halloran reported by visual that following second attack by this vessel two Japs were definitely observed in the water. One was swimming for awhile and then went under. There were no definite signs of life in the other one. One body went down alongside her fantail before recovery could be made. Additional floating objects were noticed after her subsequent attacks. At 1430 ComCruDiv Thirteen reported that the boat sent out by Mobile had picked up a block of wood, a wooden seat with Japanese marking, a brightly colored pillow with Jap writing on it and that they had seen two swimmers, both of whom apparently drowned. No bodies were recovered. A small amount of oil and bubbles were seen by the boat crew. The spot was buoyed and search continued for debris.

Underwater on the
USS *Mississinewa*, 2001

Notes from diver Chip Lambert on the search and discovery of the USS Missis-
sinewa
April 6, 2001
Location: Ulithi Atoll, Federated States of Micronesia

The wreck of the 553-foot long 25,425-ton USS Mississinewa *continued to elude
us. After seven days of continuous searching, we were down to our last two
passes before calling off the quest and surrendering to Ulithi Lagoon's inhospi-
table environment. Our team—Dr. Pat Scannon, my wife Pam and I—had
stared into the water looking for clues until it hurt, scrutinized traces on the
Hummingbird depth finder endlessly, analyzed the GPS coordinates in our
sleep—anything that might have helped reveal the ship's location. Our support
group had run out of suggestions. We had exhausted our well-researched search
area. Discouraged, sunburned, sore and dehydrated, we had only 15 minutes
before our suffering would end. We would then join the ranks of the previous
eight teams that failed to find what has been called "the last great mystery shipwreck of World War II" by naval historian James P. Delgado.*

Chip Lambert and his team could claim a number of successes: Japanese destroyers, American planes and the Japanese armed trawler sunk by a young aviator, George H. W. Bush, now the former President of the United States. While those finds had been exciting and satisfying, the team had a continuing desire to venture to Ulithi and explore the crystal lagoon where numerous war casualties awaited discovery.

The USS *Mississinewa* had been moored just inside the harbor reef when attacked. After the sinking, the ship's grave was a well-marked navigation hazard for a few years. However, when the Navy and finally the Coast Guard returned Ulithi's control to the islanders, they removed all navigational markers and destroyed all charts. The ship's location slipped into obscurity.

In 2000 the Ulithi Adventure Resort was constructed on Falalop Island. The hotel's air compressor and dive tanks as well as twice-a-week air service opened the lagoon waters as a new travel destination in the Western Pacific. At last Lambert had a base for staging and the chance to search for the wreck.

He began with Internet research and found three *Mississinewa* descendants, Mike Mair and Ron and Bob Fulleman, whose fathers had survived the oiler's demise. He pitched a logical question: "Where'd the ship sink?" But the survivors' sons didn't really know. Even though the crystal-clear waters allowed extraordinary underwater visibility, the oiler's exact location in the harbor was unknown. So despite its mammoth size—553 feet of wreckage and armaments—finding the *Miss* would be a challenge.

Over the years, many of the surviving crew members who knew more or less where the ship had sunk didn't want to reveal the location for fear that scuba divers, who often showed a lack of respect for underwater sites, might plunder the historic wreck. They felt the fifty entombed sailors deserved an undisturbed grave.

Lambert's commitment not to penetrate the vessel built trust among the descendants of the *Mississinewa* sailors. At that point Mair released a number of previously undisclosed documents for study, among them Japanese charts of the attack, ship's logs with bearings for navigational markers that had long since disappeared, and interviews with eyewitnesses. The team now had everything, it seemed—everything except the long-gone Navy mooring chart marking the ships' locations in the lagoon, or even photographs that might show where the *Miss* rode at anchor that morning.

Combing the National Archives and the Navy Yard's resources produced no additional information on *Mississinewa*'s location at the time of the *kaiten* attack. The WWII charts of Ulithi Lagoon had vanished. Eyewitness interviews, while fascinating, didn't point to the ship's resting place. Because of the military importance of the lagoon and the secrecy surrounding the *kaiten*, everything about the incident had been classified. Even the name of the lagoon had been kept secret, and many veterans who actually witnessed the attack had no idea where they were anchored until the newspapers blurted out the location.

The dive team headed for Ulithi armed with simple search gear including GPS, a depth finder and laptop computer, and a chart with the Cone of Opportunity inscribed on it.

Ulithi, at latitude 10°N, is buffeted by northern trade winds from October to May. The search for the *Mississinewa* would take place in the exposed central area of the lagoon. The Trades were blowing fifteen to twenty-five knots, unusually strong for that time of year. Despite the difficult conditions, the search officially began on Saturday, March 31, 2001.

The equatorial sun was relentless, forcing a wardrobe change after the first day. Gone were the shorts and T-shirts, now replaced by Antarctic survival gear in an attempt to cover every inch of skin to prevent sunburns. Incessant waves knocked the dive boat around, the ocean spray first soaking the electronic equipment, then evaporating, leaving everything coated with salt. Looking for shipwrecks is hard work, even in the tropical paradise of Micronesia.

Lambert noted the daily routine:

Up at 5:00 a.m. to listen for the wind. Out on the patio to watch the sunrise and observe the wave action. Nasty words describing the perpetually high winds and wave amplitude. Review the previous day's tracks and check the chart for the 15th time in preparation for the day's search grid. Great quantities of coffee and breakfast. Carry equipment out into the surf and load the boat. Rub bruises with sunblock, don all available clothes. Search. Search while eating PB and J sandwiches. Biological break. Search. A novel trace on the depth finder screen. Excitement. Into the dive gear and over the side. Disappointment. Search. Home in the dark with no lights, exhausted.

Each day's tracks were downloaded from the GPS to the computer and a portion of the search area was eliminated; the early morning hours were spent calculating the coordinates of new search areas. The continual strong winds noticeably eroded the divers' enthusiasm and energy.

April 6. After completing the survey of the Cone with no success, they were stumped. Only a few hours of water time remained, so the choice of the final search area would be the last chance to find the ship. The team pored over the charts and six days of computer-generated search patterns. They noticed two small untracked areas in the grid, but there was only enough time now to investigate one. "I made the call and we retired to prepare the gear for our last shot," Lambert says. It was a good call.

The helmsman fought the relentless wind and waves to hold the course. There was little hope of success. Suddenly the depth alarm sounded and a spike appeared on the screen. Lambert shouted, "This is it. We're here!" while pushing all the buttons on the GPS. Nobody moved. They had heard the story before.

"Turn the boat around, we just went over the ship!" he screamed. The driver responded and swung the boat 180 degrees; more spikes appeared on the screen as they crossed it again. Ecstasy was guarded. After seven brutal days, nobody dared believe it was real.

Lambert described the event:

I was over the side and descended 20 feet while waiting for [the others] to join me. I kept spinning in circles, descending, anxiously looking for some shape in the darkness below. Nothing! I was afraid it was another false alarm. Then a small mound caught my eye. Continuing down, the mound morphed into a ship, a very large, beautiful ship.

The USS *Mississinewa*, torn and twisted, lay upside down in 120 feet of water. Perfectly camouflaged, the ship's silt-coated bottom was smooth and blended with the lagoon floor. Dropping down through the water, divers saw the hull taking shape. Suddenly it exploded with fish, a living fireworks show. The bow pointed directly east, but the foredeck was vertical and rested on its port rail. A gaping hole was scooped out of the ship between the forward gun, the starboard bow gun and the number 4 tank bulkhead. Evidently the *kaiten* and the secondary explosions had torn a seventy-five-foot gash in the plates and stringers. Debris littered the lagoon floor, including what appeared to be a section of the *kaiten*. Aft of the number 4 bulkhead to the rudder, the ship was completely upside down. The bridge, well deck, cargo deck, masts and kingposts were all buried in the sand. One diver held out an American flag in honor of the fifty-plus sailors entombed within the ship.

The team swam the length of the hull. Reaching the massive seven-foot blades of the twin screws, the divers felt ready to end the dive. As they drifted away and started to rise toward the silver surface, they turned back almost as one to look at the stern. Sand drifted over the metal wreckage, and a school of orange-and-white Moorish idols darted over the ship's remains, softening the stark picture of war.

The day of horror was gone, the smoke and flames only a distant memory trapped in photographs and the minds of a few survivors. Deep in the ship, the ghosts of *Miss* sailors could sleep in peace, held in the coral embrace of Ulithi's azure lagoon.

APPENDIX D

Oil Leaks at Ulithi

Four months after the *Mississinewa* expedition in 2001, Typhoon Utro struck the Caroline Islands and Ulithi underwent a dramatic transformation: The landscape changed, the seascape was ravaged, and the *Miss* began to give up the oil stored for fifty-seven years in its bunkers.

Soon after the typhoon roared away, a Pacific Missionary Airline pilot, Peter Reichert, noticed a long dirty streak on the water as he approached for a landing. Pulling out of his descent and circling the area, he confirmed his suspicion—the streak was an oil slick. The ship had been dislodged by the storm and was disgorging a stream of thick bunker oil into the lagoon.

Within two weeks the slick had worked its way around the lagoon, and the swirling waves and wind painted the perimeter islands with globs of oily muck. The EPA/MRMD cleanup team estimated that the leak was contaminating the lagoon at a rate of approximately 360 gallons every hour. They also noted that while most of the oil was being blown through landless gaps in the barrier reef, small amounts were accumulating on the islands northeast of *Mississinewa*, at Falalop and Asor. If they couldn't stem the flow, the oil would bubble to the surface for years to come.

The Coast Guard assembled a multidisciplinary assessment team to determine the extent of the leak and the shoreline damage, cleanup strategies, the environmental resources at risk (shore-based wildlife, marine life, and breeding grounds) and what technical assistance they could provide to the local Yap government that controlled Ulithi.

Strong southwest winds made assessment very difficult but, ironically, prevented an ecological disaster by dispersing the oil. The small island population depends heavily on subsistence harvesting of seafood and native plants, and if the oil had remained within the lagoon, the finfish and shellfish would have been quickly contaminated and rendered inedible. Had the winds shifted to almost any other direction, the oil would have been driven onto the islands, and bird rookeries and turtle breeding grounds and food-producing resources would have been destroyed. Instead the two-mile slick was pushed between the islands to the open sea.

Divers rigged safety lines and conducted a systematic search of the wing tank to locate the leak. It was a huge task. The wing tanks are very large, holding 150,000 gallons, and are crisscrossed with support beams, ladders and pipes. Twenty minutes of searching found no evidence of the leak. Then as the team worked its way in pitch black to a jagged hole in the bulkhead, a diver's light swept across the funnel-shaped opening of a four-inch strum pipe just as a blob of oil was ejected. The oil leak had been found, and shortly after was plugged.

U.S. NAVY DIVERS FILL ULITHI LAGOON OIL LEAK! shouted Guam's *Pacific Daily News* on August 28, 2001.

Victory was short. The weather cleared, the seas settled, and the *Mississinewa* started leaking oil again. The now-sealed strum pipe had increased the oil pressure on the downstream four-inch stripper valve. Not only had the gate mechanism failed, which had caused the initial leak, but the bolts holding the valve bonnet together on the first fix had fractured and dissolved. Oil was now seeping out of the deteriorating case. The valve had to be sealed using much more sophisticated technology than on the first leak. A plastic garbage can was cut so it could be slipped over the pipe and valve, strapped in place and filled with cement—another finger in the dike.

The dive team turned to the task of pumping out the estimated 2,500 gallons of bunker oil trapped below the overhead shell plating. Ultimately 6,300 gallons of oil and seawater were pumped out of the hull into fifty-five-gallon oil drums.

Divers surveyed the remainder of the ship and determined the amount of oil and the integrity of the tanks. Aft of damaged number 4 tank complex, tank complexes numbers 5 through 9 were all found to be intact. Little wastage of hull plates was noted. The vulnerable area continued to be the exposed piping in the seawater-filled number 4 starboard wing tank.

When the leaks were stopped and the pooled oil removed, the Navy was ready to return to the States. Governor Vincent Figir called for immediate and effective removal of all the oil from the sunken ship to prevent the certain future catastrophic leaks. The Navy team promised to address the issue in Washington, D.C.

A few months later, in December 2001, Governor Figir notified the United States Navy supervisor of diving and salvage that the USS *Mississinewa* had developed another serious oil leak. For the third time in less than a year, oil coated the surface of Ulithi's lagoon.

The rapid recurrence of leaks, the large volume of remaining petroleum products and the vulnerability of the lagoon's marine and human residents to an oil leak convinced the Yap government it should petition the U.S. State Department to remove the remaining oil from the ship.

The ensuing monthlong mission removed 1.8 million gallons of oil from the ship, stripping twenty-three tanks and spaces by a method known as "hot tapping." The access holes were resealed at the completion of the operation. The collected oil was transported to Singapore and sold to help defray the $4.5 million operational costs.

Fifty-seven years after it sank, the USS *Mississinewa* was finally relieved of its cargo.

Underwater on the
USS *Mississinewa*, July 2013

July 2013. The wind blew over the azure waters of Ulithi Lagoon in the Caroline Islands, a part of greater Micronesia. Japan was only a three-day sail. 1944 seemed long ago and far away, but below the waves lay a sunken shipwreck that marked November 20, 1944, as a day from hell.

Michael Mair, suited up in diving gear, a tank of air on his back, was about to visit the ship where his Navy father, John Mair, a fireman second class, had been a nineteen-year-old sailor whose off-watch duty was to tend the port-side bow line on refueling. He had escaped the explosion that sent the ship to the bottom. The deathblow was caused by a *kaiten*, a Japanese suicide sub intent on one-for-one destruction: one suicide submarine for one U.S. capital ship.

"The first time I looked at the coral-encrusted anchor chains and the winches and I saw how huge the ship was, I couldn't believe this thing was sunk by one weapon."

Mair was talking about the sunken wreck of the USS *Mississinewa*, a giant Navy fleet oiler that sank in Ulithi Lagoon at the end of 1944 when the War in the Pacific was building to a terrifying crescendo. On that day, November 20, John Mair was not yet at his duty station when the ship took a hit from the submarine, erupted in flames and sank. Mair survived to tell his story, but sixty-three American shipmates died, along with the Japanese agent of doom.

The American sailors died that day when their ship exploded in balls of fire and rapid-fire munitions bursting from the immense heat. Jumping into oily water and swimming through flames licking all around the ship, Mair and the other survivors had been scooped up by rescue boats.

On July 12, 2013, Michael Mair had stepped off the plane in Yap Island in the Caroline Islands, in the far Pacific Ocean near Guam. En route to Ulithi Atoll one hundred miles to the northeast of Yap, he was part of an expedition to dive on the *Mighty Miss*, as the sailors called their ship. Mair had never seen the ship, never been to Ulithi, the atoll that for a few months was the largest anchorage in the world. Certified to dive, he was on a mission to visit the underwater site of chaos and tragedy and try to envision the day his father's world cracked open.

"The purpose of our dives," Mike said, "was to survey and look at the *Miss* and see the condition." The main motivators for the trip were Chip Lambert, who had discovered the exact location of the ship a decade earlier, and Jim Gleason, whose father is entombed on the ship. The group spent three days at Yap getting fully certified to dive.

They met with Lieutenant Governor Tony Tareg, the man who had just inherited from his uncle, Chief Pisente Talugyar, Mangyang Island, where the U.S. Navy had in 2003 built a monument to the men who died in 1944. "The *Miss* is pretty close to Mangyang Island," Mair said. "The reef fishing rights he has with his clan also include the area where the *Miss* rests, so technically he owns the sovereign territory. The U.S. government owns the ship and he owns the reef."

On the 16th the team, which included Mair, Chip and Pam Lambert, Jim Gleason and his wife Vang, Mark Hanna and his father, Judd Hanna, landed on the once-coral strip runway, now concrete, on Falalop Island at Ulithi. Most natives still alive from the WWII era had been small children in 1944. Mair brought photos and newspaper clippings from that memorable year. "They really enjoyed that. I was treated like royalty. 'We've heard about you for years and seen your picture.' One young man in his thirties, Chief Pisente's son, wanted to talk to me. His wife made a braided lei. His father had handed down my letter where I thanked him for cooperating with the Navy and for allowing the monument to be built.

"It took us time to find the ship," Mair recounted. Lambert's GPS coordinates were derived from early technology, and the team searched fruitlessly for an hour. Finally the ship's form appeared on the screen, the stern reading at a depth of 85 feet, the bow resting at 137 feet. At the time of the sinking, the bow twisted and nearly broke off at the port side, and the ship turned keel up as it rolled over and fell to the bottom.

Mair descended through cloudy water. "After I broke through thirty-five feet, the visibility was good," he said. "The sunlight penetrates all the way down and the water is so clear you don't need supplemental light. Seeing the screws and rudder come into view was a breathtaking moment."

Three other divers went down with Mair and all headed for the starboard screw (propeller). "I took a close look at the coral growth. The four flukes on the screw are seven feet long. The shaft hub, a bullet shape, is twenty-four inches in diameter—just huge. Floated up so I could see the bottom of the rudder. It jutted out from the rudder pin about twelve feet; rudder is twenty feet top to bottom, steel, very thick—ten inches—covered with coral growth and canted to starboard. Looked at the port screw."

So excited was Mair to see the ship that he broke some of the guidelines and pushed deeper toward the stern. "The stern was upside down, the top of the flat hull in pretty bright sunlight, with a little bit of coral growth. Fire foil coral nestled in the screws on the rudder. The fish were fascinating: very large tuna, thousands of streamlined fish with a colorful stripe, slim streamlined reddish fish in large schools. They circled around the starboard screw and another went around the port, and it looked like the ship was moving.

"Most exciting part for me: I happened to be floating at one hundred feet and looking at the beam of eighty-five feet, upside down, and you can't see the rear deckhouse. When Chip took pictures in 2001 there was no debris field. Now the sand had shifted and revealed the starboard side explosion at the site of the five-inch magazine. I went deep, down to the hole where the rib stringers were exposed. A big piece of hull plate was missing, measuring about six by six feet; the edge curled outward and I swam up and touched that."

Dive 2. "We went to stern area and I collected myself and saw debris on starboard side toward the stern. When the ship pancaked with the stern upside down, it crushed the stack and the rear deckhouse. Over on the star side the galley walls had squashed flat and poking out from the side, bulkhead walls with the portholes. They collapsed over the top of the stanchion railing, lying intact on beds above the galley wall plates. Stanchion rails on top of it. Not visible. There were no signs of human remains."

Mair was struck by the *kaiten*'s damage. "At the bow's starboard side, a massive gap revealed the damage from the *kaiten*, the suicide submarine. It was just an incrediblly huge hole, a V-shaped gap. The number 3 sidewing oil tank where Nishina [the submarine pilot] hit was obliterated, and the bottom hull plates are all cracked and bent. The porch—the bottom hull plate—was completely upside down."

In 2001 two large chunks of hull plating—not from the *Mississinewa*—had lain in the debris field on the starboard side. They were now gone, victim to some errant typhoon. "All I saw was sand, white sand," Mair said. He searched for any sign of the *kaiten*, but found none—whatever had been deposited on the sandy bottom was now scattered or buried in sand.

The massive damage to the ship had bent the deck plating, and the catwalks had crumpled in the explosion into a hole on the sea bottom. "On the main well deck, a stanchion ladder had blown off, a big massive piece of debris," Mair said. He swam over to the starboard 3-inch/50 gun, where Mark Hanna snapped his picture: Mair floating with his hand on the barrel encrusted with coral. The port-side gun was not visible, apparently it had fallen and was hidden in the sand.

"The current is so strong with typhoons coming through," Mair said, "any type of small debris would have been swept away a long time ago. All we saw was massive tons of steel.

"What hit me was I saw the port-side capstan on the bow covered with yellow brain coral. And I remember my dad saying the port-side tow line was where he was. I saw it and it all hit me: I'm touching the port-side capstan where my dad worked as a nineteen-year-old. It was mixed emotions, because my dad survived, but I've met families who lost men on the ship."

He felt astonished to finally come full circle. He didn't talk to his father but felt his presence all around. "I swam out and looked back at the bow. It was impressive," he said, remembering a sense of awe. "The front disappeared into the blue. And looking at the coral-encrusted anchor chains and the winches and how huge the ship was, I can't believe this thing was sunk by one weapon."

Mair, "still pinching myself," savored reconnecting with his father, a time warp of sixty-nine years and another world at war. "I'd like to talk to him now, tell him I saw the ship and the starboard side hole where the sub struck. He always talked of his fellow sailors who died. He used to say, 'I hate being called a hero—the real heroes are the boys on the ship who never made it home.'"

Although time and public indifference cause historic ships to fade in importance, USS *Mississinewa* is still a hallowed memorial. The wreck of the oiler lies on a sandy ocean seabed covered by Ulithi's placid blue waters, a haven for colorful tropical fish and anemones teeming within its shattered hull, now the final resting place for some fifty young men.

Vincent Figir, governor of Yap State in Micronesia, called for the nomination of the USS *Mississinewa* to the National Register of Historic Places on January 30, 2002. He described the *Miss* as "a significant World War II combat loss to a Japanese *kaiten* as well as a war grave" and likened its importance to other sunken U.S. and Japanese vessels already designated as National Historic Landmarks, namely the USS *Arizona* at Pearl Harbor and the Japanese fleet at Truk Lagoon. Descendants of USS *Mississinewa* survivors continue to seek National Historic Register status for the ship. That process would involve preparing the nomination paperwork and a review by the keeper of the National Register in Washington, D.C. To date neither has happened.

Many U.S. naval ships were lost in the War in the Pacific, but the *Mighty Miss* was the first ever sunk by a suicide pilot in a *kaiten*. Entangled in the oiler's debris are remnants of what appear to be the deadly *kaiten* that carried a Japanese submariner to his death and killed sixty-three American men. In its savagery and destruction, the underwater tableau at Ulithi Lagoon echoes the sketch of an aircraft carrier split in half by a *kaiten*, presented to the suicide pilots on the eve of their departure. It is all part of the legacy of war, where in painting, poetry, photography and underwater debris lies evidence of the unspeakable irony of governments who pit their soldiers and sailors against one another.

Over time the USS *Mississinewa* will succumb to the sea, as salt water takes its toll on the corroding metal. Even as the ship fades into obscurity, it rests as a tribute to America's young men who perished at Ulithi during the turbulent and tragic time of World War II. The bridge is forever silent, and the stairwells and decks once teeming with officers and men slowly yield to the waves. Memory and meaning are timeless.

NOTES

CHAPTER 1: HEAVEN SHAKER

Information on Yamamoto and the petition in blood was discussed by Toshiharu Konada, chairman, All Japan Kaiten Pilots Association, in personal letters written to Michael Mair, January–December 2001.

Quotes on the desperate situation in Japan are taken from Yokota and Harrington, *Suicide Submarine!* and Orita and Harrington, *I-Boat Captain*.

1. *If left as stands, this country will surely perish*: Konada, private correspondence to Michael Mair, 2002.
2. Information on manned torpedo development came from O'Neill, *Suicide Squads*, pp. 200–203.

CHAPTER 2: RISING SUN

Many historians have written of the attack on Pearl Harbor, and Gordon Prange's *At Dawn We Slept* is a classic, definitive account.

1. Cook and Cook, *Japan at War*, p. 69.
2. Zenji Abe, Japanese pilot; in later years he visited Pearl Harbor on December 7 anniversaries and met with American military men who were present on Oahu the day of the attack. The transcript of his personal account is on file at the USS *Arizona* Memorial, World War II Valor in the Pacific National Monument.

3. John Stephan's book *Hawaii Under the Rising Sun: Japan's Plans for Conquest After Pearl Harbor* details the extensive plans the Japanese commanders were making for occupation of Hawaii.

CHAPTER 3: MIDWAY

1. *surrounding him were two young submariners*: Toshiharu Konada, himself a *kaiten* pilot, discussed the enormous impact the defeat at Midway had on Kuroki and Nishina. Konada, personal correspondence with Michael Mair.
2. Japan's plans for the invasion and occupation of Hawaii are documented and discussed in Stephan, *Hawaii Under the Rising Sun*.
3. Balloon bombs are described in numerous articles and websites such as this one: http://news.nationalgeographic.com/news/2013/05/130527-map-video-balloon-bomb-wwii-japanese-air-current-jet-stream/.

CHAPTER 4: THE *MIGHTY MISS*

Survivor John Mair provided a great deal of background material on life aboard the USS *Mississinewa*, in interviews with his son, Mike, conducted from 1996 to 2005. Extensive information also came from Machinist's Mate c James Lewis. Other information is from interviews with *Mississinewa* sailors at 1999 *Miss* Reunion.

1. J. R. R. Tolkien fought in the Somme in World War I and saw so many men die it drove him to write as a way to expiate the horrors of war. Quote taken from an essay by Nancy Marie Ott titled "JRR Tolkien and World War I" at website http://greenbooks.theonering.net/guest/files/040102_02.html.
2. *Some of you aren't coming back*: Report *AO-59/A4-1* Serial 00547, May 18, 1944. Norfolk Navy Yard, Baltimore Repair and Conversion Branch. Report by B. N. Ward, Captain. Interviews with James Lewis, MM2c, and John Mair.
3. Biographies and recruiting stories told by *Miss* sailors at the 1999 reunion.

CHAPTER 5: CIRCLE-SIX METAL FITTING

Bio and character descriptions of Kuroki and Nishina: Konada, January 31, 2001, letter; attached four pages: "Lt. Cmdr H Kuroki and Lt. Cmdr Sekio Nishina," "Concepts of the Human Torpedo" and "Kaiten Training" by Toshiharu Konada. Other background provided by Tomoko Nishizaki, researcher and translator, email to Michael Mair on March 4, 2002.

1. *let them step forward*: These words were uttered by Kennosuke Torisu, IJN. Two sources: (1) *Silent Assassins*, History Channel, and (2) interview with Yutaka Yokota, published in the chapter "Volunteer" in Cook and Cook, eds., *Japan at War*, p. 106. Hereafter cited as Yokota, "Volunteer."

2. *Strangers will assume it is some kind of spare part or shipboard equipment*: Yokota, *Suicide Submarine!*, sub p. 21.

3. Bill Gordon, emails to Joy Waldron, 2012–2013.

4. Yokota, *Suicide Submarine!*, p. 15.

5. *Do not accept death unless by dying you can hurt the enemy severely*: Yokota, *Suicide Submarine!*, pp. 14–15.

6. *I never imagined I'd be going to a place from which I'd have absolutely no chance to return alive*: Interview with Naoji Kozu, published as the chapter "Human Torpedo" in Cook and Cook, *Japan at War*, p. 314. Hereafter cited as Kozu, "Human Torpedo."

7. *I believe that a kind of weapon such as a* kaiten, *guided by a human being who faced certain death*: Torisu, *Silent Assassins*, History Channel.

8. The effort to build an underground railroad illustrates the tremendous secrecy surrounding the *kaiten*. Masami Ono, nephew of a *kaiten* pilot killed by the USS *Underhill* in 1945, provided research, photos and maps of the secret railroad system.

CHAPTER 6: NEPTUNE'S ANCIENT ORDER OF THE DEEP

The stories of the crossing of the equator and the shipboard ceremonies were reported by many *Miss* sailors in interviews conducted by Michael Mair during the USS *Mississinewa (AO-59)* Reunion, April 14–18, 1999, Corpus Christi, Texas.

1. *That night was peaceful, until a voice from* Straus's *radar shack . . . It'll all be over in a bit*: Dan Ostrosky, RM3c, USS *Straus (DE-408)*, telephone interview with Michael Mair on November 24, 1998. The *Straus* was the flagship of ComDes-Div 65.

2. *The dog is a typical Navy dog already*: Al Bell, M1c, USS *Mississinewa (AO-59)*, letter, March 11, 1999.

3. *Schaufus, annoyed, called his bluff*: Frederick Schaufus, MM2c, USS *Mississinewa* Reunion, 1999.

4. *What color is shit?*: Gus Liveakos, MM1c, USS *Mississinewa* Reunion, 1999.

5. *You'll be in the Navy fifty years and you'll never know what I know*: Lieutenant Robert L. Rowe, navigator, USS *Mississinewa (AO-59)*, Service Record: Pers 5324a-bh 68577; letter from Jan (Rowe) Tracy to Michael Mair dated March 10, 2001; Malden, Massachusetts, newspaper clipping from December 1944.

6. *electric cipher machine (ECM) to decode messages*: Lieutenant (j.g.) Charles S. Scott, assistant communications officer, USS *Mississinewa (AO-59)*, Navy memoirs 1995; telephone interview with Michael Mair on June 3, 2006.

7. *King Neptune bellowed at Janas and Brzykcy, the recalcitrant spud sailors*: Florian "Bill" Brzykcy, F1c, USS *Mississinewa (AO-59)*, letter to Michael Mair, September 24, 1998; Bill Brzykcy died the morning after the letter was sent.

CHAPTER 7: SUICIDE SUBMARINES

1. Kuroki's death poem can be found at website http://commons.wikimedia.org/wiki/File:Death_poem_by_Kuroki_Hiroshi.jpg. Yokota and other *kaiten* recruits talked about the poem and the instructions left by Kuroki, as they were very inspiring to the young men.
2. Yokota, *Suicide Submarine!*, talked about the fuel shortages as a nearly crippling factor in *kaiten* training.
3. Kuroki's poem was accompanied by a letter to his family and lengthy, detailed recommendations for how to reconfigure the *kaiten* to prevent a similar accident in the future. He exhorted his fellow pilots to carry on the fight.
4. See Sheftall, *Blossoms in the Wind*, for training tactics.
5. *Even America, for all her industry and riches, cannot afford the loss of 100 warships*: Yokota, *Suicide Submarine!*, p.38.
6. *for we were learning much about the* kaiten *while waiting for one of our own*: Yokota, *Suicide Submarine!*, p. 39.
7. *I felt that I had myself turned into something no longer human*: Kozu, "Human Torpedo," pp. 314–315.
8. *We practiced that hard, because we valued our lives so highly*: Yokota, "Volunteer," p. 308.
9. Kozu, "Human Torpedo," p. 317.

CHAPTER 8: BATTLE STARS

1. *Bierley knew exactly why the captain had boarded in this manner*: John Bierley, telephone interview with Michael Mair on April 22, 2000.
2. Wildenburg discusses the dynamics of maneuvering large ships in close proximity in *Grey Steel and Black Oil,,* p. 174.
3. *Pharmacist's mate John Bayak toted a sea bag ashore containing baseball bats, gloves and balls*: 1999 *Miss* Reunion interviews.
4. *Did you guys really shoot down all those Jap planes?*: John Mair, F2c, speaking to the gunners on the aircraft carrier *Wasp*.
5. *We've been extremely lucky*: Morrison, *History of Naval Operations*.
6. *Tell that son of a bitch to get away*: Ensign Patrick F. Canavan, USS *Mississinewa* (*AO-59*), telephone interview with Michael Mair on February 3, 2003.

CHAPTER 9: *KAMIKAZE* WAR

1. Kozu, "Human Torpedo," p. 317.
2. *Watanabe was furious*: research document written by Hisashi Watanabe, captain of *RO-115*, and personal letter written to Michael Mair in December 1996. English translation by Minako Nakakura. Also mentioned in Orita and Harrington, *I-Boat Captain*.
3. *Other crews competing for the record were very good, very capable, but*: Yamada, "Kikusui Group Attack."

4. *Typical of the effort to reconfigure ships in support of the kaiten effort, Kitakami*: http://www.combinedfleet.com/kitakami_t.htm.

5. Minoru Yamada, personal correspondence with Michael Mair.

6. Delgado, *Khubilai Khan's Lost Fleet*. James Delgado, an underwater archaeologist and historian, has dived on the Mongol Fleet and tells the story from a historical point of view with the hands-on details only archaeology in the field can provide; his book breathes life into the events when a massive typhoon eight centuries ago in 1281 destroyed the fleet and convinced Japan they had been saved by a "divine wind"—*kamikaze*.

CHAPTER 10: KILLER STEAM, KILLER PLANES

1. Joshua Chamberlain, an icon of the Civil War, was the commander of the famed 20th Maine that defended the peaks of Little Round Top at the Battle of Gettysburg.

2. *Agonizing screams pierced the air that morning*: Herbert Daitch, S2c, telephone interview with Michael Mair on August 21, 2003, and continuous monthly telephone communication since 2003.

3. *Pharmacist's mates Kelly McCracken and Art Young sat in sick bay*: Kelly McCracken, PhM1c, USS *Mississinewa* (AO-59), letter to Michael Mair, July 19, 1998.

4. *The newly built recreation area*: Mog Mog was a very important aspect of life at Ulithi. See George Spangler, "Ulithi: Sanctuary for WWII's Pacific Fleet," *Sea Classics,* March 1998; "Building the Navy's Bases Online; Ulithi, in the Western Caroline Islands," which gives many details, http://www.microworks.net/pacific/bases/btnb_online/eniwetok.htm; and for more details, *The "Ulithi" Encyclopedia*, WVTY, the Armed Forces Radio Station, Ulithi, Western Caroline Islands, 1945 (pamphlet handed out to sailors arriving at Ulithi 1944–45).

5. *Sensing disaster, Mitchell screamed, "Pull out, you bastard, pull out!"*: Mason, *We Will Stand By You*.

CHAPTER 11: BLOSSOMS ON THE WATER

1. *The mission was given the name* Kikusui: O'Neill, *Suicide Squads*, p. 233.

2. *The Kusunoki family crest, dating from 1331*: Orita and Harrington, *I-Boat Captain*, p. 242.

3. *Lieutenant Commander Mitsuma Itakura, who had the last word*: *Silent Assassins*, History Channel.

4. *Knowing their destiny, Nishina and the other pilots*: O'Neill, *Suicide Squads*, p. 234.

5. *The kaiten pilots sat astride their weapons lashed to the decks, waving their swords*: Orita, *I-Boat Captain*, p. 243.

6. *The voice of a trained singer enriched the passing hours*: Chief Petty Officer Yukio Oka, in Orita, *I-Boat Captain*, p. 245.

7. *What they could do, the kaiten could do*: Yokota, *Suicide Submarine!*, p. 42.

CHAPTER 12: THE LAST SORTIE

1. *The rear admiral in charge of communications issued a "Well Done":*1999 *Miss* Reunion interviews.

2. Mississinewa *buzzed with scuttlebutt:* 1999 *Miss* Reunion interviews.

3. kamikaze *successfully targeted Admiral McCain's flagship:* Morrison, *History of Naval Operations in World War II.*

4. *General quarters sounded on* Boston: Florian "Bill" Brzykcy, F1c, USS *Mississinewa (AO-59),* letter to Michael Mair, September 24, 1998. Brzykcy died the morning after the letter was sent.

5. *A few days after the arrival in Ulithi . . . "and no one shoots at me":* Ray Fulleman, WT2c, USS *Mississinewa (AO-59),* personal interview with Ron Fulleman, November 28, 1998.

6. *At 1800 hours Captain Beck hailed his cargo officer from the bridge:* At issue here is a very important point that directly affected the impact of the *kaiten* attack the following morning: The centerline tanks were not purged, as they should have been. Al Bell, M1c (letter to Michael Mair, March 11, 1999, and interview at 1999 *Miss* Reunion) and Harold Ritchie (interview at 1999 *Miss* Reunion), both on the work detail shifting cargo. They were privy to the verbal exchange between Captain Beck and Lieutenant Fuller about purging the centerline tank of the volatile hundred-octane AV gas fumes.

7. *No, you guys go ahead and I'll be up there in a bit:* Rocky DeMarco, S2c, USS *Mississinewa (AO-59),* letter to Ron Fulleman, August 8, 1999.

8. *He asked his friend Joe Morris, "Where you gonna sleep tonight, kid?:* Joe Morris, EM2c (striker), USS *Mississinewa (AO-59),* telephone interview with Michael Mair, January 2000.

CHAPTER 13: *KIKUSUI* MISSION

1. *At the western entrance to Kossol Passage, the net-layer USS* Winterberry *was on alert:* Oseas, *Tales of the USS* Conklin *DE-439.*

2. Howard Higgins on the chase for a submarine, November 20, 1944: Oseas, *Tales of the USS* Conklin *DE-439.*

3. *On November 16 a Japanese high-altitude reconnaissance plane:* Orita, *I-Boat Captain,* p. 243.

4. *Watanabe will depart five minutes after Sato:* Orita, *I-Boat Captain,* p. 247.

5. *On November 20, 1944, I shall dress in a six-inch loincloth:* Uehara, *Kaiten sono Seishun-Gunzo.*

6. *It is not known if navigator Shigemoto compensated for the estimated three miles:* Yamada, *Kikusui Group Attack.*

7. *Nishina left first in kaiten number 1:* Yamada, *Kikusui Group Attack*; Toshiharu Konada, chairman, All Japan Kaiten Pilots Association, personal letters to Michael Mair, January–December 2001.

8. *Each pilot was to pursue a different attacking course after penetrating Zau Channel . . . Just after midnight on November 20, submarine I-36 was waiting at a spot about eleven nautical miles southwest of Mas Island*: The analyses of the kaiten launches from *I-47* and *I-36* come from multiple sources, and were first reported to IJN officials at the December 2, 1944, debriefing. Multiple sources: Kaiten Special Attack Forces *Kikusui* Unit Action Report (*Senken-butai*), Japanese Sixth Fleet Report, December 2, 1944; Yamada, *Kikusui Group Attack*; and Toshiharu Konada, chairman, All Japan Kaiten Pilots Association, personal letters to Michael Mair, January–December 2001.

9. *The night had grown cloudy, making astronomical observation more difficult but not impossible*: Yamada, *Kikusui Group Attack*. Konada told Mair that Japanese navigators did not use triangulation for their position, but rather celestial navigation and cross bearings.

10. *The man responsible for launching the* kaiten *was Yoshihisa Arizuka*: Yoshihisa Arizuka, chief engineer, *I-36*, interview conducted on February 8, 2001 by Mitsuharu Uehara on behalf of Michael Mair.

11. *At Ulithi, the kaiten pilots' opportunities for finding targets diminished*: Yamada, *Kikusui Group Attack*.

CHAPTER 14: DEATH AT ULITHI

The anecdotes from officers and sailors are mainly taken from interviews with *Mississinewa* sailors and interviews with *Lackawanna* sailors.

1. *On November 20, 1944, at 0418 an explosion erupted* : USS *Sumner AGS-5*, Action Report, November 25, 1944, serial 060-44. AGS5/L11-

2. *Nishina couldn't know it, but many ships had left earlier that morning as he was speeding toward the lagoon*: USS *Case* (*DD-370*) Action Report, serial 0179, November 22, 1944.

3. *"Keep an eye on it," Captain Homan growled, annoyed* : USS *Lackawanna* (*AO-40*) Reunion, October 17, 1999, St. Louis, Missouri, group interview with twenty-four former crew members of the USS *Lackawanna* (*AO-40*), who rescued fifty-nine USS *Mississinewa* (*AO-59*) sailors on November 20, 1944; Lieutenant (j.g.) Milford Romanoff, USS *Lackawanna* (*AO-40*), personal interview at the USS *Lackawanna* (*AO-40*) Reunion.

4. *Nishina's killer weapon worked as he had planned*: USS *Mississinewa* (*AO-59*) Captain Philip G. Beck, Commanding Officer's Action Report, no serial, November 26, 1944.

5. *At the moment the* Mississinewa *blew up,* Lackawanna's *cook Ulus Keeling*: The ship heeling to port was a dramatic moment described by many *Lackawanna* sailors assisting with rescue effort—Ulus Keeling, SC3c; Linus Hawkins, S1c; Willie Potter, BM2c; Bill Depoy, S2c; Joseph Fello, WT2c; Lieutenant (j.g.) Lew

Davies—and in the USS *Lackawanna* (*AO-40*) Action Report, November 20, 1944. A recap of that stunning moment when the ship turned, rolled over and sank was carried in a newspaper interview of a New Mexico sailor, Art Jaramillo, SC3c, USS *Mississinewa*, by Randles, *Albuquerque Journal*, December 7, 1991.

6. *Across the lagoon on Falalop Island several miles to the northeast, a mailman's mate*: William Assmann, MaM2c, Fleet Transfer Post Office, Falalop Island, Ulithi, telephone interview with Michael Mair, March 7, 2000.

7. *Permission granted, he snapped thirty-seven breathtaking images of the oiler's demise*: Sid Harris saw a notice in 1999 that Mike Mair placed in the VFW and American Legion magazines searching for *Miss* survivors or eyewitnesses to the sinking on November 20, 1944. He phoned Mair and said, "I have something you might like." His offering was photographs and original negatives of the *Miss* burning and sinking, and the futile firefighting efforts to save her. Captain Pingley of the *Munsee* (*ATF-107*) had given Harris permission to keep several eight-by-ten photo prints developed on board the USS *Ajax*. Harris also had kept the original negatives of thirty-seven remarkable photos he had taken with the ship's 35mm camera as firefighting was taking place the morning of November 20. Harris's photos are the only ones taken alongside the USS *Mississinewa* as it burned and sank. He nearly missed the dramatic photo he shot of the *Miss* as it rolled to port and plunged to the sea bottom—at that moment he was loading film! He quickly turned and, without aiming the camera, snapped the "death" photo of the last few seconds of the *Miss*. The photos and negatives sat on a closet shelf in Harris's New Jersey home for fifty-five years. The National Archives has only the tiny contact prints on microfilm of these photos that had been thought lost forever. In an emotional exchange at the end of the 2003 *Miss* Reunion, Sid Harris gave Michael Mair the historic negatives and photos and asked that the images be used to preserve history and eventually be donated to the United States Naval Institute. Harris died of cancer a short time later.

8. The survivors did not realize that in a few weeks their families would be reading the bad news. The photograph of the burning *Mississinewa* was released as an AP Wirephoto, published in most newspapers between December 19 and December 24, 1944; it was captioned: "TANKER BURNS IN THE MIDST OF FLEET UNITS IN THE PACIFIC—U.S Navy units, including a number of carriers, surround the burning tanker, USS *Mississinewa*, after the craft was set afire by Jap attack at an undisclosed spot in the Central Pacific. Joseph Rosenthal, Associated Press photographer with the war still picture pool, made this photo (AP Wirephoto)."

9. *Before dawn, sailors aboard the cruiser* Santa Fe *had hoisted a Kingfisher floatplane*: Blase C. Zamucen, lieutenant (j.g.), USS *Santa Fe* (*CL-60*), letter and photograph submitted to Ron Fulleman by Stephen Zamucen, son of Blase Zamucen, received on June 5, 2001; telephone interview by Michael Mair with Stephen Zamucen and sister Eva Zamucen Banchero on December 14, 2003.

CHAPTER 15: ESCAPE

Much of the tactics and reasoning of *I-36* and *I-47* captains and crews in this chapter derives from analyses by Toshiharu Konada and Minoru Yamada and Yutaka Yokota's book *Suicide Submarine!* Yokota was privy to the December 2, 1944, briefing with those two returning captains and heard the details of the *Kikusui* expedition. However, where there are discrepancies in the launch times of *I-47*, priority is given to the analyses of Konada and Yamada, as Orita's times, recollected after the war, did not agree with Japanese Sixth Fleet records and are logistically impossible to reconcile with the 0418 explosion on the reef near Pugelug Island.

1. Kozu, "Human Torpedo," p. 317.
2. *Angry and shamed at the failure, they screamed and swore*: Yoshihisa Arizuka, chief engineer, *I-36*, interview conducted on February 8, 2001, by Mitsuharu Uehara on behalf of Michael Mair.
3. *In the minutes right after the* Miss *erupted in flames, U.S. Navy destroyers and destroyer escorts made a frenzied search*: Commander Service Squadron Ten Action Report, serial 00274, December 8, 1944. Commander Service Squadron Ten Action Report, serial 00282, December 9, 1944.
4. *Seaman Eugene Cooley had awakened the moment his skivvies caught fire and scorched his skin*: Eugene Cooley, S2c, USS *Mississinewa* (*AO-59*), telephone interview with Michael Mair, November 14, 1999. Captain Beck was interviewed for an AP story where he explained that Eugene Cooley, S2c, was the only *Miss* sailor to survive forward of the bridge. Cooley dived off the bow as the centerline AV gas tank blew and survived. John Sidebottom, S1c, USS *Enoree* (*AO-69*), telephone interview with Michael Mair, January 8, 1999. John Sidebottom watched Cooley dive off the bow of the *Miss*.
5. Peter Moran story told by Frank Wilcox, interview with Michael Mair, December 16, 1999.
6. *It was Coxswain Vincent Carelli, the popular New Yorker who ran the mess hall casino*: Harold Ritchie, S1c, interview during the USS *Mississinewa* (*AO-59*) Reunion, April 14–18, 1999. Vincent Carelli regretted that he'd lost all his winnings in the escape from the ship, but he remarked that he played almost countless games of poker with *Wichita* sailors on the cruise to California, got more than a few straight flushes and won "back" thousands of dollars. *Carelli retorted, "Go to hell, sir! I'm not leaving until every man we can find is in this boat"*: Florian "Bill" Brzykcy, F1c, USS *Mississinewa* (*AO-59*), letter to Michael Mair, September 24, 1998. Brzykcy died the morning after the letter was sent.
7. *Ruwell came to the rail on the poop deck to find seaman John Costello*: William Ruwell, SK2c, USS *Mississinewa* (*AO-59*), letter to Michael Mair, August 25, 2003, in response to a detailed questionnaire, and personal interview with Michael Mair, July 24, 2003, at the 2003 USS *Mississinewa* Reunion in Seekonk, Massachusetts. Mair also talked to Bill Ruwell frequently by phone and learned that

Ruwell had been working on a manuscript about the USS *Mississinewa* for years. Mair read a partial chapter of the manuscript in 2003; the work appeared to be personal memoirs and was not published. John Costello Jr. drove from New York City to the USS *Mississinewa* Reunion in Seekonk in 2003, wishing to meet Bill Ruwell, the last man to see the junior Costello's father alive. Ruwell had left the reunion for a day and missed the Costello family; they later spoke by phone. Mike Mair reviewed the tragic events of November 20, 1944, with a large map of Ulithi and photos, and the Costello family finally learned what had happened to John Costello Sr.

CHAPTER 16: RESCUE

The anecdotes from officers and sailors are mainly taken from interviews with *Mississinewa* sailors and interviews with *Lackawanna* sailors, as well as ships' Deck Logs and Action Reports.

1. *As the launch was lashed to the port boom,* Lackawanna *sailors*: Lieutenant (j.g.) Milford Romanoff, USS *Lackawanna* (*AO-40*), personal interview at the USS *Lackawanna* (*AO-40*) Reunion, St. Louis, Missouri, October 17, 1999; Ed Miremont, S2c, personal interview at the USS *Lackawanna* (*AO-40*) Reunion, St. Louis, Missouri, October 17, 1999.
2. *"I guess I won't have to chip paint off the engine room bulkhead anymore"*: John Mair, F2c, USS *Mississinewa* (*AO-59*), personal interview with Michael Mair, September 1996.
3. *Patient transfers from nearby oilers started immediately and by 1034 twenty-four were aboard the hospital ship*: USS *Samaritan AH-10* Deck Log. November 20, 1944.
4. *"I saw my ship completely enveloped in flames over 100 feet high"*: Captain Beck, USS *Cache* (*AO-67*) Action Report, serial 004, November 24, 1944.
5. *An older officer, Navigator Lieutenant Robert Rowe, was badly burned*: Merrill McCoy, S1c, USS *Mascoma* (*AO-83*), telephone interview with Michael Mair, May 21, 2000. (Mike Mair was seated in a Dubuque, Iowa, restaurant near Mr. McCoy and noted he was wearing a *USS Mascoma* ball cap. Mair greeted Mr. McCoy and asked him about Ulithi and the sinking of the *Miss* on November 20, 1944. The gentleman was so shocked he nearly fell out of his chair. After things calmed down, Mr. McCoy consented to an interview and told about Lieutenant Robert Rowe's last moments. This interview is the only information Janet (Rowe) Tracy has learned about her father's death, which occurred when she was seven years old.
6. The hospital ship USS *Solace* was well known to U.S. Navy sailors. Daly, *U.S.S. Solace Was There.*
7. AP news story, December 18, 1944.

CHAPTER 17: THE SHADOW OF DEATH

1. Cook and Cook, *Japan at War*, p. 309.
2. Harris, *Death of a Tanker*.
3. Harris, *Death of a Tanker*.
4. *Gunner's mate Ed Loebs raced to the aft 40mm gun mount*: Ed Loebs, GM3c, USS *Menominee* (*ATF-73*), letter to Michael Mair, December 27, 2001, and phone interviews, January–December 2002.
5. *Fire consultant officer D.S. Gray reported to Commodore Kessing*: Fire Consultant Officer, Staff of Commander Battleships, US Pacific Fleet, no serial, November 20, 1944, *USS* Mississinewa (AO-59)—*Fire Fighting Operations On Board*.
6. Harris, *Death of a Tanker*.
7. *Captain Pingley wrote* Munsee's *Action Report*: USS *Munsee* (*ATF-107*) Action Report, ATF107/A12/(JWB) serial 205, November 26, 1944.
8. *As the last vestiges disappeared in the murky water, USS* Extractor *placed a buoy marker*: USS *Extractor* (*ARS-15*) Action Report, ARS15/S93, serial 101-44, November 21, 1944.
9. Pharmacist's Mate Marshall Doak, interviews with Joy Waldron, July 2, 2010, March–May 2013.
10. Marshall Doak said he found himself in the role of chaplain as well as pharmacist's mate, so he improvised prayers and said them for each dead man.
11. *Among the bodies that Arapaho sailors had recovered was* Mississinewa *sailor James Moffatt*: USS *Arapaho* (*ATF-68*) Action Report, no serial, November 21, 1944.
12. Pharmacist's mate Doak remembered with considerable detail finding the last body in the water, and he recalled his impressions of the unusual wounds. From the clothing and the man's stature he believed right away it was a Japanese combatant, although from what type of craft he didn't speculate. It is not clear at this date where Nishina's body went; it has been speculated he was buried at sea.

CHAPTER 18: MISSION FAILURE

1. Cook and Cook, *Japan at War*, p. 266.
2. Toshiharu Konada, chairman of the All Japan Kaiten Pilots Association, wrote his analysis in a document titled *Kikusui Mission—Kaiten Attacks on Ulithi*, English translation by Tomoko Nishlzaki, sent in private correspondence in 2001 to Michael Mair. Mr. Konada wrote his conclusions of the disposition of the five *kaiten* pilots who attacked Ulithi on November 20, 1944. He was critical of *I-47*'s Captain Zenji Orita's poor navigation, poor choice of launch times due to darkness, and subsequent report to Sixth Fleet. Mr. Konada was also critical of Captain Orita's interviews with *Asashi Weekly* newspaper, where Orita "relied only on his poor memory."
3. Zenji Orita, captain of *I-47*, appears to have made several errors in navigation, the times of launch, and his recollections/analysis. *Asashi Weekly* newspaper, September 15, 1949. Zenji Orita entered the newspaper essay contest, with his essay

"Human Torpedo" winning first place and a prize of 30,000 yen. This was a lot of money, as inflation in postwar Japan was significant. Orita was earning a meager living as a secretariat of a motor sailor association in his hometown of Kagoshima. Orita relied only on his memory of the *Kikusui* attack on November 20, 1944, for his essay. Orita's *kaiten* launch times as reported in the essay—0415 for Nishina, 0420 for Sato, 0425 for Watanabe, 0430 for Fukuda—are problematic with other events, such as the *kaiten* exploding on the reef near Pugelug. As Mr. Yamada stated in his 2001 essay, *I-47*'s position when its *kaiten* were launched is unknown. It was not recorded in the Sixth Fleet After Action Report. On September 18, 2000, Mr. Yamada interviewed Tadashi Ohira (a senior officer aboard *I-47* during the *Kikusui* Mission to Ulithi), who stated that precise launch times are unknown.

4. Yokota, *Suicide Submarine!*, p. 51.
5. Action Report, USS *Rall* (DE-304).
6. Action Report, USS *Rall*.
7. *Four hours after the* Miss *explosion, Captain D. A. Spencer*: USS *Wichita* (CA-45) Deck Log, November 20, 1944.
8. *Reno's captain instructed smaller vessels to set up a patrol*: USS *Reno* (CL-96) Action Report, serial 075, November 22, 1944.
9. *Yoshihisa Arizuka, the chief engineer aboard* I-36, *described the morning's attack*: Yoshihisa Arizuka, chief engineer, *I-36*, interview conducted on February 8, 2001, by Mitsuharu Uehara on behalf of Michael Mair.
10. *The Action Report from USS* Sumner *describes both explosions witnessed on November 20*: USS *Sumner* (AGS-5) Action Report, November 25, 1944, serial 060-44. AGS5/L11-1. The appropriate commands were alerted. See also memorandum, Command Western Carolines Patrol and Escort Group, January 22, 1945, A-16-3 (10)/FF12/02-cdg, serial 00209, Operational Archives, US Naval Historical Center, Washington, D.C.
11. *On December 2 a special conference was held aboard* Tsukushi Maru: Kaiten Special Attack Forces *Kikusui* Unit Action Report (*Senken-butai*), Japanese Sixth Fleet Report, December 2, 1944.
12. *a battleship apiece*: Yokota, *Suicide Submarine!*, p. 53.
13. The U.S. Navy reports provide an overview of the November 20 events, followed by authors' comments.   (1) USS *Sumner* reported an explosion on a reef at 0418 one and a half1-1/2 miles south of Pugelug Island, the southwest part of the anchorage. The event was believed at the time to be a floating Japanese mine, but the wreckage of a *kaiten* (missing its pilot compartment and warhead) was recovered by *Sumner* sailors. (2) USS *Case* (DD-370) rammed and sank the first kaiten discovered at 0538 two miles south of the entrance to Mugai Channel. It is now believed this *kaiten* would have been Fukuda from *I-47*, as his attack plan and launch time would have placed him exactly at this location. This sinking of the first *kaiten* alerted the U.S. Navy that the event was an enemy attack. (3) The *Miss* exploded at 0545–0547, depending on which deck log is referenced. The

kaiten was almost certainly piloted by Nishina. (4) The USS *Rall* depth charged and destroyed a *kaiten* at 0635 in the Northeast part of the anchorage. This was the *kaiten* of Ensign Imanishi from *I-36*. (5) A very large explosion occurred at 1132 two miles south of Pugelug Island in the southwestern part of the anchorage. The explosion, accompanied by a tall column of water on the reef, was reported by the light cruiser *Reno* and *Sumner*. The wreckage of only one *kaiten* was found in this area and was the remains of either the 0418 explosion or the 1132 explosion. Submariner Yamada thinks this pilot self-detonated, after being stranded on the reef in only nine feet of water with no hope of escape. (6) The U.S. Navy reported they spotted a *kaiten* at 2204 fifteen miles east of Falalop Island. *I-36* had jettisoned its useless *kaiten* at this location, as reported by its chief engineer. *I-36* made it safely back to Japan.

14. *I pray for your success*: Yokota, "Volunteer," p. 311.
15. *They were shed for the loss of my fellow pilots*: Yokota, "Volunteer," p. 312.

CHAPTER 19: DECEMBER 1944

1. Miss *survivors coming off other rescue ships were boarding the heavy cruiser* Wichita: USS *Wichita* (CA-45) Deck Log, Wednesday, November 22, 1944, signed by Lieutenant (j.g.) H. T. Armerding and Lieutenant (j.g.) J. W. Alcock, USNR.
2. *Two* Mississinewa *sailors met as they boarded the cruiser*: Joe Morris, EM2c (striker), USS *Mississinewa* (AO-59), telephone interview with Michael Mair, January 2000.
3. *The promise came as welcome news to survivors*: Personal interviews during the USS *Mississinewa* (AO-59) Reunion, April 14–18, 1999, Corpus Christi, Texas.
4. *Commander Philip Beck received orders on November 22 to go to Pearl Harbor*: Commander Service Squadron Ten, Duty Instructions, serial 00241, November 22, 1944.
5. *Ensign Pat Canavan had the task of selecting the men to identify bodies*: Ensign Patrick F. Canavan, USS *Mississinewa* (AO-59), telephone interview with Michael Mair, February 3, 2003.
6. *Shoot me if you have to*: p. 369 Kinsler, 1999 *Miss* Reunion.
7. Beck's article, AP, December 19, 1944.
8. Preparations to drop the bomb: http://www.ww2hc.org/articles/pacifictimeline.pdf.

CHAPTER 20: SETTING SUN

The reaction of U.S. Navy ships to the Ulithi tragedy is referenced in the many ships' Action Reports in the bibliography. The overall recommendations for change in Navy strategy and tactics for ASW defense are taken directly from Commander Service Squadron Ten Action Report, serial 00274, December 8, 1944.

1. In an interview with Joy Waldron (April 2010), Senator Inouye discussed his thoughts on the differences and similarities between World War II, in which he fought heroically, and the events of September 11, 2001.

2. The subsequent *kaiten* missions have been discussed in several Japanese military documents and analyzed by Konada, Yamada and Delgado in unpublished manuscripts.

3. Delgado, unpublished manuscript; Konada, personal correspondence.

4. Masami Ono, nephew of Jun Katsuyama, provided many details about this mission in personal correspondence with Michael Mair.

5. Delgado, unpublished manuscript.

6. The expedition to recover the *kaiten* was featured in Irving Johnson's article "Adventures with the Survey Navy," *National Geographic* vol. XCII, no. 1, July 1947, pp. 131–148.

7. Yamada Konada, personal correspondence with Michael Mair; Marshall Doak, interview with Joy Waldron.

8. Personal communication from Toshiharu Konada to Michael Mair. Mr. Konada wrote that in his research he had heard accounts of *kaiten* warheads exploding with the pilots being ejected out of the *kaiten* due to the pressure and explosive force. It seems probable Nishina was ejected from his *kaiten* and his body had no injuries except for the face being sheared off when his head hit the edge of the hatch coaming.

EPILOGUE

1. J.R.R. Tolkien fought in the Somme in World War I and saw so many men die it drove him to write as a way to expiate the horrors of war. Quote taken from an essay by Nancy Marie Ott titled "JRR Tolkien and World War I" at website: http://greenbooks.theonering.net/guest/files/040102_02.html.

2. Toshiharu Konada, private correspondence with James P. Delgado, September 27, 2002.

3. Kennosuke Torisu, IJN officer, in Evans, *The Japanese Navy*, chapter 14.

4. Yokota, *Suicide Submarine!*, p. 250.

5. Toshiharu Konada, personal correspondence to James P. Delgado, September 27, 2002.

6. Toshiharu Konada, personal correspondence to James P. Delgado, September 27, 2002.

BIBLIOGRAPHY

BOOKS

Andrews, Lewis. *Tempest, Fire & Foe.* Narwhale Press, 1999; Trafford Publishing, 2004.

Astor, Gerald. *Operation Iceberg.* Dell Books, 1995

Boyd, Carl, and Akihiko Yoshida. *The Japanese Submarine Force and World War II.* Annapolis, Maryland: Naval Institute Press, 1995.

Boyne, Walter J. *Clash of Titans: World War II at Sea.* New York: Simon and Schuster, 1995.

Carter, Rear Admiral Worrall Reed. *Beans, Bullets and Black Oil: The Story of Fleet Logistics Afloat in the Pacific During World War II.* Naval War College Press, 1998.

Cook, Haruko Taya, and Theodore F. Cook. *Japan at War, An Oral History.* New York: The New Press, 1992.

Daly, H.C. *U.S.S.* Solace *Was There: The History of a Hospital Ship During World War II.* Bloomington, Indiana: Balboa Publishing Corp., a division of Hay House Publishing, 1991.

Delgado, James P. *Khubilai Khan's Lost Fleet: In Search of a Legendary Armada.* Berkley: University of California Press, 2010.

Delgado, James P. *Silent Killers: Submarines and Underwater Warfare.* Oxford, United Kingdon: Osprey Publishing, 2011.

Delgado, James P. *Tokko: The Manned Torpedo Program.* Unpublished manuscript; used with permission.

Evans, David C., ed. *The Japanese Navy in World War II.* Chapter 14, "Japanese Submarine Tactics and the Kaiten," Kennosuke Torisu. Annapolis, Maryland: Naval Institute Press, 1969, 1986.

Harris, Simon. *Death of a Tanker.* Unpublished memoir, 1944.

Hashimoto, Mochitsura. *Sunk! The Story of the Japanese Submarine Fleet, 1941–1945.* Translated by E. H. M. Colegrave. New York: Henry Holt, 1954.

I-Go Sensuikan; Kaiten Type I. Gakushukenkyusha, January 20, 1998.

Jane's Fighting Ships of World War II—1998 Edition. New York: Crescent Books, a division of Random House Publishing, 1998.

Kaiten: The Wills Left by Kaiten Pilots. Kaiten-kai Society. Tokyo: *Kaiten kanko-kai,* March 1976.

Konada, Toshiharu. Four-part document: "Lt. Cmdr H Kuroki and Lt. Cmdr Sekio Nishina," "Concepts of the Human Torpedo" and "Kaiten Training." January 31, 2001, letter to Michael Mair.

Konada, Toshiharu. "Wolves Above and the Enemy Below." *Kikusui* Mission—*Kaiten* attacks on Ulithi. Unpublished essay, February 2002.

Konada, Toshiharu. *Maruroku Kanamono: Hardware Zero Six.* Unpublished Paper, 2000.

Maeda, Masahiro. *The Idea of Kaiten—Human Torpedo.* Tokyo: Kensho Kanko-kai, 1985.

Mason, Theodore C. *We Will Stand By You, Serving in the Pawnee, 1942–1945.* Annapolis, Maryland: Naval Institute Press, Blue Jacket Books, 1990.

"Memory of I-36." *Kaiten-kai* Society Tokyo: *Kaiten Kanko-kai,* 1984.

Morrison, Samuel Eliot. *History of Naval Operations in World War II.* Volume XII, Leyte (June 1944–January 1945) 1958. Castle Books, 2001.

Nitobe, Inazo. *Bushidō: The Soul of Japan.* Tokyo: The Student Company, 1905.

O'Neill, Richard. *Suicide Squads: WWII.* New York: St. Martin's Press, 1981.

Orita, Zenji, and Joseph D. Harringon. *I-Boat Captain.* Canoga Park, California: Major Books, 1976.

Oseas, Eileen. *Tales of the USS* Conklin DE-439. McNamara, self-published, 2000.

Ott, Nancy Marie. "JRR Tolkien and World War I." Essay. Website: http://greenbooks .theonering.net/guest/files/040102_02.html.

Prange, Gordon W. *At Dawn We Slept.* New York: McGraw Hill, 1981.

Prange, Gordon William, Donald M. Goldstein, and Katherine V. Dillon. *Miracle at Midway.* New York: Penguin Books, 1982–1983.

Report *AO-59/A4-1,* serial 00547, May 18, 1944. Norfolk Navy Yard, Baltimore Repair and Conversion Branch. Report by B. N. Ward, Captain.

Rohwer, Jurgen. *Chronology of the War at Sea 1939–1945: The Naval History of World War Two.* Annapolis, Maryland: Naval Institute Press, 2005.

Scott, Lieutenant (j.g.) Charles S., assistant communications officer, USS *Mississinewa* (*AO-59*). Unpublished Navy Memoirs 1995. Telephone interview (with Michael Mair), June 3, 2006.

Sheftall, M.G. *Blossoms in the Wind: Human Legacies of the Kamikaze.* New York: New American Library, 2005.

Shigemote, Shunichi, Navigator of *I-47. Kaiten Hasshin.* Nagasawa, Michio: Kojiin-sha, April 1, 1989.

Stephan, John J. *Hawaii Under the Rising Sun: Japan's Plans for Conquest After Pearl Harbor.* Honolulu: University of Hawaii Press, 1984.

Toll, Ian W. *Pacific Crucible: War at Sea in the Pacific, 1941–1942.* New York: W. W. Norton & Company, November 14, 2011.

Torisu, Kennosuke. *Human Torpedo, Kaiten and Young Men.* Tokyo: Shinchosha, 1960.

Torisu, Kennosuke. *Human Torpedo, Special Attack Weapon Kaiten.* Tokyo: Shincho-sha, 1983.

Uehara, Mitsuharu. *Kaiten sono Seishun-Gunzo. Tokushu-Senkoutei no Otoko-tachi* (Kaiten, Its Youthful Group: Men of the Special Attack Submarines). Tokyo: Toshimitsu Hoshi Publishing Co., 2000.

The "Ulithi" Encyclopedia. WVTY, the Armed Forces Radio Station, Ulithi, Western Caroline Islands, 1945.

USS Mississinewa AO 59 *War Diary.* May 18–31, 1944; June 1–30, 1944; July 1–31, 1944; August 1–31, 1944; September 1–30, 1944; October 1–31, 1944.

Watanabe, Hisashi, Captain of *RO-115.* Research document and personal letter to Michael Mair, December 1996. English translation by Minako Nakakura.

Wildenburg, Thomas. *Grey Steel and Black Oil: Fast Tankers and Replenishment at Sea in the US Navy 1912–1995.* Annapolis, Maryland: Naval Institute Press, 1996.

Yamada, Lieutenant Minoru, Navigator of *I-53.* "Kikusui Group Attack on Ulithi Atoll." Unpublished essay sent to Michael Mair in February 2002. English translation by Tomoko Nishizaki.

Yokota, Yutaka, and Joseph D. Harrington. "Kaiten . . . Japan's Human Torpedoes." U.S. Naval Institute *Proceedings* 88 (January 1962): 55–67.

Yokota, Yutaka, with Joseph Harrington. *The* Kaiten *Weapon.* New York: Ballantine Books, 1962.

Yokota, Yutaka, and Joseph D. Harrington. *Suicide Submarine!* New York: Ballantine Books, 1962.

ARTICLES

Associated Press (AP) Wirephoto. "Tanker Burns in the Midst of Fleet Units in the Pacific." Photocredit Joseph Rosenthal. Published December 18–24, 1944, in the *Los Angeles Times* (December 18, 1944), the *Honolulu Star Bulletin* (December 19 and 20, 1944) and other newspapers around the world.

"Blast Kills 6, Five Children, Pastor's Wife in Explosion: Fishing Jaunt Proves Fatal to Bly Residents," *Klamath Falls Herald and News,* May 7, 1945, page 1.

Jaramillo, Art, SC3c, USS *Mississinewa (AO-59).* No headline, Jaramillo feature by Slim Randles. *Albuquerque Journal,* Albuquerque, New Mexico, December 7, 1991.

Johnson, Irving. "Adventures with the Survey Navy," *National Geographic* XCII, no. 1 (July 1947): 131–148.

Juillerat, Lee. "Mitchell Monument: A Place Remembered." *Service & Sacrifice: Klamath Basin Life Through Two World Wars (Journal of the Shaw Historical Library*, Vol. 17), 2003.

Zenji, Orita. "Kaiten Kikusui Attack." *Asahi Weekly* newspaper, September 15, 1949.

BROADCAST

History Channel. *Silent Assassins*. History Channel and Greystone Productions—Silent Service, December 2000.

Torisu, Kennosuke. *Silent Assassins*. History Channel, 2004.

INTERVIEWS

Arizuka, Yoshihisa, Chief Engineer, *I-36*. Interview February 8, 2001, by Mitsuharu Uehara on behalf of Michael Mair.

Bierley, Lieutenant John, Medical Officer, USS *Mississinewa* (*AO-59*). Telephone interview with Michael Mair on April 22, 2000.

Delgado, James P., Historian. May–June 2013 (Joy Waldron).

Doak, Marshall, Pharmacist's Mate on USS *Arapaho*. July 2010, April–May 2013 (Joy Waldron).

Inouye, Daniel, late Senator from Hawaii. April 15, 2010 (Joy Waldron).

Scott, Lieutenant (j.g.) Charles S., Assistant Communications Officer, USS *Mississinewa* (*AO-59*). Unpublished Navy Memoirs 1995. Telephone interview (Michael Mair), June 3, 2006.

Yamada, Minoru and Michael Mair, 2000-2007.

Zikewich, Joe, S2c, of USS *Lexington CV16*. April 14–18, 1999, during USS *Mississinewa* (*AO-59*) Reunion (Michael Mair).

Interviews of *Miss* Sailors During the USS *Mississinewa* (*AO-59*) Reunion, April 14–18, 1999, Corpus Christi, Texas:

Bayak, John PhM2c

Bell, Al M1c

Caplinger, Fred SK1c

Cuevas, Fernando "Cookie" S2c (ship's cook)

Cunningham, James "Jim" S2c

D'Anna, John S2c (ship's cook striker)

Fulleman, Ray WT2c

Gimmeson, William "Bill" S2c

Givens, Earl T. S2c

Glaser, Lawrence SM1c

Hammond, J. P. "James" S2c (radar striker)

Kinsler, Ed S2c (radar striker)

Lewis, James "Jim" MM2c
Liveakos, Gus MM1c
Ritchie, Harold S1c
Schaufus, Frederick "Fred" MM2c
Whitten, Winston MM1c
Van Orden, Earle S2c (quartermaster striker)
Vulgamore, Robert "Bob" F1c

USS *Lackawanna AO-40* Reunion Association, October 17, 1999, St. Louis, Missouri, Personal Interviews by Michael Mair with the Following Men:
Anson, Jim SF3C
Bir, Claude SK2c
Davies, Lew Lieutenant j.g. Navigator
Factor, Jim F2c
Fello, Joe WT3c
Grimes, Stanley QM
Hawkins, Linus S1c
Kaiser, Fred RM3c
Miremont, Ed RM2c
Moore, Bobby SM3c
Newman, Paul GM2c
Milford, Romanoff Lt. j.g.
Simon, Clarence SM3c
Wicker, Tom ENS.
Williams, Harold "H.B." WT2c

PERSONAL CORRESPONDENCE
Delgado, James P., and Joy Waldron, March–June 2013.
Gordon, William, Wesleyan University, and Joy Waldron, 2012, 2013.
Harris, Simon "Sid", SK2c, USS *Munsee* (*ATF-107*). Letter to Michael Mair, March 1, 2000.
Konada, Toshiharu, Chairman, All Japan Kaiten Pilots Association. Letter to James P. Delgado, September 27, 2002.
Konada, Toshiharu. Personal letters to Michael Mair, January–December 2001.
Konada, Toshiharu. E-mail to Michael Mair, February 13, 2004.
Konada, Toshiharu. *"Kikusui* Mission—*Kaiten* Attacks on Ulithi." Mr. Konada wrote his analysis of the disposition of the five *kaiten* pilots who attacked Ulithi on November 20, 1944. Mr. Konada was critical of *I-47*'s Captain Zenji Orita's poor navigation, poor choice of launch times due to darkness and subsequent report to Sixth Fleet. Mr. Konada was also critical of Captain Orita's interviews with *Asashi Weekly* newspaper, where Orita relied only on his poor memory. English translation by Tomoko Nishlzaki.

Loebs, Ed, GM3c, USS *Menominee* (*ATF-73*). Letter to Michael Mair, December 27, 2001; frequent e-mail and telephone communication, 2001–2013.

Tareg, Tony, Lieutenant Governor of Yap, native of Mog Mog. Letter to Michael Mair, February 26, 2002. Ongoing e-mail communication with Mair, 1998–present.

Watanabe, Hisashi, Captain of *RO-115*. Research document and personal letter written to Michael Mair in December 1996. English translation by Minako Nakakura.

Yamada, Minoru, and Michael Mair, 2001–2007.

TRANSLATION

English translation and research professionally provided by Tomoko Nishizaki for Michael Mair in 2001 from the following sources: (1) Kaiten sono Seishun-Gunzo. *Tokushu-Senkoutei no Otoko-tachi*. English: *Kaiten, Its Youthful Group* (translation Youthful Group refers to "Young *Kaiten* Pilots"). Subtitle in English: *Men of the Special Attack Submarines*. Author: Mitsuharu Uehara. Publisher: Toshimitsu Hoshi. Publishing Company: Shounsha, March 25, 2000. (2) Letters and research of Toshiharu Konada. (3) Letters and research of Minoru Yamada.

U.S. AND JAPANESE OFFICIAL ACTION REPORTS AND DECK LOGS; REPORTS AND CORRESPONDENCE

Action Reports—Imperial Japanese Navy

"Kaiten Special Attack Forces *Kikusui* Unit Action Report" (*Senken-butai*).

Japanese Sixth Fleet Report, December 2, 1944.

Action Reports—U.S. Navy

Commander Destroyer Squadron Four. Action Report, Serial 071. November 24, 1944. *Subject:* USS *Cummings* (*DD365*)—Anti-submarine Action Report of 20 November 1944.

Commander Service Squadron Ten Action Report, Serial 00274. December 8, 1944. Torpedoing of USS *Mississinewa* and Events in Connection Therewith. Covers Sinking of *Mississinewa* in Ulithi Harbor and Various Measures Taken by Vessels Present in Area. Period 20 November 1944.

Commander Service Squadron Ten Action Report, Serial 00282. December 9, 1944. Highlights of Events Occurring at Ulithi. Brief Summary of Events Which Occurred on 20 November 1944, the Torpedoing of USS *Mississinewa*, Rescue of Survivors and Anti-Submarine Actions in Which Three Japanese Midget Submarines are claimed to Have Been Sunk.

USS *Arapaho* (*ATF-68*). Action Report, no serial, 21 November 1944.

USS *Mississinewa* (*AO-59*)—Report of fire in.

USS *Cache* (*AO- 67*). Action Report, Serial 004, 24 November 1944. Action Report, Instant to torpedoing of *USS Mississinewa*. Covers Rescue Operations Following Torpedoing and Sinking in Ulithi Harbor on 20 November 1944.

USS *Case* (*DD-370*). Action Report, Serial 0179. November 22, 1944. Anti-submarine Action of Surface Ship, Report of: Forwards One ASW-1 Form Report and Detailed Narrative Covering Action of 20 November 1944 at 0532 GCT in Lat. 9. 56.30 N, Long. 139.44 E, While on Patrol (sortie) from Ulithi Lagoon via Mugai Channel in Task Group Consisting of Cruiser Division 5 & Destroyer Division 7. Midget Submarine Surfaced and Was Rammed by USS *Case*.

USS *Extractor* (*ARS-15*). Action Report, ARS15/S93, Serial 101-44. 21 November 1944. Fire Fighting-report of.

USS *Gilligan* (*DE-508*). Anti-submarine Action of Surface Ship. November 20, 1944.

USS *Lackawanna* (*AO- 40*). Action Report, 20 November 1944.

USS *Lipan* (*ATF-85*). Action Report, ATF/S93/ahr, Serial 378. 20 November 1944. Fire Fighting and Salvage Operation.

USS *LST-225*. Action Report, January 14, 1945, Serial 003-45. Operational Archives, US Naval Historical Center, Washington, D.C. Analysis of debris correctly interpreted that "the craft was a one-man human torpedo of a new type rather than the two-man midget submarine of the Pearl Harbor type." The appropriate commands were alerted. See memorandum, Command Western Carolines Patrol and Escort Group, 22 January 1945, A-16-3 (10)/FF12/02-cdg, Serial 00209, Operational Archives, US Naval Historical Center, Washington, D.C.

USS *Menominee* (*ATF-73*). Action Report, Serial 479. 20 November 1944. Explosion and subsequent fire on board *USS Mississinewa* (*AO-59*).

USS *Mississinewa* (*AO-59*). Captain Philip G. Beck, Commanding Officer's Action Report, No Serial. 26 November 1944. Covers Torpedoing with Resultant Sinking While At Anchor in Ulithi Harbor, 20 November 1944.

USS *Mobile* (*CL-63*). Action Report *CL63/A4-3/A16-3*, Serial 033. To: Commander Task Group 38.3 (Commander Carrier Division One) Subject: Japanese Submarines in the Anchorage at the Ulithi Islands, Morning of 20 November 1944 (East Longitude Date) Enclosure: (A) Wood and Metal Seat, Block of Wood *and* Pillow from Japanese Submarine (forwarded by Commander Cruiser Division Thirteen).

USS *Munsee* (*ATF-107*). Action Report, ATF107/A12/(JWB), Serial 205. 26 November 1944. Fire Fighting, Report onUSS *Mississinewa* (*AO-59*).

USS *Pensacola* (*CA-2 4*). Action Report, Serial 0159 (*CA24/ A12- 1/ A16- 3*). Engagement with Enemy Submarine(s) by Units of Task Group 57.9 on 20 November 1944.

USS *Rall* (*DE-304*). Action Report, No Serial. 20 November 1944. Anti-Submarine Action by Surface Ship, Report of: Two ASW-1 Form Reports of Action on 20 November 1944 in Ulithi Harbor at 0647 and 0653, Resulting in Sinking of Japanese Midget Submarine.

USS *Reno* (*CL-96*). Action Report, Serial 075. November 22, 1944. Subject: Operations in Southern Anchorage during Submarine Attack on Ulithi Atoll 20 November 1944.

USS *Ringness* (*APD-100*). Action Report, April 28, 1945, Serial 450, Operational Archives, US Naval Historical Center, Washington, D.C.

USS *Sumner* (*AGS-5*). Action Report, November 25, 1944, Serial 060-44. AGS5/L11-Subject: Explosion, Southern Anchorage, November 20—Report of. Operational Archives, US Naval Historical Center, Washington, D.C. The appropriate commands were alerted. See memorandum, Command Western Carolines Patrol and Escort Group, 22 January 1945, A-16-3 (10)/FF12/02-cdg, Serial 00209, Operational Archives, US Naval Historical Center, Washington, D.C.

USS *Underhill* (*DE-682*). Action Report, July 30, 1945, No Serial, Operational Archives, US Naval Historical Center, Washington, D.C.

USS *Vigilance* (*AM- 324*). Action Report, Am324/A16-3/A9-8, Serial 032. November 20, 1944. Enemy Midget Submarine, Visual Contact, 20 November 1944—Report on.

CORRESPONDENCE REPORTS

Beck, Captain Philip. (Handwritten document re purging tanks on USS *Mississinewa*) SECRET and CONFIDENTIAL. Serial number 10871, written November 26, 1944, officially received by U.S. Navy January 8, 1945.

DECK LOGS

LCI-79 Deck Log. November 20, 1944.

USS *Mississinewa* (*AO-59*) Deck Log.

USS *Pamanset* (*AO- 85*) Deck Log. Monday November 20, 1944. Signed by Lieutenant (j.g.) Arthur J. Gregory, USNR.

USS *Samaritan* Deck Log. Thursday November 23, 1944. Signed by Ensign W. A. Naprstek, USNR.

USS *Samaritan* (*AH-10*) Deck Log. November 20, 1944.

USS *Santa Fe* (*CL- 60*) Deck Log. Monday November 20, 1944. Signed by Lieutenant (j.g.) J. R. Simpson, USNR.

USS *Solace* (*AH-5*) Deck Log. November 20 and 22, 1944.

USS *Tallulah* (*AO-50*) Deck Log. November 20, 1944.

USS *Tappahannock* (*AO-43*) Deck Log. November 20 and 22, 1944.

USS *Wichita* (*CA-45*) Deck Log. December 8–10, 13–16, 20, 1944.

USS *Wichita* (*CA-45*) Deck Log. November 22, 1944. Signed by Lieutenant (j.g.) H. T. Armerding and Lieutenant (j.g.) J. W. Alcock, USNR.

WEBSITES

Atom Bombs, Preparation For, December 17, 1944 Timeline
http://www.ww2hc.org/articles/pacifictimeline.pdf

Balloon Bombs
http://news.nationalgeographic.com/news/2013/05/130527-map-video-balloon-bomb-wwii-japanese-air-current-jet-stream/

http://www.oregonencyclopedia.org/entry/view/balloon_bombs/
http://legionmagazine.com/en/index.php/2009/08/the-west-coast-balloon-attack-air-force-part-34/

Bombardment of Iwo Jima, December 8, 1944
http://www.uwec.edu/duckswsm/pacifictime.html

Japanese Suicide Attacks at Sea
http://www.ww2pacific.com/suicide.html

J.R.R. Tolkien, WWI Experiences and Relation to His Writing
Ott, Nancy Marie. "JRR Tolkien and World War I." Essay. Website: http://greenbooks.theonering.net/guest/files/040102_02.html

Kaiten
http://en.wikipedia.org/wiki/*Kaiten* (*Kaiten* Types 1-4 schematic, measurements, deployments)
http://www.geocities.jp/torikai007/1945/*kaiten*.html
http://www.history.navy.mil/library/online/kye_japnavalshipbldg.htm (Japan Shipbuilding sites)
http://wgordon.web.wesleyan.edu/kamikaze/monuments/saku/ (Monument in Saku City, Japan to Sekio)

Kaiten Memorial Museum, Ozushima, Japan
http://photoguide.jp/pix/thumbnails.php?album=873
http://www.kamikazeimages.net/museums/*kaiten*/index.htm

Kuroki, Death Poem Of, Copyright Expired = Public Domain
http://commons.wikimedia.org/wiki/File:Death_poem_by_Kuroki_Hiroshi.jpg

Nishina and Other *Kaiten* Pilots
http://www.kamikazeimages.net/japanese/index.htm (Japanese views, by Bill Gordon, 2004)
http://www.kamikazeimages.net/books/related/hashimoto/index.htm

Ulithi Lagoon, Map
http://upload.wikimedia.org/wikipedia/commons/7/73/Ulithi.jpg

U.S. Ships Sunk by Japan Special Attack Weapons
http://en.wikipedia.org/wiki/List_of_Allied_vessels_struck_by_Japanese_special_attack_weapons#Kaiten

Zenji Abe, Pilot at Pearl Harbor
http://www.historynet.com/lieutenant-zenji-abe-a-japanese-pilot-remembers.htm

MISCELLANEOUS SOURCES
Valor in the Pacific National Monument kindly provided transcriptions of interviews from Japanese pilots who took part in the Pearl Harbor attack; the interviews were taken over the years and included pilot Zenji Abe.

INDEX

Page numbers in *italics* indicate maps.